M000314657

Battling Siki

BATTLING SIKI

A TALE OF

Ring Fixes,

RACE,

and Murder

IN THE 1920s

Peter Benson

THE UNIVERSITY OF ARKANSAS PRESS • FAYETTEVILLE • 2006

Copyright © 2006 by The University of Arkansas Press

ISBN-10: 1-55728-816-X
ISBN-13: 1-55728-816-5

All rights reserved
Manufactured in the United States of America

10   09   08   07   06   5   4   3   2   1

Text design by Ellen Beeler

◉ The paper used in this publication meets the minimum requirements of the American National Standard for Permanence of Paper for Printed Library Materials Z39.48-1984.

Library of Congress Cataloging-in-Publication Data

Benson, Peter.
    Battling Siki : a tale of ring fixes, race, and murder in the 1920s / Peter Benson.
        p. cm.
    Includes bibliographical references and index.
    ISBN 1-55728-816-X (hardcover : alk. paper)
    1. Siki, Battling, 1897–1925. 2. Boxers (Sports)—Senegal—Biography.
    3. Boxing—Corrupt practices. I. Title.
    GV1132.S6B46 2006
    796.83092—dc22

                                                                    2005036072

For Peter E. Benson, 1914–2001

Contents

Acknowledgments

I am deeply grateful to the individuals who helped me find and gain access to materials during my period of research for this book, including especially Hendrick Henrichs of the Faculty of Letters at the University of Utrecht, who took time out from his own research to visit Dutch archives on my behalf. I am grateful as well to his nephew Damien Hope, to Babacar Ndiaye, Marie-Hélène Jeanmonod, René Jeanmonod, and Nodira Alimkhodjaeva. Mamadou Niang was very generous in sharing photographs with me. Bill Cayton and Steve Lott generously allowed me to watch videos at the offices of Big Fights, Inc. A number of other individuals served as informants in my research, including Oumy Ball, Oumar Ly, Dominick Scibetta, and my father C.W.O. Peter E. Benson, U.S. Marine Corps, retired. The reference staffs of many libraries greatly aided my hunt for materials, including the Bibliothèque Nationale de France, Bibliothèque Publique et Univesitaire of Geneva, the Research Division of the New York Public Library, Atlanta Fulton Public Library, Columbus Metropolitan Library, Key West Public Library, Manchester (New Hampshire) City Library, Los Angeles Public Library, Montclair Public Library, Buffalo and Erie County Public Library, Memphis Shelby County Public Library, Wheeling Public Library, Allentown Public Library, Rochester Public Library, City of Saint Paul Public Library, Minnesota Historical Society Library, and the Cleveland Public Library. I am also deeply grateful to Pino Mitrani and Nathalie Simonnot, and to Philippe and Dominique Certain, who put me up in Paris during several trips I made to do research there, and whose warmth and gracious hospitality made my stay in the French capital a pleasure. The library staff at Fairleigh Dickinson University, Teaneck, New Jersey, also helped me a great deal. Two reference librarians in particular, Leila Rogers and Judith Katz, worked tirelessly on my behalf. For translations of Dutch materials I was greatly aided by Andrew Groeneveld and by my mother-in-law, Liliane De Michely, and her former colleagues at the International Telecommunications Union. Many friends and colleagues aided me by reading drafts of the manuscript of this book, sometimes making suggestions for its improvement. Two boxing trainers, Kenny Jones and Dominick Scibetta, worked long hours with me in the gym teaching me things about boxing that you cannot learn just by watching.

I especially appreciate the opportunity they gave me to spar again against challenging opponents. This book benefited immeasurably from their influence. Lastly, I would like to thank my wife, Dominique, not only for her help with French materials, but also for her support, patience, and encouragement over the long gestation period this book turned out to have.

Preface

Early in 1991, when I was Fulbright professor at the Université Chiekh Anta Diop in Dakar, Senegal, my wife and I went on the slow-moving, rattletrap train that heads north along the West African coastline, just a few miles inland, to a terminus far in the north of Senegal, at Saint-Louis. Now a sleepy backwater, Saint-Louis had been one of the oldest outposts of France's colonial empire, one of its first colonies along the African coast, and for a time its most important. We had flipped through our guidebooks, read up on its history, and tried to imagine what it had been like there fifty or a hundred years before, when it was a thriving and important place, rather than the half-forgotten relic it was now. We read about Louis Faidherbe, who'd flung a steel bridge rated then an engineering marvel between that island outpost and the mainland, who'd planned there his inland campaigns of conquest along the Senegal River, building what would become a huge West African empire. After some seven dyspeptic hours in a wobbly second-class carriage, I found myself, among a crush of Africans, lugging a suitcase across that bridge, astonishingly little changed from the nineteenth-century drawings of it. The island spread out behind it didn't look much different either, with its string of low, whitewashed houses baking in the sun like so many coconut cakes.

We unpacked our suitcases in the Hôtel de la Poste, by the administrative center in the old colonial quarter, with its shady veranda and quiet inner courtyard. We hung up our clothes and went for a walk to get a feeling for the town. Anticipating a crush at the train station, we had left Dakar at dawn and had little to eat or drink since. I had lived in Africa for five years already and learned mostly to love it, though you couldn't help but hate it sometimes too, to hate, for instance, how it made any white person a twenty-four-hour target for unwanted attention, open game for anybody who wished to demand, beg, steal, or hustle anything of value you had and they lacked. I loved Africa too—most of all in those moments when it showed its kind heart, its human warmth, such as for instance the time when, up country in Sierra Leone in Kabala, a town whose language I didn't speak, I'd gone onto a brightly painted veranda, thinking the paint job must be meant to attract customers, and that therefore this must be some sort of local chop shop. I'd sat down at a table, and when a woman had come out, mimed that I was hungry and wanted something to eat. She brought out a delicious groundnut stew, and only when I'd eaten it and tried to give her money (which she refused) did I realize that this wasn't a restaurant at all but the home of a very ordinary and not especially well-off family.

And here I was in Saint-Louis looking for just what I'd been looking for in Sierra Leone, a modest chop shop—for a cold drink, perhaps a plate of the national dish, *cebu jen*—rice with fish. No beggars, street hawkers, or con men followed us. Calm and indolence prevailed. Within a few hundred yards of the hotel, we came across a small café-restaurant. It looked like a place mostly for Africans, not expatriates or tourists—a bit spare, but clean. That suited us. Inside the café, to our surprise, the walls were covered with enlarged photos and drawings of a black boxer, a world champion from years before. The boxer was someone from the 1920s, but I didn't recognize him, couldn't place him. I asked the waiter who he was. "BATT-Lem," he said. "BATT-Lem Siki." The café, it turned out, was named for him, dedicated to his memory. He'd been born in Saint-Louis. Apparently he was some sort of national hero in Senegal. I searched my recollections. This made no sense. What world champion from the 1920s would I not have heard of? After all, I'd fed off boxing books from the time I was a kid.

I'd started going to boxing matches virtually from birth. My father, a career soldier in the U.S. Marine Corps, had boxed professionally, and coached the boxing team at every base we followed him to throughout my childhood. When I was seven he started taking me to the fieldhouse at Camp Lejeune in North Carolina, where he trained his boxers. His boxers adopted me as a sort of mascot, especially the bantamweight Ron Decost, who'd get down in a crouch so we were nearly chin to chin, to spar with me. Decost later went on to a professional career. Another fighter on that team, Bob Fosmire, later ranked among the top-ten professional middleweights in the world. Fosmire, Decost, and two other fighters came to my First Communion at the base chapel and chipped in to give me a silver Saint-Christopher's medal.

The following year the Camp Lejeune team won the All-Marine title. By then I'd graduated to fighting exhibitions against other kids from the base during intermission of the team's tournaments. My photo appeared in the camp newspaper. (I got plaudits in tournament write-ups—stuff like "Pete Benson Jr. showed the crowd a future star," and "some good left jabs and right hands by Benson, who is only eight years old"—but then the editor was a pal of my dad's). That year my dad coached the All-Marine boxing team, the first to ever win the All-Service title. After Lejeune, he quit coaching and bought a house in Connecticut, where he was assigned to a Marine Reserve unit. I still shadowboxed imaginary bouts in the basement, yet I wasn't training and dreaded those times when my dad would come home and suddenly spring on me that some friend of his had a PAL or YMCA tournament lined up in a nearby town, and wouldn't I like to fill in for some kid who was sick (yeah, sick my ass, I thought—try afraid)?

He was always after me to fight in the Golden Gloves, as he had when he was eighteen, but I played high school football instead and made the all-conference team at middle linebacker. That seemed to satisfy him. I was still fascinated with boxing, however. I read and reread every boxing book in the house. I read *Bill Stern's Favorite Boxing Stories* so many times that both covers fell off. Once, in the kitchen of our house, I remember my father playfully sparring me, imitating the style of Benny Leonard, the lightweight champion from the 1920s, skipping nimbly from side to side, turning this way and that, pushing my shoulder or hooking my elbow with an open hand, so I was always off balance, never at an angle where I could touch him. I remember evenings spent watching the snowstorm figures of fighters on the Friday night "Gilette Cavalcade of Sports," the image so fuzzy you could barely tell the black fighters from the white—which was ironic in a way, for that was the moment in boxing history that saw a sudden dominance of the sport by black fighters.

Nearly all the boxing champions of my own generation would be persons of color, including one, middleweight and light-heavyweight champion Dick Tiger (real name Richard Ihetu), who was Nigerian. If anyone had asked me who was the first African to win a world title, I suppose I would have guessed Dick Tiger. But I would have been wrong. In 1991 when I got back to Dakar, I went poking around the library at the American Cultural Center, trying to find out about the guy whose pictures I'd seen at the café in Saint-Louis. And sure enough, there he was: Battling Siki, world light-heavyweight champion from September 1922 to March 1923. He'd won the title in one of the most spectacular upsets the sport had ever seen, an upset to rival James J. Braddock's defeat of Max Baer for the heavyweight title in 1935 or Buster Douglas's defeat of Mike Tyson for the heavyweight title in 1990, an utter annihilation of one of the great athletic idols of his day, the darling of French boulevard society, Georges Carpentier.

Battling Siki! Of course! The guy the sportswriters used to call "the Singular Senegalese." As the story started to come back to me it, seemed stranger and stranger that I hadn't been able to place him. For god's sake, *Bill Stern's Favorite Boxing Stories* had a whole chapter about him. He'd been an oddball, a drunken eccentric who couldn't resist his impulsive nature, who won the title in a freak outburst of savage anger, then so lost control of himself in celebrating his triumphant fortune that he went on the skids, became a lush and a bum. The bright lights of the civilized world dazzled him, made him lose his head. Stern had described him picking fights with total strangers on the street just for the fun of it and finally getting himself murdered after a free-for-all in a New York speakeasy before he reached the age of thirty. A primitive savage, a brutal child with a talent for violence, that was Battling Siki. At least, it was the Battling Siki in *Bill Stern's Favorite Boxing Stories.*

The story I'd swallowed whole as a child didn't make much sense as an adult. I'd lived and worked in Africa for five years, stayed in African homes, eaten with African families, drunk beers and eaten roast meat for endless hours with African colleagues and friends. I thought it pretty unlikely that Battling Siki had been anything like the savage child Bill Stern had described. Then I had a sort of epiphany. I realized why I hadn't been able to place Battling Siki. His story had been filed away in memory under the wrong code, like a book languishing for years on the wrong library shelf. I suspected his story might be a concrete embodiment of what the post-structuralist and post-colonialist critics had said about the power of language, specifically the language of race, to render certain realities unimaginable, unspeakable. I wanted to find out what Battling Siki's reality was or at least to thoroughly take apart the myth that had for so long buried his identity under an oddball caricature.

I was already working on another manuscript, but filed away the idea that I'd find out someday how a false Siki had been enshrined in the sport's collective memory. I was conscious of the lessons of semiotic theory. I wouldn't find the "real" Battling Siki. He was dead. All we had left were the words that had been written about him. But I could deconstruct them, set them against each other, and thereby recover glimpses of a different Battling Siki than the one in *Bill Stern's Favorite Boxing Stories,* or, for that matter, in all the other books that have passed along the image of "the Singular Senegalese."

As I began doing research and drafting early chapters of this book, I came to understand how grossly the writers of his own day had misrepresented Siki, both as a fighter and as a man. I took up boxing again at a gym in Teaneck, New Jersey, a year before my father died, rediscovering the pain, fear, and discipline of the ring with two trainers and an assortment of sparring mates much younger than I, some of them professional fighters. In a way, stepping into the ring again was as necessary a part of writing this book as the research I did on three continents over the course of several years.

The ring teaches humility, an awareness of how hard a test is not just boxing but life, how wrong it is to disparage anyone with guts enough to face its moments of brutal truth. Siki, I would learn, had been more than just a fierce and skillful ring warrior. He had faced harder realities outside the ring, confronting valiantly the terrors of modern technological warfare, speaking out against the cruel racism of his day, even openly defying it, at a time and in a place where to do so courted violent retribution. Not that he was some sort of pasteboard hero. He had flaws and eccentricities to go along with his heroism. But no shortcoming of his own ultimately killed him. The only thing "singular" about Siki was his refusal to meekly play along with the fix, not just the fix black men so often were asked to accommodate in the ring, but also the fix they had to deal with in life. And that, in the end, is what makes his story unique.

CHAPTER ONE

The Savage Battler
and Clever Little Mike

An Irishman, in Dublin, on Saint Patrick's Day

The weeks leading up to Saint Patrick's Day in March 1923 in Dublin, Ireland, weren't much more violent than the weeks and months preceding them. Yet that made them violent enough. In his recollection a year later of the immediate circumstances of the first big fight to be held in Ireland in more than twelve years, Nat Fleischer, in *Ring* magazine, would muse, "It is doubtful whether a boxing contest was ever staged under such conditions. . . . Spectators walked to the theater between rows of guards. Armored cars loomed around corners. Machine guns poked their noses from points of vantage."[1] Actually, Fleischer understates the reality. Just two hours after the world champion's arrival in the Irish capital to defend his title, at 9:30 P.M., heavy rifle fire broke out throughout Dublin. Machine guns popped up on rooftops and in alleyways, raking city hall, Fowler Hall in Parnell Square, the Bank of Ireland, and other buildings. Rifles peppered a foot patrol near Christ Church Place.[2] Three days later, as the world champion, Senegalese light-heavyweight Battling Siki, trained for the match not far away, a bomb blew up the Irish Free State's Customs and Excise Office at 4 Boresford Place, blasting in the door, caving in walls, collapsing the main stairway, dropping upper floors into the basement, and reducing "great portions of the building" to "debris," killing one policeman and injuring another in the process.[3] In the week that followed, Criminal Investigations Division (CID, the equivalent of the American FBI) officers in major cities throughout the United Kingdom rounded up hundreds of Irish nationalists, fingered by informers as part of a network supplying arms to the Irish Revolutionary Army, driving them to Liverpool and Clyde and loading them in great secrecy aboard cruisers and destroyers for deportation to unknown destinations. Within days they would turn up in Dublin, held under strict secrecy at the city's Mountjoy Prison. Just days before the fight, a bomb thrown from the roof of the telephone exchange wounded the military guard. The same night, as mobs of fight fans arrived from England, a patron at Dublin's Theater Royale shot Commandant Bolster, an intelligence officer from the Wellington Barracks, in the chest. The wounded man staggered from the theater and fell bleeding in the street.[4]

On March 14, three days before the fight, as a gesture of firmness, the government executed seven men for revolutionary activity. The next day, rebel leaders declared a national period of mourning, forbidding public celebrations on Saint Patrick's Day—including the light-heavyweight championship bout. For good measure they hit back with their own executions, shooting down a guard at Glengarriffe Parade, near Mountjoy Prison, and a soldier of the Eighth Infantry Battalion returning to barracks by Charlemont Bridge.[5] The government in Dublin, "hardly agreeing that the present regime was a calamity for the country," threw the challenge back in their faces, disdaining the warning.[6] To ensure the safety of the boxers, promoters, and visitors, the authorities turned La Scala Theater, the movie palace where the fight would take place, into a fort. Military patrols circulated on the streets, stopping suspects for questioning. Guards flanked the doors of important buildings. "Siki," said the *Petit Parisien*, "for the first time in his life had a military guard of honor." In fact, a police guard followed Siki wherever he went, mostly to protect him from photographers hoping to shoot bootleg newsreels, as well as "crowds of autograph hunters."[7]

The day before the match, the Free State Government released a document captured in a raid on a Dublin house, addressed by "O.C. Brigade" to "O.C. Battn. 111," giving new regulations from the Republican general headquarters (GHQ) to "meet the desperate and more barbarous attempts being adopted by the enemy." Any further government executions would provoke shoot-on-sight orders against any Free State Parliament member who had voted for them, against all National Army officers, and "certain members of the Senate, legal advisers to the Government who have been connected with Court Martial, judges and solicitors, members of the CID forces, and 'aggressive civilian supporters of the Free State Government's policy of executions.'" The GHQ also directed its agents to institute a general campaign of arson, burning the homes of any senator who had backed the harsh crackdown on nationalists fighting to free the country from English overlords.[8]

The same day, Siki himself received a death threat—written in Gaelic. The authorities considered conveying him to the fight in an armored car.[9]

In light of the nationalist heroes' martyrdom, who on earth would want to go to a prizefight anyway, especially on the feast day of the Irish patron saint? Even the hierarchy of the Irish church voiced its displeasure.[10] You'd think that machine-gun rounds, terrorist bombs, and a grisly round of executions, not to mention the antagonism of the church, might turn the sporting public off to the upcoming fight, but in fact when the train carrying the world's champion pulled into Dublin's Kingsbridge Station at 7:00 P.M. on March 5, 1923, the detachment of soldiers stationed outside the gates could hardly restrain the crowd. "What's all the commotion about?" a reporter for the *Irish Times* overheard a bystander ask. "Ah, that's Siki; he's just after arriving," the soldier answered. Once inside the station, the "jostling crowd of men and women" rushed the private carriage carrying the world title-holder.[11] When he came down the steps they called out his name and clapped him on the back, delighted to have a chance to "catch a glimpse of his face." The muscular black man grinned in acknowledgment. Though he spoke five languages, none of them was English—or Gaelic. His blonde Dutch wife beamed alongside him, as grateful as the champ himself for the tumultuous welcome. When Siki's party managed to push through the crowd to promoter T. Singleton's waiting automobile, impatient admirers jumped onto the running board, flattening faces against the glass, hoping for one last gawk at the famous face. Siki took the whole thing in "great humor." At the promoters' offices, another crowd awaited to gape at the fighter and his "pleasant-faced young" wife. All the *Irish Times* could elicit from the champ was a shrug. His manager, Charles Brouillet, interceded: "Siki is very pleased at his reception. From what we have seen of Ireland, we like it very well. We had a good crossing from Cherbourg. Siki did a bit of training on the boat yesterday." Asked if his boxer was ready, he joked that on the train National Army soldiers searching for hidden weapons had felt his biceps and "decided to go no further. What more dangerous weapons could they find?"[12]

The glee of Irish fans at the sight of the world champion was predictable. In the tumult of revolutionary violence Dublin's fight fans had waited a long time to sate their hunger for a fight of real international consequence. Ireland's place in boxing history was nearly as long and momentous as England's, going back to 1833, when Irish champion Simon Byrne fought the longest heavyweight battle in ring history, ninety-eight rounds, over three hours and sixteen minutes, before he succumbed to English champion James "Deaf" Burke. Byrne died of his injuries soon thereafter.[13] The latest light-heavyweight champion's new manager, Brouillet, who had piloted his career less than two months, displayed an adroitness in at least at one vital feature of the manager's trade—reading public ardor. Ignoring threats of impending violence, he did something really unexampled in that fight-mad town. He booked a hall in the middle of the city, held training sessions there, and charged fans admission on a sliding scale, from one to three shillings. So intense was public curiosity that he sold out the sessions, packing over one thousand onlookers per day into the hall. Eventually, more than twice as many Dubliners would see Siki sparring, hitting the bags, wrestling, working with the medicine ball and Indian clubs, doing calisthenics and standing leaps, than would actually see the fight itself. Inspired by his example, Siki's opponent, Irish-American Mike McTigue, temporarily repatriated to the land of his birth, would hold training sessions of his own, and though you could have seen McTigue train for free a few weeks before, each day a full five hundred fans gladly paid for the privilege.[14]

The glee that greeted Siki in Dublin contrasted weirdly with the attitude toward him that trailed in the wake of journalists pouring into Dublin from London, Paris, and Rome, or, for that matter, with the notion of him holding sway in faraway Boston and New York, both of which had been proposed as rival venues to host the new champion's first title defense. The only reason Siki was fighting in Dublin at all, in fact, was because of the storm of controversy, and abuse, that had inundated him in other places.

Only a clever stratagem by Brouillet, in fact, had fixed it so that Siki could arrive in Dublin with those essential accouterments intact that made the trip worthwhile: his French and European boxing titles, his world title, a visa, and a boxing license. Life had been no stroll in the park lately for Battling Siki, world champion. First there had been the little matter of getting paid for the fight back in September 1922 when he'd won the title, flattening French national hero, matinee idol, and anointed sporting icon Georges Carpentier, in one of the most amazing upsets in the history of boxing. Then there had been the French Boxing Federation's sudden decision to strip him of his French titles and license to box, over an alleged altercation with a rival manager. When an irate, and flat broke, Siki poured fuel on the fire by announcing to anyone who would listen that the title fight had been fixed, a huge scandal that would come to be called *l'affaire Siki* ensued, involving even the French Chamber of Deputies, dragged unwillingly into a debate over the chicanery of the clique that ran French boxing and the fate of a recently obscure black boxer.

And that hadn't even been the half of it. As the vitriol and feelings of abused vindication spread, even racially tolerant France rapidly came to treat the once-popular boxer as a *bête noire*. He was denounced as a drunk, a thug who enjoyed assaulting strangers, including the police, in the cafés and on the streets, who enjoyed brutalizing his own blue-eyed bride. He was said to have been caught peddling cocaine, to have behaved lewdly in the company of a minor, in short to have been a public disgrace, a permanent blot upon the sport of boxing. The *Fédération Française de Boxe* (FFB), after a long, drawn-out commission of inquiry, finally ruled, on January 15, that "in their souls and in their consciences they had the absolute conviction that the match of 24 September [between Siki and Carpentier] had not been preceded by any agreement" to "fix the result."[15]

Siki himself had refused to testify before a commission that announced beforehand it wouldn't reconsider his suspension or investigate the money he insisted was still owed him. One -by -one other witnesses who might shed light upon what happened the night of the alleged fix went mum.[16] What happened next happened behind tightly closed, locked doors. Within twenty-four hours Siki's manager Brouillet was telling any journalist who would listen that the "8e Chambre" (*Correctionnelle*—in other words, the city court), on February 15, would show up with "a revelation that he characterized as sensational."[17] Whatever the well-guarded revelation was, the threat worked, for exactly one month later, when the FFB's board met again, instead of requesting that the pasteboard International Boxing Union (IBU) strip Siki of his European titles and world title, the FFB reinstated his French boxing license and recommended that his world and European titles be restored. It was all part of a general amnesty, they claimed, to celebrate the twentieth anniversary of their founding. Sure! When the congress of the IBU (which in fact consisted of exactly three people, representing France, Belgium, and Italy) met a few days later, it reaffirmed Siki's claim to the light-heavyweight championship of the world.[18]

For months, the French boxing public had been demanding a rematch between Siki and Carpentier. Siki had promised to give them one for free, if his license to box were reinstated. The profits could be given to charity. Carpentier had agreed. But by the time the FFB called off the dogs and let Siki alone, Brouillet had cut a deal for Siki to fight McTigue in Dublin. François Descamps, Carpentier's preternaturally cunning manager, had by then pulled the plug on the agreement to fight for free, alleging that he'd never made any such promise—until someone came forward with a letter affixed to his bona fide signature promising exactly that.[19] Meanwhile, the endless flood of proffered, then withdrawn charges and vaguely attributed innuendo against the boxer had so poisoned the well that Siki had been banned from country after country. He'd had a match set up with England's heavyweight champion, Joe Beckett, until their Foreign Office abruptly forbade it, explaining that such a spectacle might inspire riots among sub-jects in its colonial empire.[20] Other nations promptly followed suit, banning Siki personally or all mixed-race boxing in general. Even Holland, where Siki had campaigned for more than a year and been something of a sporting idol, where, in his own words, *"comme le roi nègre Malicoco"* (like the nigger king of Malicoco), he'd been feted and idolized, had latterly decided it would no longer have him.[21]

The American sporting press still smarted from the indignities of hav-ing to witness for nearly seven years the one-sided triumphs and extra-pugilistic lifestyle of an unrepentant champion of color, the African American Jack Johnson, and did not bother to suppress its glee at each new rumor of a Siki outrage. Siki atrocity stories got big play everywhere, from Minneapolis to Memphis, Boston to Buffalo. When the New York Boxing Commission, whose lead other state commissions followed, expressed outrage over tales of Siki's behavior and talked of banning him, Siki's fortunes began to look less rosy across the water as well.[22]

Siki went to Dublin because if he wanted to get paid for fighting he had little other choice. He didn't go to Dublin because he'd never heard of Saint Patrick's Day or was ignorant of the fact that a civil war raged there. Nevertheless, boxing writers soon enshrined an opposite reading. It's the one thing you can count on anyone remembering about Battling Siki, all these years after his death. Siki? Wasn't he the guy who, "in all innocence,"[23] ignorant of "the ominously Celtic overtones of his opponent's name," and perhaps even unaware of "the special significance of the date," came up with the "comical plan"[24] of "fighting an Irishman in Dublin on Saint Patrick's Day"?[25] "Boxing buffs still chuckle," Nigel Collins notes, "at the stupidity (or was it brazenness?)" of Siki's mistake. Never mind that this was not the first time, as Nat Fleischer points out, that a world champion defended his title in Ireland against an Irishman on Saint Patrick's Day, and that the earlier champion, though he fought under the name Tommy Burns, was, like Siki, a foreigner, a Canadian, whose real name was Noah Brusso.[26]

Neither McTigue nor his diminutive, cigar-chomping manager, Joe "Yussel the Muscle" Jacobs, had any idea of winning the world light-heavyweight championship, and they didn't bother to pretend they did. Jacobs told the *Irish Times* about his plans for the future, once this bout was over. Assuming his man made a good showing against the world champion, he figured to get Mike a shot against British middleweight champ Roland Todd. That fight alone ought to be worth $500 or 1000. Then, God willing, he hoped to get a shot on the Fourth of July against Johnny Wilson, the middleweight world champion who fought out of East Harlem in New York City. If McTigue won the light-heavyweight title, he'd have no reason to fight Wilson or Todd—but that possibility doesn't seem to have occurred to Jacobs. He wanted his boy to make a good showing against the light-heavyweight champ as a springboard for later middleweight bouts. Period.[27] He didn't even mention the possibility of defending the light-heavyweight crown. Why should he? Anyone who'd seen Mike box knew he was no slugger. He was one of the best defensive boxers in the world, slippery, elusive, almost impossible to hit with a clean shot. But he never stood still long enough to clock anyone else with a punch harder than your Sunday School teacher might—if you failed to memorize your catechism properly.

If you look over McTigue's record, you find that he'd fought past and future champions, including Harry Greb and Battling Levinsky. But he fought them in full retreat, in "no decision" bouts (where victory could come only by knockout). No-decision contests had originated in a quirk of New York boxing laws during the period from 1900 to 1911 when boxing was permitted only in private clubs, and persisted from 1911 to 1920 under the Frawley Law, which permitted only exhibitions. The rendering of a formal decision disqualified a bout as an exhibition. All New York matches between 1900 and 1920 thus were "no decision" affairs, but even after the passage of New York's 1920 Walker Law, allowing decisions, some managers continued to mandate "no decision" bouts. Some distrusted corrupt referees. Others, like Jacobs, used no-decision bouts to protect their fighters' records. And nothing, even before passage of the Walker Law, stopped a boxer from fighting in states where decisions were allowed.[28]

For most of his career, McTigue was a prize-ring Houdini, an escape artist who inflicted minimal suffering, but kept his record unblemished by seldom risking a decision. McTigue fought thirty-six no-decision fights over the course of his career and won only twenty-four decisions, a greater percentage of such bouts than any ring contemporary, with the exception of Al McCoy, the infamous "cheese" champion of pre-Walker Law days, who prolonged his reign as middleweight champ nearly four years by fighting only no-decision bouts. Kid Norfolk, in contrast, who fought many McTigue opponents, won nineteen decisions, with fifteen no-decision bouts, out of fifty-eight fights between 1914 and 1922. Against Siki, Jacobs had one thought in mind—for Mike to slip, duck, and move, firing back when he could do so in absolute safety. The possibility of winning a decision seemed remote, of winning by knockout unimaginable. Whether McTigue's mob-connected manager also took the precaution, in case his boy kept off the canvas, of "reaching" the referee before the bout is a matter of speculation.[29]

Jacobs was never one to set much store by the niceties of ring campaigning. He was as cute as they came at working referees, paying off journalists, rigging decisions. When McTigue fought Tommy Loughran in New York City, where "newspaper decisions" in no-decision bouts could win gamblers tens of thousands of dollars, Loughran cut McTigue's eye in an early round. He whispered to McTigue in a clinch not to worry, he'd lay off the injury, figuring he'd get a decision without needless brutality. He dominated every round. After the fight McTigue said, "You beat me tonight but you won't get the decision tomorrow.... My manager sent the reports out at eight-thirty." The fight hadn't started until ten! Jacobs had snuck into the telegraph office and written the writers' stories for them before the bout even began.[30] Bill Stern tells of Jacobs threatening mob retaliation over a decision that didn't go McTigue's way in Georgia.[31] A week before the Dublin fight, odds were two to one for Siki. But Irish fans had an abrupt change of heart in the last days before fight night, pouring bets in on McTigue, dropping the odds to seven to five.[32] Did they perhaps hear rumors about the fight being in the bag?

As for Siki himself, what he may have thought about the upcoming battle is obscured in the haze of legend. Years later, an old friend of his, sportswriter Gaston Bénac, would tell what he purported to be the true tale of how Siki came to be in Ireland at all. Caught between two managers with rival claims to his allegiance, suffering a recently sprained ankle, Siki, Bénac swore, was balking at fulfilling his contract. One of his managers, faced with a forfeit and unpleasant penalties, came up with a ruse, enticing Siki with a willing lady of the evening, getting him falling-down drunk, paying accomplices to lug him aboard ship "like a sack of coal."[33] They were safely out of sight of land before Siki woke up. As his head began to clear, Siki, always the good sport, said, "Aw, I just pretended to pass out, but I'm very glad to have tricked Deprémond."[34]

Just twenty-four hours before Siki went into the ring in Ireland against McTigue, the boat that had carried Siki across the channel docked at its final destination, Hoboken, New Jersey, where an enterprising local journalist hustled down to the docks to quiz the sailors about what Siki had been like, how he'd behaved on the boat. A few were glad enough to spin a yarn. Sure, they said. They'd seen Siki, and he was just as wild and crazy as advertised. Why, he'd been carried onto the boat "kicking like a roped calf," drunk as a lord, after a week-long bender. His poor wife, trailing in his wake, had a black eye to show for his distemper. Once aboard, they'd locked him in a cabin, which he'd promptly wrecked, bellowing for strong liquors.[35]

Yet another recollection, by patronizing English boxing aficionado Fred Dartnel (Lord Melford), had Siki sweating out a fit of paranoia in the hours before the match, sure that the Irish referee, the promoter, his own manager, and the international sanctioning board were out to get him. He wouldn't

Mike McTigue. (Author's collection.)

even weigh in, Lord Melford recalled (a fact confirmed by news reports), so worried was he that someone had reached the referee. After all, without a weigh-in the fight couldn't, by the IBU's own rules, be an official championship bout. He insisted on being paid his share of the purse in advance and then secreted it in a belt underneath his ring togs. "Thus equipped," said Melford, he "went forth to battle," though he made it harder on himself in the ring, since he wouldn't allow his seconds to douse him with water between rounds, for fear of spoiling the banknotes under his waistband.[36] For years rumors would also persist that armed men at ringside had threatened Siki before and during the bout. Siki himself would tell the African-American journalist William White, "The Irish soldiers told me if I hurt Monsieur McTigue they would shoot me. I didn't want to get shot. I saw enough shooting in the war."[37]

The gunfire he'd heard in the city all week ought to have been enough to make him jumpy to start with, and what he saw on the way to the fight couldn't have calmed his nerves. *New York Times* and *New York Herald* correspondents described a surreal scene on the streets that night, with army platoons patrolling the neighborhood of La Scala Theater, and a cordon of soldiers surrounding the building, forcing two long columns of ticket holders sporting shamrocks to file down a side street near the bombed-out main post office. When they reached the theater doors they found CID officers waiting to question and search them, one by one. Despite the whiff of danger in the air, incredibly, an even bigger crowd marked time beyond the barriers, non-ticket holders hoping to barter, bribe, or buy their way in—or failing that at least to share the vicarious excitement at second hand. Moments after the greatest part of the crowd had made it through the doors, a bomb exploded in a tenement in nearby Moor Lane, badly injuring two children, blowing out windows and doors in adjacent buildings, and raining glass from the skylights overhead into the hall itself.[38] Outside the theater, fans ran for cover. Inside, rumors spread of open warfare erupting.[39] For once, patrons had the rare experience of sharing the rush of adrenalin that fighters feel on the way into the ring. Before the fight began, a theater manager came forward to proclaim that patrons would be asked to remain seated for hours after the contest ended, to give police a chance to sweep the streets, hunting for terrorists.[40]

The French Jack Johnson

The two fighters made their way down the aisles at 8:00 P.M. (The start time had been moved up to accommodate the hordes of foreign press who had deadlines to meet and trains to catch). Siki wore a purple robe, which he stripped off to reveal a sash around his waist in the French tricolor, McTigue, a slate-blue gown, which he doffed to show off tights of Kelly green.[41] What happened next is a bit difficult to piece together, so thoroughly has it been reshaped by wishful thinking, rationalization, and outright hallucination.

The huge throng of press at ringside, like many white boxing fans, had strange mixed feelings where Siki was concerned, feelings at once of fascination, revulsion, longing, and dread. The first few years after World War I had seen a rising vogue for all things black, latterly labeled by scholars "Negrophilia."[42] Seen against the futility of white civilization, epitomized in the Great War, blackness took on a powerful allure. Negrophilia accepted, even exulted in, racial stereotypes born in the past century, when Gobineau had insisted that the white race, alone capable of civilization, would succumb to the lure of more vital "lesser races," dooming their own species to destruction via mixed-race mating.[43] By the 1920s, far from shunning blacks, whites came to see them as more primal, more real than whites. Whites longed to hear black music, read black poetry, watch blacks dance, share black laughter—and yes, see blacks fight in the ring.

Siki's stunning triumph over French national idol, war hero, and cinema celebrity Georges Carpentier had been a defining symbolic moment. It made him at once hero and anathema. His victory had kindled street battles between elated blacks and American sailors in Montmartre, Paris's seamy quarter of cabarets, prostitutes, and drugs. It both shocked white sensibilities and fit neatly into evolving prejudices. A brutal savage, so the media spun the tale, in an outburst of instinctual rage, had overcome a skillful practitioner of the "sweet science" of self-defense. When, months later, Siki disclosed the fight had been set up for a fix, he tarnished what little luster white "civilization" had left. The press, worldwide, reacted by sneering not only at Siki's allegation but also at the man himself, mocking him as a simple-minded primitive who couldn't deal with the sophistication of civilization. In America they lampooned him in language borrowed from the minstrel show character "Zip Coon," who appeared on stage in spats, lorgnette, and motley colors. Though nearly every picture of Siki that survives finds him wearing a well-tailored suit and tie, no reference to him was complete without sidelong mention of a tuxedo, top hat, cane, and bright red or purple opera cape. He was routinely referred to as a "child of the jungle," though in fact, as he put it himself, he had "never even *seen* a jungle."[44]

Though Irish fans seem to have accepted Siki simply as a boxer, the international press wrote him up in much the same style as, decades earlier, P. T. Barnum had touted his sideshow attraction the "Wild Man of Borneo."

Impersonated in the 1880s, under sworn secrecy and a bushy wig, by African American brothers from Long Island, Hiram and Barney Davis, Barnum's Wild Man was made out to be a monster of lust and rage.[45] The press similarly anticipated, from Siki, outbursts of bestial fury. No matter what the outcome of the bout, that angle would find its way into their stories. It was too good to pass up. Some also came wanting badly for the man the *New York Times* called "the French Jack Johnson" to be put in his place—not just beaten but thrashed. Their judgment of the final outcome is colored by that desire.[46]

Jack Johnson had taken the heavyweight title in 1908, the very year Siki arrived in France. Johnson wasn't the first black champion, but he was unquestionably the most controversial. Boxing had been integrated, so to speak, since African American Tom Molineaux lost challenges for England's heavyweight title to Tom Cribb in 1810 and 1811.[47] But once the notion of a world title was cooked up and "Boston Strongman" John L. Sullivan claimed it, thrashing Paddy Ryan in nine rounds in 1882, a color line was firmly drawn. "I will not fight a negro," Sullivan said. "I never have, and I never shall."[48] The great West Indian heavyweight Peter Jackson never got a shot at the title, though in 1891 he'd held Jim Corbett, Sullivan's successor, to a bloody sixty-one-round draw. Even Johnson never faced a black title challenger, though his toughest pre-championship fights had been against black boxers Sam Langford, Sam McVey, and Joe Jeannette. The lighter weight classes were a bit more open. By the time ragged street boy Louis Fall first stepped into a professional ring in 1913, five men of color had held world titles. "Little Chocolate," George Dixon, won the bantam- and featherweight crowns in the 1890s, Joe Gans the lightweight crown in 1902, "Barbados Demon" Joe Walcott (not to be confused with the New Jersey heavyweight who later borrowed his name) the welterweight crown in 1901, yielding it to another black man, the "Dixie Kid," Aaron Brown, in 1904.

Siki's story, as the *New York Times* pointed out, mirrored Johnson's in many ways. Siki really seemed in 1923 to be what the biographer Al-Tony Gilmore calls Johnson—the "bad nigger" *par excellence,* "dangerous and difficult" enough to defy whites, ignore death threats, refuse to be cowed. Promoter Tex Rickard had deliberately pitched the Jack Johnson / Jim Jeffries bout in 1910 as a battle for racial supremacy, unwittingly provoking racial carnage when Johnson brutalized the popular ex-champion. Across America whites assaulted blacks, lynched them, burned down homes. In New York City, three thousand whites mustered on Eighth Avenue, between Thirty-seventh and Thirty-ninth Streets, kicking and beating any black in reach.[49] Ultimately, white America made Johnson pay for his temerity, forcing his flight into exile by prosecuting him under the Mann Act, intended to prevent "white slavery" (forced kidnapping into prostitution of white women). Johnson's real sin had been rubbing America's nose in its racial illusions. Whites—especially those who stood to profit from boxing's roaring success—recalled his reign with horror. The million-dollar promoter Tex Rickard put it plainly: "We can't have a nigger heavyweight champion." A black champion wasn't "worth a bucket of warm piss."[50]

To many, Siki seemed potentially worse than Johnson. Like Johnson, he liked to flaunt his money, dress ostentatiously, be everything but humble and obsequious.[51] Siki too had married a white woman and even fathered her child. And Siki was not just black but Senegalese, at a time when to be Senegalese meant to be downright terrifying. The war had left a lingering image of the *tirailleurs sénégalais* (Senegalese riflemen) as pitiless mercenaries, killing gleefully with specially designed mini-machetes (their famous *coupe-coupe*), murdering prisoners, and carrying lopped-off ears as trophies.[52] In America, where the war years had witnessed the rebirth of the Ku Klux Klan, Siki's triumph seemed particularly malign. Glorified by a popular book and yet more popular film, *The Birth of a Nation,* the Klan had begun a covert war against blacks and others deemed inferior. A broad public credited pseudo-scientific treatises such as Madison Grant's *The Passing of the Great Race* (1916), which argued that living side by side with inferior species invited "race suicide" for dominant Nordic races. When Siki won the title, New York's *Literary Digest* ran an editorial entitled "Battling Siki as a Dark Cloud on the Horizon" bemoaning the immense error France had made in letting its national hero risk his title against a black man. In a sense Siki's triumph was more perilous than Johnson's, for Johnson's victory had threatened white prestige only in America—while Siki's menaced white mastery on a global scale. His victory came just as 850,000 black French troops were demobilized and as France proclaimed African conscripts would fill out the ranks even of its peacetime army. "The permeation of the most warlike nations of Africa by hundreds of thousands of veterans of the World War," warned the *Digest,* "reinforced yearly from the 206,000 called up.... for training in the most up-to-date military science, is of serious import for France and for the world."[53] It quoted a French writer who observed with horror that Africans "ceased to regard white Frenchmen as unquestionably superiors. Our military glories no longer dazzle them." In Siki, blacks now had a fresh symbol of black superiority.

Siki also, however, unlike Johnson, provoked not only hostility but also fascination—partly because his brutality was represented as instinctual, not malicious. In the wake of the war, the French, moved by a debt of gratitude to men who had "*versé le sang*" (spilled blood) for France, began to cultivate an image of the Senegalese not as beasts of prey but simple, guileless children. French advertising played up that notion in dozens of familiar images. One, for a hot breakfast drink, Banania, depicted a grinning *tirailleur*, in a red fez, declaring in pidgin dialect, "y a bon Banania"—which translates roughly as "there is good, Banania." After the war, when American soldiers attacked ex-*tirailleurs* seen with Montmartre prostitutes, the French whores defied them, backed by their pimps' fists, crying, "You shits! It's France here, not Chicago." "First of all," cried one huge pimp, "they make us puke, these Sammies [as in *Uncle* Sam]! The Senegalese, whether they're niggers or not, in any case, they fought for us!"[54]

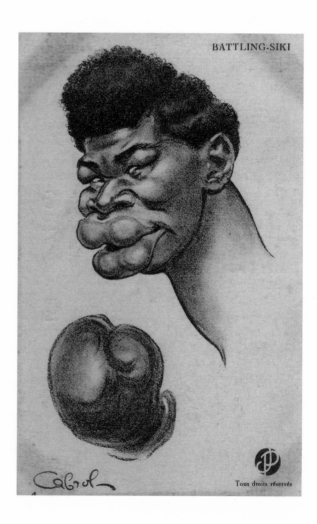

BATTLING-SIKI

French caricature of Battling Siki, 1923. (Publications I. P. Paris.)

War-weary Irish fans, on the night of March 17, 1923, came to the Siki/McTigue contest happy to have a chance again to see championship boxing in their battle-scarred capital city, but the sporting press came primed to see a test of racial verities. What really happened, therefore, becomes a bit difficult to fathom through the fog of their prejudices. A newsreel of the fight still exists.[55] Though heavily edited, it does allow you to get a clear impression of the tenor of the match, leaving a few distinct images. First, it leaves you with an image of the muscular Siki, in the early rounds, firing heavy punches at the fleeing specter of a pale, almost scrawny McTigue, who skitters away like a crab, twisted sideways, ducking and dodging, flicking up a jab that has about as much impetus as a crab's feeler. In the middle rounds, Siki continues to chase his pale rival, who pokes his jab straight out like a halfback stiff-arming a linebacker. Siki, irritated, paws it away, then returns to the assault, still missing more than he's landing, but landing hard to the body and head when he does land. In the late rounds, McTigue suddenly and unexpectedly, for an instant, turns the tables, stepping straight inside after a huffing and puffing Siki misses, sticking one, two, three neat straight counters. But then that's it. The film shows no other bursts of aggression from McTigue—and even this brief assault is neither sanguinary nor stunning. Siki, though clearly exhausted, goes straight back to the offensive.

One looks in vain for resolution to the mystery of what really happened in the ring in the next day's round-by-round accounts. So great are the disparities that even lining up the details from the various reports side-by-side in separate columns one comes away scratching one's head, wondering how so many different fights could have occurred at once in the same ring. The *New York Herald* writer, for instance, called the fight "one of the most grueling fights in the modern history of the British prize ring"[56]—and he was right in one sense: this was the last championship fight ever staged over a twenty-round distance. Thereafter, championship fights never again went past fifteen rounds. The *New York Times,* however, called the bout "a tame affair" and the *Irish Times* labeled it "disappointing."[57] For some writers, the early rounds were all Siki. Some (most notably the *Paris Herald*) have him swarming over McTigue, who barely weathers the storm. Some (the *New York Times,* for instance) have McTigue standing his ground at intervals, gamely firing back. The *Irish Times'* description of round four offers a fair sample of the more plausible representations of the early rounds:

> Continuing his aggressive tactics, Siki landed twice on the body and head; but still McTigue was content to act merely on the defensive. Later on in some in-fighting the colored man got home on the body. So far it was Siki's fight, but the Irishman was meeting his fierce

onslaughts with amazing coolness, wonderful skill, faultless ringcraft and resource.

Their reporter said flatly that Siki won every round through round six. The French papers, many of which had been disparaging Siki for months, said he dominated the early action, though they praised McTigue's clever defense. *Le Populaire* had Siki dominating the first ten rounds, as did the Paris edition of the *New York Herald.* The English heavyweight champion Joe Beckett, who had been scheduled to fight Siki himself until the British Home Office banned the bout, commenting on the fight for the *New York Times,* said that as late as the beginning of round seventeen he and others at ringside thought McTigue had stayed so passively on the defensive that he no longer had any chance to win, since he had no knockout punch. In the eleventh round, Siki split open a gash in McTigue's right eyebrow and in the twelfth, reported *Le Populaire,* he tagged McTigue there again, "making the blood flow."[58] Bizarrely, both the *New York Herald,* Paris, and the *London Times* claim McTigue scored a phantom knockdown in this round. The newsreel of the fight records no knockdowns by either fighter, and no other ringside report makes mention of one. In fact, the *New York World* says plainly, "Neither man was floored or badly damaged at any time."[59] The *Paris Herald* and the *London Times* accounts show other strange similarities as well, suggesting that one was lifted from the other by a not very scrupulous or careful hand. The *Herald's* story, for example, insists, "At the opening of the fourth round, Siki landed two heavy rights on McTigue's jaw." The *London Times* echoes the *Herald,* but weirdly reverses the polarity: "In the fourth round, McTigue scored with two heavy rights to the jaw."[60]

McTigue's big moment (phantom knockdowns aside) didn't really come until round eighteen, when most reports credit that sudden, sharp counterattack the newsreel showcases. Some stories (most notably one later run in the *Boxing Blade*) play up these punches as nearly knocking Siki out, insisting that "only an unsuspected . . . ability to take punishment . . . enabled Siki to be on his feet" at the bell, but the *Irish Times'* matter- of-fact wording rings truer: "Siki was cleverly countered by McTigue, who . . . penetrated the black's defense with rights and lefts to the head and body."[61] The *New York Times* thought Siki was "well ahead on points" as the bell rang for round nineteen. The *Irish Times* had him "driving his man to the ropes" in that round, landing to the head and jaw as McTigue "sidestepped out of danger." Though the *New York Times* said the nineteenth "began badly for Siki," who was "getting all the punishment," it called it "neither's round" and had both men landing about evenly at the final bell.[62]

An early round in the Siki/ McTigue bout, March 17, 1923. Siki is set to throw his signature left-hand swing as McTigue covers up.

Even if you somehow reconcile all the inconsistencies in the reporting of the fight, you're left with boxing's familiar conundrum: Do you credit more the man forcing the action, landing the heavier blows, or the man using quick hands, deceptive feet, and a bobbing head to make the other miss? Some judges tend, by instinct, to favor light-hitting boxers, others heavy-hitting sluggers (witness the dispute recently over the decision in the rematch between Shane Mosley and Oscar De LaHoya). In Siki's day too, this issue was much debated. Nat Fleischer, founder of *Ring* magazine (the "boxing bible"), published a pamphlet in 1933 entitled *How to Judge and How to Referee a Fight*. In it, he cautions would-be arbiters not to be fooled by "the man whose aggressiveness consists of simply boring in, of forcing the battle by keeping on top of his opponent, but fails to land effective blows." He adds, "Defense, good guarding, slipping, ducking, and good countering—all should be given their proper credit in the award of points."[63] Before the advent of the "ten-point must system" (which gives the winner of a round ten points, the loser normally nine or eight), decisions were awarded on a "rounds" not a "points" basis. Referees or judges turned in scorecards quantifying each round based primarily on the number of "effective blows" delivered by each boxer—but also on intangibles. Only the total number of rounds won or lost counted toward picking a winner. Some cards left room, in the column under each fighter's name, only for "W" (for won the round), "L" (for lost the round), or "E" (for an even round). On cards where points were awarded, the scorer might give points for "effective blows," and also, in separate columns, for intangibles such as "ring generalship," "aggressiveness," or "defense." But points were totaled only within the round, toward deciding who'd won that round. A running total wasn't kept to decide the fight as a whole. The bottom line on scoring cards read simply "rounds won, rounds lost, rounds even."

Fleischer duplicates judge Charles F. Mathison's scorecard for the 1932 Jack Sharkey / Max Schmeling heavyweight title match. Its columns (in order of importance) are "Clean Effective Punches, Ring Generalship, Aggressiveness, Defense," plus a fifth to deduct for fouls. *Ring generalship* meant "the ability to quickly grasp and take advantage of every opportunity offered; the capacity to cope with all kinds of situations which may arise; to force an opponent to adopt a style of boxing at which he is not particularly skillful." *Aggressiveness* credited the fighter who was "pressing the fight" and "busier" (threw more punches) over a fighter backing up, throwing fewer punches.[64] *Defense* meant blocking punches or making a rival miss.

But Mathison's scorecard for the Sharkey / Schmeling bout reveals a strange split between the code and its application. In round one, Mathison gives Sharkey three points, and Schmeling two, for "clean effective blows," and gives Schmeling additional single points for "ring generalship," "aggressiveness," and "defense." Go ahead, add them up. You get Sharkey three points, Schmeling five. But Mathison gave the round to Sharkey! And in fact, in each round, though he noted down points in every category, the only ones he counted in deciding who won the round were those for "clean effective punches." Thus the split. The system seems to credit intangibles, to value "science" equally with brute infliction of pain. But the scorer ignores his own code. Only pain counts, not style. "The referee and the judges," Fleischer writes, "should award the points for . . . clean hits with the knuckled part of the gloves. Blows landed on vulnerable parts of the body should receive greater credit than those landed elsewhere." In other words, if you want to write something down in the other columns—style points, if you will—go ahead. But when it comes to deciding who won the fight, credit only those "clean hits with the knuckled part of the glove." Pay attention to who inflicted the most "damage," via knockdowns or cuts, who landed the hardest blows, who looked "fresh" (as Mathison said of Schmeling), and who looked "pretty well mussed up" (as Mathison said of Sharkey).[65] But give the fight to the man who hurt the other man the most.

In fact, in the 1920s the referee was often the sole judge, and he didn't actually count blows. He was too busy enforcing the rules in the ring. The *Police Gazette* recounts a tale of a too-literal-minded referee who handled several bouts in Coney Island and tried to actually add up every blow landed or blocked: "He had a pair of counters, one in each hand, and clicked off points, first for one, and then the other." But when the two men really started to sling leather, the referee gave up clicking his counters and went back to scoring the fight the way referees always had, by trusting his overall impression.[66]

The report of the Siki / McTigue championship fight that is the "thickest" (to use the anthropologist Clifford Geertz's term), with the most specific detail, in the *Irish Times,* gives the fight to Siki. That paper, moreover, was hardly partial to Siki. For the sake of science, however, it's interesting to score the fight based on an eclectic approach, using Fleischer's New York scorecard, crediting every punch the chief commentators said they saw, totaling them, and filling out a score card as if all four accounts together equaled a single judge. I omit, in doing so, the *London Times* and the *Chicago Defender* accounts, since both were lifted from the *New York Herald,* but I do include the *Herald,* along with the *New York Times, Le Populaire,* and *Irish Times* accounts. I credit punches landed in the first column and add a point to that column whenever an account specifically mentions "aggressiveness" (one fighter carrying the fight); in the second column I add a point whenever an account specifically mentions "clever sparring and good defense." Though several accounts mention warnings for low blows or kidney punches, none mention points being deducted. Thus that column remains blank. The following scorecard tabulates the result:

Battling Siki					Mike McTigue			
Rounds Won / Lost / Even	Aggres-siveness and Clean Hitting	Clever Sparring and Good Defense	Fouls, Clinching, Holding (—)	Rounds	Fouls, Clinching, Holding (—)	Clever Sparring and Good Defense	Aggres-siveness and Clean Hitting	Rounds Won / Lost / Even
W	9			1		1		L
W	2			2		1		L
W	9			3		2	4	L
W	7			4		2		L
W	5			5		2		L
L	2			6		1	4	W
W	3			7		1	1	L
W	4			8		1	2	L
L	3			9			4	W
L	1			10			3	W
W	5			11				L
W	6			12			1	L
L	3			13		1	3	W
L	2			14			4	W
L	3			15		1	4	W
W	4			16			1	L
L	2			17			7	W
L	1			18			10	W
W	8			19			1	L
L	3			20			4	W
11–9	82*			Totals		13	53*	9–11

*Note: Scoring totals are higher than they might normally be, since they score all the blows seen in all the various accounts of the fight; thus, if three reporters saw the same McTigue uppercut, for instance, it might be scored three times.

Had the reporters at ringside scored the fight together, exactly as they described it, they would have credited Siki with successfully defending his title. If you score the fight based only on "aggressiveness and clean hitting" (as seems to have been the case in the Sharkey / Schmeling fight), without giving credit for "clever sparring and good defense," the composite score gives Siki eleven rounds, McTigue eight, with one even. If instead you use the New York State card's additional scoring categories, giving McTigue credit for any mention of "clever sparring and good defense," you get eleven rounds for Siki, nine for McTigue. The *National Police Gazette,* boxing's original authority, however, observed, "Men who have gone into the question of points generally allow one point when a fighter leads and lands a blow and a half point if the antagonist is clever enough to counter and reach the mark."[67] Scored on those principles the fight would go lopsidedly Siki's way.

In our own day as well as Siki's, one final consideration comes into play. Siki was the world champion. In title fights, close decisions, by an unwritten law, go to the champion. Lightweight champion Willie Ritchie complained bitterly of a breach of this very assumption by referee Eugene Corri in Ritchie's title fight with Freddie Welsh in London in 1914, when Corri, acting as the sole judge, handed Welsh the title by a single point, scoring every round but one a draw.[68] Against Siki, English heavyweight Joe Beckett observed, McTigue showed he had "a jolly good defense at that!" But Siki had been the one "doing all the forcing." "Throughout the fight," Beckett said, McTigue "kept showing us what he can do, but I would have liked to see him do it."[69] In other words, though he sparred adeptly at times, he'd never really hurt Siki. The English press, the *Petit Parisien* reported, was universally acclaiming "the strength, suppleness, and the combative spirit" of the Senegalese, and even those who thought McTigue had won admitted his margin had been slender indeed.[70]

English referee Jack Smith's scorecard for the Siki / McTigue bout is lost to science, but when the final bell sounded he strode over to McTigue and raised his arm in triumph. One of McTigue's corner men, overcome by his emotions (one of which no doubt was astonishment), dropped to the floor unconscious. The Irish fighter's jubilant fans rushed into the ring to hoist him on their shoulders. But not everyone was so happy with the result. The *Petit Parisien* said the verdict was "badly enough received," that "violent protests arose within the hall," and that "the Irish [fans] themselves were not the last to show their discontentment." Siki fumed, complaining that he'd won the first seventeen rounds, and only faded in the final rounds because he'd run out of gas. In his dressing room he stalked back and forth, seething, waiting for the Irish police to give him the word that it was okay to leave the theater. Inside the hall the fans waited too—for the soldiers to finish sweeping the streets so they could head for the exits. When the last of them finally made it out through the doors, at 11:30 P.M., more than two hours after the fight ended, a sudden burst of revolver fire set the whole throng into a stampede.[71]

Siki himself was practically the last man to leave the arena. He would wait more than two weeks before finding his way back to France. "I am informed on good authority," wrote Frank Withers in the *Chicago Defender,* "that Siki is patiently awaiting the arrival of an American boat to sail for France, as he will not be allowed on British soil."[72] Siki would tell the Parisian sporting paper *L'Auto* that England's malicious maneuver in preventing him from transiting via England had cost him dearly. When he finally did book passage, on the Irish tramp steamer *Finola,* he was forced to pay an exorbitant 10,000-franc fee and spend four full days at sea. The American press couldn't resist laughing up its sleeve, blaming Siki himself for his predicament, though as the *Defender* noted the incident reflected badly on England, not on Siki.[73] Siki himself, chastened but retaining his self-deprecating humor, merely quipped, "I will never go to Ireland again, unless I can cross by way of England. I lost so much weight during the ocean trip to Ireland and back that I am now a middleweight."[74]

Back in Paris, Siki turned up at *L'Auto*'s offices with Louis Anastasie, the Continental Sporting Club proprietor, in tow, swearing he'd had it with Brouillet. "I have no manager now and I'll have nothing more to do with Brouillet," he said.[75] Months later Siki would insinuate Brouillet had stiffed him: "As for M. Brouillet, since the McTigue affair I've never seen him again. I'm told he stayed in Dublin to discuss with the promoters the cost of the cinema for my match with the Irishman; he knows that until that affair is settled he has nothing to hope for from me."[76] He spoke with equal bitterness of his treatment by the English. "I am very happy to be in Paris," he said, "and you can believe that the English have made me realize how cruel they are. I will retain a very bad memory of that adventure."[77] Of his future plans, Siki commented, "First of all I need a manager! On that subject I am in agreement with M. Anastasie, because I have great confidence in him, and I don't believe I can find a better one. Apart from that, tomorrow I'll go and see M. Rousseau, president of the FFB, and ask his advice." As for fighting again in Ireland, Siki said, he had nothing against the idea, in fact he'd "accepted in principle" to fight Bartley Madden there three weeks hence, but he hadn't signed anything and would go through with it only if the British authorities would permit him to pass through England, so he wouldn't again have to suffer four days of seasickness coming and going.

CHAPTER TWO

"The Wild Man of the Boulevards"

Lions and Leopards

In the spring of 1923, a lot of people in the boxing world drew a long sigh of relief. Battling Siki had lost. Maybe now he'd dry up and blow away. But then gradually they began to realize something. Siki was drawing nearly as much ink now that he'd lost his title as he had when he held it. The newspapers turned every thinnest bit of Siki gossip into a story. They played up stuff that wouldn't be news at all if someone else did it, running it not in the sports pages but the front section. When Siki got in a brawl with some waiters who taunted him for losing his title, in a fashionable restaurant in Montmartre (called, of all things, Le Rat Mort), the fracas got running coverage worldwide, even though no charges were filed against him.[1] So did another incident when Siki was accused of firing a pistol (which turned out to be just a starter's pistol, loaded with blanks) in a cabaret. In that instance, he did have to listen to the magistrate's "spiritual and indulgent indictment" and hear himself condemned, with a condescending smile, to pay a fine of three hundred francs (less than thirty dollars).[2]

Managers work like demons to get anything they can about their boy in print. Anything to fix in the public mind a persona, any hook to make their fighter real, to get the public to care about whether he wins or loses. And journalists are cynical. They toss away two-thirds of the tripe they're fed by publicity-hungry managers and promoters. But even though Siki's managers, busy fighting among themselves about who held a valid contract, hardly had time to push the fighter's name under the noses of the press, there Siki was in the papers anyway—everywhere, all the time. You could hardly keep him out of print. Carpentier, for all his celebrity, didn't have the pull on the public fancy Siki had. And McTigue, poor Mike McTigue, had hardly any at all. Though boxing's money men might now safely give the black fighter the cold shoulder, they suddenly discovered it wasn't at all in their interest to do so.

It would be easy enough, for instance, to arrange a Mike McTigue/ Georges Carpentier fight. But who'd pay to see it? Carpentier was primarily a counter-puncher, with a famously potent right hand. But McTigue figured never to get within smelling distance of that right hand. He was a certified Houdini of an escape artist. You had to figure Carp would win, unless McTigue's manager, Joe "Yussel the Muscle" Jacobs, engineered another miraculous decision in his boy's favor. But it would be no fight for purists, and it would be hard to make the public care enough about it to show up at the ticket windows. McTigue seemed genial enough, plucky enough, in the way that a schoolboy stealing apples from a farmer's orchard is plucky. But who'd pay to see a schoolboy stealing apples?

Let's face it, boxing fans choose their heroes in ways that have little to do with heroism of the Sir Galahad variety. They aren't drawn by heroes of noble brow, pure reputation, and sterling character. They've been in fights themselves, many of them. They've also ducked down side streets to avoid guys they didn't dare confront once or twice in life. A hero, to them, is someone so fierce, so inured to pain, or so desperate, that he won't feel the fear fans themselves would, won't break under the pain, will be frightening, not frightened. The boxing writers, in 1922, when the astonishing fact broke over them that they had as their new world champion not only a black man but an outspoken and flamboyant one, had bent heaven and earth to fix as quickly as possible in the public mind the idea that this guy had won only because he was a childish savage, a creature of strange fits of violence, impervious to pain. They'd done so because they wanted to protect the public from recognizing a chink in the armor of racial dominance, but their propaganda against Siki had an unexpected, opposite effect. A large part of the boxing public became fascinated with their manufactured icon of racial inferiority and took it instead for a perverse kind of superiority. If Siki was, as advertised, a gorilla in boxing shorts, a primitive throwback to the times when men were savage predators, then great! When can we get a chance to watch him? Who can we run out there to face him first?

And they didn't really want him in there with a slick escape artist, a slippery jab- and-duck type. They wanted King Kong against Tarzan.[3] It's no accident at all that Fleischer would later label Siki "the pugilistic King Kong of Paris," or an "imitation King Kong."[4] But he had the polarity exactly reversed. King Kong was an imitation Siki.

McTigue holed up in Dublin throughout the spring, intent on facing his first challenger on home ground. Siki tried to hold him to his promise of a rematch, but wanted it elsewhere, with judges who could be counted on to wait until they'd watched the fight to decide who won it. Carpentier, much as he wanted the title back, didn't feel like chasing it to Dublin either. When Carpentier finally agreed to fight McTigue in New York in July, McTigue's U.S. manager, Joe Jacobs, fired off a cable to his boy to get on the next boat back to New York—leaving his pregnant wife behind in Ireland. But the boxing public remained a lot more interested in a rematch between Siki and Carpentier than in either of them fighting McTigue. Carpentier postponed the McTigue bout until August.[5] In Paris, the French Boxing Federation and the sporting papers were making a huge fuss: Hey, what happened to the free rematch between Siki and Carpentier? What happened to giving the whole purse to Madame Curie?

But Carpentier's slick pilot, François Descamps, had no intention of letting his *poulain* risk his neck for free, no matter how badly reneging on their promise made them look. And Siki wasn't all that keen on the idea either. He'd hardly made anything on his title victory against Carpentier, had lived off various managers' and promoters' advances for all those lean months between the Carpentier fight and the Dublin debacle, and then had returned to France to . . . nothing much at all.[6] He'd fought everyone of any stature in Europe. Apart from a few English heavyweights, he'd cleaned out the top-three weight classes. He had a few fights lined up—one against English light-heavyweight Ted Moore, a solid fighter, but not one to capture the fans' imagination; another against Marcel Nilles, whom both he and Carpentier had already beaten; and another against Emile Morelle, the journeyman light-heavyweight the French boxing board had installed as French champion after they'd stripped Siki of that title the previous autumn. None of these fights was going to make anyone rich—and more and more the deluge of publicity surrounding Siki's every move made it clear that against the right opponent a Siki match might well make someone rich.

The right opponent. But who? The obvious choice was Dempsey—whose reputation for ferocity even overmatched Siki's, though his personality outside the ring was hardly as colorful. But the problem with a Dempsey match was that a huge portion of the public would be up in arms to stop it. Though most people gave Siki little chance against Dempsey, they remembered far too well the last time a black fighter had held the heavyweight championship, an equally flamboyant character by the name of Jack Johnson. Siki, with his white wife and his readiness to take on white hecklers outside the ring, reminded them far too readily of "L'il Arthur," as the ex-heavyweight champion liked to call himself. They'd made the mistake once of matching Siki against a white champion who was supposed to handle him easily. They weren't likely to make that error again. Tex Rickard had promised Siki three big bouts in America, against top light-heavyweights and heavyweights, dangling the names of Harry Greb, Gene Tunney, Jack Dempsey, and Harry Wills, but the match he really wanted to make was with one of the toughest black fighters on the planet, Kid Norfolk.

Meanwhile, the Siki bubble went sailing along without so much as a puff of promotional hot air from the boxing fraternity to drive it. And just when it seemed public interest in Siki might flag, along came the notorious lion story. Like the story of the savage innocent who knew no better than to fight an Irishman in Dublin on Saint Patrick's Day, it's a tale that has taken on a life of its own, outliving nearly every other memory of the Senegalese fighter. The U.S. press, once it had gotten over its initial hair-raising astonishment and racial anxiety, had taken up Siki as a running gag, building up the least bit of mischief the young man got into. Siki's shenanigans with his pet lions fit the bill perfectly. There was nothing especially out of the ordinary, mind you, about a professional fighter keeping exotic pets. As one of the great boxing writers of all time, A. J. Liebling, comments in "The University of Eighth Avenue," it had become a kind of tradition among boxers to mark ring triumphs with the adoption of an exotic animal. Lightweight champion Jack McAuliffe did his daily twenty miles of roadwork with a monkey perched on his shoulder. The monkey also sat in his corner during bouts and would leap on his back to help him celebrate as the referee raised his hand in victory.[7] Ruby Bob Fitzsimmons, who defeated Gentleman Jim Corbett for the heavy-weight championship in 1897, kept a pet lion at his ranch.[8] The very year that Siki got his lion cubs, Jack Dempsey was photographed with an ocelot he kept as a mascot while training to fight Luis Firpo.[9]

Siki's lions started out as a freak on the young fighter's part when he first got back from Dublin, a bit at loose ends, looking to distract himself from the loss of his title. Bénac, as usual, is ready with an account that benefits from an insider's familiarity, even if the insider in question reshapes the past at times to improve his story. In *Champions dans la coulisse,* Bénac recalls that he and Siki had befriended a couple of animal trainers named Marcel and "Martha the Corsican." Soon the pair had Siki taking exotic animals off their hands. Siki had been back barely twenty-four hours from Dublin when a reporter for *L'Auto* headed out to his modest middle-class house in suburban Vanves to interview him. When Mrs. Siki came out to the front gate to answer his ring, the reporter saw through the grill an exotic menagerie in the courtyard that included two huge Great Danes, a donkey, and a giant Percheron horse. She said her husband had told her he bought the animals with the intention of reselling them for a profit. She smiled and didn't seem to think much of her husband's commercial expectations. A few weeks later, a *L'Auto* reporter would witness Siki appearing at the same front gate with a full-grown lion in a cage, again swearing that he meant to sell it. He only gave up on the idea when he couldn't fit the cage through the gate to his house.[10]

Soon Siki heard his pals Marcel and Martha had gotten in a shipment of lion cubs, and this time he acquired them not with the idea of selling them, but of keeping them as pets. Bénac swears the two-year-old animals were essentially "inoffensive," but they got into serious mischief all the same, mauling someone's pet dog at the gym where Siki trained. Bénac also confirms one part of the story that soon became a favorite of the U.S. press (though Siki himself would deny it) testifying that Siki, at least on one occasion, maltreated his pets by giving each a glass of Pernod to drink in the Café Madrid, declaring, "now I've baptized them."[11] The French newspapers at the time, however, though they had plenty to say about Siki and his cubs, mention no such stunts. The *New York Times* does recount a tale about one of Siki's cubs leaping the bar at Maxim's and bolting down the stairs into the cellar, where neither Siki nor the waiters felt much like poking around to roust him out. Siki sent word to Marcel to come do the honors.[12] Another time, at the Neuily Fair, a cub clawed an innocuous passerby, one M. Munier, who filed a lawsuit seeking forty thousand francs in damages and interest.[13] Siki, by now, was getting a bit sick of his pets. Asked by a *L'Auto* reporter how they were doing, he replied that he'd have to get rid of them. They were becoming too much of a distraction to his training.[14]

The cubs were about half the size of Siki's two Great Danes, but they sure did make a stir in the few months he had them. They'd already made it into nearly every newspaper in the world when one of them playfully bit Siki on the hand, and though the wound was reported by *L'Auto* to be "light,"[15] it became infected, forcing his manager, Lucien Defrémont, to cancel the pending bout with English light-heavyweight Ted Moore.[16] The further away from their sources these stories travel, both in time and space, the less they resemble the actual incidents. Siki's cubs become full-grown lions and leopards, whom Siki, the writers urge, tries to raise strictly on absinthe, who turn on him and attack him violently, who send patrons fleeing at a run, screaming in terror, from cafés on the Boulevard Montparnasse. The *Newark Evening News,* for instance, pumped the lion-cub-bites-hand story full of hot air as follows:

> Battling Siki...has been bitten by a lion in a circus and therefore the
> bout between him and the British middleweight Moore, which was to
> have been held May 27 in Marseilles, has been postponed.... Of late
> Siki has deserted the squared circle for the circus sideshows in an
> endeavor to carry out his ambition to become as prominent as a wild
> animal tamer as he has been a man-mauler. A few days ago the
> Senegalese was severely bitten by a lion cub which he had dragged
> into a café from a nearby menagerie. He was said to have been
> attempting to force refreshments down the beast's throat.[17]

At first Siki seems to have enjoyed the attention his exotic pets brought. He
didn't much like being the butt of newsmen's jokes, but he couldn't help seeing how neatly other people's prejudices worked to his profit. In an era when
so-called savages were all the vogue, stunts like walking a lion cub on a leash
sold tickets. Siki wasn't alone in playing the exotic primitive. The African
American artists Bricktop and Josephine Baker played that role too. Baker
had first caught the public eye as a chorus girl in Noble Sisle's "Shuffle
Along" because of a manic way she had of thrashing her legs akimbo and
crossing her eyes at the end of a number. When she first appeared in Paris
in 1925 she caused a sensation by dancing an "Egyptian number" at the
Théâtre des Champs Elysées with bare breasts and nothing but a bunch of
feathers (or sometimes bananas) covering her genitals. Eroticism was thus
represented as somehow African—and if one crossed one's eyes, too, one
could perhaps buy the illusion that she hadn't grown up in a one-room
shack in Missouri, where she'd hunted food in trash cans, but was a raw
force of nature, fresh from the jungles of some distant exotic land. Baker
became so popular in Paris that white women even copied her straightened,
slicked-back hair. Siki too, it happens, was adept at the trick of suddenly
twisting his eyeballs into opposite quadrants, and did so, when prompted,
for newsreel cameras. He even went Baker one better, for he could roll them
in opposite directions, like loose marbles in a child's puzzle game.

  Siki's identity allowed whites to have it both ways, to indulge in what
they took to be a spectacle of savagery run wild, while reassuring themselves the alleged primitive would revert outside the ring to a docile innocent. Like Baker, Siki was affable, easygoing, unfazed by racial stereotyping.
Like black minstrel show artists forced by the conventions of the genre to
perform in black face, he was willing, when it suited him, to "black up," "play
the coon." But the imposture wearied—especially when he felt he'd been
short-changed of his share of the take. "I am tired of fighting for glory," Siki
told an American reporter in July 1923. "I got only chicken feed when I beat
Carpentier. Why don't they let up on me? I need money for my family." He

called his treatment by the French boxing board "persecution," a "plea" the *New York Times* labeled "pathetic."[18] But he had a point. Siki's first manager, Eli Lepart, had just come out of the woodwork to demand a cut of his winnings. Lepart had handled Siki back in the days when he was a ham-and-egg fighter taking whatever was offered in shabby dens in the south of France. He'd helped Siki, Lepart insisted, pushed him along, given him handouts when he was a nobody. Now that he was somebody, Lepart wanted his 30 percent.

Didn't everybody? Siki had for years been caught in the grips of the same conundrum: how did you escape from a manager who was getting you nowhere and find one both capable and willing to get you fights that would pay? Since when was a contract valid in perpetuity? His with Charlie Hellers had been provisional, for just one year. Lepart hadn't squawked when Hellers had started directing Siki's career, getting him fights all over hell and gone. He hadn't said a word even when Siki signed to fight Carpentier—since he fully expected Siki to lose. It wasn't until Siki astonished the world by winning a world title that Lepart had suddenly turned up intent on enforcing a contract he'd allowed to lapse more than a year before.

The Fédération Française de Boxe, as a result, had yet another effective method to rein Siki in. The previous winter they'd lifted his French title, ostensibly to punish him for roughing up a rival manager, but really so they could hold a tourney among other top light-heavyweights and hand the winner Siki's rightful laurels. In short order, the International Boxing Union (IBU), which the FFB's head, Paul Rousseau, largely controlled, had followed suit, lifting Siki's European titles. When the IBU restored them in February 1923, the FFB didn't follow suit with his French title. Now they were withholding it as a bribe: If he wanted it back (and if he wanted to keep his license), he had to challenge the pretender to his title, a mediocre fighter from Metz named Emile Morelle. Then he had to challenge the man he'd beaten the year before in an elimination fight for the right to face Carpentier, heavyweight Marcel Nilles. Then, in September, he had to go through with his promise to fight Carpentier for free.[19] As for the rival claims to the rights to manage or promote his fights, the FFB insisted that from now on Siki could sign nothing except in their offices, in the presence of Rousseau himself. There was some logic to this. Trusting none of his official managers, after all the times they'd short-changed or lied to him, Siki was far too ready to offer his exclusive services to casual acquaintances or friends. Bénac recalled how many times Siki had handed him a slip of paper with his signature on it, saying, "Here, you'll be my sole manager now."[20] But the FFB's action provoked a storm of petitions and counter-petitions, from rival claimants and Siki himself. The

FFB responded by threatening to ban Siki for life from fighting in France if he refused to fight Morelle, Nilles, and Carpentier, as Brouillet had promised on his behalf.[21]

Siki himself pointed out to *L'Auto,* just days before the scheduled match with Morelle, that his behavior hadn't been as erratic as it was made out to be. He'd studiously respected the FFB's strictures. According to Siki,

> Ever since my requalification, I've promised to sign nothing except in the presence of the president [of the FFB]. I signed in front of him a contract to fight Morelle similar to the one that the manager of Morelle signed. Right now I'm training with M. Anastasie, at the Pelleport Stadium. I recognize in this way that he fulfills the conditions of his contract and have not the least idea of failing him in any of my responsibilities towards him. M. Defrémont is very much occupied with his business; he cannot therefore give me all of his attention, but he has promised me not to abandon me on the eve or the day of the match. If he keeps his promise, then I will declare myself satisfied.

How men (such as Brouillet and Lepart) who hadn't kept their end of the bargain could now come forward and demand a cut of his winnings was more than Siki could fathom. For them now "to pretend to prevent me from boxing, under the pretext that they didn't sign my contracts," he fumed, was ridiculous. "The courts will decide whether the attention that they gave me merits the stipend that they claim. They will equally say who is or who are my real managers; I don't really think I need more than one; if the court insists on giving me several, then they can divide the percentage of the one most favored. These are questions that have nothing to do with the fight I want to combat."[22]

When Siki climbed through the ropes in Paris's Vélodrome d'Hiver (Winter Bicycle Arena) to face Morelle on June 16, 1923, he wasn't in shape.[23] He'd been spending more time with his exotic pets than in a gym. Bénac tells us he'd also been carrying on an extramarital affair with a sixteen-year-old gypsy girl, going nearly every night to the dangerous quarter where she lived, near a stone quarry (in Belleville?), battling rivals armed with knives and revolvers, and finally taking along his two Great Danes to protect him— until one night gypsy rivals stabbed them to death.[24]

The crowd greeted Siki with both applause and scattered whistles of derision. On the one hand, as *L'Auto* put it, they were thrilled to see Siki "in flesh and bone" for the first time in a Paris ring since his stunning destruction of Carpentier. But they were also put out by the Senegalese boxer's refusal to conform to FFB rules. The very day before, spooked by some last-minute specter of shady dealings, Siki had announced, via an open letter to the press, that he would not show up for the fight unless his light-heavyweight world title wasn't on the line. When the FFB refused to accede, he turned up for the weigh-in but declined, as he had in Dublin, to mount the scale. Maybe he knew he was overweight. He had, after all, hardly trained. But in light of what was to happen in the fight, he may also have heard rumors that someone had "reached" the referee. The FFB was the one sanctioning body actively upholding Siki's claim to the light-heavyweight title. Defying them risked losing that support. On the other hand, as *L'Auto* pointed out, the FFB had behaved erratically toward Siki, going through with the "masquerade" of an elimination tourney for Siki's French title even as it was re-anointing Siki as world champion. How, logically, could a French light-heavyweight be champion of the world without being champion of France?[25]

Siki spent the early rounds doing what was guaranteed to make a short fight of it, pressuring Morelle, pounding him to the body. In the second and third rounds, he floored Morelle with right hands to the chin. In the sixth, he dropped him again with a brutal shot to the gut. Morelle's corner protested the punch was low. The referee told Morelle he had a two-minute respite to recover from the blow. Siki, in his corner, grinned, laughed, waved to the crowd, assuming he'd won by knockout.[26] At ringside, Rousseau, the FFB president, meanwhile, was busy feeding the scribes some information he hadn't shared with Siki: he'd decided to withdraw for good the FFB's recognition of Siki as world champion. Then suddenly the referee signaled a disqualification. For the second time in a row in a Paris ring, a one-sided Siki victory was abruptly reversed via one man's ruling. As Morelle's handlers carried him from the ring, the fans began to hurl abuse. Had there been no foul call, they'd have celebrated the fulfillment of their expectations, a brutal knockout win. But now they were incensed. Did this savage think there were no rules?

The following morning, *L'Auto,* which so recently had taken his part, denounced Siki as a man who had failed to "honor his engagements." "He does not understand," they editorialized, "that the ring is something very perilous and that it doesn't accord its favors—which is to say glory and success—except on condition that one shows oneself worthy." One day Siki would live to regret wasting his best years in this way.[27] *L'Auto* would not go so far, however, as to suggest that Siki really was a dirty fighter—because if there was one thing he was not, it was that. It's impossible to know at this remove whether Siki really did foul Morelle, or whether Morelle simply took the easy way out of a fight he was on his way to losing, but if Siki did punch low, he didn't do so deliberately. If he were the sort to foul deliberately, he would have fouled Carpentier, who'd pulled every dirty trick in the book on him the year before.

By early August, with Rousseau urging the IBU to force Siki to go through with his commitments, Siki was threatening to back out of his fight with Nilles. Already banned in half the countries on the continent, as well as England, if he ducked out of this bout Siki would be down to precisely two places where he could still fight: Ireland and America. And for that matter Carpentier, if he reneged on his offer to fight Siki for the glory of French science, would be in nearly the same boat—though at least he hadn't been banned in England (which wasn't an IBU member).

Rousseau was playing a weak card, however. The FFB and IBU had both insisted the fight in Dublin hadn't been for a world title, since no official challenge had been issued and neither Siki nor McTigue had weighed in. But virtually every American boxing commission, relieved no longer to have to deal with a black world champion, recognized McTigue. Rousseau had been dangling his own recognition before Siki as a means to lure him into going through with fighting Carpentier—but now that he'd dropped that inducement, what motive did Siki have to follow FFB orders? Rousseau threatened a lifelong ban on Siki if he ducked out of the Nilles bout, set for July 8—but it began to look more and more as if he might do just that. He'd have a tough time convincing race-phobic America to grant him a license when he was under a lifetime ban in his home country, but maybe the smell of lucre would entice them. Then American promoter Tex Rickard abruptly declared that the big-money bouts he'd promised Siki depended on his showing against Nilles, and all at once the fight was on again.

A wonderfully sharp newsreel still exists, showing the entire bout.[28] In it Siki looks lethargic at first, crouched in a shell, covering up, while the hulking Nilles stamps after him like a rhino, in an old-fashioned English stance, bolt upright, turned completely sideways, left arm extended like a battering ram, right foot directly behind his left, propelling him forward in rapid jumps. He moves with surprising speed, despite his ungainly style, and twists the whole weight of his torso into his straight right hand. Siki hadn't done especially well against Nilles the year before, scraping by with a close decision win. Carpentier, in contrast, had knocked Nilles out. For all of the first round and the opening moments of the second the newsreel shows a bout that seems one-sided, with Nilles doing all the punching, Siki crouching, blocking. Then all at once Nilles hesitates at the wrong instant, and before you can blink Siki snaps a left hook, followed by a huge right-hand swing that cuts the air like a whip, sending his towering foe crashing to the canvas as if he'd been whacked behind the ear with a two-by-four. That final blow leaves Nilles flat on his stomach, twitching like a fresh-caught mackerel. He will have to be carried from the ring, and it will take nearly ten minutes to revive him.[29]

After Siki's dramatic knockout of Nilles, French fans were greedier than ever for a rematch with Carpentier. "Siki, more powerful, more supple than ever," *Le Populaire* enthused, "would be for Carpentier a rugged rival, and if he boxes as he did yesterday, he would be [a] formidable [one]."[30] McTigue, meanwhile, had an offer of twenty thousand pounds to fight Carpentier in England. But what he really wanted, and felt he deserved as newly anointed champion, was that series of three big fights in America Rickard had promised Siki. McTigue put on such a poor showing, however, in Philadelphia in a "limited round," no-decision bout against one of the light-heavyweight division's rising stars, Tommy Loughran, that Rickard gave him the cold shoulder. Bantamweight contender Charlie Phil Rosenberg, one of the era's most popular fighters, put it bluntly, "People pay to see blood. Well, I either gave them my blood or somebody else's."[31] With McTigue, the fans got instead a

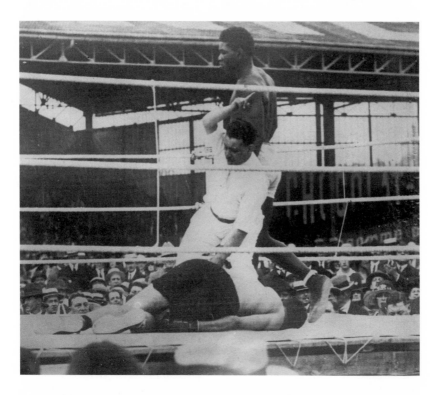

Siki knocks out Marcel Nilles, Paris, July 8, 1923. (Author's collection.)

game of hare and hounds. His manager, Joe Jacobs, knew fans would only pay big money to see McTigue fight one man. When Irish promoter Patrick McCarten offered him $100,000 or 45 percent of the gate receipts for a Siki rematch in September in Dublin, he quickly signed on the dotted line—and crossed his fingers hoping Siki would too.[32]

It remained to be seen whether Siki would. In many ways the logical destination for him was America, not Ireland. France seemed determined to offer him no inducements to stay. The boxing establishment there had made up its mind to force him to fight for free. And when he'd enriched the scientific coffers, they seemed to mean to force him to dole out handouts to a queue of lapsed managers noisily demanding their share of the spoils. Coming so quickly on the heels of the putrid decision in Dublin, the disqualification against Morelle soured Siki further on his chances for fair treatment in a European ring. What did that leave but America?

Yet in July 1923, the idea of going to America must have filled Siki with disquiet. The behavior of Americans in Paris toward blacks had become notorious. The French were hardly free from prejudices themselves, but at least during the war their image of the Senegalese had evolved from fearsome beasts of prey to simple, innocent children. But if French indulgence for Siki's behavior had more than a hint of condescension, it stood in stark contrast to the bitter anger and contempt Siki suffered from the huge colony of Americans lured to Paris by the surging value of the dollar. When Siki first won the title, black American papers had gleefully reported how white women mobbed him and kissed him on the streets. White Americans had been swift to retaliate, assaulting anyone they suspected of celebrating his triumph openly, especially persons of color from throughout the French colonies.[33] Siki more than once exacted vengeance with his fists for such affronts to him personally.[34]

Now there were fresh outrages. American tourists had begun using the power of the dollar to bully French tour operators and restauranteurs into segregating persons of color—usually discreetly, but sometimes with blatant disregard for French proprieties. At the Moulin Rouge fistfights erupted when American tourists jumped black men seen dancing with white women. One dance hall, the Bal Tabarin, began trumpeting itself as "the only place in town that admits only white people."[35] In July 1923 a scandal arose when a group of American tourists tried to expel from a tour bus a party of black French colonial soldiers, whose loyal service during the war left the French with a debt of honor that equaled their sense of indebtedness to America itself.[36] Then came a worse enormity. Unruly American diners at an elegant Paris restaurant confronted two African brothers, princes of the royal family of Dahomey, one a medical student who'd won the *Croix de Guerre* for heroism during the war, the other a lawyer, both dining quietly in evening clothes. Insisting the presence of the Africans somehow befouled the ambiance, the Americans demanded they leave, browbeating the proprietor into collusion. When the two men resisted and were thrown out by force, they continued their protest on the street, enlisting passers-by to their cause, who threatened to invade the restaurant, turn out the Americans, and trash the place to pay back the owner for toadying to such people.[37]

For days French papers bellowed outrage. "It is unacceptable that such moral values could show themselves in our country," bristled *Le Peuple*. "Racial prejudice isn't accepted in France.... Let us hope that energetic penalties will make certain foreigners understand that Montmartre... is still governed by French administrative law, and that a black citizen has there the same rights as a white citizen—even if the latter is very American, very drunk, and very rich."[38] "Hatred of blacks," *Le Populaire* fumed, "shouldn't be an article of exportation. That some Americans ignore all sentiment of humanity towards blacks and set against them a thousand odious regulations is something extremely regrettable, against which we can do nothing. But that they try to transplant their customs to our country, that they try to order us around and impose their habits here ... should arouse anyone of liberal spirit."[39] "If they don't like our ways," roared Blaise Diagne, the Senegalese deputy, "they can stay at home."[40]

Nor was this the first inkling France had of American racial enmity. The French public had heard with horror as far back as the summer of 1919 of street warfare in twenty-six U.S. cities, including Chicago, where fifteen whites and twenty-three blacks were killed and black areas burned and looted.[41] In January 1923, *Le Matin* ran a front-page series from a Texas correspondent about the rebirth of the Ku Klux Klan. We must be wary, the writer warned, for this oddball sect seems intent on exporting its program. He gave a graphic account of a lynching and a tarring and feathering. We laughed, he mused, when we first heard of this cult, with its idiotic names for an army of fantastic dignitaries (Grand Titans, Grand Dragons, Imperial Sorcerers), its secret meetings, its acolytes draped in sheets, peering though eyeholes in pillow-case hoods. Nothing so ridiculous could last long, we thought. But it had not only lasted. It had spread like wildfire.[42] In October 1919, the major newspaper in Toulouse told of a secret black army in Arkansas said to have fifty thousand boxes of ammunition secreted for an uprising to butcher whites.[43]

It's understandable, therefore, that Siki was in no hurry to quit France for America. At one point he actually posted a formal challenge (with a forfeit of five hundred francs) to Carpentier for his European heavyweight title, apparently meaning to make the best of a bad job and at least try to win a title, if he couldn't get paid for fighting.[44] But when the two met to discuss the match in the offices of the *Echo des sports,* Carpentier answered Siki's "hello Georges" by turning his back on him and marching out the door.[45] Meanwhile, ex-manager Eli Lepart continued to press his claim, hauling Siki into court, demanding a 30 percent share of every purse he'd earned in the past year and a half. Siki's lawyer, Alcide Delmont, managed to bargain Lepart down to a flat fee for a signed release, 35,000 francs—more than $2,000—equivalent to Siki's entire purse for defeating Carpentier, but substantially less than the 200,000 francs Lepart originally demanded.[46] Soon the promoter for the Morelle fight had also gotten into the act, suing Siki for 60,000 francs, claiming Siki's open letter declaring he wouldn't show up for the fight had hurt ticket sales. When Siki returned to Paris in early August from a junket to Bordeaux, where he'd flattened in the third round in a bullfight arena another pretender to French boxing laurels, a light-heavyweight named Marmouget, he'd finally made up his mind to take his chances on the other side of the pond.[47] Carpentier, he'd heard, was heading for America in any case. As Sparrow Robertson of the *Herald* put it, "Siki has cleaned them all up in Europe."[48] He had no one left to fight there.

Siki set sail on August 25 on the liner *Berengaria,* accompanied by Defrémont and two sparring partners, but not his wife and child.[49] Before Siki left, he told a *New York Times* reporter:

> I am making negotiations for an exhibition tour of America, but as yet nothing has been definitely decided. Yesterday a wealthy gentleman wanted to take me over there and make a fortune for me, and just today another wanted to put a guarantee of 500,000 francs in the bank for me at the moment I set sail. Still another has come along with a fairy tale, but I let them talk. My manager, Defrémont, will make all the arrangements for me.[50]

The final lines are telling. Though routinely portrayed, in America at least, as simple-minded to the point of being childish, Siki in fact was nothing of the sort. He knew a "fairy tale" when someone tried to feed him one. He equally categorized as "fairy tales" the "yarns told about his [alleged] pranks in Paris."[51] His recent tribulations had sobered him—both literally and figuratively. Even as antipathetic an observer as the *Herald*'s Sparrow Robertson noted that lately Siki was promenading through Montmartre "with eyes front all the time," bypassing the seedy dives he'd once frequented. About the only potable likely to turn his head was mineral water.[52]

"You know, I am perfectly peaceful and good now," Siki told the *Times* reporter. "I rarely go out and I want to be a gentleman." Another assertion widely reported in U.S. papers had him insisting, "I'm serious now, and am thinking only of boxing."[53]

The Young Man with the Bushy Hair

The man who came down the gangway from the Cunard liner *Berengaria* on September 1, 1923, was a letdown to the scribes and newsreel photographers lined up to record America's first real look at "the wild man of the boulevards" (as they liked to call him).[54] Smaller and more slender than they'd expected, dressed in a dark gray suit, black fedora, dark tie, and brown shoes, Siki might have been mistaken for a department store clerk, if it weren't for the bright yellow pocket handkerchief and ivory-handled cane he also sported—and if it weren't for the fact that America's racial order excluded people of his color from such a calling.[55] The reporters plied him with questions, but discovered he spoke no English and wasn't much more voluble when quizzed in French. Fellow passengers interrupted his curt answers, breaking in to shake his hand and wish him luck. Siki, it turned out, had been a great favorite on shipboard. He'd made an especially big hit with the children and the crew. The day before he'd staged a boxing exhibition on deck, donating the proceeds to the sailors' relief fund. Also on hand to welcome Siki was his recent nemesis, new light-heavyweight champion Mike McTigue, alert to the chance for real lucre that Siki's notoriety offered. McTigue was only too glad to tell the scribes Siki was "a great fighter" who "hit harder than any man in the game." "You haven't seen any of those fellows on the other side of the water fighting him, have you?" he added.[56]

The newsmen finally got a rise out of Siki when they turned the subject to his drinking, his alleged abuse of his pet lion, and his generally uproarious behavior. Well, he admitted affably enough, and in perfectly proper French, he did like wine better than water. And yes, perhaps he had been "just the least bit happy-go-lucky in the old care-free days," but now "all this was past." He was "walking the straight and narrow from this time on." He'd left the lion home, "for fear of being misunderstood," and by the way, he "resented" the nonsense the press had written about him forcing the animal to drink: "The lion was his pet and he wouldn't mistreat it."[57]

By a weirdly prophetic coincidence that was really no coincidence at all, since lately it was becoming commonplace, at the moment Siki's boat docked seven men sat in a row on wooden crates in front of a store on nearby Tenth

Avenue, as police cars screamed up, sirens wailing. The men roosted calmly, barely looking up, feigning indifference. We have a report of a shooting, the cops said. Did you boys see or hear anything? "Shooting?" they answered. "No shooting around here; not that we've heard of." The cops were about to walk off and leave them to their strange lassitude when the middle guy in the row of loiterers suddenly slumped forward. When the police propped him back up they saw blood coursing down his shirtfront. Hours later, in the French Hospital on West Thirty-fourth Street, when detectives tried to find out who shot him, he snarled, "I'll tell you nothing. Get away from me."[58] Hell's Kitchen's code of violent retribution didn't involve confiding in the officers of the law—as Siki himself would one day learn. He too would one day be found bleeding on these sidewalks, he too would wind up in French Hospital, and he too would know better than to spill the real story of what happened. But we're getting ahead of our story.

William White of the *Chicago Defender* is clearly bemused by the notorious foreign boxer he's just met. He's surprised, despite all the "malicious" tales he's read in the white press, to find the young man "genial," with "a whimsical way of expressing himself." He strikes White as being like "a big overgrown kid." Hardly the hulking gorilla the white press imagines, this fellow Siki in fact is "small-bodied, small-waisted, trim-limbed," and only about 5 foot 10. He does, however, have powerful shoulders, and "the largest pair of biceps we ever saw"; when he flexes his arms they pop up like a pair of derby hats.[59]

But the thing that startles White the most is the young fighter's hair. It's the wildest thing he's ever seen. Why the young man's mop must be four inches long, left unconked and uncombed, at a time when the only options for black male hair are either severely straightened locks or a close-shaved stubble. Siki's mop, on the other hand, is "a mass somewhat uneven," which, when he doffs his hat, leaves an inch-deep groove from his hatband, like an inscribed halo. When White asks if he'd consider getting it cut, Siki protests that he wears it that way because it suits his wife, whipping out a pocket photo of her and their infant son.

The hair marks the young stranger wherever he goes. Nobody in Manhattan wears a coif like that—so Siki, who loves to stroll the streets with a bottle of wine wrapped in a newspaper under his arm, draws gawking crowds everywhere. In answer to another reporter, who wonders what he might do when he retires from boxing, Siki hooks his thumbs under his armpits in mock parody and answers, "I don't know—promenade maybe."[60] He seems to drink the wine, White observes, only moderately, and insists the authorities genially looked the other way when he came into the country, allowing him to import ninety-four bottles for his private use.

But though Siki doesn't drink much himself, the wine is disappearing fast, for the young man is generous with his supply, even to casual acquaintances. White notes with tolerant amusement that Siki, if moderate in his drinking, is not so restrained either in his smoking or his skirt chasing. He seems always to have a cigarette in his mouth, and his eyes dart after every passing female, especially if she's white. "To women of his own color," White observes, "he pays little attention." Siki's strange color-blindness extends as well to boxing. When grilled about the bouts his manager is trying to line up—against Dempsey, Kid Norfolk, George Godfrey, Harry Wills—Siki admits, to White's astonishment, that he hadn't known, and isn't terribly happy to learn, that of the four only Dempsey is white. He doesn't want to fight blacks. He prefers whites. He knows better how to fight them. Siki really had fought few other blacks, but unfamiliarity wasn't the real reason he preferred whites. He would tell another writer, "I don't like fight colored man; can't get big money."[61]

In several weeks on U.S. soil, Siki had given the dailies remarkably little to build a story around. He'd wrecked no cafés, provoked no riots, knocked out no policemen, committed no felonious assaults. Well, he'd been arrested once—but that affair was almost laughable. Booked to a string of Vaudeville appearances for Jack Goldberg's review, Siki had sold out the house for nearly a week before the cops suddenly arrived to shut down the performance. So primed had the public been for an incident linking the words *Siki* and *police* that a crowd quickly gathered, totally blocking the street outside the Lafayette Theater on 131st Street, where Siki had been putting on a training exhibition with his sparring partners.[62] New York's boxing laws were a bit murky in the twenties. The sport had been outlawed there for eleven years, in punishment for its history of crooked fights and domination by gamblers, then reinstated, but on an exhibition-only basis that made the rendering of decisions illegal. It wasn't until 1920, under the instigation of state senator Jimmy Walker, the future mayor of New York City, that decision bouts were again made legal.[63] But the Walker Law set strict rules for the staging of bouts. Unknowingly, Siki had broken them. He'd put on the same training exhibition hundreds of times in Europe, with calisthenics, rope jumping, bag work, a few quick rounds of sparring—nothing by any stretch of the imagination like a real match—but he still was led away by a squad of police, and hit with a one-hundred-dollar fine. As one of the arresting officers confided, he could have avoided the penalty by the plain expedient of not taping his hands or wearing gloves. It was that simple.[64]

Battling Siki. (Author's collection.)

Siki wasn't finding much that was simple in the United States. He could get bouts, he was learning, only if he was willing to fight black fighters. And until he got a boxing license he couldn't fight even them. Meanwhile, he had time on his hands and nothing much to do with it. White tells us that though Siki and his entourage were lodging inexpensively in a Yonkers hotel, he'd already found a favorite haunt in Harlem, the Scaleberg Café on 131st Street. His manager, Lucien Defrémont, was finding New York State boxing commissioner William Muldoon no easy person to deal with. Muldoon, a bit of a character himself, was leery of granting a license to a man he regarded as a freakish oddball likely to bring discredit on the sport. An ex-carnival muscle man and wrestler who once billed himself as the world's strongest man, Muldoon had strong-armed dipsomaniac bare-knuckle champion John L. Sullivan into walking the straight and narrow in the weeks leading up to his toughest fight, against Jake Kilrain.[65] Like Sullivan himself, Muldoon was no friend of interracial boxing. Before Siki even arrived on American shores he'd issued dour pronouncements about Siki's putative unfitness to appear before the public in an American ring. Now Muldoon was stringing Defrémont along, telling him Siki had to prove he wasn't the public nuisance he was said to be, that he knew how to behave.

Muldoon is best remembered these days as the man who blocked Jack Dempsey's bout with the fighter many regarded as his toughest rival, black heavyweight Harry Wills. Though Tex Rickard had arranged the match, he didn't fight very hard to save it. He feared it might provoke riots, as had the Jack Johnson / Jim Jeffries match. The heavyweight title was political dynamite. "It was all right to have colored champions in the lighter divisions," mused Dempsey, "like Joe Gans or somebody like that. But many people, accustomed to Sullivan, Corbett, Fitzsimmons and Jeffries, considered it an insult to the white race that Johnson should hold the heavyweight title—and Johnson didn't do much to make them think any other way."[66] For public consumption, Muldoon pretended to be outraged by Rickard's proposed high admission prices. Nat Fleischer's Dempsey biography replays Muldoon's spurious rhetoric: "Whether the men responsible admit it or not, they have come dangerously near accomplishing the abolition of boxing. The talk of millions and hundreds of thousands for a ring exhibition where the heavyweight title is at stake is repulsive."[67] The first "mixed bout" in New York in many years was staged under Muldoon's watch, in March 1923, between heavyweights George Godfrey and Jack Renault, but Godfrey got the fight only because he promised to "carry" his white rival.[68]

Meanwhile, Siki himself, restive at Defrémont's failures, was hearing on all sides the dulcet voices of would-be managers: sign with me, kid. This Defrémont guy can't get you the fights you deserve. He doesn't know his way around the New York fight scene like I do. As Siki's final comment before he left France indicates, he heard this kind of chatter all the time. But it began to make sense. Defrémont, after all, was a timber merchant, not a real boxing manager, and the validity in America of a contract signed in France was questionable anyway. When McTigue had gone to Ireland, he'd taken on an Irish pilot. His American manager, Joe Jacobs, had split the manager's share. Why shouldn't Siki sign with someone who could cut the Gordian knot of delays and obfuscations keeping him out of an American ring? Defrémont hardly seemed to be holding up his end anyway. He was basically just leaping at whatever Tex Rickard offered. He'd signed an agreement for Siki to fight Harry Wills, then another for him to fight George Godfrey, both hulking black heavyweights, even though Siki had said he didn't want to fight black fighters, and even though Wills, whose manager was hot in pursuit of a title fight with Dempsey, had shown little interest in his fighting Siki.[69]

Godfrey, the "Leiperville Shadow,"[70] whom Defrémont had signed Siki to fight in Philadelphia on October 8, was a genial colossus whose willingness to accommodate himself to fixes ingratiated him to gangsters.[71] Jack Johnson's erstwhile black rival, Sam Langford, had discovered Godfrey, then just a teenager, in a Chicago gym and Johnson had taken him along on an exhibition tour. He'd abandoned the young heavyweight, however, when Godfrey began to make him look bad in the ring. Though Godfrey's eventual record would be spotted with suspicious losses that probably were dives, at 240 pounds, he was a daunting opponent for the 170-pound Siki. Working as Dempsey's chief sparring mate a month earlier, before the Firpo match, Godfrey had decked the world champion for what would have been a knockout—if Dempsey's handlers hadn't been too busy ministering to their fallen meal ticket to bother counting to ten.[72] Harry Wills was nearly as big as Godfrey and an even more powerful slugger. Defrémont, in searching for potential rivals, seemed concerned only with making a few quick bucks, even if he got Siki killed in the process, not with getting him the fights he wanted, against Dempsey, Carpentier, or McTigue.

E. W. Ferguson, boxing columnist of the *Montreal Herald,* came away from his first meeting with the notorious "wild man of the boulevards" with the same favorable impression as the *Defender*'s William White. The young man, on his way to a series of exhibitions in Quebec City, seemed "quiet-spoken, well-behaved." Could this really be the same young boxer whose "stormy and erratic disposition" had wreaked havoc across the water? Ferguson saw not the least hint in this "astonishingly quiet" and "reserved" fellow of the man said to have left a trail of destruction, the man whose charges of an attempted fix in the Carpentier fight had made him "a national figure in France, even outside of pugilistic circles," his fate debated in the French parliament, and finally the object of an international incident with the British Home Office. Imagine! "A Chamber ... quarreling over a colored prize-fighter!" And yet, Ferguson wondered if Siki hadn't been "the object of persecution," "more sinned against than sinning," his misdeeds "grossly exaggerated." When Ferguson pressed him about the stories of ferocious lions on leashes Siki laughed and said the beast in question had been nothing but "a wee suckling cub."[73]

Whether a walking terror or a choirboy, Canadian fans were thrilled to have Battling Siki in their midst, especially since his arrival afforded a first glimpse as well of forty-three-year-old former heavyweight champion Jack Johnson, who was to be his opponent in the exhibition series. Johnson, Ferguson observed, seemed hardly to have changed since his days as champion. He still dressed ostentatiously, still shaved his head bald, still flashed his famous gold-toothed grin, and at 220 pounds looked, if anything, more trim and fit than he had on the day he lost his title in April 1915. Though these were only exhibitions, the Siki / Johnson encounters had a historic feeling, as of an old generation set aside, with no good grace, for a new one. In Quebec City and Sherbrooke, the first stops on the Siki / Johnson exhibition tour, fans were delighted to find that "L'il Arthur" had lost none of his defensive skill. He spent six 2-minute rounds in the ring with Siki, alternately going into a defensive shell, then grabbing the smaller man, pinning his arms, and wrestling him off balance, all the while grinning broadly at the crowd. Siki, despite this being a mere exhibition, went after L'il Arthur for the first minute of each round with the ferocity of a man avenging an insult— but Johnson kept him at bay, stabbing jabs to his face, then tying him up and showboating, mugging for the crowd, risking nothing like a sustained counter-assault.[74] Siki should not have taken Johnson's showboating personally. He was just as apt to play to the crowd himself, to wave and grin, call out wisecracks—as he'd done in the Morelle bout.

But something about the way Johnson was playing him for a fool didn't set well with Siki, and rumors reached the *Montreal Herald* of bad blood between the two.[75] You'd think Johnson would have been glad to give a break to the young black champion, the first in any division to even get a shot at a title, much less win one, since Johnson won his own. But he wasn't made that way. He'd never given any black rivals from pre-championship days, Langford, Sam McVey, or Joe Jeannette, a shot at his title, preferring to face mediocre white challengers. Moreover, Johnson may have disliked Siki for the very good reason that Siki and he were too much alike. He'd never been the sort to relish standing in another man's shadow.

By the time the Siki / Johnson exhibition tour returned to Montreal, the *Herald* columnist E. W. Ferguson had reason to revise his original estimation of the soft-spoken fellow he'd met the week before. On fight night at the Mount Royal Arena Siki showed up in a yellow leather overcoat, with a cigarette dangling from his lips, and further offended Ferguson's sensibilities by grousing about the spare accommodations, trying to slip a few chance acquaintances past the doorman, and parading through the stands before the bout glad-handing patrons. When he did make his way to the dressing room, Siki lounged about in a bright red silk robe and "dainty slippers" that Ferguson speculated must have been picked up in the red light district. He was "quiet enough" when the mayor and a city alderman appeared to wish him luck, but suddenly dashed into the arena when he heard that an old friend from Paris, Robert Distaillon, a rugged war hero who, like Siki, bore the scars to prove it, was having a tough time in his preliminary bout.[76] Siki shouted encouragement from ringside to his friend, who badly needed it, for he was on his way to an eighth-round knockout loss. By then ringside police had coaxed the overstimulated African fighter back to his dressing room.[77]

Ferguson, plainly embarrassed at having defended this eccentric fellow, next had to witness an altercation in the corridors behind the arena, as Siki, fist cocked, threatened his own handlers, including "his management," which Ferguson labeled "numerous." Défrémont must have been one of the group, since his two other fighters, Robert Diamond and Charles Raymond, went along on the junket, but Siki may have had another pilot along as well, for just days before he left New York, the boxing commission upheld as legal Siki's freshly inked contract with an American manager, Gene Sennet.[78] Ferguson doesn't specify what the altercation was about, but it isn't hard to guess, since just days later Siki would part company from Defrémont and Sennet both when they sold his contract to a new American pilot. Ferguson describes the fracas as ending with Siki pounding on the door of another dressing room, but doesn't say whose or why. It's not hard to figure out. It must have been Johnson's. The *Montreal Herald* reports that the deal for the exhibition had the two men sharing 50 percent of the gate receipts or three thousand dollars, whichever was higher, but doesn't specify who got what from that sum. As in Ireland, Siki was no doubt adamant that he wanted to be paid before stepping into the ring.

Whatever he said in the hallway, or inside that dressing room, it must not have endeared him to Johnson, for L'il Arthur was, if anything, even more vocal and contemptuous in this bout than the earlier one. At one point he lay "negligently" against the ropes, dropping his arms, as Siki glared and beckoned him to come to the middle of the ring and fight. More than once Johnson rabbit-punched Siki behind the neck. When he called "come on and mix," Siki tried to oblige him by plastering him with whirlwind combinations, but as in the earlier exhibition, Johnson frustrated him by blocking well, slipping punches, shoving his much-lighter rival off balance. The next day, when the entire company, including Johnson, entrained at Bonaventure Station on the Rutland Railway for New York, another fracas broke out, and Siki was actually put off the train at the first stop, St. Lambert.[79] The New York papers jumped all over the story, spinning it as another drunken-savage-slugs-it-out-with-cops tale, but when the Montreal scribes finally ran down Siki himself, he told a different story. The scrap had been over money, fifteen hundred dollars he insisted had been stolen from him. He didn't say by whom, but the inference is clear. He hadn't been paid for the exhibitions.[80] His managers had either stiffed him outright or put him off, pending a settlement of accounts for expenses. The whole deal was complicated by the fact that they were about to sell Siki's contract. Just days later they would announce they'd let it go for six thousand dollars to a shirtwaist manufacturer from the West Side of Manhattan named Robert Levy.[81]

Meanwhile, the New York papers had just the sort of Siki story they'd been longing for, a wild-man-gone-rabid yarn, a savage-lost-in-civilization scoop. And Siki really was nearly on the bum for a day or two. The first night after the altercation on the train, the *Montreal Herald* reported, the poor guy had made the rounds of the big (and therefore white) hotels, trying to get a room, but was turned away from every one.[82] Finally, after wandering the streets for hours, picking up the usual new friends and casual cronies along the way, he wound up at a cheap boardinghouse on St. Dominique Street. By morning, chastened but unbowed, he was cabling New York, trying to run down whoever was his pilot these days, knowing that the deal to sell his contract couldn't go through without him. When he got no answer, he talked local promoter Aleck Moore into advancing him the price of a ticket in return for his signature on a contract. Moore returned with Siki to New York, bent on pursuing his brand-new claim.[83]

Though he'd been about as tractable in New York City as any young fighter was likely to be, Siki's latest managerial complication was the last straw for the New York boxing czar William Muldoon. Faced with a whole clan of rival managers, he declared Sennet's contract valid, and accepted as equally valid the sale of that contract to Robert Levy, who up to now had mostly occupied himself with the business of making sure the seams were sewed straight at his factory in the garment district. Muldoon did make one final stipulation, moreover, which was far from the liking of Siki himself. He ordered the young fighter to go through with the one fight Sennet had signed for on his behalf: against the man many considered the toughest light-heavyweight on the planet, Kid Norfolk, in Madison Square Garden, just ten days hence, on October 26.

CHAPTER THREE

"The Leopard...his Spots, the Ethiopian...his Skin"

With Becoming Dignity

To hear the million-dollar-gate man Tex Rickard tell the story, this quixotic young fellow from the land of the palm trees, Battling Siki, has put Mr. Rickard seriously out of pocket with his shenanigans. Twice in a matter of weeks Siki has insisted on a last-minute postponement of his scheduled bout with Kid Norfolk, the Baltimore light-heavyweight, erstwhile heavyweight, and all-around roughneck Siki's manager signed for him to fight. Siki has trekked down to the state boxing commission offices for weeks with a string of managers in tow, much to the exasperation of Commissioner William Muldoon. Each time, it's the same story. He doesn't want to fight Norfolk, doesn't believe he's obligated to, and in any case is in no shape to take on anyone in Norfolk's class right now. The postponements have come so late in the game Rickard hasn't had time to find a substitute and has had to eat the loss.

In each tête-à-tête with the mercurial African and his entourage, Muldoon has stuck to his guns. When he signed for Siki to fight Norfolk, Gene Sennet was the young man's legitimate American manager. The sale of Siki's contract was bona fide, but that does not invalidate the deal to fight Norfolk. Like it or not, new pilot or not, Siki must go through with the bout. Siki's latest manager, shirtwaist manufacturer Bob Levy, has inherited that obligation with the contract. And as for Siki being in shape to fight, why he'd damned well better get in shape. Muldoon, ex-physical fitness guru that he is, isn't putting up with any guff on that score. To him, this is the same story he went through with another pugilist with a fondness for alcohol, the great John L.

Sullivan. A firm hand, constant oversight, and a stubborn demeanor did the trick then. It will now. Muldoon lays it on the line: He'll grant a postponement, but only for four weeks, until November 20. And in the meantime he's withholding Siki's boxing license. He'll keep it in his desk drawer until the day of the fight. Siki will then have to report to the commission offices and prove he's in shape. Otherwise, Muldoon will tear it up and call off the bout. And Muldoon swears he'll rip up the license even sooner if Siki fails to conduct himself "with becoming dignity."[1]

This, of course, is all for the benefit of the press. Muldoon isn't likely to learn much about Siki's physical condition by feeling his biceps or having him do a few jumping jacks in the commission offices. The fight is scheduled to go fifteen rounds. The only way Siki could prove he's in shape for that grueling ordeal would be to stage a full training session of equivalent intensity under Muldoon's nose. He isn't about to do that on the day of the fight.

Anyone who knew anything about the fight game knew Muldoon was grandstanding. Whoever heard of a fight being postponed because one fighter wasn't in shape? Harry Greb fought the last few fights of his career blind in one eye. Sam Langford kept on fighting even after his vision had deteriorated to the point where all he could see were dim shadows. Mickey Walker was falling-down drunk when he went into the ring to fight Paul Swiderski in Louisville in 1930.[2] In 1923 one of the top heavyweights in the country, Billy Miske, was still fighting even though he was dying of Bright's disease. Though a urinalysis would have disclosed his debilitating kidney ailment, Miske got the Michigan boxing board's approval to challenge Jack Dempsey, one of the most brutal body punchers in boxing.[3] Miske had been set to fight ex-champion Jack Johnson as well. That bout had been canceled—not out of concern for Miske's weakened condition, but because the New Jersey commissioner thought it would be a "lowdown disgrace" to sanction a fight involving the disreputable ex-champion![4]

Muldoon's grandstanding was partly political (meant to reassure the public that the newly reinstated sport of boxing was being rigorously overseen), partly self-serving (the ex-carnival strongman liked being in the public eye), but all this fuss wasn't much fun for new pilot Bob Levy, whose late-blooming interest in boxing threatened to distract him from his real love, baseball. Once a gifted amateur ballplayer himself, Levy was a passionate New York Giants baseball fan, and Siki's return from Canada coincided with a dramatic and troubling turn in the fortunes of his beloved team, at that moment in the process of losing the World Series, for the first time, to an upstart team from the Bronx led by a bandy-legged former Boston Red Sox hurler named Babe Ruth. When Levy recovered from his chagrin, he discovered that the managerial contract for the celebrated foreign boxer that he'd purchased for six thousand dollars came with constricting strings attached, in the form of rival claimants, a signed obligation for a bout already twice postponed, and an out-of-shape boxer adamant in his refusal to fight the man the commission insisted he must fight. It took Levy, novice to the boxing game that he was, a full week and a half to set about mending fences and making the best of this bad job.

He had no easy task. Siki was telling Levy, Muldoon, and anyone else who cared to listen that he didn't want to fight Norfolk at all. He wanted Carpentier, McTigue, or some other white light-heavyweight, such as Tom Gibbons or Gene Tunney. If he must fight Norfolk, he wanted "two or three minor bouts" first.[5] If Siki had known a bit more about the New York boxing scene he'd have realized he was wasting his time. The first interracial bout in recent memory had taken place just eight months before, in March 1923, between George Godfrey and Jack Renault, but even his promise to carry his white rival wouldn't have won Godfrey that dubious honor, had not a boxing manager from Oregon, George P. Moore, forced Muldoon's hand by doing some amateur sleuthing and instigating a one-man revolution.[6] Moore had spent weeks chasing phantom bouts for black bantamweight Danny Edwards in 1922. Every time he seemed close to a deal, a hitch appeared. Suspicious, Moore started poking around in the murky depths of the boxing game and somehow got hands on a letter from Commissioner Muldoon to his Philadelphia counterpart spelling out how black fighters were kept out of the ring with whites. The *Chicago Defender* outlined how the system worked. When pressed by reporters, Muldoon would insist that it was the promoters who'd "failed to present a mixed program for the commission's approval." Yet when Moore asked promoters what was going on, every one, "from Tex Rickard down," insisted he didn't dare risk mixed-race bouts "for fear of losing [his] boxing license, which strongly indicated the promoters got their instructions when the licenses were issued."[7] Undaunted, Moore, with two allies, city alderman George Harris and Port of New York tax inspector Charles W. Anderson, pushed mixed-race boxing as a political issue. When Governor Alfred A. Smith, in the closing speech of his 1923 reelection campaign, couldn't explain why top challenger Harry Wills was denied a shot at Dempsey's heavyweight title he was nearly booed off the stage at Harlem's Liberty Hall.[8] Finally, when promoter Jim Buckley of the Pioneer Athletic Club on West Twenty-fourth Street filed for a mixed-race bout in 1922, two of three commissioners voted to approve it.[9] The lone dissenter? Muldoon.

A year later, Muldoon would gladly have forbid Siki from fighting white boxers—if he dared. But he didn't have to. Instead he could just refuse to nullify the contract for Siki to fight Norfolk. He laid down the law. No Norfolk bout, no boxing license! And he added that he was serious about Siki acting with "becoming dignity," too. Any more shenanigans and he'd bar Siki from New York rings for good. And since most other state boxing boards followed New York's lead, the young African would have a tough time fighting any-where if New York excluded him.[10] The next day an incident in a Harlem speakeasy late at night gave Muldoon additional excuse for throwing cold water on talk of the young African fighting whites.

The episode was murky at best. Though it involved all the requisite ele-ments for a rousing savage-loose-in-civilization tale—a late-night encounter in a café, excessive alcohol, bared fists, police intervention, an arrest on charges of intoxication and assault—the elements were strangely jumbled. The morning after the incident, the *New York Times* reported simply that late at night at Siki's favorite hangout, the Scaleberg Café on Seventh Avenue and 131st Street, he and another black man, one Lieutenant Oswald Desverney (or Des Vernie), had gotten into an altercation, whereupon Desverney had pulled out a .45 caliber revolver and threatened to shoot Siki, who had promptly retreated to the 135th Street Police Station and fetched detectives, who arrested Desverney.[11] It wasn't so astonishing that a famous boxer would be involved in such an incident. As welterweight and later middle-weight champion Mickey Walker observed, once a boxer won a title, he could count on being a target for foolhardy strangers. "If you stay at home," he mused, "it's peaceful and nice, but if you go around where the lively life is in town ... you're going to be challenged to a fight at least three times a night, three drinks in a guy and they're going to be the fighter."[12]

A few days later a more baroque tale emerged in the pages of Harlem's own weekly, the *Amsterdam News*. Siki, it turned out, really hadn't done anything especially provocative, unless giving a fellow veteran of the great war a Gothic kiss on the cheek might be considered a provocative act.[13] Desverney, however, had been charged with violating the Sullivan Act (prohibiting concealed firearms) and two counts of felonious assault, for he'd not only threatened to shoot Siki, but leveled his weapon as well at Detective William Boyle.[14] This was no joke in Harlem in 1923, where over the last two years several police officers had been murdered by assailants firing from ambush.[15] Desverney begged for leniency, citing his war record, denying malicious intent. He'd just been "showing" Siki his weapon, he said, "during a conversation about Jack Dempsey," when Siki, half-drunk, had "jabbed him in the side." At that point he "threw his coat aside and showed ... his army revolver in the holster, whereupon Siki left."[16] The reference to Dempsey suggests what really happened. Desverney said, "Aw, you couldn't beat Dempsey"—whereupon Siki jumped from his stool to show his new buddy how quick his hands were. Siki's prompt effort at reconciliation suggests the poke in the ribs was good-natured. And the fact that Desverney pointed his weapon at Detective Boyle suggests that he, not Siki, was the one who escalated the encounter into real violence.

To understand the absurdity of Siki being barred from boxing for such an offense, you have to consider that white pugilists were hardly known for their "becoming dignity" in public. Mickey Walker, for instance, once went on a week-long bender with a fellow drunkard, sleeping between debauches on the floor in the back room of bars, neither bathing nor eating nor changing clothes.[17] After his losing battle to middleweight champion Harry Greb, he and Greb, meeting by accident that night in a bar, went on a pub crawl together that ended in a fistfight on the street in front of gangster Bill Duffy's Silver Slipper Club on Forty-eighth Street.[18] Greb himself was in so many barroom brawls, biographer James J. Fair tells us, that he had the art of the sucker punch down to a near science, as did Jack Dempsey.[19] Dempsey was once hauled out by his ankles from under the bed in a speakeasy's back room when the cops raided the joint.[20] His first wife admitted in court to having supported her then-penniless husband by plying the trade of streetwalker. Dempsey's manager, Doc Kearns, later alleged that Dempsey had in fact been her pimp.[21] Million-dollar-manager Tex Rickard, the very man who would promote the fight Muldoon was threatening to cancel, had been at the center of a major scandal when he was charged with luring underage girls into sexual trysts at a swimming pool above the old Madison Square Garden.[22] Muldoon never threatened to ban Greb, Walker, Dempsey, or Rickard from the boxing game. But then, they were white.

If he cared to see what Sennet, Defrémont, and Levy had gotten him into, Siki might have strolled over any time to see Kid Norfolk training at Grupp's Gym on 116th Street. Had he dropped by there, he might have been even more reluctant to go through with the match, for Norfolk well merited his reputation as one of the best counterpunchers, and ugliest customers, in boxing. Harry Greb had found that out the hard way in their 1921 bout, when Norfolk paid him back for thumbing him in the eye by retaliating with such vehemence that he blinded Greb in one eye. Greb, despite the injury, went right on with his boxing career, making cornerman Happy Allbacker swear to keep his secret.[23] He even fought a rematch with Norfolk in 1924, and when he did no better than in their first encounter, pulled a fast one to avoid further suffering, maneuvering Norfolk into a corner and hitting him after the bell, giving Allbacker an excuse to leap onto the ring apron and crack Norfolk over the head with a bottle. Greb lost by disqualification, but still had one eye left intact.[24] So tough a foe was Greb himself that Doc Kearns, Dempsey's manager, flat out refused to let Dempsey fight him. The "human windmill's" unorthodox style gave everyone fits. Kearns wanted "no traffic with that son-of-a-bitch."[25] Greb, however, was one of the white fighters Siki proposed fighting instead of Norfolk.

Few boxing fans of our era have had a chance to see films of Kid Norfolk in the ring. A rare newsreel of one of his fights, against longtime Dempsey sparring partner Big Bill Tate in 1920, still exists. Watching it gives one a real sense of why Norfolk was the most feared fighter in the light-heavyweight ranks, and why even a lot of heavyweights wanted nothing to do with him. Norfolk's style at once startles you and seems familiar. You can't help but note how herky-jerky and spasmodic it is. Tate towers over him—but hardly seems to dare to throw a real punch—mostly contenting himself with poking long-armed jabs while leaning well back, out of harm's reach, snatching his hand back after each punch as if he'd scalded it. He knows what's coming and wants that hand in front of his face to defend against it. Norfolk, squat, coal black, bullet-headed, broad in the shoulders, his v-shaped back all knots of muscle, poises on his toes with his front foot nearly touching Tate's, rocking side to side, with unpredictable, staccato jerks, like a mongoose luring a snake. It's as if he's daring Tate to strike—and as if Tate is scared to take his dare. Each time Tate throws a half-hearted right, Norfolk bobs under it vaulting his taut body upward like a coiled spring, twisting that powerful back into doubled, even tripled hooks, that explode with thudding force. Sometimes he throws rights, too, cleaning up his combinations with brutal efficiency.

He's scary, this guy. He reminds you of a smaller, more agile, more compact Joe Frazier, his head movement quicker, usually to his right, away from Tate's right hand. Because of that constantly bobbing head, he takes fewer punches than Frazier did. Tate, though he knocked out fading ring immortal Sam Langford, is having no luck touching Norfolk. Norfolk hardly ever throws a jab, his disdain of that weapon baiting his rival, luring him into reaching, shifting his weight forward, exposing ribs or chin, so that Norfolk can dart in, mongoose style, and strike. Big and powerful as he is, Tate seems to have only one goal in mind: to keep Norfolk on the end of that long jab. He doesn't dare to muscle in on the squat light-heavyweight, though Norfolk does everything he can to tempt him to try.

Few people in New York had seen both Norfolk and Siki fight. But anyone who had would warrant this bout for a barn-burner. Both were fierce, give-no-quarter punchers. And Siki was not likely to sit outside and bide his time, as Tate did. His style was full frontal assault. Nor was Norfolk the kind

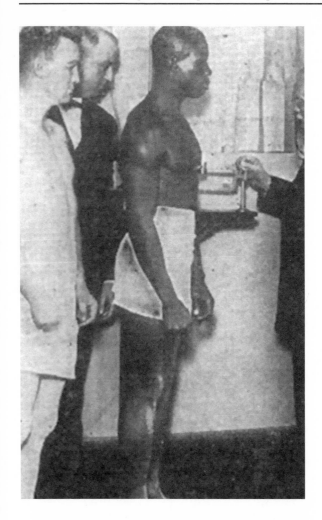

Kid Norfolk weighing in for his 1924 bout with Tommy Gibbons. (Author's collection.)

of fighter you could back up. The more Siki came after him, the more furiously Norfolk would wing those counters of his. But Siki wasn't the kind to quit coming forward either. Siki had one of the best chins in boxing, as did Norfolk. Something had to give, yet nothing would. Yes, this fight figured to be a war—if only Siki could get in good enough shape in the four weeks that remained before fight night, November 20.

Lots of people who followed boxing in New York doubted his chances of doing so. The *Amsterdam News* columnist Romeo L. Dougherty had been one of the few newsmen willing to spell out what had really gone on. "Poor, poor Battling Siki" had been fleeced, "managed" by a succession of hustlers, each taking their cut while making no effort at all to get him the fights he wanted and deserved, conniving with the boxing club proprietors to freeze the "black Frenchman" out until, "flat broke," he'd be forced to take a fight he didn't want and couldn't win. Meanwhile, Siki had been frequenting some of the worst dives in Harlem, being fed "some of the vilest liquor on record" by false friends who had anything but his best interests at heart. When the boxing clan finally did maneuver the "poor black half savage from Senegal" into a ring, if it was against Kid Norfolk or someone of that caliber, "after they count him out there will be nothing left for him to do but grab a steamer as quick as possible for that dear Paree."[26] Anyone, Dougherty implied, who thought Siki's recent travails an accident was a sucker.

Meanwhile, Siki's new manager, Bob Levy, seemed curiously lax about getting his fighter into training camp. He dawdled away a full week before he got Siki across the river to a boxing camp in Summit, New Jersey, and another week before he found a professional trainer to work with him. Until an old-timer from the boxing game, Tom Goodman (his claim to fame that he'd once trained Sam Langford), finally joined them in Summit, a little over a week before the fight. Levy had simply let Siki set his own routine and work out with whomever was handy—a dangerous stratagem for a fighter facing one of the toughest tests of his career. But then what did Bob Levy know about boxing? He was a baseball man.

See That Tree There?

It's Friday, November 2, 1923, and a young light-heavyweight from Georgia, just eighteen years old (though he tells everyone he's nineteen), has been called into the ring to be introduced to the crowd before the Madison Square Garden main event between Floyd Johnson and Jack Renault. He strolls across the ring in his nice suit, blond hair neatly slicked back, blue eyes glinting, but as he turns to wave to the stands, a shy smile creeping onto his lips, a chorus of boos builds, overwhelming the spattering of applause. The crowd's enmity startles him, freezing that smile awkwardly in place as he goes stiffly through the rest of the ritual, turning to each quadrant, hand upraised, face flushed. Columnist George B. Underwood doubts he'll ever forget this image: the poor kid with that sickly half smile plastered on his mug, his face "all red and flustered." It's hardly his fault that a whole arena full of fans hate him.[27] The young boxer is only the occasion of the fans' ire, not their real target. They're not angry at him but at the alarming national movement that is backing him, and that has stirred up a campaign of hatred against many of them. In 1923, after all, most of New York's fan base for the sport of boxing is ethnic. And the nationwide organization so ardently behind the Georgia schoolboy, the Ku Klux Klan, has no more use for ethnic Americans than for blacks. To make matters worse, the Klan has lately been making a big push to spread its membership into the North, with startling success.

Catholics, blacks, and Jews might have despised the Klan's race and ethnic baiting, but it appealed to nativists in northern cities. Ultimately, New York City would have the twelfth-highest Klan membership of any city in the United States. In 1927, the Klan's attempt to take part in the Queens Memorial Day parade and wreath-laying ceremony would provoke a riot. Motorists attempted to run down Klan marchers and spectators hurled stones, snatched away banners, even stole the Klan's memorial wreath.[28] Outside New York City, Klan candidates evenly contested elections against Democrats and Republicans. "Few are heard to denounce the Klan in this section," wrote H. J. Adamson in the *New York Evening Post*. "One never knows whether or not one is talking to a member."[29] Leading ministers throughout New York City sang the praises of the Klan. A robed Klansman even delivered the sermon at Brooklyn's Washington Avenue Baptist Church.[30] As national membership surged to five million in 1925, the Klan elected mayors, sheriffs, councilmen, judges, even governors (in Indiana, Texas, and Oregon).

Hardly anyone in boxing had heard of the Klan boxer with the sickly half-smile until a month earlier, when the combination of two pushy, garrulous parents and the silent backing of the "the invisible empire" (the Klan's membership rolls were secret) had gotten him a shot at the light-heavyweight title. The young man, Billy Stribling, had fought well that night, carrying the fight to Mike McTigue for the full ten rounds. The crowd had been unanimous in its insistence that "Young Stribling" (as he was called in the ring) had won. They had reason enough to be incensed, in a way. McTigue had scampered away for most of the fight, hardly throwing a menacing punch, just as he'd done in Dublin against Siki. But McTigue showed spunk just going down there in the first place, set up by his normally cagey pilot, Joe Jacobs, to face the eighteen-year-old Georgian in the heart of Klan territory. At the 1923 Texas State Fair, where two hundred thousand had turned out for "Klan day," Imperial Wizard H. W. Evans had spoken of "three powerful and numerous elements" that would forever defy "every fundamental element of assimilation."[31] Blacks, he said, could never "attain the Anglo-Saxon level." "Both biology and anthropology prove it. The low mentality of savage ancestors" was "inherent in the blood of the colored race." To "the Jew," another "absolutely unblendable element," love of country, "as the Anglo-Saxon feels it," was inconceivable.[32] Catholics were slavish followers of a religion that "thrives on ignorance."[33] Yet here was Jacobs hand-delivering to the Georgia Klan specimens of two of its three leading types of ethnic undesirable. You had to wonder what he could have been thinking. If Siki's excursion to Dublin at the height of the Irish Civil War was pixilated, what was this? Insane?

The night before the bout the Irish fighter watched out his hotel window as cars rolled through the town square sporting canary banners taunting "McTigue is yellow." When Jacobs threatened to call off the bout, Columbus mayor John Paul Jones waved toward the square and asked, "See that tree there? You want your fighter to swing from it?" Five thousand Klansmen had been ordered to attend—"to make sure that everything was all right."[34] The diminutive Jacobs, Bill Stern swears, chomping a cigar, said, "Go ahead and hang me.... But lemme tell you, I guarantee that if you hang me there will be some guys down here from N'Yawk that will blow this here whole dump right off the map!"[35] Stern pretends to believe that Jacobs was bluffing, but he really did have the mob ties to make good on threats of violence. Jones, unawed, told referee Harry Ertle, imported from New York by Jacobs to make sure his boy left with his title intact, that the eighteen-year-old local marvel "had to win"—or else.[36]

When word got out that McTigue might call off the bout, five hundred men stormed the hotel and threatened to kill him. McTigue, undaunted, went out onto his balcony in the wee hours of morning to shout to the thugs in the square below, "I'm not yellow. I'll flog your kid with one hand." The scene got so ugly, related the *New York Leader*'s Ed Sullivan (the same who later hosted a popular television variety show), that Fort Benning sent reinforcements for the detachment of military police it had dispatched to keep order. Angry mobs were no joke in Georgia. In Savannah, three months before, two thousand men stormed the county jail, intent on lynching a black man accused of molesting a white woman. When the fire department turned hoses on them, they hurled bricks. When the state militia fired over their heads, they took cover and fired back. Finally, a machine gun dispersed the rioters. Klan lynchings became so common in 1923 that Missouri congressman Leonidas C. Dyer began a campaign for a Federal anti-lynching act.[37] To combat Oklahoma's eruption of Klan vigilantism Governor Jack Walton declared martial law. When a storm of press enmity followed, Walton tried to censor the newspapers. The Klan-controlled state legislature sought to impeach him, despite his threat to arrest them en masse.[38] In Cedar Lawn, New York, Klan death threats made a mockery of the trial of a man accused of murdering seven-year-old Howard Rothenberg.[39]

On the night of the McTigue / Stribling fight, referee Harry Ertle kept faith with Jacobs at great risk to his health, dutifully declaring the bout a draw, and ducking under the storm of invective hurled his way. Then, with the Georgia boxing faithful becoming more and more menacing, he abruptly reversed himself, allowing Mayor Jones to hop into the ring and raise the challenger's hand in victory. Back in New York, McTigue put on his own display of chutzpah, telling his mob-connected manager Jacobs to take a walk, swearing he'd never fight again under Jacobs's management, and defying him to try to enforce the contract McTigue insisted Jacobs had tricked him into signing in the first place. According to his story, Jacobs had assured him their deal would be a straight 30 percent cut for Jacobs, with expenses to be paid out of his end. McTigue was to have final approval of any contract for a specific opponent. So far a standard deal—except that Jacobs, according to McTigue, then also pulled the standard ploy, telling him, Here, kid. Just sign this blank sheet of paper. That'll make it all go quicker. I'll get my secretary to type it up just the way we agreed to it, over your signature, then I'll file it with the commission and everything will be hunky-dory.

But when McTigue went to the commission offices to see for himself what he'd allegedly signed, he discovered that his official contract called for expenses to be taken out of his end of the profits and denied him any say in whom he fought or when. With that kind of deal duly filed in the commission offices, Jacobs had casually stiffed McTigue in Georgia, paying him not the $7,000 promised, but only $3,800, which was a lot bigger deduction than you could justify for gym fees, lineament rub, a couple weeks' stipends for sparring partners, train fare, and one night in a mediocre hotel.[40] To make matters worse, now Jacobs was insisting McTigue had to fight Gene Tunney, the man who would one day relieve Dempsey of his heavyweight crown, even though McTigue had a broken bone in his hand. When Jacobs had a doctor take off the cast and certify McTigue would be ready to fight once the injury "baked out," McTigue said no dice and made the sawbones wrap it back up in plaster of Paris. He knew what he'd be in for in the ring with Tunney. I'll fight him, he said. When my hand heals. Meanwhile he hit Jacobs with a lawsuit, seeking $50,000 in damages for inept management.[41]

If anyone should have sued his pilot for mismanagement it was Battling Siki, not Mike McTigue. By mid-November, with old-timer Tom Goodman in camp, Siki was finally getting around to sparring. Until then, by Levy's and Goodman's own account, he'd pretty much stuck to road work and calisthenics. The fight camp where Siki was training, run by a Turkish couple named Bey, had just been set up a few weeks before, apparently with encouragement and financial backing from ex-middleweight champ Johnny Wilson—which is another way of saying with encouragement and financial backing from the mob. Wilson (real name John Panica) had grown up in

Italian East Harlem, where he was schoolmates with future crime kingpin Frank Costello. Costello found him his first manager, East Harlem gangster Vincent Morell.[42] When Morell was gunned down in a 1920 mob hit Wilson's management passed to other mob figures, including downtown mobsters Owney Madden and Bill Duffy. For a time Wilson even fronted for Duffy's Silver Slipper Club.[43]

According to the middleweight champ Mickey Walker, Madden secretly managed many top boxers, including Primo Carnera, Bob Olin, Ace Hudkins, Pancho Villa, Maxie Rosenbloom, Jimmy Braddock, and Leo Lomski, as well as top managers Joe Jacobs and Joe Gould.[44] Boxing had always attracted gamblers and fixers, but in the four years since the Prohibition Amendment huge bootlegging profits had given the hustlers and fixers wads of play money to invest in their pet sport. Walker, who himself worked for bootleggers, recounts how the mob moved in. Madden and Bill Dwyer ran much of New York's illicit alcohol trade, smuggling from Long Island beaches, while in New Jersey, Pete Reilly, Larry Coyle, Big Red Dempsey, and Herman Black controlled the traffic. Walker for some reason left out other key players, Willie Moretti of Fort Lee and Longy Zwillman of Newark. Zwillman ran bookmaking and numbers, and, protected by political connections in the port of Newark, was personally responsible for about 40 percent of all the illegal liquor smuggled into the United States.[45] In Manhattan, Frank Costello, who ran a huge fleet of rum runners with Dwyer that for a time even included a seaplane, was also one of the city's biggest bookmakers.[46] The same men infiltrated the nightclub scene and the boxing game. Coyle owned a Brooklyn club, "The Fallen Angel." Reilly managed top boxers. Reilly's light-heavyweight, Jack Delaney, would win the world title in 1926. Five featherweights Reilly managed would win world titles, too. One, Battling Battalino, recalls how Reilly strong-armed his original manager and then forced Battalino to throw a title fight against his chief rival, Freddie Miller. Only later would Battalino learn that Reilly had taken over Miller's management as well.[47]

In 1923, Walker said, Owney Madden, an Englishman of Irish origin with roots in the tough Hell's Kitchen Irish gang, "went into the bootlegging and boxing rackets" in a big way, muscling in on Harlem's top nightclub, the Cotton Club, with gangster / boxing manager Bill Duffy. Madden controlled Joe Jacobs, McTigue's manager—and also called the shots behind the scenes for the fighter Jacobs was trying to force McTigue to fight, Gene Tunney. Tunney, also of Irish stock, was raised in Greenwich Village, a region taken over by Madden's gang. Though Billy Gibson, who also handled lightweight champ Benny Leonard, nominally ran Tunney's career, actually Madden pulled the strings behind the scenes. After the rackets squad forced

Madden out of New York, retired heavyweight champ Tunney would fly down to golf with the exiled mob boss in Hot Springs, Arkansas, the regional vice capital from which he continued to run his illicit empire.[48] So thick were Madden and boxing manager Joe Gould that Gould picked him up at the gate of Sing Sing when he was released after serving a murder sentence. Trainer Ray Arcel went yet further in his loyalty to Madden, arranging a fight card featuring future champion Kid Berg inside prison walls to help Madden while away his lonely incarceration.[49]

New York gangs had begun as ethnic enforcers, ruling rival turfs. Though black gangs such as the Fly Boys and the Long Bridge Boys once tyrannized their own neighborhoods, Irish, Jewish, and Italian gangs now held sway. By no accident, many boxers were also Irish, Jewish, or Italian. Ring battles mirrored street warfare and fitted easily into a street culture built around blood sports of all sorts. In the 1870s, the most popular betting sport had been rat-baiting, which charged as much as five dollars admission (boxing bouts charged fifty cents) to let spectators watch a champion terrier savage a hundred or so panicked rodents. A top dog's purse might reach $125. Boxing only began to rival the allure of rat-baiting when gang leader Owney Geoghegan began matching his behemoth waiters in a small ring on the dance floor at his Hurdy Gurdy Bar on the Bowery for a five-dollar purse.[50] The most popular New York fighter of the 1920s, lightweight champ Benny Leonard (real name Benjamin Leiner), only took up boxing as a sidelight to street fighting in the Lower East Side ghetto where he lived. Leonard, though small for his age, became "the feared leader of his 'pack.'"[51] When manager / promoter Billy Gibson got him his first few bouts, Leonard's old gang strong-armed people to sell tickets.

As street thugs evolved into big-time racketeers and rumrunners, boxing was evolving into big-time entertainment. By the 1920s its popularity was soaring. Fourth-quarter revenues for 1923, the *New York Tribune* reported, nearly 2.5 million dollars, had "broken all records."[52] Even in the era before 1910, when boxing was still technically illegal, it had been lucrative enough for gamblers that a turf war raged among rival syndicates. So routinely were matches fixed that referees had the right to "call off all bets" if the boxers' efforts seemed in any way dubious.[53] By the 1920s, with boxing selling out 100,000-seat stadiums and attracting million-dollar live gates, a slickly engineered fix could be worth millions of dollars—hence the fascination of racketeers with the sport. By 1925, the year the East Side hood Waxie Gordon muscled in on the popular lightweight Ruby ("the Jewel of the Ghetto") Goldstein's contract, few top boxers, Goldstein attested, lacked a mob sponsor.[54]

When Battling Siki and his manager arrived in the first week of November 1923 at the Beys' training camp in Summit, New Jersey, they had their first up-close encounter with the mobsters who ran boxing behind the scenes—if they hadn't already met them in New York. Levy, let us not forget, ran a clothing factory in Manhattan's garment district, where two kingpins of the midtown mob, Arnold Rothstein and Lepke Buchalter, ran an aggressive and deadly protection racket that collected its tithe from anyone doing business there. If he hadn't run into New York's illicit high rollers before, Levy assuredly did now, for around the same time he and Siki arrived at the Bey's brand-new training camp so did East Harlem's (and Frank Costello's) favorite son Johnny Wilson, who'd lost his middleweight title just two months before to Harry Greb. Wilson put up the money to help Bey, a retired Turkish diplomat with thinning gray hair and small mustache, set up his camp. Levy had at first taken Siki to ex-lightweight champion Freddy Welsh's camp a few miles away, but Welsh, in ill-health, nearly bankrupt, abruptly closed it, sending his clientele to the Beys.[55] While waiting for Levy to find him a trainer, Siki in fact trained with Wilson.[56]

The Beys' camp would ultimately become a huge success. Mme. Sitky Bey, a superb cook, became famous for the way she watched after "her boys" the boxers. An impressive roster of champions trained there. Mickey Walker at times virtually lived there.[57] When Siki arrived, however, in November 1923, the Beys were still refitting their barn to turn it into a rude gym. The haphazard facilities and Levy's dawdling over finding a trainer set back Siki's preparation further. When Levy invited the New York boxing writers to Summit to see him train, he'd just begun doing real sparring—eight days before the fight! Levy, who owned up to "a lack of experience in handling boxers," said he'd "merely regulate[d]" Siki's hours and "systematize[d] his activities" until then. Otherwise, he let Siki train himself. He wasn't about to "interfere with the routine of the former titleholder."[58] When Levy finally hired Tom Goodman, Goodman let Siki carry on as before. He seemed eager to train, Goodman observed. He "ran the entire camp bowlegged on the road," and "in the gym . . . never seemed to know when to stop."[59]

Dominick Scibetta, who manages and trains professional fighters in New Jersey, works his fighters into shape by using a combination of calisthenics, bag work, work with the punch pads, rope jumping, and sparring. Like most trainers, he sets a timer for three-minute exercise intervals and one-minute rests, to approximate the intervals of stress and recovery in a real fight, but he pushes his fighters to work harder as the bout approaches, shifting the exercise intervals to four minutes, the rests to thirty seconds. Before a crowd in a big arena, with adrenalin flowing, fighters burn energy twice as fast as in the gym. He overtrains to compensate. His general rule of thumb,

originally adapted from Al Certo, who trained Scibetta when he fought professionally, is to have fighters spar ten times as many rounds in the gym as
they will fight in the bout, and have the sparring sessions peak about two
weeks before with a workout to match the intensity of a real bout. By that
classic rule of thumb, Siki should have sparred around 150 rounds in the
gym to get ready for Kid Norfolk, and his training should have peaked with
a fifteen-round session on or about November 6. Instead, he hadn't even
started sparring then! A week later, with just a week's training left, his entire
workout consisted of three rounds skipping rope, one on the speed bag, and
three sparring—barely seven rounds in total!

Siki did at least start doing road work three weeks before the fight. He
ran, Goodman said, three to seven miles a day.[60] Not bad—if he'd started
weeks earlier. C.W.O. Peter E. Benson, U.S.M.C., who coached the U.S. Marine
boxing team to its first All-Service title in 1956, had his amateur boxers run
five to seven miles daily, mixing in quarter-mile sprints—but they fought
only three-round bouts. They sparred three or four rounds daily too, and
worked two or three more on the heavy bag.[61] Mickey Walker would later
spell out the regime needed for a ten-round main event: five to ten miles of
road work (half walking, half running hard), "stomach exercises to harden
you up," eight or ten rounds sparring, additional rounds on the heavy bag.[62]
Yet on November 12, when Siki ought to have been near the end of his training cycle, he wasn't working the heavy bag at all, and was sparring just three
rounds.

Scibetta feels it takes two or three months to get a boxer ready for a big
bout, especially if he's starting from scratch. The first month is devoted
mostly to conditioning, with some two- or three-round sparring sessions
thrown in. The really hard sparring begins in the second month. Ferdie
Pacheco writes, "A fighter usually trains for a big match from four to six
weeks,"[63] but he's referring to a fighter who is already in shape. Siki had
done next to nothing for two months, then some haphazard sparring in
Canada against Jack Johnson. The key period for him to peak for the fight
should have been between October 8 and November 6, a period during
which he did no sparring and had no trainer. He didn't start sparring again
until eight days before the fight![64] If ever there were a recipe for disaster in
the ring, this was it!

The Singular Senegalese

If Bob Levy didn't know much about training a fighter, he knew plenty about
publicity. A black boxer might be different from a shirtwaist, but Levy was a
quick study where selling was concerned. He stood the writers an ample

buffet on the veranda of the hundred-year-old farmhouse where the Beys lived and housed their cauliflower congregation, all for the sake of feeding them a line of corn about the young boxer they'd lately amused themselves by nicknaming "the Singular Senegalese." Just a few weeks before the *Tribune* sports editor Bill McGeehan had coined that moniker, forever after automatically associated with Siki's name. McGeehan was also the wordsmith who (with Siki in mind) had coined the farcical label "Senegambians" for all athletes of color, a phrase, as Kahn notes, intended to suggest, in the coded lexicon of the era, "a figure out of a jungle, probably half lowland gorilla."[65]

Wilbur Wood of the *New York Herald,* appropriating McGeehan's witticism, amused readers with sallies about "Senegambians" climbing down from palm trees to conk each other on the head with coconuts, quipping, "The singular Senegalese has settled down to his work at Summit, N.J. where there are plenty of trees that he can swing from when in the mood."[66] McGeehan also had great fun with jibes about Siki's drinking, alleging that it was unfair to deprive Siki of his usual mode of training, "consisting principally of elbow work before a polished mahogany bar," adding a facetious mock quotation from Siki: "It is unfair that I cannot train in my usual way, which is to develop the elbow muscle. When I return to that dear France it may be that I will be unable to bend the elbow and then I shall be lost."[67]

Levy's commercial instincts told him that you couldn't buy this kind of publicity for hard cash (which, by the way, was precisely how many boxing promoters *did* secure press coverage). The image of Siki as a berserk yet harmless savage wasn't the sort of thing Levy would have paid someone to print (he knew Siki chafed under such depictions), but it was precisely what was likely to sell out the fight on November 20. After they sampled Madame Bey's food, the newsmen followed Levy to the barn, where a crowd of tourists from the Jersey shore were waiting. Their admission fee permitted them to see Siki work "like a whirlwind with the skipping rope" and speed bag, then spar somewhat ineffectively with Jack Taylor.[68] The *Herald*'s Wilbur Wood called Siki "extraordinarily light on his feet for a man of his size." Even his unorthodox style, Wood thought, might work in his favor. And he sure could hit! "His attack," wrote Wood, "consists of terrific hooks and swings for the body with either hand and an occasional left or right swing for the jaw. There was plenty of power behind his punches and several times he swung Taylor around."[69] Siki liked to fake a right to land a left hook, and also had a decent uppercut. Though he was strong enough to push his sparring partner around, Siki, Wood noted, "was wide open on defense and Taylor had no trouble reaching him with straight lefts." He missed far too often as well. His timing was off. Wood still picked Siki to win, envisioning a dramatic bout that would make the "rough and ready slugger . . . a big card," a major draw. Siki's sparring mate, Taylor, had twice fought Norfolk, holding him to a draw in 1922 and losing a decision in March 1923. He'd been sent to camp by the same George P. Moore who the year before had bared the conspiracy against interracial boxing.

Before the assembled scribes on Madame Bey's porch, Levy tried to explain away Siki's lackluster sparring. It was his first session. He'd spent his first week in camp "getting all the 'paint' out of his system." Goodman had been "running him over the hills around here until his tongue hung out." He'd lost a dozen pounds in the process. He was in top condition now. The writers took that assertion with a pinch of salt. Yeah? Was Levy sure his wild man wasn't slipping out of his cage at night to lap up home-cooked alcohol?[70] No, no! Levy said. Believe me! My wild man's completely tame these days. Siki sat on exhibit, listening to the scribes' laughter, unsure what Levy was saying. Finally he got a chance to speak, through an interpreter, though only the *New York World* saw fit to report his words. Someone complimented his uppercut. "That is the blow with which I wore Carpentier down," Siki answered, "and it is the one that will bring defeat to Mr. Norfolk." The newsmen chortled. "*Mr.* Norfolk"? Huh?

Then "Papa Bob" Levy took over again, working at selling the fight along the very lines the writers seemed inclined to play up themselves. It wasn't in Levy's interest to eradicate the vestiges of the Siki-the-savage-throwback myth. That, after all, was what had so fascinated the public about this fight in the first place. Instead, he tacitly accepted the Wild Man of Borneo image—adopting for himself the role of man-tamer. Asked how he managed to keep his wayward protégé in line, Levy said he had "used a lot of psychology stuff on him, and so far the results have been all that I could ask. He has a big heart and responds to good treatment." Since coming under his influence, Levy insisted, the savage Senegalese had become "gentle as a lamb": "He promised me that he would be good, and so far he has kept his word."[71] The reporters scribbled away. Wow! Simple savage meekly submits to civilized rule! Great stuff! Sid Mercer later summed up the manager's attitude: "Levy keeps in close touch with his protégé, indulges many of his boyish whims, but knows where to draw the line." Siki had "accepted his American manager as a master and obeys his orders faithfully."[72]

Later that day, Siki's opponent, whose real name was Willie Ward (he called himself Kid Norfolk after his city of birth), "enthused a large crowd" with ten rounds of fast sparring against Panama Joe Gans, Clem Johnson, and Billy Shade at Grupp's Gym on 116th Street.[73] Ward had started boxing in Baltimore, but hadn't made a sensation until he went to Colon, to entertain

Siki publicity photo, September 1923, on the El Platform,
New York City. (Courtesy of Mamadou Niang.)

Panama Canal workers. When leading U.S. heavyweights went down there hoping to pick up a few easy dollars they ran into a "black thunderbolt." He went twenty rounds with Jack Johnson's old rival Sam McVey, twice flattened ex-"white hope"Arthur Pelkey, and took twenty-round decisions from Jeff Clark and Big Bill Tate. Leo P. Flynn got the raw young fellow's name on a contract in 1917, promising to bring him north to win a world title. But even though Willie beat top heavyweights Gunboat Smith, Billy Miske, John Lester Johnson, Tut Jackson, and the Jamaica Kid, those wins brought him no nearer a title shot.[74] For years, Norfolk proclaimed that he, not Carpentier, was the real world champion, but only the black press took him seriously. If Rickard was on the level, maybe that was over. Maybe now he'd get a shot at McTigue. Norfolk had had seven fights in the last seven months, but for this bout, at the Garden against an ex-champion, Flynn was taking no chances: he'd stepped up Norfolk's training even before the match was signed. Kid Norfolk couldn't be in better shape. The *New York Daily News* ran a staged photo of him chinning himself, showing quadriceps that stood out like a football player's thigh pads.[75]

The day after Levy hosted the press at the Beys' camp, he was at it again, pumping more newspaper columns full of hot air. He sent an invitation to Ward and Flynn to come to Summit to watch Siki train. Siki would "be glad to demonstrate some of the punches he expects to bring into action next Tuesday evening." Nor did he expect a return invitation. Goodman knew all Kid Norfolk's "tricks" and had "tipped... off the whole works."[76] The invitation was an inside joke. Tough as Kid Norfolk was, he'd suffered two humiliating defeats by early-round knockout—one the year before against Harry Wills, the other early in his career against Sam Langford. Langford had prefaced his knockout of Norfolk with a derisive gesture that became boxing legend. At the beginning of round two Langford extended his arms to touch gloves. Hey! Norfolk said. I thought we were only supposed to do that before the *last* round. Kid, this *is* the last round! Langford answered and summarily flattened his young rival.[77] Goodman had trained Langford. As for Flynn, he was celebrated for his keen analysis of fighters' styles and took special trouble to scout rivals. Dempsey, whom Flynn would manage for his 1927 fight with Jack Sharkey, called Flynn's advice the crucial factor in his victory: "Leo knocked out Jack Sharkey for me, just by going out and finding out something about him."[78] You could bet that, by hook or by crook, he'd found out all he needed to know about Siki's style.

When the writers came back for a second look on the eve of the fight, Jack Lawrence said Siki "mauled" his sparring partners.[79] Sid Mercer thought his hook his best punch:

He bends low—almost to the floor—and as he straightens up and closes on his opponent he unleashes powerful punches. His left hand is especially dangerous. He has learned to hook with it from different angles and without drawing back his arm or otherwise warning an opponent.[80]

Siki's sparring mates, Mercer noted, stepped inside his whistling right and "let it curl over their necks harmlessly," though they found it harder to slip his left hook. Siki seemed weak, moreover, at in-fighting. His most devastating blow in Europe, the punch he'd used to knock out Marcel Nilles, was a "right hand swing," thrown from a sideways stance, with a whiplike torsion. A French instructional manual describes its technique:

The swing or *coup balancé* is a punch that was greatly employed in the English style; it is thrown with a twisting of the body while ducking the head to the right if the punch is thrown with the left, and vice versa. The arm at first is completely unflexed but bends slightly just before arriving at its target; the nails are turned to the outside; it is the first joints of the finger that hit; certain English boxers hit with the back of the hand.[81]

Still photographs freeze the eccentric punch, showing its practitioners winding up to throw it, arms drawn back behind them, like discus throwers. The Dixie Kid used the blow with great success in France before the war. Marcel Petit was still teaching it in 1972, long after it was made illegal. Petit showed how to turn the fist counterclockwise, so that it landed back-handed, striking with the first metacarpal bones.[82] Indeed, both legal and illegal versions of the punch turned up in matches late in the modern era. A photograph of Luis Rodriguez fighting Fraser Scott in August 1971, for instance, shows Rodriguez winding up to throw a classic right-hand swing. It might be a sucker punch, but landed flush, fully extended, it had about the effect of a torpedo detonating a fishing smack.

Since it had to be thrown across the full extension of the body, it was easy to slip. Jack Johnson had no trouble in 1914 with "white hope" Frank Moran's celebrated right-hand swing (which Moran so loved that he nicknamed it "my Mary Ann"). Johnson stepped inside it and landed short lefts. By 1923, that maneuver had become a basic part of the boxing repertoire. A 1924 English primer, *Boxing Taught through the Slow-Motion Film,* illustrated this counterpunch with newsreel frames from the Billy Wells / Tom Berry fight.[83] Fifty years later Marcel Petit suggested as a counter the "*esquive rotative,*" or circular duck—which was in fact Kid Norfolk's signature move, a semicircular rotation of the torso down and away from the blow, and then upward to deliver a hook.[84] Norfolk's power made a swing a risky punch to employ against him. It was dangerous in other ways too. As Fleischer noted, the extreme torsion of the arm delivering the punch could snap tendons or bones.[85] Siki had success with such a vintage punch because he mixed it in unexpectedly from a modern stance and because he had quick reflexes. But if he missed with it against Norfolk, he'd pay dearly.

If Siki was worried, he didn't show it. In New York a few days before the fight to see Tex Rickard, he told reporters he'd "flatten" Kid Norfolk in eight or nine rounds. In return, he wanted Rickard's promise of a match against one of four white fighters: McTigue, Tom Gibbons, Gene Tunney, or Harry Greb. Sure, Rickard promised. Good as done. Afterward, Levy bundled his fighter back to Jersey. With days left to fight night, Siki was at last ready to tackle a workout rivaling the grind of a fifteen-round fight. He sweated through seven rounds shadow boxing, skipping rope, and hitting the heavy bag, eight rounds sparring with Jack Taylor and Battling Thomas. At Grupp's, a confident Norfolk also sparred eight rounds, but he'd been sparring for months and was winding down, not peaking.

As the fight drew nearer the New York writers stepped up the intensity of their jawing. Of the lot, Ford C. Frick, in his *Evening Journal* column, best succeeded in fixing Siki's persona in public memory. Twenty years later, as president of baseball's National League, Frick would defend Jackie Robinson against a threatened boycott by white ballplayers, but in 1923 he took as much delight as McGeehan or Wood in concocting a racialist fable around Siki's origins. Siki, he said, was a savage "born to the dank jungle of Senegal," where he had heard "the wail of the witch doctor and the boom of the tom-tom," an influence that had recently "fade[d] away before the witching melody and the glowing lights of the Rue de l'Opera." A "pitiful waif" and "cultural orphan" dazzled "by the allure of civilization," Siki had become "a slave to his own popularity and a victim of his own birth and breeding." Men who knew him would "remark sagely and with much shaking of heads, that the leopard cannot change his spots, nor the Ethiopian his skin."[86] Though Frick worked his way down to admitting that, in person, Siki had "little of the flamboyant," just "a broad smile and an apparent desire to be friendly," he nevertheless dismissed him as a fellow who was "nervous, flighty, change-able as the wind that sweeps the New Jersey heights where he is quartered," a freak who brought to mind "a jungle chimpanzee, aping, mimicking, copy-ing," yet never quite getting straight the ways and manners of civilized humanity. A product of a debased heritage, faced with strange new customs, he showed "a wistful, distrait manner that is at times almost pathetic."

For Siki, *heritage* had a very different meaning. In his Wolof culture a man inherits specific qualities from his mother and father, still others according to his position as first-, second-, or third-born. Heritage is primarily passed on through *meen* (mother's milk), which determines *derat* (blood), *soox* (flesh), *jiko* (character), *xel* (intelligence), and *ndëmm* (the spiritual power which determines destiny). The Wolof saying is not "like father like son," but *doom ja, nday ja* (like mother like son). From his father, the son inherits *yax* (bones), *siddit* (nerves), *fit* (courage), and *nooxoor* (a lesser spiritual force). Thus, courage, though an absolute duty, is a lesser virtue than intelligence, destiny, and blood lineage. Heroism is defined by readiness to fight to defend one's culture, to endure suffering without complaint. Greed is a failure in one's duty to share openhandedly. The attributes of manhood, ritualized and tested in the Wolof rite of passage, the circumcision ceremony, are *fit* (courage), *mun* (patient endurance), *jom* (modest discretion), and *kolëre* (loyalty and group allegiance).[87] No respect is reserved for a "beautiful machine of combat" or "beast of the jungle." Wolof male virtues are not instinctual or physical, but social, intellectual. The terms of Frick's portrayal would have made Siki no hero to his own people. In Wolof terms, virtue comes from control and restraint, not unbridled impulse. Nor would they have made Siki a true hero in 1923 America. They were traits of a funhouse heroism, marked by outlandish singularity, at once repulsive and intriguing.

In his essay on Siki, Gerald Early sees racial stereotyping as a type of mirror, projecting a distorted self-image. The white sees the black as his binary opposite, his troubling other self.[88] Mirrors do fool us, after all, on a primal level. Umberto Eco, in discussing Freud's "mirror stage," explains how displacement of the self necessitates a leap of understanding. As children, such displacements disorient us. As adults they bring vicarious pleasure (for example, via fun-house mirrors). But only if we can "decide (for the sake of playing) to accept that we have three eyes or an enormous stomach or very short legs, just as we accept a fairy tale," and can conceive that "the mirror, which usually tells the truth, is lying," mentally correcting for the distortion.[89] In representations of racial primitivism, one decides (for the sake of playing) to envision a "secret, yet defective" other self, a creature of unbounded appetite. The illusion brings pleasure—since this distorted self, this ape man, is not really me but another human being whose identity I've stolen—as Frick steals Siki's in writing:

> Into his life there is written nothing of fineness. Born a savage he has been unable to cast aside those things which are his savage heritage. In his habits and beliefs and ideas and actions there is little to praise, much to condemn. Yet in the moment of his flitting fame and in the hours of his deepest depravity, he has lived ever to the letter of his gospel, which is—to be unusual. And that makes him a personality.[90]

Frick thereby savors counterfeit delight. He imagines that *enfant terrible,* the simultaneously oral and phallic child, consumed at once by rage and lust. Racism is a peculiar case of the fun-house mirror phenomenon, precisely because the racist does not mentally amend the distortions of race. He cannot help, on some level, but see the truth through the distortions, yet sets himself no obligation to correct them. What is a minstrel show, after all, but a fun-house mirror one pretends to believe is a real human being?

If Bob Levy had cared to, days after his arrival in Summit he might have strolled over to the high school auditorium to see the annual Summit Show, put on by the Calvary Church choir, joining hundreds applauding the "loose-jointed, nimble-footed" dancing of Harold Baldwin, the "hit of the show." He might have cheered black-faced local representations of the "droll humor of the Negro" in songs such as "The Big Brown Bear," "Kentucky Babe," "I Dunno," and "Doan Yo' Cry Ma Honey." Perhaps he might have agreed with the *Summit Herald and Summit Record* that the men playing "Bones" and "Tambo" were "full of 'wim, wigor, and witality.'"[91] Why not? A minstrel show was fun. It let you indulge what you took to be primal instincts. The visual images of the minstrel show informed popular conceptions of Siki too. A cartoon in the new *Ring* magazine depicted him as a grinning, woolly-headed "dark planet," eclipsing an open-mouthed, horrified white "star," Carpentier.[92] Siki's cartoon lips and eyes were grease-paint gray circles, imitating not African features but a white mummer's parody of them. Nor was America alone guilty of such travesty. Yginy's perfume *Le Golliwog* was sold in a round bottle with protruding black feet; its label featured painted black hands and a leopard-pattern collar, its cap a black-face minstrel's head, with pale circles for eyes, an elliptical mouth, and a shock of bushy hair.

Though he read little English, comments such as McGeehan's, Wood's, and Frick's reached Siki, who told Jack Lawrence of the *New York Tribune* that he meant to show American fight fans in the ring that he was "no freak imported from the jungles of Africa as a circus attraction."[93] To their credit, the editors of *L'Auto* had asked Siki, soon after he won his title, to write a letter to their readers, who hardly knew him at all outside the ring, defining for them his identity and giving impressions of his life. "We find here all the frankness, and the genial mischievousness [*bonne gaminerie*] of the Sengalese," the editors advised, smoothing away some of the edge from Siki's ironic commentary. The editors had asked Siki if he was afraid to so risk self exposure in print, and Siki's answer, which *L'Auto* took pains to assure its readers was his own composition (by affixing a facsimile of his signature), began "I have never been afraid. Therefore, you [should] understand that I am not going to start today, as I have to relate to the readers of

L'Auto who I am. "To begin with," he wrote, "the readers of *L'Auto* are friends for me." He had felt very much "among friends" three days before when he'd visited the magazine's offices. Then he went straight to the issue which, for him, was most troubling, the image that had been created of him as an illiterate and inarticulate savage:

> First of all, I am not a cannibal. An evening newspaper, recently, seized the occasion of an interview to have me speaking pidgin [*"pètit negre"*]. That's ridiculous. I speak and I write French like the average French person. And also, am I not Friench? I consider myself doubly so, being Sengalese. I should say that since my great victory over Georges Carpentier, I perceive that I am very much a son of France, the great![94]

Strangely, the drawing that accompanied Frick's *Evening Journal* column offered a counter-image to his verbal representations, featuring an artfully limned sketch that gave Siki an entirely normal haircut, an intelligent glint in his eyes, and a sculpted profile. Siki looked gentle, handsome, almost boyish. His forehead was broad, his eyes widely spaced. His hair was neatly groomed, a razor part on one side. For once an artist had not given him liver lips, a gorilla nose, a scowl. The artist, Carl Meyer, had posed Siki in an on-guard stance, in gym togs and hand wraps, his left well extended. It was a first-class job, inked in thousands of fine lines and swirls. It must have taken Meyer a week to do. Okay, he couldn't resist a few doodles around the margins to remind readers of the Siki myth—including a cartoon of a lope-legged, grinning imbecile walking a leopard on a leash. But then, Levy was probably happy enough to have that doodle in there. That Siki sold tickets, not the handsome fellow with the trim hairdo.

And Kid Norfolk—or rather Willie Ward, the real human being behind the ring persona—did he imagine he was fighting a savage beast? The Baltimore fighter was a bit flamboyant himself, famous for his impossibly limber bows to the crowd, and nonstop loquacity. Years later he liked to tell the gang at Stillman's Gym, "There is nobody here that can discuss a question from an intelligent point of view." Or, reverting to dialect, to threaten, "I going to whip you with words, I going to make the hair whirl on you goddam haid."[95] The newsmen might want to ruminate on trainer Leo P. Flynn's famed ability to read a boxer's style, but Ward had actually done his own scouting. Hearing Siki was fighting Jack Johnson in Montreal, he'd hopped a train north, without saying a word to his trainer. The *New York World* repeats, in classic minstrel-show idiom, his report to Flynn on what he'd seen: "Misto Leo, dat Sikiman A'm gwine to fight am a putty good fightuh. Doan let anybody tell YOU he am a suckuh."

Yeah? Flynn responded. Who wised you up to that?

"Nobuddy wises lil' Keed No'foak up," Norfolk replied. "Keed No'foak wises hesef up. Ah jess took a lil' run up into Canada and Ah see dis Sikiman chase big Jack Johnson all ober de ring. DAT'S what Ah SEE and DAT'S what Ah KNOWS. Ah ain't meeting no suckuh."[96]

Siki and Norfolk probably met for the first time at the Madison Square Garden weigh-in the morning of the fight. Later that afternoon at the boxing commission offices, at a second weigh-in, Norfolk was holding court, "beaming," "almost cockily confident," telling reporters he hit harder than Siki, was in top shape, and "would take off his hat to no man so far as [ring] cleverness was concerned." Hey, what do you think of the odds? someone asked. They had once been one to two for Siki but were now seven to five—and dropping. He laughed. Seven to five? People must be foolish! Hey, he said. I've got two thousand dollars in my pocket. Anybody want to bet on Siki? One guy took the action. By the time he stepped into the ring, Ward would have $3,800 down on himself.

Then Fall walked in, and silenced Norfolk with an almost cocky exuberance. "He fairly bubbled over with good humor," said the *Evening Telegram,* "joked in French, tickled his opponent, and made a wild swing at him to show what he was going to do in the ring." Ward turned "serious, . . . not quite knowing how to take this wild man from the jungle."

Ticket sales picked up as fight night neared. So did wagering. The betting had once held at nearly two to one for Norfolk. But now, as genial manager "Pa" Levy succeeded in replacing the standard wild-man-goes-berserk tales with his own savage-tamed-by-civilization yarn, the odds swung Siki's way. By the opening bell they'd reach six to five in his favor.[97] Two days before the fight, Harry Newman, in the brand-new slangy *New York Sunday News,* wrote, "The Battler has been signed to go fifteen rounds against squat Kid Norfolk in Madison Square Garden, and if the Battler cops he will be right in line to grab himself plenty of dough; if he blows the works . . . it means that he is through for good." A win meant "another tilt with Carpentier, which will net him a fortune, but a reverse would put him on his ankles and the walking ain't so good these days."[98] Other papers aired similar forebodings. If Siki read them he must have wondered: Was he kidding himself? Could he really beat one of the sport's most brutal counterpunchers on only the minimum of training? If he'd had an inkling of the gory ordeal awaiting him a few hours hence, he might well have let Rickard keep his money—and his promises.

CHAPTER FOUR

"A First-Class Fighting Man"

Boy, You're Lonely!

At 9:50 P.M. on November 20 Robert Levy and two black corner men escorted a beautifully muscled young man with slender legs and a "boyish smile" up the aisle of Madison Square Garden on the northeast corner of Twenty-third Street.[1] Siki, in good spirits, turned to wave to the crowd, glad to be back in a big arena after so many aborted matches. He crossed the ring, "slapped his opponent jocularly on the back," and made as if, gloves and all, to "tickle" him.[2] The voice of short, bald-headed announcer Joe Humphreys cut through the hilarity—a voice so penetrating it reached the back balconies without a microphone: "Ladies and gentlemen! Our main event! In this corner, weighing 174 pounds, the colored light-heavyweight champion of the world, KI . . . I . . . ID Norfolk! . . . NOR . . . folk! And in this corner, weighing 172 pounds, the former light-heavyweight champion of the world, BAT . . . tling SIKI! . . . SI . . . ki!"

Yells for Norfolk drifted from the balconies. A roar for Siki rose from the bright ringside ranks. All fashionable New York seemed to be there— gangsters and entertainers, politicians and gamblers, men in open-faced evening jackets, women in splendid gowns—all come to watch a spectacle of blood and pain. Even the photographers who jumped onto the ring apron were dressed as if for a dinner party. The largest crowd of the indoor season, 12,180 strong, paid $59,894, an average toll of nearly $5.00 a head[3]—when $5.00 could buy you dinner for two at the fashionable Hotel Vanderbilt.[4] The classic Harry Greb / Gene Tunney battle, in the same arena two weeks later, would draw only 11,097.

With two black men contesting the main event, black New York was out in force too. "The cabarets of Lenox Avenue," Seabury Lawrence wrote, "will be practically deserted this evening."[5] Kid Norfolk, after all, was a credit to the Race. If he wasn't a Bible-citing deacon like future middleweight champion Tiger Flowers, he at least never courted public opprobrium. The rude uproar from ringside that greeted the foreign boxer nettled and astonished the Race. How had Battling Siki become the darling of fashionable white New York? Whatever the reason, Levy was glad. Rickard had insisted future bouts depended on this one. The *Evening Journal*'s Sid Mercer had speculated, "A victory tomorrow night may be worth a fortune to Siki; a defeat may rush him toward oblivion."[6] For tonight's work, Siki would get somewhere between $15,000 and $17,968, Norfolk $11,379—huge purses for black fighters in a non-title bout.[7] When this was over, Siki would be, after Levy's cut, $9,000 richer.[8] In 1923 that was more than the yearly salary of nine day laborers,[9] almost enough to buy four new Packard touring cars.[10] McTigue, the world champion, made only $7,500 for his junket to Georgia. Rickard needed a big crowd to turn a profit. Even with a near sellout the boxers were getting almost half the gate.

Levy knew that to get big purses, three things had to happen: this fight had to nearly sell out; Siki had to give the fans what they'd come to see; and Siki had to win. One down, two to go. To satisfy condition two, he'd have to come out steaming. After all the crowd had heard about how "something suddenly snapped" and the Senegalese had "gone berserk" against Carpentier, they wouldn't be satisfied unless they thought they saw foam on his lips. He'd also have to show himself to be "game." Norfolk, a rough customer, gave rivals something to remember him by. Witness what he'd done to Greb. Fans came to the Garden expecting to see Siki get hurt, wanting to see how he'd take it.

The third condition would be the hardest. Even under ordinary conditions Kid Norfolk was a tough rival. And conditions weren't ordinary. For some strange reason Goodman was missing on fight night. Maybe Levy didn't want to pay him, or maybe he was ill. Waiting for the bell for round one, Fall listened to his novice manager repeat Goodman's training lessons by rote. Norfolk would slip Siki's right and would hook to the body and head. Inside, he'd throw uppercuts. With his edge in stamina, Siki would have to get him in trouble early. If he didn't, it would be a long night. Siki had chased all over Europe winning fight after fight he'd been picked to lose, beating the Belgian, German, Italian, and French heavyweight champions. Siki believed in himself, believed in his *ndëmm* (spiritual destiny). Still, it must not have been easy standing there, as his seconds stepped through the ropes, set to begin the toughest fight of his career.

Any fighter who tells you he doesn't feel fear before a bout, Mickey Walker said flatly, is a liar.[11] Ex-heavyweight champ Jack Sharkey explained how it feels to wait for the bell for round one: "Lonely? You don't know what it's like to be lonely.... The seconds are out of the ring but you're in there with a guy who wants to hurt you and a referee who can't help you. Boy, you're lonely!"[12] Thomas Hauser repeats an analogy an (unnamed) modern champion made in describing how a fighter holds in fear against a tough opponent. He compared it to the way he'd felt at seventeen when he was suddenly afflicted with diarrhea on a date with a pretty girl. He couldn't find a restroom and was terrified he'd lose control of his bowels: "I fought it. It was like every ounce of strength I had was working to keep it in. I had to keep it in because if I shitted in my pants in front of this girl, I'd die.... I could hardly talk and I felt it slipping, but I held it in.... That's the kind of effort you need in the ring."[13]

Whatever his apprehensions, Siki rushed out at Norfolk from the opening bell "at a furious pace," the *Chicago Defender* reports, "swinging lefts and rights for the head," intent on giving the fans what they'd come to see.[14] Norfolk clinched. Heads lowered, the two men twisted torsos, "socking hard to the ribs."[15] Both the *Times* and *Evening Journal* saw Siki score to the head and body. But Norfolk counterattacked, sticking jabs, pounding body shots, and throwing uppercuts. The *Daily News* columnist Harry Newman shook his head over a strange anomaly the next day: the writers' scorecards added up to nearly identical round tallies, but apart from the dramatic final round, they hardly scored a single other round the same.[16] The *Times,* the *Evening Post,* and the *Evening Journal* had round one even. But the "thickest" account (to resurrect Clifford Geertz's term), in the *Daily News,* gave Norfolk the round.

The *Daily News* has Siki missing several "left-hand swings." Since a "swing" is usually thrown from a radical sideways stance, a right-handed boxer has to go southpaw, drawing his left foot back, to throw a left swing. Newman has Siki, late in the round, landing body shots, but taking his share too, along with uppercuts that bloodied his nose. Though the details are murky, an impression emerges of Siki rushing Norfolk, landing to the body and head as the crowd roared—but of Norfolk slipping punches and landing hooks and uppercuts. Both men worked well in the clinches. For Siki, that was a good sign. But Norfolk gave as good as he got, and between rounds, it was Siki's corner men who were pushing gauze up his gushing nose.

Siki had a battle ahead. He hadn't established physical dominance, hadn't been able to back Norfolk up. But he'd won twenty-nine bouts in a row before he fought McTigue, and lost just one (on a foul) since then. He came out again in round two at a "furious pace" *(Boxing Blade)*, landing heavily.

Two papers (the *Evening Journal* and the *Daily News*) saw Siki catch Norfolk with a hard left hook to the jaw and score well in the clinches. The *Evening Journal* saw him batter Norfolk to the body, "swinging with both hands in primitive fashion"as Norfolk tried to keep him off with his jab.[17] The *Daily News* related, "Siki rushed Norfolk into a corner, but the Kid drove him back with two straight lefts to the mouth." Norfolk blocked a left to the head, but Siki "stung" him with another to the mouth. The *Evening Post* and the *News* called the round even, the *Evening Journal* and the *Herald* gave it to Siki.

Siki had reason to feel good about some things. He'd out-worked Norfolk in the clinches, landed well to the body, and scored with his left hook. He'd avoided the uppercut Norfolk had caught him with in the first round, but was still getting hit with counters. Whenever he cocked back his arm for a right-hand swing, Norfolk caught him with a left. Two of the best corner men in boxing, Flynn and Dai Dollings, nodded close to Norfolk's face, reminding him of what he'd planned to do. Siki had only "the crudest of seconding," two inept helpers and novice manager Levy, who was "trembling like an aspen leaf before the first gong" and "still ... shaking when the final bell clanged."[18]

The third round became a back-and-forth slugfest, with Norfolk sticking his jab, shooting counters to the face and body, as Siki, spurred by the crowd, swung menacing hooks and swings, often missing, but landing heavily too. The *Tribune*'s Jack Lawrence described him "swatting Norfolk solidly on the jaw with both hands" as the crowd "howled" for a knockout and Flynn shouted advice to help Norfolk weather the storm.[19] The *Evening Journal* and the *Daily News* gave the round narrowly to Norfolk. The *Evening Post* and the *Tribune* had it for Siki. The *Times* called an equal number of punches for each man. All agreed about the punishing pace. A typical passage, from the *Daily News,* gives the feeling:

> Siki dropped over a hard right to Norfolk's ear at close quarters, but Norfolk was back with a hard right under the heart. Siki hooked a left to Norfolk's ear and ripped a right to the stomach. Norfolk tried to force the battle along the ropes, but Siki landed another left to the face. Norfolk drove a straight left to Siki's mouth and followed it with a hard right to the ribs.

A brutal back-and-forth combat might normally auger well for the younger man. Yet ringside observers saw bad omens. Siki was fading after the furious combinations he threw to start each round, Sid Mercer observed, and missing more and more.[20]

In Norfolk's corner, Flynn saw Siki's fatigue. When the bell rang he sent Norfolk charging out "with fire in his eyes," opening a cut over Siki's left eye "with almost his first blow" (Jack Lawrence) and scoring with his jab. Newman said Siki stormed back, attacking throughout the round, firing hook after hook, swing after swing, missing more and more, and with each miss suffering malicious punishment. Siki "was strong and kept plunging in with sweeping blows to Norfolk's head," but Norfolk twisted his whole weight into his shots to Siki's stomach, and Mercer saw him snap Siki's head back with three or four uppercuts, splitting his lip. Newman described Siki floundering about, "trying desperately to land a haymaker," tiring after each flurry, a sluggish target for shots to the body and head. Mercer saw Siki turn to his corner with his face "a smear of blood." Frantic seconds wiped the gore and clumsily daubed the cuts with astringent. Siki was hurt, and he was limp with fatigue. His handlers were all talking at once. Don't clinch with him! Levy said. Fight him from the outside.[21] It was true Siki was getting beat up on the inside, but he didn't have the legs to stick and run for eleven rounds. Siki needed to find a way to take back the fight, just over one-quarter gone. If he didn't hurt Norfolk soon, what had begun as a back-and-forth slugfest could turn into one-sided carnage.

In the glittering ringside ranks, men stood, pumped clenched fists, shouted. This was something like it! This was what they'd come to see! The men in the splendid evening coats had more than an aesthetic interest. Many were gamblers or racketeers. Among them, no doubt, were two West Side mob chieftains (they went to every big fight), Owney "the Killer" Madden and George Jean "Big Frenchie" De Mange, though no newspaper said so. Madden made sure the writers knew better than to put his name in print. Bookmaker and rumrunner Frank Costello undoubtedly was there too, along with Longy Zwillman and Willie Moretti, who ran New Jersey's biggest gambling rackets. Years later the *New York World Telegraph and Sun* would report, when Costello was shot in the head by Vincent "the Chin" Galante, that the hit had been ordered by a Midwestern gambling syndicate reluctant to pay off on $150,000 Costello had won betting on Sugar Ray Robinson to take back his middleweight title from Gene Fullmer.[22] Moretti and Zwillman had working partnerships with brother mobsters across the river. Moretti was an ardent sports fan and Zwillman liked to host political bigshots at big fights. New Jersey governor Harold Hoffman would later tell Estes Kefauver's senate rackets committee that he'd often been Zwillman's guest at Madison Square Garden boxing shows.[23]

Madden, whose uncle had been a Liverpool booth fighter, and who would in time control five world champions, often so far forgot himself at bouts that he jumped up and shadowboxed. His apartment sported a speedbag—mostly for brass-knuckle practice.[24] The elegant crowd had hoped to see Siki lose control and tear Norfolk limb from limb. Again and again in the early rounds they'd jumped to their feet screaming, sure they were about to witness a savage apotheosis. A blood frenzy filled the hall, not of the fighters but of the fans. The crowd waited, tense, expectant, for each sixty-second respite to end, and a fresh three-minute fit of violence to begin. They'd come, like sideshow patrons, hoping to see the wild man goaded into breaking down the bars, seizing and throttling a victim. They hoped pure rage would overcome control. But seeing it thwarted also brought a weird satisfaction.

Meanwhile, in the ring, an all too mechanical tragedy of broken flesh, blood-soaked gauze, and cotton swabs dabbed in white paste played itself out. Even the most seasoned cut man works frantically in the seconds between rounds. He may have to close as many as three bad cuts, so well that only a hard, direct hit will reopen them. Nat Fleischer would one day cite Bob Levy as an example of how a clever cut man could save a fighter. In Tommy Loughran's 1933 bout with Ray Impellitiere, referee Pete Hartley had waved his arms to stop the carnage, but Loughran, blood coursing down his chest from a cut lip, protested so fiercely Hartley let him go on, warning he'd stop the bout if the cut reopened. Levy and Joe Smith, working Loughran's corner, did their work so well that the huge gash never bled another drop. They literally won Loughran the fight.[25]

Ironically, Levy's chagrin over his work as Siki's cut man a decade before may have shamed him into mastering the trade. If by the early thirties he'd become one of the best in the business, in 1923 he was surely the worst. "Levy's hand shook when he attempted to apply the collodium to Siki's wounds, and not only that but he misjudged the time and as the gong would ring would attempt to jab on the collodium, or whatever it was, as Siki was rising from the chair," the *Evening Telegram* reported. "It is a wonder Siki's eye wasn't put out." To make matters worse, one of Levy's helpers "kept wiping Siki's wounds with the same blood-soaked and unkempt towel. He pawed Siki's face and nose and shut off his breath. Siki several times had to shake his head and push his handlers away in order to get his wind." He'd have been better off with no handlers at all.

In the 1920s, with no one regulating their trade, top corner men such as "Doc" Bagley, Dai Dollings, Paddy Mullins, Dan Morgan, and Jack Kearns formed a tiny secret society, concocting remedies of legendary ingenuity to stop cuts, restore gut-sick or winded fighters, or revive men knocked senseless. Many nostrums were dangerous, even in expert hands. A veteran second could often close a cut just by squeezing the edges tightly together,[26] but most depended on medication. A favored remedy was adrenalin, swabbed inside the nose or mouth, or pressed against the skin on a gauze pad.[27] But though adrenalin promotes clotting, it also raises blood pressure and pulse, often radically. Some trainers burned lesions shut with caustic substances. One called "dynamite" (ferric chloride) left permanent scars.[28] Levy most likely treated Siki with a coagulant called Monsel's solution made popular by Owney Madden crony Lou Brix, who used it in the corner of Benny Leonard, Charley Phil Rosenberg, and Gene Tunney. Brix's application of Monsel's solution to Tunney's cut eye in his Philadelphia fight against Dempsey so completely closed the wound it virtually healed by the final bell. Levy and Joe Smith used Monsel's solution on Loughran in 1933. Dispensed on the skin or inside the mouth or nose it formed a crust so hard a surgeon had to cut it off with a scalpel after the fight to avoid infection. A few drops of Monsel's remedy on an eye could also blind a fighter.[29]

Bleeding profusely, encircled by inept novices flourishing toxic substances, Siki risked more than the loss of a crucial match. A gauze pad had to be held over a fighter's eye until Monsel's remedy dried, to prevent errant drops from blinding him. If the nostrum on those swabs Levy jabbed at Siki as he rose from his stool was not collodium (an unlikely remedy for a fresh cut) but Monsel's solution, Levy could have blinded him. A heavyweight who fought Kid Norfolk three times would become a familiar sight on New York sidewalks, cup in hand, placard around his neck reading, "I am totally blind. Please help Jamaica Kid, former sparring partner of Jack Dempsey."[30] Bantamweight champ Pete Herman also ended his career blind, as did Siki's onetime stablemate, French welterweight Francis Charles.

Wilbur Wood in the *New York Herald* said Siki "came out fast" for round five, slamming lefts to Norfolk's head, giving the impression he might end the fight then and there.[31] But Norfolk survived the onslaught and stung Siki to the face and body.[32] Siki rallied, but his blows were wild. Levy's inability to stop the flow of blood, said George B. Underwood, had left him "not only blinded from the cut over his eye, but at times ... nearly choked from the flow of blood from lips, mouth, and nose."[33] No observer mentioned Norfolk's talented thumb, but Newman saw Siki came out of one clinch with his left eye closed. By round's end Norfolk was landing whenever he pleased. Choking on his own blood, half-blind, Siki held on in the clinches, as Norfolk landed blows that "nearly doubled [him] into the shape of a jackknife."[34] Jack Lawrence of the *Tribune* says referee Eddie Purdy warned Norfolk again and again for hitting low. In that era before rubber groin protectors, low blows could rip an intestine or rupture a testicle. Referees stopped bouts for low blows, awarding victory to the man fouled. In 1930, Max Schmeling won the heavyweight title in that manner—even though the referee hadn't seen the punch land.[35] Eddie Purdy, however, wasn't one to pay much mind to fouls. When Mickey Walker fought Harry Greb in 1925, Greb worked every dirty trick in the book while "putting a sour eye" on Purdy. When Purdy twisted an ankle, Greb took advantage of his incapacity by fouling yet more brazenly.[36]

Siki, perhaps aware of Purdy's laissez faire attitude, grinned, waved Purdy away, and beckoned Norfolk to come on. Norfolk launched an immediate assault, landing a left to the face, a right to the body. Siki winced and fired back, connecting at the bell with a shot that "sent Norfolk back on his heels."[37] The *Herald* gave the round to Siki. The *Evening Journal,* the *Daily News,* and the *Tribune* gave it to Norfolk. The *Times'* punch count, subtracting for the low blow, would make it even. Round five might have encouraged Siki. As badly as he was hurt, he still rallied, landing one the most vicious punches of the fight. But Norfolk could keep firing his counters longer than Siki could keep up his furious rushes. Sid Mercer thought he saw another factor swing Norfolk's way. He was sure Siki had injured his hand landing an overhand right to the top of Norfolk's head.

The sixth round began, said Mercer, with a weary Siki for the first time backing away. When he missed a left, Norfolk landed a hook that sent him reeling. Siki came back with long lefts to the head. Then Norfolk got inside and stayed there, jolting Siki. The *Times* saw both men land lefts to the ribs.[38] Newman of the *Daily News* saw Siki, toward round's end, force Norfolk to the ropes and land left and right swings to the body. Most accounts gave Norfolk the edge. Jack Lawrence called the round even.

In the seventh, flat-footed, "arm-weary"(*Evening Journal),* "blinded . . . with left jabs" (*Times*), his nose bloodied (*Chicago Defender*), Siki kept tossing left swings, though (said Newman) he'd landed few so far. When Norfolk reopened the cut over his eye, Siki seemed to Mercer to "revert to cave-man tactics," smashing lefts to the body. Newman saw him hook a left to Norfolk's ear, but Norfolk retaliate to Siki's ribs. Norfolk came out of a clinch with a bloody mouth but staggered Siki with a hard right to the chin and three lefts to the mouth at the bell. Every account gave Norfolk the round. "Papa" Bob Levy must have seen his fighter's disorientation, for he slipped Siki a dram of scotch. Alcohol was a common tonic for athletes in that era. Even Tour de France riders drank red wine during race stages, on the theory it "restored the blood." Siki could maybe have used a real transfusion instead. Under Levy's inept handling, he must have lost a quart of blood.

Levy ought to have brought down the swelling in Siki's eye (Kearns suggests) with ice or, if that failed, by opening a small slit in the swollen tissue with the corner of well-taped razor. To revive Siki if he were stunned, Levy should have splashed cold water in his face, or stuck smelling salts under his nose.[39] Fleischer suggests ice on the back, or chafing the face or the limbs to restore blood flow.[40] Ferdie Pacheco urges seconds to get men past exhaustion by massaging their necks, back, and legs, or rubbing them with sponges and ice.[41] Rather than doping a fading man, he advises, "Ask the referee to stop the bout." Why risk permanent disability? "Pa" Levy and his helpers, meanwhile, were wiping Siki's face with a gory rag and leaving him choking on his own blood. That he may have been in no condition to continue seems not to have occurred to them. The fight was not quite half over, but Siki had already taken more punishment than most men would in a dozen tough fights.

Buzzed over by a swarm of novices, Siki might have been forgiven had he thrown in the towel. His chances were fading with each round against the superbly conditioned athlete across the blood-spattered canvas. Every trainer has his own strategy for rekindling a fighter's will to win. Some appeal to greed or pride. In Siki's day, some, like Levy, poured a few fingers of whiskey down a disheartened man's throat. Some even dabbed cocaine up his nose.[42] Others mocked their man's inadequacies, as Kearns said he did with Dempsey.[43] Whitey Bimstein jeered one fading fighter, "If you done your roadwork right you wouldn't feel this way. I hope he kills you."[44] But Levy just kept telling Siki to stay out of the clinches and left him to rally his own fading spirits.[45]

It didn't much matter. Siki wasn't the sort to give in to weakness. He'd survived rifle fire, poison gas, high explosive shells, malaria, and dysentery. What was this in comparison? In the morning, his eye might be swollen shut, his senses addled. His ribs might ache when he coughed. He might leave the ring blind, too, or in a coma. He risked as well initiating the process of slow cerebral atrophy that ends in *dementia puglistica*—but who knew much about that in 1923? Deep inside, despite the patent and not so patent risks, Siki found the restorative that mattered most, a summoning of his own will.

At the bell for the eighth, Norfolk "tore after" Siki, "tossing his left" into Siki's face.[46] Siki turned the tables and "nearly upset" him with two hard left hooks to the chin, but Norfolk plunged back in. The *Times* saw him land with both hands to the body, then blind Siki with "snappy rights and lefts to the face."[47] At round's end, Siki lashed out, catching Norfolk to the jaw with a right-left combination. It had been the roughest round of the fight, with the nearly thirteen thousand patrons on their feet throughout, screaming for blood. Wood, Mercer, and Newman all gave the round to Siki. One more combination at the right moment, said the *Times,* and he might have knocked Norfolk out.

In Siki's corner, with everyone getting in each other's way, everyone talking at once, "keep it up" was about all the counsel Siki got. In Norfolk's corner, you'd expect Flynn to be saying, "Okay, you let him take that round. Now relax and forget it. Go back to what was working." In fact, however, Flynn seems to have seen how much energy Siki had squandered and decided to try to end it then and there. At the bell Norfolk charged after Siki, who, from sheer exhaustion, backed away. Newman said Norfolk "nearly swept the Battler out of the ring" with lefts to the mouth. Jack Lawrence saw him "put across a vicious shot to the chin that made the Battler's legs waver." Mercer saw him hammer Siki to the kidneys. Siki kept retreating, holding Norfolk off with his jab.

Between rounds Siki swallowed another "three fingers of Johnny Walkers"[48] and at the bell for the tenth came out fast, dancing, tossing his left hook,[49] until Norfolk caught him with a right to the jaw[50] and doubled him up with blows to the stomach. Even so, Siki kept trying to land the heavy blow that might reverse the fight's fortunes. For the fans, this was the bout's most spectacular round. Siki "fought like a wounded tiger," Underwood said. Mercer said Norfolk's punches "splashed the blood" from Siki's "battered face." Newman saw a "series of right and left smashes" send Siki "staggering," followed by "stinging blows to the kidneys." By round's end, Siki was utterly drained, his right eye nearly closed.[51] The fans, in an uproar, were now shouting not for Norfolk's blood but for Siki's. "After the eighth round," Wood deemed, "Siki never had a chance." The crowd sensed that and settled in to enjoy the gore.

"A Beautiful Evening's Socking"

The boxers Siki most reminds one of these days, Ricardo Mayorga and Manny Pacquiao, have both scored spectacular upsets over men who held all the advantages in technique, footwork, and style. A tough, relentless fighter, with a granite jaw, a knockout punch, and fierce determination can overcome stylistic flaws, as happened three times in 2003, when Mayorga beat Vernon Forrest twice, and Pacquiao knocked out Marco Antonio Barerra. But a fighter like Mayorga or Pacquiao must be in top shape to keep up the relentless assault that overcomes a deficit in technique. Like Siki, Mayorga is not averse to conning the writers into believing he trains on cigarettes and wine. He's even been known to puff a celebratory butt in the ring after a victory. But don't let the hype fool you. For a big fight he turns up in superb shape. With Siki, you can't help but wonder what if... What if Siki had seasoned corner men, a few more weeks in camp? Might not he have pounded out a victory over his ring-wise rival just as Mayorga did over Forrest or Pacquiao over Barrera? For the first ten rounds, in shape or not, Siki made things more than interesting for Kid Norfolk. The *New York Herald* judged the bout "anybody's fight" at that juncture. The next four, however, would tell a different story and set the stage for one of the most memorable final rounds a Garden crowd had ever witnessed.

Those rounds are painful to consider in light of what we now know about the effects of ring combat. The human brain, soft, pliable, fluid-filled, with a "firm jelly-like consistency," is attached at its base to nerves and blood vessels of the spinal column, but only tenuously anchored to the skull by spidery strands of tissue and "thin elastic veins." A stunning blow can send the brain slamming against "sharp inward projections" of the cranium with a torsion reaching 520 m/s^2, producing a "'swirling' effect" as one hemisphere hurls into another, impeding neurological function, tearing its casing, inducing superficial bleeding, and, when the blood clots, a blockage of blood flow.[52] Knockout blows don't provoke the worst chronic injury. Rather, an accumulation of punches over the course of a career scars the brain, shrinks it (through loss of surface gray matter and inner white matter), and leaves permanent lesions in the folds of the fluid-filled central cavity, the septum.[53]

Fights like this one, where endless series of blows followed devastating single punches, were tailor-made for permanent injury. A hard punch typically produces "'grogginess' and a sensation of weakness or paralysis." Observers "may see a weakening of the boxer's legs," "a lack of focusing of the eyes." If the referee misses such signs, worse damage may follow. The fluid filling the brain weakens its tissue, swelling blood vessels, which sometimes break, or lose their ability to adapt to "a drop in perfusion pressure." Each new blow adds worse injury—and Siki suffered a remorseless series of such blows that night. The blood splattered on the boxers' trunks thrilled the crowd. They didn't consider the blood seeping inside both men's skulls.

If the late rounds are painful to consider, they were thrilling to watch. The crowd that had roared for Norfolk's blood in the early going now shouted with equal fervor for Siki's. The eleventh and twelfth rounds were agony for him. As Norfolk's confidence grew, Siki, utterly spent, reflexes deserting him, kept trying to mount fresh assaults. Mercer speaks of Norfolk going after him at the bell for round eleven, landing lefts to the head that "had him hanging on." Dead game, Siki kept firing, missing badly. When Norfolk drove a right uppercut, Siki "flopped against the ropes but came back for more." When he tried to escape, Norfolk pursued him "throwing punches from every direction,"[54] staggering Siki with a left to the jaw.[55] When Norfolk again landed a low blow, Siki protested. Purdy ignored him. Siki wrestled Norfolk across the ring but a stiff left to the face had him "spitting blood." With "nothing left," he was "reeling around," both eyes swollen nearly shut, taking everything Norfolk threw.[56]

As the twelfth opened, Norfolk staggered Siki with a left hook and doubled him over with a punch that Siki again protested was low, shaking his glove and muttering in French to Purdy, who snarled "go ahead and fight." In a clinch, Norfolk landed "a dozen short uppercuts."[57] Siki managed only a "feeble" right.[58] Seasoned boxers learn to "ride a punch," softening the blow by pulling the head away. One of the crucial effects of repeated neural damage, however, is a loss of reflexes. Thus, the more a fighter is hit, the more solidly each punch lands.[59] By now, Siki was being hurt badly with each successive blow. But "Pa" Levy was reluctant to call a halt. His 30 percent cut barely covered his investment to buy Siki's contract. If Siki lost on a TKO, how would he recoup his expenses? Siki's marketability might survive a decision loss. A knockout was another story.

Siki went out for the last three rounds with one eye battered shut, the other nearly so, and blood streaming from his mouth and nose, intent on landing the knockout combination that had eluded him so far. The closed eye affected his peripheral vison and depth perception. The blood in his mouth and nose choked him. Norfolk "pranced around," looking spry,[60] but when he missed a left hook, Siki "rallied spectacularly,"[61] landing a "vicious uppercut," a "smashing [left] hook," and a right to the head.[62] When the rally spent itself, however, Norfolk went back to punishing Siki. Siki tried more and more wildly to connect with a haymaker, unleashing a final rally near the bell.[63] The *Boxing Blade* implied Siki dominated the round. The other papers gave it to Norfolk.

The crowd thought they'd witnessed Battling Siki's last stand, but he rallied yet more desperately in the final rounds. In the fourteenth he leaped in and "drove a corking left" to Norfolk's head.[64] As Norfolk hung on, Siki "ripped another left" to the face coming out of the clinch and whacked a left hook to Norfolk's jaw. Norfolk clinched and winked at his corner, as if to say, Okay, he hit me a couple cracks. But it doesn't change a thing. Siki cut short his gesture with a crisp hook, but when Siki's stamina faded, Norfolk again went back to work. The round ended with them trading shots in a long clinch as Norfolk snapped off a dozen short uppercuts that Mercer said "tilted Siki's chin back."[65]

In the final round, Siki all at once "lash[ed] out with terrific rights and lefts," with "no regard for the consequences of leaving himself open,"[66] landing one stunning blow, a "long left swing" that the *Times* said almost knocked Norfolk out of the ring.[67] Heartened, he "chased Norfolk around swinging both hands" as the fans roared.[68] The huge crowd, largest of the season, would carry this moment with them as they streamed out the exits. The *Evening Journal* cartoonist Hal Coffman fixed it in memory for thousands who weren't present, depicting a "lumbering Siki" (actually he was quick on his feet) with a gorilla-like upper torso, wide neck, and shaggy head. The cartoon-Siki leans forward, pivoting on his front foot. His arm, in mid-follow-through, crooked at a ninety-degree angle, moves parallel to the plane of the floor in a classic left hook. Norfolk, elevated off the ground, flies through the air, his torso bending the top rope, arms flopping like a rag doll's, a hapless victim flung aside by a raging Borneo wild man.

Wilbur Wood saw "a sickly, silly sort of grin" on Norfolk's face as he flopped against the ropes, where Siki pursued him "and pounded the temporarily bewildered Norfolk around the ring working furiously with both hands." The roaring crowd urged Siki on as he stung Norfolk with a "solid left hook to the jaw" and "staggered" him with a right. Again Norfolk "backed to the ropes, laughing foolishly."[69] Somehow Norfolk rode out the storm. At the bell, the two men stood toe to toe, lashing out with lefts and rights. And so the bloody, vicious ordeal ended.

The *Evening Journal* contrived to give the round to Norfolk, though its round-by-round credited Siki with landing more and harder punches. The *Daily News* made it even, though it too called more blows for Siki. Jack Lawrence of the *Tribune* gave Siki the round. After the bell, Siki clasped his hands over his head, as the crowd roared its admiration. To the wonder of reporters, as referee Purdy and judges Eddie Becker and Tommy Shortell tallied their cards, the fans chanted, "Draw! Draw! Draw!" Ring announcer Humphries instead intoned, "The winner, by unanimous decison... Ki... id Nor... folk! Nor... folk!"

The crowd couldn't seem to make up its mind whether to boo or cheer. Finally, they decided to cheer. After all, it had been a hell of a fight—the knock-down-drag-out of the year, better even than Firpo / Dempsey from the standpoint of sustained violence over a full fifteen rounds. Neither man had knocked the other down, but they'd splashed the ring with gore and stunned each other time and again. "Siki dealt out plenty of stiff wallops to head and body," wrote Wilbur Wood. Norfolk had blocked many, but enough had landed "to have stopped the Kid if he had been anything but a sturdy warrior." Both men, the *Chicago Defender* said, "gave and received blows that should have killed an ordinary man."[70] The *Evening Telegram*'s Underwood judged the bout "as hectic a combat as two colored boxers have waged" since John Jeannette and Sam Langford staged their epic battle before the war.

After the verdict, Siki "walked briskly across the ring, slapped Norfolk on the back, and congratulated him."[71] He crawled through the ropes, "trying to smile, through bloody lips," as the crowd's cheers thundered down.[72] The fight had been closer than some writers pretended, but the outcome was as plain as the gore on Siki's face. Wood wrote, "Siki was a sorry sight when he trudged to his corner at the end of the final round. Both eyes were nearly closed and there was a nasty cut alongside his left optic. His nose and mouth were bleeding promiscuously." The real pain would catch up with Siki in the morning. Levy, however, already wore a "very pained expression" as he left the arena.[73] Many credited him with costing his boxer the fight: by neither giving him time to get in shape nor arranging for a good corner man. "One good handler," Underwood observed. "'Doc' Bagley, Dai Dollings [who worked Norfolk's corner], Paddy Mullins, Dan Morgan, Jack Kearns, for instance, might have made a big difference."

The day after the fight, Mercer found Siki at a theater district hotel, hardly up to a stroll down Broadway, but thankful for the cheers the fans had accorded him.[74] Reporters caught up with Levy at the Garden, where he insisted that despite last night's "unpalatable surprise," Siki would stay in the United States. He was "more determined than ever" to show American fans "his best fighting form."[75] Newman insisted Siki said he'd leave for Holland that Saturday, returning to the United States "inside of a month." "The Senegalese thumper" declared that it would "be different the next time around"; "if he ever gets another poke at Norfolk he will knock him silly."[76]

Levy now blamed Siki's loss on scanty training, admitting, "He was not at his best, although, under the circumstances, he was in as good physical condition as possible." His lack of fitness showed "in each round when, after starting strong, he would fall into clinches before a minute's activity."[77] Wilbur Wood seemed to exculpate Levy in observing that Siki "fights in his own way and has been fighting that way for so long that he hardly will change much now."[78]

The way the newspapers received Siki's losing effort boded well, at least. He'd "made a hit" with his "gameness and good nature," Sid Mercer wrote, adding, with no apparent irony, "The Senegalese has that indefinable ring attraction the promoters call 'color.' Siki 'gets over' the ropes with his smile and his boyish nature. He can take a licking and smile through it."[79] The *Times* called the bout a "privilege" to watch, and Rickard began talking up the very opponents—Gibbons, McTigue, Tunney, and Greb—he'd dangled as rewards for Siki if he *won*. Levy got offers from Atlanta (against Tiger Flowers) and Havana.[80] In defeat, Siki "emerged ... so popular that he is far more in demand by matchmakers than his conqueror, Kid Norfolk." Sid Mercer summed up the feelings of many:

> Though outpointed in practically every round . . . , Battling Siki . . . displayed one quality that won the sympathies of nearly 13,000 boxing fans. . . . That quality is gameness. Siki has plenty of it. He proved it during the great war when he was twice decorated for courage. Last night he proved it again when he endured a fearful beating, yet never took a backward step except from sheer weariness.[81]

Seabury Lawrence gave Norfolk credit for superb ring generalship and infighting, but thought it "doubtful" he'd beat Siki again if Siki got in shape and worked with a top trainer.[82] Walter Trumbull mused wryly, "Now Willie Ward is no gentle playmate. There are a lot of white gentlemen in the boxing game who want no part of Willie. It is true that he sometimes loses a bout to an invisible punch [a hint at an alleged dive against Harry Wills], but ordinarily Willie is as safe to mingle with as a barrel of black powder."[83] Leo Flynn said Norfolk had spent fifteen rounds trying to set up Siki for a right but Siki "never failed to cover his chin with that left shoulder. And he can sock."

"Far from being the crude, unschooled, wide open boxer some reports would have had us believe," Underwood mused, Siki had "boxed fairly cleverly and skillfully and flashed a world of power and speed." He boxed in an "orthodox fashion too, not in that weird jungle style, with the low crouches and animal-like springs accredited him."[84] Siki would "make it interesting for any man of his weight in the world. He will be no cinch for Gene Tunney, Tom Gibbons, or Harry Greb. Make no mistake about that," he added. "The Siki who fought Norfolk the other night would whip Mike McTigue the best day Mike ever saw in the ring."[85] The *World*'s Hype Igoe observed, "Siki won a place in the respect of all lovers of gameness, willingness, and determination. Fighting Norfolk as he did, with no fights under his belt, his was a worthy performance."[86] Hal Coffman's cartoon's caption put a final exclamation point on the bout: "Yes, Siki sure did receive a beautiful evening's socking, but he showed a lot of the boys and girls that he is as game as they come. And that's something, I'll say."[87]

Underwood began his piece by quoting Rudyard Kipling, "So, 'ere's to you, Fuzzy Wuzzy, at your 'ome in the Soudan; / You're a pore benighted 'eathen, but a first-class fighting man." Elsewhere he called Siki "the kinky headed coon from Senegal," but he clearly intended the Kipling allusion as a compliment. He added, "It took 'a first-class fighting man' to take the licking Siki did from Norfolk and keep plunging right back in for more. Siki showed a ring courage thoroughly in keeping with the gallantry on the larger field of war which won him both the *Croix de Guerre* and the ribbon of the Legion of Honor."[88]

The allusion is interesting, for Kipling's "Fuzzy-Wuzzies" were in fact followers of a Muslim religious leader, Muhammad Ahmad, the "Mahdi" (literally "the expected one"), fighting not, as Kipling's poetic speaker has it, out of blind fanaticism or savage indifference to danger, but nationalistic fervor. Battling Siki shared such sentiments. His own ring cognomen, which he'd chosen himself when just a teenaged novice, recalled an anti-colonial insurrection from about the same period. Kipling's poem was, moreover, a familiar schoolroom declamation piece in the 1920s. Many of Underwood's readers would have heard echoing behind the quoted lines others he'd left out—about a "big black boundin' beggar" with a "'ayrick 'ead of 'air" who might be born a warrior but also much resembled an "india-rubber idiot on the spree." That Underwood's sally resonated with readers is evident from the alacrity with which other writers echoed it, nationwide.[89]

As Underwood himself observed, there was nothing odd about Siki's style in the ring. Nevertheless, sportswriters would again and again describe him as having India-rubber reflexes, or leaping and whirling about the ring like a dervish. And of course, though the notion of a heedless, impossible bravery would adhere permanently to the boxer Battling Siki, linked to it equally indelibly would be the notion of Siki as a fantastic "idiot on a spree" whose courage was of a piece with his freakishness. Damned with quaint praise, Siki would never, as Gerald Early recognized in his essay on the boxer, seem quite real to boxing writers or fans. It's strange how much more interesting we find our own illusions than others' truths. In Siki's case, America's racial illusions obscured a simple verity about the life he'd led to that point: that the courage and toughness the writers saw were real, but their sources came from a heritage they did not begin to comprehend.

CHAPTER FIVE

"Tough Luck!"

Amadou M'barick Fall and Battling Siki

S iki said it often enough. No, he wasn't a "child of the jungle" bedazzled by civilization. In fact, the only jungles he'd ever seen had been on movie screens. As he put it himself, "A lot of newspaper people have written that I have a jungle style of fighting—that I am a chimpanzee who has been taught to wear gloves. That kind of thing hurts me. I was never anywhere but in a big city in my life. I have never even *seen* a jungle."[1] In fact, there were then, and are still, more trees on the island of Manhattan than on the two contiguous sandbar islands on which stand the city of his birth, Saint-Louis du Sénégal. When Siki tried to describe his real origins, the writers nodded their heads, said "sure, sure, kid," and went right on writing that he'd climbed down from a coconut palm. Fifty years later, in a sudden, guilty burst of nostalgia when George Foreman became the first world champion to defend his title in Africa, a few boxing writers resurrected the legacy of Battling Siki, the first African to win a world's title, and the boxing world finally heard what Siki had so vehemently said.[2] No, he wasn't a jungle-bred savage. But still they couldn't quite shed their notion of Siki the "India-rubber idiot on a spree." It fit too well with their preconception about the origins of his "unquenchable fighting spirit."

In a way, Siki's fighting spirit came both from his heritage and in spite of it. His parents, Oulimata and Assane Fall, had imagined a very different destiny for him. His cousin Oumar Sarr, shortly before his death, told Niek Koppen[3] that at Siki's baptism his parents had named him Amadou, a version of the Muslim prophet's name.[4] Senegalese fathers usually choose a

89

son's name, though they may cede that right to the mother as a mark of favor. It often honors a relative, friend, or religious figure—but may record a propitious incident of his conception or birth.[5] A father may also ask the *marabout* at the child's *ngente,* the Wolof baptism, to choose the name. Often, the *marabout* finds a propitious Koranic verse, chooses a name from that verse, writes the verse on a slate with ink made of harmless herbs, washes it off with water, and gives the mixture to the baby to drink, sweetened with honey. But whatever stratagems his parents employed at the future Battling Siki's *ngente* didn't work, for the name Amadou never stuck, and their son, fully grown, would have little use for formal religion.

Instead of Amadou the child soon was being called by a name that better fit him, one of Toucouleur origin, M'barick. The Toucouleur word *m'baré* means *to kill,* and gives rise to a Wolof derivative, *bèré,* to wrestle. Fall's cousin Oumar Sarr told Niek Koppen, "He was a very, very turbulent child," suggesting the name *M'barick* was a nickname, marking the boy's early truculence.[6] Both Nat Fleischer[7] and the *New York Times*[8] aver that at some point colonial African soldiers (*tirailleurs sénégalais*) in Saint-Louis nicknamed young Fall "Baye." In Wolof, "baay" means "grandfather," and is a common nickname for infants, particularly those named after a grandfather (dead ancestors are believed to be reborn within the family). But "Baye" may also refer to the *Baye Fall,* a fractious Muslim sect devoted to the Senegalese holy man, poet, and nationalist Cheikh Amadou Bamba. Since Bamba's acolytes were fervent militants, that name too might suggest the boy's combative behavior. It seems appropriate in other ways as well, for the *Baye Fall* wore long uncombed locks and motley clothing, symbolic of Bamba's years of suffering when the French sent him into exile. What better name for the future "Battling Siki," whose public image was marked by flamboyant attire and a shock of unruly hair?

The name "Louis," which Siki later used in private life, probably wasn't chosen by his parents. In Saint-Louis du Sénégal only the *métis citoyens*— mixed-race descendants of colonial officers and their mistresses—gave children Christian first names. Those of pure African descent gave their children Muslim names or names derived from traditional African usage. Many, however, picked up Christian names later at mission schools (Saint-Louis had two). Perhaps a mission schoolteacher assigned young Fall the name Louis, not in honor of *Louis le Grand,* but, like the town itself, after the sainted Louis IX, an ethnic zealot who led bloody crusades against the "infidels" in the thirteenth century. Later, perhaps when he served with the Eighth Colonial Regiment of Toulon during the war, Fall may have adopted another Christian given name, since the *New York Times* insisted the boxer's real first name was Philippe.

Saint-Louis, the windswept settlement in the arid north of Senegal where Amadou M'barick Fall was born, was hardly the "jungle" Frick presumed. France's main colonial outpost (and military citadel) on Africa's west coast, founded in 1659, it had, by the turn of the century, become administrative center to a vast West African empire, including much of present-day Niger, Dahomey, Chad, Ivory Coast, Guinea, Burkina Faso, and Mauritania. Its coaling station refueled ships bound for Europe or Brazil. By the 1920s, it would boast a seaplane base.

Its white population, shrunk in the nineteenth century to less than 2 percent, rebounded in the twentieth, but the *habitants,* Europeanized Africans and persons of mixed race, dominated public life.[9] Saint-Louis was really two towns, on parallel sandbar islands at the mouth of the *fleuve Sénégal:* Guet Ndar, a mile-long outer islet just one hundred meters wide, where Muslim fishermen, with strong ties to mainland Wolof and Peul cultures, crowded in family compounds; and behind it, Ndar itself, a tiny inner islet (less than a mile and a half long), with a grid of white stone bungalows encircling cool inner patios, where masters occupied balconied upper floors and servants lived below. The master might be European, Arab, African *assimilé,* or a mixed-race descendant of French merchants and their mistresses.

The ocean pounded endlessly the *Langue de Barbarie,* the outer island where M'barick Fall was born, shrinking its contours by 1930 to barely half its width in Fall's day. Typhoons regularly swept away half the dwellings on an island barely two meters above sea level. Though his cousin would show Niek Koppen a putative brick and cement birthplace, Fall probably, like most people in Guet Ndar, was born in a square hut with a conical thatched roof, two circular holes eighteen inches in diameter for windows, and a cloth curtain for a door—one among several within the reed palisade of a family compound. Such houses were often built of mismatched materials: "Reeds with tin or corrugated sheet metal, rope made of Baobab fiber with nails and iron wire, boards with stone or cloth fabric."[10]

Guet Ndar defined itself by the sea. In the 1930s, it sent forty tons of fresh fish daily to the covered market and thirty-five tons to the smoke sheds to be shipped in pirogues up the Senegal River. The industry employed a hundred sailmakers, three hundred ropemakers, two hundred netmakers, and fifty smoke shed tenders. Though a few hundred francs framed a dwelling and 15 more added a roof, fishing clans pooled resources to raise the 750 to 2,000 francs a pirogue cost, or the 5,000 an imported net could set you back.[11] Fishing was the all-consuming reality. Even today a favorite *jeux de mots* of Dakar political cartoons in *Le Cafard Libéré* represents the nation, Sénégal, as *"sunu gaal,"* our tipsy, overcrowded fishing boat. M'barick Fall's father Assane went out each dawn, as did most men from Guet Ndar, to launch a precarious long-nosed pirogue. Two men working in tandem muscled the boat into crashing surf, timing the breakers, and set off to tow heavy nets upon the turbulent Atlantic. Leca tells of giant sea turtles surfacing among the boats and of fishermen so reckless they threw themselves onto the turtles' backs, overturning the turtles so they could be wrestled into the boats.[12]

On a good day in dry season, when fish were plentiful, two men could fill a pirogue to the gunnels in an hour, dispatching the fish with blows from iron bars, for a big *capitaine* (barracuda) could chomp off toes or fingers. In the struggle against wind, wave, and flailing fish, boats capsized, and men were swept overboard. Assane Fall one day fell victim to such an accident among the anonymous waves. A bleak stretch of the *langue de Barberie* south of town, then as now, was given over to the fishermen's graveyard, where fishnets toss from wooden stakes, memorializing lost men. Often a torn net was all the sea returned. After her husband's death, Oulimata Fall supported herself by one of the trades open to women: salting and preserving the catch, dying indigo cloth, selling basic goods in the covered market between Guet Ndar and Ndar Tuti at the island's north end.[13] By some accounts, she was part of a polygamous household where a half-dozen co-wives nurtured twenty-two children.[14] If so, her fatherless son had the succor of an extended clan of half-brothers, half-sisters, cousins of every degree—the interlocking web of consanguinity so important in Wolof culture. Still, he, his siblings, and his *ndey* (his mother and her co-wives or kinswomen) struggled to get by. Life was hardscrabble, tenuous. He learned to fight his own battles on the streets. African soldiers of the *tirailleur* battalion, whose camp was a few hundred meters away, may have called him "Baye Fall" as a joke, equating his shaggy poverty with the militant self-sacrifice of the Muslim sect, as he ran wild with other boys, dressed in nothing but a *gemba,* a loin cloth.

Soon thereafter he was brought to Europe and abandoned, though the story of how that happened exists in a maze of versions. According to one, the ten-year-old Amadou M'barick "Baye" Fall and a gang of other boys dove for coins tossed into the sea by passengers hanging over the rail of an ocean liner.[15] A woman passenger took a fancy to the boy. By some accounts she was Dutch,[16] by others French,[17] by others German.[18] One said Fall himself had no idea whether his patroness—who arrived not by boat but by train from Dakar—was German or Dutch.[19] Some accounts call her old,[20] one even says young Fall was brought to France by *"un fonctionnaire colonial"*—a (male) colonial administrator.[21] Most accounts have the stranger offer to take young Fall to Europe on a whim. Bénac's version, the most complete, gives the scene thus:

> While waiting for the health formalities to be completed, the passengers amused themselves by throwing silver or nickel coins at little blacks who dove into the clear water to depths of twenty meters and brought them back to the surface, showing them in triumph at the tips of their fingers. One of them, a kid ten or twelve years old, already well-muscled for his age, showed himself to be more talented than the others. A rich Dutch passenger noticed it and, once she had reached dry land, called him to her side: "—What's your name?"
>
> "—Louis Siki Fall."
>
> "—What do you do? Do you have a trade?" A vague gesture was the only answer of the little Negro. "—Would you be willing to come with me to Europe?"
>
> "—Oh, yes!"
>
> "—But what would your parents say?" Another vague movement of the shoulders is his only response.[22]

From there accounts diverge. Some declare the woman—whose name Nat Fleischer and Nigel Collins give as Elaine Grosse[23]—was an actress,[24] some a dancer,[25] some a singer.[26] Some say she took up with the boy because she was impressed by his pert intellect[27] or moved by his poverty.[28] Bénac hints precocious social deviance, calling the boy "resourceful, eccentric, and a devilish liar."[29] In some versions, his savior was rich[30] and meant to educate him ("to give to little Siki an adequate instruction by making him follow the course of the Lycee, to make of Siki an educated and well-mannered little boy, like the others of his age").[31] Others depict her as impressed by his looks or anatomical attributes.[32] In some versions she meant to employ him in her house,[33] or give him a part in her show.[34] By some accounts, Fall's benefactress had to talk his parents into letting him leave.[35] By others, she paid them.[36] By yet others, he left in secret.[37]

Many accounts say his benefactress died soon after his arrival in France,[38] one says four years later.[39] Others say she enrolled him in school in Marseille.[40] Yet others say French customs authorities prevented her from taking her young charge with her any farther, since he hadn't proper papers.[41] She reluctantly continued her homeward journey (or left her home in the south of France to go on tour in Eastern Europe) without him, leaving behind a note for 1,000 (or 3,000, or 6,000, or 10,000) francs (or 30,000 marks) to give him a start in life.[42]

Some accounts portray the benefactress as dressing young Fall in an exotic costume and putting him into service ("in a page boy's uniform of bottle green")[43] before he committed some fault for which she turned him out of the house. Other accounts leave a salacious odor lingering. John McCallum and John Lardner both allege that young Fall's mistress chose his surname (which they give as "Phal") "for reasons based on classical Greek" (a reference to *phallus*).[44] In fact, *Fall* is one of the most common Senegalese surnames, but what writer could pass up a chance to hint at the racial myth that assigned black males oversized penises and monstrous sexual appetites? Eventually, in every account but McCallum's (which has Fall returning to work as her servant after the war), the boy runs through his patron's money and makes his own way on the streets.

Georges Peeters asserts Fall left Senegal at the age of eight. But he gives Fall's birth date as December 16, 1899,[45] as does De Lafrete in *L'Echo de Paris*.[46] Fall listed his age on his New York City marriage certificate, on July 23, 1924, as twenty-three—implying he'd been born between July 24, 1900, and July 23, 1901. More likely birth dates, fitting better with the dates for his first professional fights and enlistment in the army, are either September 16, 1897 (supplied by *L'Auto*)[47] or September 26, 1897 (given by the *Petit Parisien*).[48] Fall probably left Senegal (as Peeters implies) in 1908, when he was ten or eleven years old, not eight.[49]

By that time he'd almost certainly undergone the Wolof circumcision rite. Fall's family would hardly have allowed him to leave had he not attained symbolic adult status. The focal point for boys' education into Wolof conceptions of maleness, testing and interiorizing courage, patient endurance, modest discretion, and loyalty or group allegiance, the circumcision ceremony also ritually affirmed *yax* and *siddit,* bones and nerves—symbolizing underlying substance and external emotional control.[50] Without them, the boy would be unable to take destiny in his own hands. Popular tradition holds that Fall attended both mission and Koranic school. In the former, he'd have learned about the civilizing mission of French culture, with its ideal of *liberté, égalité,* and *fraternité.*[51] In the latter, he'd have learned of the duty, enjoined in the *Koran,* to defend the true faith. When the Great War came, all three ethics would play a role in justifying the sacrifices Africans would make.

In 1908, Amadou M'barick Louis Fall, though just ten years old, had made a basic life choice: to leave his homeland. His name, M'barick, along with his cousin's comment, offer clues to why he did so. In a world where external calm and control were a *borom jom*'s cardinal virtues, an inability to master emotions, to hold one's tongue, and move without urgent commotion were anathema. M'barick Fall's bull-in-a-china-shop persona was therefore problematic. As an adult, he wasn't guilty of two-thirds of the misconduct attributed to him. Yet if young Fall's nature weren't somehow flawed, Guet Ndar wouldn't have nicknamed him "M'barick." As Magel observes, a *borom jom* (man of virtue) exhibits *jom* (inner tranquility and self-restraint), *revtal* (control of inner urges and external behavior), and *wax bu denga* (reserved speech). Placid, dignified, he has no need to rush; no ill-considered words spill from his mouth.[52] Young Fall's nickname suggests he was the opposite—a child whose inner demons thrust to the surface, driving him to rush into things, to act rashly, and to speak recklessly.

Fall's Senegal had a rigid caste system, dividing people into *geer* (free-born farmer), *gewël* (griot), *tëgg* (smith), or *wuude* (artisan). Caste also marked you as descended from *mbuur* (aristocrats) or *jaam* (slaves, outcasts).[53] We don't know which M'barick Fall was, but his name gives a clue. Black men enslaved by Arab peoples from the north often passed on the name Fall to descendants.[54] Thus Fall may well have been casteless, and that in itself would have given him good reason to leave. We do know the urchin from Guet Ndar was no one's ideal of a proper Wolof man (for he was a *man*, in Wolof terms). The nickname suggests Guet Ndar foresaw trouble for this fellow who, though he'd undergone the rite of passage to manhood, had not learned its lesson of placid restraint. As an adolescent fighting to make his way in an alien city, he'd need *jom* and *revtal*—as well as *fit* and *mun*—to survive.

Old Marseille was as turbulent as he was, a place of gangsters, thugs, corruption (*La Dépêche* of June 28, 1914, for instance, describes six thugs arriving in a taxi with pistols blazing to rob a *cantine* and then shooting it out with police; the November and December 1922 *L'Echo de Paris* tells of fights with pistols and knives littering the streets with corpses). Fall survived in this world by becoming as tough as it was—and by boxing. The sport's popularity was growing rapidly in the south of France, making heroes of local boxers like Jean Poésy, Paul Latil, and Paul Buisson. After a barkeep from Aix-en-Provence, Victor Frégier, set up the Palais des Sports, behind the *Bourse,* at the turn of the century, boxing clubs thrived. M'barick Fall, hardly more than a boy, was drawn to the sport, working any job he could—stevedore, restaurant doorman, locksmith, messenger—to allow him to spend free time hanging around Premierland boxing club on rue du Lycée, where his first teacher was Latil. He became "le benjamin de la salle," the gym's youngest boxer.[55]

Restive, he wandered to Toulon, where Honoré de Bruyère trained him, then in 1912 moved on to Nice, where he washed dishes in a restaurant.[56] He went to Bordeaux and, roving an amusement park, came upon the boxing booth of Frank and Jim Roose, who entered him in their lists.[57] Bénac has him in May 1913 returning to Nice, a skinny lightweight: "thin to the point of being scrawny,... ill-treated, mauled by punches, ill-fed on a mess tin of cooking water in which a bone and some crusts of bread had been soaked, and which he ate sitting on the shafts of a wagon."[58] Dispirited, he wanted badly to find a new manager. A fighter named Richardson (Bénac spells it "Richarson") introduced him to the boxers who founded Boxland Toulousian: Pessieto, Jean Audouy, and Orientis. He quit the booths and began training with them.

On Place Masséna, Fall met former amateur champ Gideon Gastaud, who offered to help him turn pro.[59] It was then that Fall chose the ring name Battling Siki,[60] probably in memory of the Nyamwezi leader who had, from his Tabora stronghold, in what is now Tanzania, held out tenaciously against German conquest until his death in 1893.[61] Thus, in yet another form, the boxer's name affirms the idea of resistance and struggle. His first fight as Battling Siki, at Grasse, north of Cannes, earned the rock-bottom fee (L'Auto makes it 3 francs 50; Bénac, 3 francs),[62] but Siki thrilled the crowd, scoring a knockout.[63] At Nice, soon afterward, Gastaud matched him at the Parisiana Club against his first established fighter, Mario Gall.[64] By now, says Bénac, he was making 10 francs per fight.[65] A little later, Siki left the Côte d'Azur for Toulouse, where Bénac gives him an inauspicious debut on November 13, 1913: a loss via a foul against a fighter named Pirroud, followed by a loss on points in a return bout.[66]

Despite Siki's up-and-down record, Bénac says, "One senses in him natural qualities, his footwork is excellent, he is supple, and very strong."[67] In 1914, built up to 70 kilos (154 lbs.), Siki fought his trainer Audouy (who around the same time fought a draw with Georges Carpentier) and barely lost on points. Thereafter, writes Bénac, "He begins to find his rhythm and, punch by punch, wins two victories by knockout." The first victims were a boxer named Billy from Narbonne and Siki's old trainer and patron Frank Roose.[68]

The *Ring Record Book* lists seven professional bouts in 1913, five more in 1914, with seven victories (four knockouts, three decisions), one draw, and three losses (two by decision, one on a foul).[69] Years later *L'Auto* would refer to Siki as "the terrifying black boxer from before the war," calling him a "rough slugger" who made "a brilliant start," but they were probably shilling for his manager Eli Lepart.[70] Once Lepart was no longer handling him, *L'Auto* would dismiss the novice Siki as "a little boxer without glory who contested a few matches of no importance."[71] Before the war Siki was seen as a crude but willing slugger who knew little more than the rudiments of the "noble art." Still, though just a teenager, he'd fought some of France's best boxers. He'd twice knocked out sturdy heavyweight Pierre Nicolas. The

Féderation Française de Boxe later ranked Frederick Henrys, who beat Siki on a foul in 1913, among France's top three welterweights, and Jean Audouy, who beat Siki by decision in 1914, as one of its top three middleweights.[72]

Siki got his first taste of American-style boxing during the war in American Expeditionary Force (AEF) camps in the south of France. One opponent, African American sergeant Jack Townsend of the 325th Field Artillery, would face George Godfrey in New York City just a few days after Siki fought Kid Norfolk there.[73] Sparrow Robertson recalled Siki during that period as "a willing Negro battler who toured the camps, meeting the best heavyweights of the American Army."[74]

The Black *Marsouin*

On April 25, 1915, the soldiers on the wretched troopship, under sultry 8:30 A.M. sunshine, watched in awe as a crescendo of satanic fire rained down on the Turkish coast. They heard the screaming shells from ancient battlewagons and sleek new dreadnoughts dueling with coastal artillery picketing the crumbling stone fort on the Asia Minor side of the straits. This wasn't their first bombardment. The past November, they'd watched a faltering barrage hit enemy positions before they crawled out of their wretched pits in the Champagne sector of the Western front to slog through the muck into gusts of machine-gun fire. Months later they'd been on the other end of a barrage, waiting, numb with terror, as German artillery pounded their trenches along the same ridgeline. But this was different. This was unearthly. In the distance they could see a steam *chaloupe* tugging a string of boats, against the currents spilling from the Dardanelles, toward the inferno falling like diabolic reprisal on the crumbling fort. Would anyone live through the fire and brimstone descending upon that pathetic stone relic?

They had no idea what a naval bombardment could do. They knew the edge attackers had in a normal assault when a field artillery barrage lifted and dazed, deafened survivors crawled from their burrows to creep to blasted forward trenches. But no one, in the history of warfare, had mounted an amphibious assault of this size—into the teeth of machine guns and high-explosive shells. The men of Toulon's Eighth Colonial Regiment, baking under the sun in shipboard reserve, did not envy their brother soldiers in the Sixth Colonial. On the deck of the creaky old freighter, among a sea of sweaty men, a black soldier watched the dawn spectacle.

Barely seventeen, Private Louis M'barick Fall had already made his debuts both as a main-event prizefighter and a trained killer. He saw a sea of black faces aboard another troopship—the *tirailleurs sénégalais*. On his own ship nearly all the faces were white. French regulars called the men in units like his *les vieux marsouins* ("the old porpoises"), mocking the exotic regiments who'd fought on the outskirts of empire. The *marsouins* in turn gossiped about the *tirailleurs,* calling them "savages" and "vicious killers," yet recounting rumors that under the terrifying fire of heavy artillery they were prone to panic and flee. Private Fall himself had played with *tirailleurs* as a boy. He'd seen their camp wives in the markets of Saint-Louis. He knew they were just men, like others. In Champagne, he'd seldom seen an enemy. The real enemy was the frigid cold, the shuddering ground you clung to as the shells screamed down. Who didn't want to bolt and run?

As the naval shelling lifted, the fragile string of boats straggled into the lee of the fortress. African soldiers flopped over the sides. It was safer to swim for it, rifles strapped to their backs, than to drift ashore like targets in a carnival arcade. Burdened with gear, they waded under the dead angles of Koum-Kalé citadel, clambered the walls, hesitated under heavy fire, then vanished into the fortress. On the boats Fall's comrades wondered: Would this day bring triumph or disaster? In fact, it would bring both; for on the European side of the straits, the British landings were going very badly indeed, and it was into that debacle, on the night of May 6, that Private Fall's own regiment would be hurled. They too swung down rope ladders to tossing boats, watched a fiery shoreline, like a Medieval hell, grow closer. In the surf at Cape Helles, gripping mooring lines, the *marsouins* struggled to keep their feet. They barely had time to drag ashore ammunition and food under artillery fire from Turkish lines a mile and a half away before the order came for an assault. The whole brigade moved forward, the Toulon regiment in its vanguard. Private Fall and his mates shambled across sand heaped with wrecked equipment and littered with dead men and pack animals. As they passed through the French left flank, they heard the cries of the wounded and saw corpses and mangled body parts. The first line, then the second, shuffling forward weighted with gear, melted under rifle and machine-gun fire. Only the third reached the enemy, seizing outlying trenches, gaining a few hundred yards of ground.[75]

The Eighth Colonial's orders were to climb the dry stream bed of Kérévès Déré, take the Turkish trenches, then swing onto a rocky spur, following the ravine toward the distant heights of the town of Krithia. Their goal was to turn the Turkish flank and link with the British on their left, but it might as well have been to take Constantinople itself. The British, in khaki, watched, incredulous, as blue-coated ranks went forward, banners waving, bugles blowing, drums beating, like troops in a heroic painting. It might have been inspiring if it was not so absurd. Private Fall's Eighth Colonial, said Du Bert, "covered itself with glory." Charging Hill 300, men fell by the dozens, but the lead battalions overran the first Turkish line. There, their officers butchered, one hundred meters short of their goal, they faltered. Dragging the wounded, they crawled back to the first trench line. Precariously in advance of their own lines, they watched French assaults fall apart, one after another, and waited—for relief, for food, water, ammunition, for orders. Finally Colonel Frèrejean sent forward his reserve, the Senegalese. Hundreds died.[76]

Fall left behind no memoir of this day, but a fellow Senegalese, Bakary Diallo, tells of his own emotions under fire, dispelling Kipling and Underwood's alluring fable of the fearless African savage. He tells us frankly he was terrified by the risks he had to take, but ashamed to show any sign of panic.[77] For three days and nights, the Eighth Colonial hung on, as French assaults swept past. Finally, the night of May 9, the Turkish commander sent forward a human-wave assault, its apex striking the exposed trench where the Eighth Colonial huddled. The Turks came through in the darkness, silent, fast, unencumbered by gear (they were issued no cartridges, to force them to close with the enemy). Private Fall and his comrades fired at shadows, threw grenades at sounds, killed in the filthy darkness with knives, rifle butts, and bayonets.[78] By May 10, the Eighth Colonial had suffered 1,095 casualties— two-thirds of its men. Most battalion commanders were dead. Two battalions had only two officers left.[79] The division of which Fall's regiment was a part had lost 9,000 of its 14,000 men, and 200 officers.[80]

Those who survived graduated to the slow torture of trench life. One *tirailleur*, Baïdi, a Toucouleur from the fishing village of Podor, who like M'barick Fall had swum expertly as a boy in the Senegal River, spoke of the misery of life in the trenches: "There's nobody to find good a war like this one, a war for staying always in the same place, in the ground, without walking, washing, sleeping, nothing. There is nobody French, nobody Senegalese, nobody German."[81] Typhus and dysentery savaged the ranks. Even dying seemed better than living like a rat in a hole. Said one *tirailleur*, "One has to get used to living in utter rottenness, especially where the soil is rocky, denuded of organic matter, and the enemy trench is built of corpses, where one must pass a terrain where Turkish corpses . . . are in a state of utter decomposition."[82] Front soldiers came to hate the grinding claustrophobia of trench life.

Most depictions link Fall's enlistment in the French army in 1914 to his truculent and restless nature. Nat Fleischer, who probably based his account of Fall's war service on an interview (he uses the phrase "according to his story"), said Fall was "a good soldier, so far as bravery went, but the curse of irresponsibility, which afterward was to prove his undoing, as well as his penchant for breaking the boundaries of discipline, were the malign agents that kept him from further distinguishing himself."[83] All accounts agree about two basic facts: that Fall served on nearly every front and left the service in 1919 decorated with the *Croix de Guerre* and *Médaille Militaire.* A comrade from the war later said Fall had won the *Croix de Guerre* with two palms and the *Médaille Militaire* with "seven citations for conspicuous bravery, wounds with shrapnel and bayonets."[84] Some sources supply dates: August 23, 1914, for his enlistment, November 12, 1914, for his arrival on the front.[85]

Though Fleischer often defended black boxers from calumny, he seems to have bought the "primitive savage" reading of Siki's personality. In *Black Dynamite,* volume 3, he calls Siki "a veritable jungle-child, a throwback to the primitive."[86] In *Fifty Years at Ringside,* he writes, "Perhaps Siki was only half human."[87] That judgment colors his accounts of Siki's life. He has Siki "eager to join the army and fight for France"—which was probably true, though not for the reasons Fleischer imagines. As Thiam explains, Saint-Louisiens often *were* eager to serve, though most West Africans were loath to risk death defending French soil, and many resisted recruiting efforts. Saint-Louisiens, however, saw themselves as French and longed to be accepted as such. The "long cultural cohabitation," Thiam relates, had fashioned the "miracle" of creating colonized peoples who thought themselves more French than the French themselves and who demanded their rights and duties as citizens, including the right and duty to fight for France.[88] Though they'd sent a representative to the French Chamber of Deputies since 1792, the *originaires* still were not fully recognized as French citizens. Nationalistic young Saint-Louisiens were therefore eager not simply to enlist, but even to be *drafted.* After April 1915, when they were finally granted that honor, though only in French West African units, nearly five thousand were called to serve in the butchery.[89]

According to *L'Auto*'s Special Editon, Fall enlisted "in the 8th Colonial of Toulon. " Bénac, however, asserts that "Siki enlisted in the *tirailleurs séné-galais.*"[90] *Le Petit Parisien* holds he "enlisted as a volunteer and left for the front in a regiment of heavy artillery."[91] *L'Auto* and Peeters chorus, "Rifleman/machine-gunner, [then] grenadier, he fought on every front."[92] As an *originaire* of one of the four communes, Fall shouldn't have been allowed to enlist in a *régiment colonial.* The colonial regiments were made up of reservists, recruits from continental France, and veterans of colonial campaigns, not colonized peoples,[93] though *tirailleur sénégalais* battalions were often attached to colonial regiments. Du Bert describes the Eighth Colonial's makeup: "elite officers, beloved of their men, and noncommissioned officers worthy of them, old-timers, raw recruits who reached draft age in 1915, reservists, and Senegalese."[94]

The Eighth Colonial got its first taste of the horrors of war one month after its arrival on the Champagne front, west of the Argonne forest.[95] Five days before Christmas in 1914 they launched an ill-conceived assault along the *Main de Massiges,* a group of ridges stretching southwest of the town, like a four-fingered left hand, pressed palm-down, its fingers trailing behind the lines.[96] The Toulon men were caught in enfilading fire as Germans poured forth in counterattacks. They fled, leaving behind more than a thousand men, the dead grotesquely contorted, perforated with bullets that had converged from three sides. The following September, fresh from the horrors of Gallipoli, the regiment found itself again in trenches along the murky creek they'd waded in 1914. The late September weather near the town of Massiges was chill, the terrain slimy. Private Fall and his mates went forward hunched under a pelting rain.[97] The fire was murderous, progress slow. Again and again, for three days, they slithered up from the muck and struggled forward. The slaughter gained nothing more than the positions they'd held in February. Stuck there, perched atop the middle-finger ridge, the Eighth Colonial paid for its temerity. With range coordinates laid out precisely during their tenure there, the Germans shelled the *marsouins* day and night.[98] Ernst Jünger speaks of the experience of such fire. It's as if, he says, you're tied to a post as someone swings a sledge hammer at your skull, barely missing, sending splinters flying.[99] The sense of helpless terror, he says, is indescribable.

Finally, on November 3, after a storm of artillery, German assault waves trudged forward. When the shelling lifted, the Eighth Colonial soldiers saw knots of gray phantoms moving through nightmarish dust and smoke. Soon, they suffered worse horrors, for this attack, for the first time in any war, featured a new toy from the purveyors of death, the flame-thrower. Assault teams sprayed jets of burning oil over their trenches as desperate *marsouins* tossed grenades. The eerily picturesque struggle went on all night. Somehow they repelled the attack. But when dawn brought more long spouts of flame they scrambled down the slope to huddle in holes at the foot of the ridge, pounded by artillery as they waited for the next assault.[100]

Leed, in his study of the psychopathology of infantry service in the Great War, explains how the hardest thing to bear was waiting, in degrading squalor, under artillery fire, impotent to strike back. With no recourse to conditioned aggressive instincts, stuck within claustrophobic horizons, front soldiers developed a psychology of victimization whose only relief was rage, at times turned inward, at times outward upon the machine of war itself.[101] Yet if one credits Nat Fleischer, one must imagine Private Fall sorry to leave the muck of Champagne, the glee of mass carnage. "Private Siki," he insists, liked to be a soldier. It suited him, satisfied his wants, stripped away the trappings of civilized life. Promoted to corporal for valor, he was twice demoted because he "was given a short leave of absence and deliberately overstayed his allotted time so he might be reduced to the ranks."[102]

Perhaps Fall was twice demoted for overstaying leaves. But if he told Fleischer he'd overstayed leaves on purpose, he would hardly have said he did so because he loved being a private. That part smells fishier than a *Guet Ndar* smoke shed. As Blond explains, furloughs, held out as rewards for good soldiering, often spawned emotional crises, giving men a taste of ordinary life scant kilometers from the squalor of the trenches. With little money, facing a return to the carnage, many, unable to tolerate the illusory sanity of civilian life, refused them.[103] Others, despondent when their furlough was up, went awol. If Private Fall did overstay his leave in spring 1915, he wasn't alone—and he hardly did so because he liked the killing.

Yet Fleischer links all of Fall's actions to blood lust, even those for which he won his medals. "Siki," he insists, was "decorated for capturing nine Germans single-handed":

> [He] surprised the Germans while they were eating, compelled them to lay down their rifles, collected the weapons, carried them, and marched the Huns ahead of him to the French lines. En route, however, he guessed that his prisoners were planning a mass attack on him, according to his story, and he didn't care about taking on such heavy odds. He might kill a couple of them, but it was pretty certain that the survivors would get him. So he dropped his burden of captured weapons and at the point of a gun ordered his prisoners into a big shell hole. They obeyed and as soon as the last man had dropped down out of sight, Siki tossed a couple of grenades down on top of them. The resultant explosions were accompanied by yells of pain, then silence. Siki picked up the nine rifles and proceeded to the French lines.[104]

It's a great story—but not very plausible, and not only because of its vagueness as to time, place, and circumstance. (What, for instance, was "Private Siki" doing wandering alone behind German lines?) Still, any front soldier stuck with prisoners might well kill them, despite the conventions of "civilized" war. Ernst Jünger, a German officer whose unit faced Fall's Eighth Colonial in the Somme, tells how front-line soldiers, burdened with prisoners who must be brought to the rear along communications trenches under continuous shelling, loath to risk their own lives, often simply shot them.[105]

Nor is Fleischer's the only entry in the how-Siki-got-his-medals sweepstakes. McCallum pedals another version, representing Siki as a "well-drilled mercenary" drafted into a stranger's war:

> Louis Phal liked the army. He had been conscripted into the Eighth Colonial Infantry Regiment of the French Army and distinguished himself as the bravest soldier in his outfit. When his unit was pinned down by machine gun fire, he cheerfully obliterated the hornet's nest, permitting his regiment to advance.[106]

When the *New Orleans Times-Picayune* asked Fall about his war record, he peeled off his shirt and rolled up his pant legs to display "several wounds from bayonets, shrapnel and machine gun bullets." He added that he'd been "sliced down the back by a saber" and had "four brothers in the war, three of whom were killed in action."[107] He told the *Allentown Morning Call* he'd been knifed in the belly, bayoneted in the legs, and had grenade fragments everywhere.[108] He showed a *Providence Journal* writer a scar on his head from the blow of a rifle butt and said he'd been wounded fifteen times.[109]

French sources are mostly silent. They repeatedly confirm that he'd won a *Médaille Militaire* and *Croix de Guerre*. But the French postwar prize ring had a glut of heroes, including Ercole Balzac, Eugene Criqui, and Leon Bernstein, all *Médaille Militaire* and *Croix de Guerre* recipients; as well as Georges Carpentier, Edouard Brochet, Hubert Desruelles, and Jean Poésy, all Legion of Honor winners.[110] Records for World War I *Croix de Guerre* and *Médaille Militaire* recipients are notoriously deficient. No official registry exists. Instead, one depends upon regimental histories, compiled by surviving senior officers. The *Livre d'or de l'effort colonial* for *tirailleurs* lists several medal winners named Fall, giving units and the text of citations—but none named Louis or M'barick. The regimental history has no Fall in its medal list.[111] However, errors were legion in memorial volumes. African names were often misspelled, inverted, or replaced by nicknames.

Not that it matters. Their medal citations describe in nearly identical terms the heroism of Adioema Fall, Diarra Fall, Madiougo Fall, Mafal Fall, Mahmoud Fall, and Samba Laobe Fall. The formula marks obedient soldiering, not solitary heroics, privileges loyalty, duty, staunchness ("a very beautiful attitude under fire"), self-sacrifice (*grièvement blessé*—gravely injured— is the obligatory phrase). When one scans the citations, one finds a truth about these men: they were not praised for uncommon skill at the game of war, but singular submission to it—for obeying orders, staying put, suffering unflinchingly. Du Bert tells of one *tirailleur* whose rare act of courage was to remain upright under fire because an officer told him not to break a basketful of eggs, another who continued to obey his lieutenant's final order to bring him water hours after the lieutenant was dead.[112] As a soldier with the colonial artillery at Gallipoli observed, the men on the front came to regard medal ceremonies as a joke. As the war dragged on, they were handed out "by the shovelful" as an antidote to poor morale.[113] Private Louis M'barick Fall's heroism was like others' heroism—a courage that faced suffering, went forward in spite of fear and futility, stayed put when ordered to, risked death without flinching. Magel, discussing the virtues of a Wolof *borom jom* (man of honor), names *ñemeñ* (courage) first, but makes *revtal* (emotional control) equally important. A *borom jom* kept his composure (*seday*) no matter what fear he held inside.[114] Fall's family would have been proud of him for that—as they would never have been of a savage killer taking infantile delight in carnage.

Kill, Kill All!

Fall's status as a black soldier in a white regiment gave him an oddly equivocal standing, particularly in light of the fact that the colonial regiment had attached to it segregated, all-black battalions whose reputations among white regiments were unsavory at best. The *tirailleurs,* moreover, didn't always bother to disillusion their white compatriots. Leed describes one *tirailleur* battalion marching past quick-step, grinning, muttering vehemently under their breaths, "We'll kill them, we'll cut off their heads." Hustled along the narrow lanes in tight formation, hardly given a chance to look right or left, shut in camps far from the white regiments alongside whom they would move forward to the assault, the *tirailleurs* took the occasion to put on a show, waving their *coupe-coupe*, chanting "no prisoners, kill, kill all." Like most front soldiers they preferred the identity of predatory killers to that of passive victims of a random machine of death.[115] But like Kipling's "Fuzzy-Wuzzies," the *tirailleurs* were given credit only for bravery of a hysterical kind—the bravery of an ignorant savage.

Henri Barbuse in *Le Feu* recalls his own first encounter with *tirailleurs:* "We look at them and fall silent. We don't call out greetings to them, not these ones. They intimidate us, and even frighten us a little.... We notice certain typical *bicot* [pejorative for exotic foreigners] traits: their predatory relentlessness on the assault, their thirst to get to close quarters, their taste for giving no quarter." The *tirailleurs* obligingly act out their role in pantomime:

They lift their arms: "Kam'rad! Kam'rad!" and mimic thrusting a bayo-
net in front of them, at the height of the stomach, and then of pulling
it out, from lower down, with the aid of their foot. One *tirailleur*...
laughs broadly in his helmeted turban, and repeats, while shaking his
head no, "Not Kam'rad. No, never Kam'rad! Cut off head!"

"Rest irritates them, you know," one soldier ventures; "they live for nothing
but the moment when an officer sets his watch and says, let's go. Deep
down, they're the true soldiers. We aren't soldiers at all, we're men."[116]
Ingold tells of panicked Germans surrendering at the mere sight of the
Africans, hands stiffly upraised as they jumped into enemy trenches, scurry-
ing toward the safety of white enemies in the rear.[117]

The *tirailleurs'* founder, General Charles Mangin, had created their
image, arguing as early as 1911 that African infantry were superior to whites
because they had not been enfeebled by factory work.[118] Their primitive
nervous systems, he thought, made them insensible to pain, capable of
prodigious endurance.[119] He commanded *tirailleur* battalions in Morocco and
campaigned tirelessly for a black army corps on the eve of the Great War. He
dabbled in racial selection, recruiting among ethnic groups (Wolofs, Sérères,
Bambaras, Diolas, Bagnouns, Balantes, Laobés, Soccés, Peuhls, Toucouleurs)
believed especially warlike.[120] He decked out his *tirailleurs* in red fezzes
because he believed they took childlike delight in bright colors, furnished
them with short swords (the famous *coupe-coupe*) because he believed such
weapons suited their blood-thirsty spirit, and encouraged white officers to
communicate with them in crude pidgin because he believed their linguistic
capacities to be rudimentary. Mangin's racial stereotypes gave the French
high command an excuse to use the black soldiers as cannon fodder.
Housed in squalid barracks, treated in fetid infirmaries, sent to attack in
freezing weather, the *tirailleurs,* black deputy Blaise Diagne charged in 1917,
often lost four times as many men as the white battalions alongside whom
they fought.[121]

Mangin's notions stuck in the public mind because they filled a human
need to misread modern warfare, to assign inhuman brutality not to the
effects of technological ingenuity, but to a group of savage outsiders.
German officer Rheinhold Eichacker, for instance, gave his impressions of an
assault by a *tirailleur* battalion:

> Entire bodies and single limbs, now showing in the harsh glare, now
> sinking in the shadows, came nearer and nearer. Strong, wild fellows,
> their log-like, fat, black skulls wrapped in pieces of dirty rags.
> Showing their grinning teeth like panthers, with their bellies drawn in
> and their necks stretched forward.

Some came forward armed only with knives. To Eichacker they seemed:

> Monsters all, in their confused hatred. Frightful their distorted, dark grimaces. Horrible their unnaturally wide-opened, burning, bloodshot eyes. Eyes that seem like terrible beings themselves. Like unearthly, hell-born beings. Eyes that seemed to run ahead of their owners, lashed, unchained, no longer to be restrained. On they came like dogs gone mad and cats spitting and yowling, with a burning lust for human blood, with a cruel dissemblance of their beastly malice.[122]

As they came forward, the black soldiers in the lead tripped over the wire and "fell headlong,... somersaulting like clowns in the circus." Still caught in the wire, trying to rise, some "jerked themselves further, crawling, gliding like snakes." A jumble of images spills out, by turns weirdly excremental ("log-like, fat, black"), Gothic ("unnaturally wide-opened, burning, bloodshot eyes"), absurdist ("somersaulting like clowns"). The dark men change forms like mythological monsters: ravening leopards become feral cats, rabid dogs, gliding snakes. Eyes detach, mutate into vicious dogs. Eichacker hears "the stamping and snorting of thousands of panting beasts."[123] Look, he seems to say, at the cruel trick the French have played us: assaulting us with our own psychoses, harrowing us with our own nightmares.

To an artillery spotter watching from an airplane the morning of July 1, 1916, the assault in the French sector of the Somme seemed weirdly picturesque. The single-race battalions formed contrasting black and white patterns, like a sand painting, remaining neatly intact until they hit the wire. The artillery showed off a new trick, edging a "curtain of fire" a hundred yards in front of the first wave, to give the German defenders no time to recover. But when it jumped too far ahead, machine guns opened up, and the neat patterns dissolved into a salt-and-pepper swarm.[124]

The men of Private Fall's regiment climbed over the parapet that morning weighed down with more than sixty pounds of equipment: food, water, gas mask, wire cutter, trenching tool, ammunition—enough to live in a bare field for a week. They walked into the maw of an inferno, hoping their gunners had the timing right. Down the ridge to the left black battalions moved up along Cappy Herbécourt Road; others to the right crossed the shattered fields of Bussus farm. Then the artillery jerked too far ahead, leaving the wire untouched, and German gunners scrambled from bombproofs to set up machine guns. Bullets buzzed like flights of metal insects. The soldiers worked free from the wire with agonizing slowness, weighted with packs. Men fell, twisting in pain. They reached a trench line, stabbing, shooting the few survivors. The plan, this time, hadn't been to send men forward at any cost, but to crush the first line under the weight of artillery, bite off a chunk of terrain, move the artillery up, crush the next line under heavy shells, then send in the infantry again. But the artillery had failed—and men went on across widening distances, chasing defense lines that dissolved before they reached them, only to materialize farther away. All hope of a breakout gone, they steeled themselves for a kind of war they knew too well. They worked through the village of Becquincourt, moved up a road parallel to the Cappy Herbécourt Road, dropping into a valley below Herbécourt. There, a mile from their starting point, panting with fatigue, parched with thirst, they halted. Tomorrow, the element of surprise gone, they'd advance again. They'd had all they could stomach for one day.

The multilayered German fortifications, hugging high ground in deep parallel lines, with elaborate underground shelters, strongholds, redoubts, communications trenches, double belts of wire, were mirrored by an equally elaborate second line, two or three miles to the rear.[125] On July 1, the British bit off only a half-mile-wide chunk of German ground north of Fricourt, and gained not an inch at Beaumont-Hamel, despite 57,470 casualties (a 50 percent toll).[126] The French, to the south, did overrun the front-line trenches, pushing the Germans back a mile across the whole front, overrunning Méréaucourt and Herbécourt woods, amid ghastly slaughter.[127] General Ferdinand Foch had hoped his new strategy would let him leave his first wave longer in the field.[128] When the plan collapsed, and one attack followed on the heels of the last, French commander in chief General Joseph Joffre left his first wave out there anyway. After days without food or sleep, under constant fire, the men felt hardly human. Private Fall's Eighth Colonial, their numbers depleted, chain of command ravaged, by then barely deserved to be called a regiment.

An African soldier named Ahmat whom Lucie Cousturier spoke with on the eve of his departure for the front in 1918 expressed to her a philosophy that was far more likely Private Fall's than the one Fleischer assigns him. "Maybe the war won't end," Ahmat said. "Maybe God has said, die, for all the soldiers." Ahmat intended, nevertheless, to go on with life "all the same as if I were soon going back to Senegal . . . And then . . . if it's death, *tant pis!*" From the front he wrote to her that "all that time he was always tired, always a little sick."[129] Before he was killed in July 1918, he was, like Fall, twice decorated for bravery.

At dawn, July 4, so exhausted they seemed more like a band of zombies than a regiment, the *marsouins* rose from their holes. In four days they'd advanced nearly three miles, but now they were dying over scraps of ground no bigger than a *potager* (kitchen garden). Fall's Eighth Colonial fought through the village of Flaucourt, with its clutch of ruined cottages, wrecked mill, and smashed *sucrerie* (sugar factory), its jagged brick walls a fine mark for artillery. Every meter of earth was booby-trapped, every cottage ransacked, every well purposely fouled. When the wind was right, chlorine gas wafted over, leaving a "beautiful green patina," littering the ground with dead moles, rats, and snails, and leaving horses and men heaving through seared lungs.[130]

This part of battle, when soldiers died for nothing, was hardest. They went forward because they had to, but took no extra risks. Their effectiveness blunted, first the Eighth Colonial Regiment, then the entire First Colonial Army Corps were withdrawn—for the first of many times in this campaign. The Somme turned the tide of war, swelling the current of death toward Germany's defeat. But to the soldiers of Fall's regiment as they finally departed from this bottomless pit of misery in September 1916, it seemed worse than even Gallipoli: more futile, more inept, more horrifying. Their commander, General Robert-Georges Nivelle, would a year later provoke wholesale mutiny by sending men forward at Chemin des Dames in another such "using up" assault, across impossible terrain, in miserable weather, with little artillery support.

By then, however, Private Fall and his comrades had attained the dream of every soldier in this dismal war: a billet in a "quiet sector," where artillery shells fell each day at precisely the same time, generously short of the mark; where soldiers built cooking fires without drawing the prompt mortar round such insolence would invite in Champagne; and where a man might expose himself to hunt small game in No Man's Land, or just to relieve himself, without anybody disturbing him with an uncivil round. "Live and let live" was the motto on the "quiet" fronts—and of all the utterly dormant fronts, Macedonia in December 1916, where five Allied armies—French, British, Italian, Russian, and Serb—cooled their heels, took the cake.[131]

The Eighth Colonial soldiers soon learned why the Tommies called Salonika "the birdcage." Hemmed by impossible mountains and intricate fortifications, every move scrutinized by enemy spotters, you did feel like a squab in a pen.[132] The Germans called it their "largest internment camp."[133] In a region of vile weather, supplied by a single-track railway from an inadequate port, British soldiers suffered nearly 500,000 hospitalizations, most for malaria, only 18,187 for combat wounds. In 1917, of 600,000 men, only about 100,000 were fit for duty.[134] It might be a "quiet sector," but life among the swamps and frigid mountains, with no solace but bad wine, was grim. When brief fits of violence came, the outnumbered Bulgarians, behind intricate defense works, fought a death-accountant's war, eyeing the bottom line: lives taken / lives lost. In March 1917, their return on investment improved when Fall's Eighth Colonial Regiment assaulted the Cerna River bend, storming a rocky ridge. Caught by flanking machine-gun fire among the boulder fields, one battalion reached *piton rocheux*, only to be routed by counterattacking Germans' bayonets and grenades.[135] Days later, sent into the same inhuman fire, another battalion barely cleared its own parapet before being ripped apart. Others made it to the wire only to be pinned among the rocks, waiting for darkness to slip back to their lines.

In September 1918, allied commander Franchet d'Esperey made another try at prying open the bars of the birdcage. With the German divisions that had stiffened their lines gone to the Western Front, the Bulgarians, ravaged by disease and short rations, were hit by assault waves between the 2,092 meter *Dzena Massif* and the Vardar River, as Private Fall's Eighth Colonial waited to launch a second-wave attack. Five times Krantza peak was taken, lost, retaken. By midnight, as counterattacks fell apart, the birdcage was sprung for good. Bulgarian staff officers rallied fleeing regiments around *Dzena Massif.* But on the twentieth, the Eighth Colonial, with its attached Eighty-fifth *tirailleur* battalion, turned their flank, and by 9:00 A.M. on the twenty-first a mad scramble had begun, scattering Eighth Colonial Battalions all over the map.[136] Eric Leed tells of how the vision of a breakout formed a defining fantasy for front-line soldiers, an almost sexual release of pent-up violence.[137] When the *percée* (piercing) came, the twenty-year-old black private in the Eighth Colonial Regiment, who'd lived for years in a hole, risking death again and again over a few hundred yards of soil, was suddenly free. Just like that, the stalemate was over.

But if Fall and his mates awaited a congratulatory backslap and "*bien fait mes mecs*"—with maybe a train ticket to Marseille thrown in—they could think again. The abrupt collapse left a perilous political void. Exhausted regiments trudged across rugged terrain with few roads, into Serbia, then to the Bosnian border, then Sofia.[138] Finally, at Nicoli-Plevna, south of the Danube, Private Fall and his comrades heard of the armistice on the Western Front. A week later, when King Ferdinand's forces marched into Bucharest, Fall's colonial division accompanied them.[139] The Toulon *marsouins* stayed put through the spring, in commandeered barracks, longing for home.

Private's Fall's only real home, since age eleven, had been a boxing gym. When he returned he'd start over almost from scratch. Who remembered Battling Siki's victories over Pierre Nicolas, Jules Perroud, and Jean Audouy five years before? He'd lost nearly five years of his life, and in return had gotten just one thing, a lesson: you were either the guy with the hammer or the guy tied to the post. And if you found a way to get that hammer in your hand, you swung it for all you were worth. If you were the guy tied to the post, well, as the *tirailleur* Ahmat had said, "*tant pis pour toi*"—tough luck for you.

CHAPTER SIX

"A Hero, Perhaps..."

Loving Lijntje

One top French welterweight of Siki's era, Francis Charles, spoke of his own return from the war: "They called me a hero. Joined up at seventeen in September 1914. Wounded May 23, 1916, at the Fort of Douamont. Amazing medals. Medal of Verdun, *Croix de Guerre, Médaille Militaire.* I'm telling you!... A hero, perhaps. A *con* [a jerk, an asshole] for sure!"[1] Siki's volatile and self-destructive pattern of postwar behavior suggests he too carried back from war private demons. But though show-and-tell patter about his war record was standard at prefight press conferences in America, Siki did not divulge his real emotional burdens from the war. In any case, America was too caught up in romanticizing its own role—and had fixed too firmly its image of the Senegalese—to care. A prime example is John W. Thomason's best-selling *Fix Bayonets,* with its vision of "wild black Mohammadans" who "swept [the] front line like a hunting pack," "slew with barbaric leaps and lunges and a shrill barbaric yapping," "enjoyed themselves" in battle, took no prisoners, and found the killing "only too palpably their mission in life."[2]

Of 134,000 Africans who fought the war, 30,000 were killed. Those who survived, though they had a right to stay in France, usually left for their home countries. France offered little inducement to stay. Ex-*tirailleurs* were typically shuttled into ill-paid agricultural "apprenticeships."[3] Most trades were closed to them. Marseille's maritime unions struck in 1920 to protest the hiring of a Senegalese *graisseur* (oiler). The strike spread to the whole south of France. "Note that the Senegalese in question is a brave *poilu,*" mused

L'Express du Midi, "who fought conscientiously during the war and who had very well the right to take work."[4] Even white ex-*poilus* found life tough. *La Dépêche* of Toulouse told of a soldier shot to death for stealing an apple.[5] The killer got five years in prison and a fine.

Siki said he washed dishes after he left the army in 1919. Bénac says he was a *"chasseur"* (page boy) in Toulouse's Hotel Albrighi.[6] But he was soon back in the ring. Outlawed during the war (fighting for money seemed obscene as thousands were being butchered in the trenches), boxing had somehow gone on. Men boxed in the camps—or munitions factories, such as one on rue Vivienne near the Paris Bourse. Fernand Vianney recalled bouts staged in private clubs run by Philippe Roth, where the purses were disguised as gifts: "'An anonymous donor offers five francs to the winner,' the classic formula."[7] The Duke of Case and Prince of Massena held covert matches in their homes. When the sport was officially revived, in 1919, the first big bout in the south of France, at Béziers on June 14, matched Georges Carpentier against the black American Battling Robinson.[8]

The *Ring Record Book* says Siki's first postwar fight (probably in December 1919) was against powerful slugger Eugène Stuber, a prewar French titleholder. Siki startled everyone by going toe to toe and dropping Stuber for the count in the second round. Weeks later, *La Dépêche* noted that "the Negro champion Battling Siki," already with his eye on the French middleweight title, had signed for a ten-round bout on December 29 at the théâtre des Nouveautés against the "champion of the *Côte d'Azur,* Léonard."[9] The *Ring Record Book* and *Le Sporting* list this fight as a draw, but months later *La Dépêche* calls Léonard "champion of the Côte d'Azur and victor over Battling Siki"—so perhaps the men fought twice.[10] *Le Sporting* describes one twelve-round encounter in the *"coquet"* (adorable) théâtre des Nouveautés, a "fierce" brawl between two "rude combatants," which Siki "dominated at long range, thanks to his footwork," though "manhandled" a bit inside. Léonard got the nod, a decision many in the hall protested.[11]

Two weeks later, Siki fought Jean Audouy, ranked in the *"première série"* (first rank) of the French Boxing Federation's official rankings—below only French middleweight champ Ercole Balzac, who'd beaten him for the title six months before.[12] Siki himself was not even listed in the *"troisième série"* (third rank), though Stuber, whom he'd beaten handily, made the second. In theory fighters could only fight men in the same or adjoining ranks, but on February 16 Siki fought Audouy, and though Audouy had out-pointed him before the war in Toulouse, this time Siki staggered his former trainer in the second round and stopped him in the fourth. He also beat (by decision) the Marseille welterweight Henrys, who'd beaten him on a foul before the war.

Siki seems also to have been forced to engage in a fix around that time. Bénac writes, "He goes down to Marseille and can do no better than a draw with [Constant] Barrick, some gangsters of the period having threatened to cut him down if he won."[13] Writing years after the fact Bénac often flubs details, but he knew Siki personally, so the fix may well have taken place, either then or in 1921, when the *Ring Record Book* lists a ten-round fight with Barrick that Siki won by decision.

Despite victories over top fighters, Siki did not seem any different from the *rude cogneur* (crude slugger) Provençale fans had known before the war. He'd moved up in the caliber of opponents, but his postwar record—three wins, one loss, two draws—was uninspiring. His rise to the top ranks of European boxing really only began when he arrived in Paris in March 1920 with manager Eli Lepart and scored a series of startling victories that had the sporting paper *L'Auto* vaunting "the redoubtable Senegalese... a dangerous man who boxes with extraordinary power."[14] *L'Auto* may have liked Siki's slash-and-burn style, his image as a fierce Senegalese trailing war medals. But it may also have been paid to boost him. In December 1922 *Le Gaulois* said Paris papers had for years taken money from managers to puff their fighters.

A March 22, 1920, *L'Auto* advertisement gives Siki's first Paris bout, at the Nouveau Cirque, third billing, below two others, though his foe, Léon Derenzy, a former French amateur champion, had three recent wins there (the latest by TKO) and a large following.[15] A photo reveals a spindly-legged guy with long arms, a pointed chin, and oft-broken nose.[16] Now he was set to face "this slugger of the first-rank who is Battling Siki, the victor over Léonard, over Stuber (by knockout in the 2nd round, if you please), over Audouy by technical knockout, over Perroud by knockout." *L'Auto* cited training camp reports that "certain people... place great hopes in [Siki]...." —poor mouth praise indeed if Lepart really had paid them off. Siki didn't disappoint, however, dropping Derenzy in the first and second rounds before putting him away in the third for good.[17] Within days, *L'Auto* was puffing the second coming of the "terrible Sénégalais"—against "scientific and powerful" heavyweight Maurice Lefèvre—in a co-headliner this time. Could Lefèvre, who'd beaten Derenzy, stand up to the ferocious African. "We don't dare say," *L'Auto* hedged, though luckily Lefèvre wasn't one to "get demoralized easily."[18] It was a good thing he wasn't. Siki staggered his heavier rival in the opening round with a hard right and seemed about to put him away for good. But Lefèvre got on his bicycle for the next few rounds, dodging and ducking as Siki tried to drop him for the count. By the late rounds, Lefèvre was counterattacking to the body as Siki teed off to the head, trying for a knockout. Lefèvre barely made it to the final bell. A week later, *L'Auto* was still chirruping, "It took all the courage, all the admirable resistance, all the tight defense of Maurice Lefèvre to save him from a knockout."[19]

Despite this notable victory, *L'Auto* still wasn't exactly lavish in its praise, calling Siki "a combatant perhaps not always elegant, but of undoubted power and perfectly put together," and concluding that he faced the fight of his life against his next rival, "that... punching machine that is K. O. Marchand." The Select Boxing Club main event, his first fifteen-rounder, would allow Siki to "test himself to the limit." The shock of the collision promised "beautiful sensations."[20] Marchand had dispatched most recent rivals in the early rounds, but U.S. Marine private Gene Tunney, a year earlier, had taken a train to Paris expressly to fight him—and though warned he risked getting his head handed to him, easily outboxed Marchand. Even so, the man who later beat Dempsey hadn't put Marchand down. Siki, knowing he faced a tough opponent, took on a new trainer and worked hard to diversify his arsenal. So keen was fan interest that *L'Auto* ran a front-page photo spread, observing, "Battling Siki is really counting on doing the impossible."[21]

The next day *L'Auto* ate its words: "We thought it was going a bit too fast to match Siki with a crack [boxer] like K.O. Marchand. We were wrong."[22] Siki had come out swinging. Even when Marchand landed a vicious low blow, Siki waved off the foul and went back to the attack. By the eighth, he'd dropped Marchand for the count. *L'Auto* gasped, "His decisive victory has classified him as a man of the first rank who may do even better yet." Siki wasn't around to read the plaudits. He was on a train to Anvers, where he beat Belgian champ Jeff de Paus in a fierce fight that had *L'Auto* hailing him "the public's idol," a "loyal combatant... who gives [himself] from the first round to the last."[23] Matched days later against Belgian René de Vos, Siki for once really was pushed to his limits. A "young revelation," on the verge of a brilliant career, de Vos stares out from his publicity photo, eyes eager, hair parted in the middle, plastered with brillantine. Burly, thick-waisted, with heavy upper thighs and short muscular arms, he'd beaten Dutch champion Piet Hobin and twice bested Belgian champion Jean Leroi and former French champion Eustache. He'd lost only once, to Hobin in 1919.

After a slow opening round, the boxers settled into a pattern, Siki trying to land his right as de Vos bulled inside to work the body. De Vos's body punches, *L'Auto* noted, had the effect of neutralizing Siki's normal attack, and he "misse[d] many wild swings."[24] By the fifth, Siki was wading through the Belgian's left and landing heavily. By the late rounds he was doubling his hook to de Vos's ribs and chin, but de Vos kept scoring too. De Vos fought back fiercely in the final rounds, but Siki won a close decision. He'd forced the fight and landed the heavier blows, especially in the eighth, when he had de Vos in real trouble. It had been an exciting fight, but one Siki had nearly lost.

Siki decamped from Paris soon after, intending to stay away only a few months, escaping the summer doldrums that infected the Paris sporting scene—as well as a new tax on boxing tickets that had clubs closing their doors in protest. His next bout, in Rotterdam, one of the most dramatic held there, pitted him against Holland's best-known boxer, Dutch middleweight champ Willem Westbroek. It took place May 2, just days after Siki's punishing bout with de Vos. In his fictionalized Siki biography, Stol speaks of Dutch boxing in 1920 as at a rudimentary (*kinderschoenen*—literally infant's shoes) stage, having been introduced by English soldiers during the war. He styles Siki an instant sensation, a fast, unorthodox fighter whose withering rallies were unlike anything Rotterdam had ever seen. The Dutch bouts, Stol muses, were mere sparring sessions to Siki, easy sources of cash. He goes perhaps a bit far—though in the makeshift ring at Circus-Schouwburg, site of many of former *sergeant-boksinstructeur* (sergeant-boxing instructor) Westbroek's triumphs (he'd won eighteen of twenty), Siki struck the partisan throng dumb by flattening their hometown hero in the seventh.[25]

Siki was back in Paris a week later, in time to watch American middleweight Jeff Smith beat French middleweight champ Ercole Balzac. Smith had been one of a group of superb middleweights victimized during the prewar no-decision era, when men like Al McCoy and Mike O'Dowd acquired world titles by luck or intrigue and held onto them by a patent ruse: since only a knockout could dethrone them, they stalled through lackluster bouts against mediocre rivals.[26] The clever artistry of boxers like Smith and Mike Gibbons, meanwhile, went unrewarded. Smith's European tour in 1913 had featured a memorable twenty-round clash with Georges Carpentier, whose decision win spurred his rise to prominence. On fight night, hoping for a chance to follow Carpentier's example, Siki made a brash move: When the announcer called him into the ring to be introduced, he loudly defied either man to fight him. Asked why he'd made a gesture then considered insolent, he told *L'Auto:*

> Say well that I am capable, not only, as Balzac said he was, of beating Jeff Smith by knockout, but of putting on a performance that will astonish everyone. People smiled Saturday night when I got up into the ring to challenge the winner. They were wrong, and I'm ready to prove it with the gloves on my hands. I'm capable of getting up [off the canvas] ten times without being counted out. Jeff Smith doesn't frighten me and he'll see what a difference there is between an

American nigger and a French nigger. If Jeff wants it, I'm ready to
meet his last victim with this as the condition: the whole purse to
Balzac if I don't knock him out inside the limit of the fight. Up until
now, apart from K. O. Marchand and de Vos, I've gone up against no
one but heavyweights. I weigh 73 kilos (161 pounds) and can make
the middleweight limit if I'm asked to.[27]

Siki sounds almost arrogant: betting his whole purse he could knock out
Balzac, as if the French champion were a rube in a carnival boxing booth! Yet
Siki's words betray trepidation too. Why else would he envision Smith
knocking him down ten times?

Siki's bravado, reminiscent of latter-day heavyweight Muhammad Ali,
may have its origin in Wolof culture. Traditional Senegalese wrestlers, for
instance, steel themselves for combat with displays of bravura virility.[28]
Gérard Salem evokes the "sense of audacity and provocation" of a star
wrestler's arrival, carried into the arena on the arms of supporters, dancing
a taunting, macho dance, offering an "incessant play of provocations,"
threats, and insults that sometimes provoke "veritable psychological melt-
downs of [rival] wrestlers ... seized by fear or doubt."[29] Some reports say
Siki did, in fact, himself later wrestle—though they may confuse him with
Reginald Siki, a professional wrestler who borrowed his ring name.

The racial epithet Siki used shocks us now. The postwar French press
referred to him routinely as le nègre sénégalais, the closest English equivalent of which is "the Senegalese nigger." But semantic equivalents are
deceptive. Signification is mapped by usage—and nègre was used differently than its English equivalent. It appeared often in print and remained
until very recently in widespread French usage in expressions such as tête
de nègre (nigger head), for a kind of bon-bon; nègre-en-chemise (nigger-in-a-
shirt), for a dessert made with lady fingers and ice cream; and petit-nègre
(little-nigger), for a stereotypical dialect. Yet like nigger, nègre implied derision or disdain. How could Siki, so ready to resent affronts to his dignity,
call himself such a thing? Was the phrase a deliberate linguistic provocation? He knew Smith's chief sparring partner, African American welterweight Jimmy Lyggett. Was he, with some irony, throwing the phrase nègre
américain in Lyggett's face, and in Smith's face the imputation that he
thought blacks easy to defeat because he only knew the putatively inferior
American kind?

A year later, in his letter to L'Auto after he won the world's title, Siki
would mock French attitudes toward race yet more directly. "I was afraid, it's
true, that my victory over the popular Georges Carpentier would not please
sports fans," he would write, pretending to acquiesce in the racial status

quo. "I was afraid that my color.... [Ellipsis Siki's] Not at all! It's fine, very fine indeed! It's even a little too fine.... Fortunately Charley Hellers is around! He's my guardian angel...." He added, again with tongue in cheek,

> So, I am Senegalese and I am proud of it. One day, one morning, twenty-three years ago, I made my appearance in the world. It was in Saint-Louis. It was very hot, it seems. I was black, but I wasn't aware of that, because where I was from, it was very fashionable. Everyone was of a dusky color. First of all, don't we say that black is a good color to wear? It wasn't until later, until much later, when I came to France, to Marseille, that there were people around with white skins. Right away I found that color to be very disagreeable and ridiculous and I thought: "It's loathsome to be white like these whites here. What paleness! They aren't cooked enough...." [Ellipsis in the original] I was happy to be black. For me whites were beings that hadn't been cooked enough.[30]

Instead of a Smith bout, however, all Siki got offered was a rematch with K. O. Marchand, on the undercard of Ercole Balzac's tilt with Gabriel Pionnier at the Cirque de Paris. French promoters still didn't know what to make of Siki. His string of triumphs left them short of credible rivals—unless they let him fight for a French title—and that seemed going a bit far. Martiniquen heavyweight Paul Hams was to fight Paul Journée for the French title that month, but somehow "Battling Siki, Middleweight Champion of France" was harder to swallow. Perhaps promoters balked at the risk of having not one but two champions of color.

Or perhaps the image of a brutal *tirailleur* that clung to Siki categorized him as more a novelty act than a serious contender. The phrase *"nos braves Sénégalais"* might make French eyes glisten with tears, with its immediate association "who spilled their blood for France." But every other connotation that clung to the word *Senegalese* was negative. Nineteenth-century literature of black exoticism had pictured "an unhealthy and morbid Africa, peopled by naked and lustful savages." Now that image gave place to "the myth of the 'nigger child,' laughing and innocent." Though the new *"indigènophiles"* were "full of indulgence for those 'overgrown children' to whom France brings 'civilization,'" their notions could take a nasty turn. They compared the *"nègres,"* Dewitte writes, to "wild animals, they complacently describe cannibalism, they return to the supposed atavistic laziness of Africans, they ridicule the 'trained monkeys' who copy the manners of the whites and dress themselves up in European fashion."[31] Either way, whether it saw him as laughing innocent or vile brute, France's gut reaction was: Not him! Not Battling Siki! Not as French champion!

When Marchand backed out, fight night (May 29) found Siki instead facing Smith's sparring partner, *"nègre américain"* Jimmy Lyggett. Siki, who outweighed his rival by ten kilos (22 pounds), came out confident and aggressive. But although he dropped Lyggett for a nine count in round two, by the sixth the American was trading vicious straight lefts and hooks with the bigger man. By the final round, however, Siki had Lyggett holding on for dear life, and Siki easily got the decision.[32] By June, Siki was chief sparring mate for brawny heavyweight Paul Journée, prepping him for his bout with Hams.[33] *L'Auto* talked up a rematch with Lefèvre—but when it fell through Siki returned to Rotterdam, lured by manager / promoter Henri Mionnet, whom Stol says Siki met during the war. Against Bertes Ahaus, a hulking heavyweight nicknamed the Schellingwoude Giant, he again came close to a knockout, but settled for a decision win. A week later, Siki fought Daan Holtcamp, a bearlike ex-wrestler with only a rudimentary knowledge of boxing. Stol writes, "In a street-fighting style the man from the Hague tries to bring to bear his natural strength. [But] his illusions about defeating a real boxer come to an end in the third round in Rotterdam."[34] The end came via an abrupt cerebral concussion.

A week later, Siki gave Westbroek a chance to redeem himself. At first the packed house thought the Dutch champion might well do so. But once the swift and supple *neger* (as *Het Stadion* styled him—the Dutch equivalent of *nègre*) began backing Westbroek up, the crowd began to urge on the foreigner, hoping for a knockout. Siki did his best to oblige, dropping the Dutch fighter with a right hook to the face. But he bounced up and fought back, stinging Siki with a hook to the jaw. The crowd shrieked—for the Dutch fighter this time.[35] Their cheers reversed polarity again when a right exploded in Westbroek's face, dropping him for good.

Stol represents this as the moment Siki met his first great love, Lijntje van Appelteer. Stol arranges their meeting, disposing private events against the backdrop of Siki's known matches. He supplies fortuitous coincidences. Both spend time near the docks—she as a volunteer at a *Zeemanshuis* (sailor's home—she also works as secretary at a law firm), he at seaside bars, refuges for the down-and-out, human oddities, street artists, con men, boxers, and prostitutes.[36] Lijntje's father's boardinghouse on Van Oldebarnevelt Street abuts Mionnet's gymnasium. Both take long walks: his a symptom of alienation in a foreign country, hers of revulsion against the boorish amusements of its bourgeois *jongen* (young people). Stol supplies a happy affinity, a sentimental chemistry when the two pass on the street. He writes, "Before she realizes it herself, she says hello to him. The first thing that strikes Louis about her is that she does not look at him with scorn, but fixes him in her eyes in a pleasant way." Still, his self-confidence falters. "A young white girl who speaks to him in such a way!" It's too strange![37]

Lijntje is patrician, literary, repelled by violence, the wayward daughter of propriety. Her great-uncle, Baron van Heckeren van Brandenburg, served for fifteen years as burgemeister in her native town. Siki is a product of the streets, boisterous, crude, with a talent for violence. Yet she likes his mysterious smile, uncertain laughter, sees through his coarse exterior. Stol's narrator relates, "On first sight, his deep-set eyes give him a surly and hard air, but that's only an impression, because there is no hardness in Louis's glance."[38] Stol, at least, tries to construct a different "Louis" (as he habitually refers to Siki), not a savage machine of lust and violence, but a shy, vulnerable outsider trying to adapt to an alien culture.

Stol links Louis's meeting with Lijntje to his most memorable Rotterdam triumph, the win over Westbroek. Lijntje is swept along in the triumphal procession of her new man, a virile force of nature from a distant realm so unlike "that bourgeois place that was the Netherlands."[39] There is perhaps inadvertent irony here: Stol's tone suggests he joins Lijntje in her admiration of Louis's triumphs. Yet he represents the black champion as meekly indulging the crowd's prejudices. His Louis "pulls a comic nigger-mug and raises his gloved hands."[40] Then he leaps into the crowd to look for Lijntje. She wonders: Was that all? It's over? The narrator relates, "He laughed at her reaction, stretched himself out, and beat his chest with his two fists. 'Me Siki,' he cried at the top of his lungs in a tone somewhere between pride and comic self-mockery."[41] Stol's Louis kisses Lijntje then and there—making their first embrace a sideshow—and she blushes, partly from pleasure (*blijdschap*), partly from excitement (*opwinding*).

Stol is kinder, at least, to Siki than is the Italian novelist Orio Vergani in his 1929 novel, *Io, povero Negro,* where the only fortuity worth mentioning is of a female in heat meeting a male in rut. Was there ever a subject for life discourse so endlessly lacerated by the impositions of language as Siki? He says it best himself: "To the whole world, I am a savage. I sometimes let them believe that. But, gentlemen, it's not true."[42] Vergani's African boxer, George Boykin, like Siki, is adopted by a white benefactress, fights the Great War, and wins the light-heavyweight title in a bout closely mirroring Siki's triumph over Carpentier. But Vergani's account of Boykin's birth tips off his take on race: "The birth of a white baby is considered one of the most important things in the world. But nobody is particularly interested in the birth of negro babies, with their large heads and shriveled legs."[43] Vergani's descriptions of larvae-like black infants hint at the uncouth animal his Boykin will be.

If Stol's Lijntje sees depths of sensitivity beneath Louis's crude surface, Boykin's white lover sweats out her own lechery as she listens to him pounding a punching bag behind a closed door. She steals into the room where he sleeps on a sweaty mat, clamps a hand over his mouth, touches him intimately, asks, "Are you afraid?"[44] For her, he's a cipher, an erotic toy. "She'd never looked at him before," we're told. "He was not a man." Vergani's Boykin (the name is no accident) is terrified of white females. Her nearness brings "a fear at once sweet and tormenting, a feeling of something illimitable, of something which he did not know, but which it would be so fine to understand." Even in the dark she overawes him. One idea possesses him: she is white, "white as the day, as the line of the horizon, as the underpart of a bird's wing."[45]

In *The Wretched of the Earth*, Frantz Fanon tells us that in the neurosis of race, the stronger the sexual taboo, the stronger the obsession. He writes of "a look of lust, a look of envy" that the colonized turns secretly upon the colonizer's possessions—particularly the colonizer's wife.[46] In *Black Skin, White Masks*, he recalls fellow Antilleans whose "dominant concern" on arrival in France had been to have sex with white women, a "ritual of initiation into 'authentic' manhood" they must immediately fulfill.[47] Fanon cites René Maran, who, in *Un homme pareil aux autres*, speaks of Antilleans who married whites "not so much out of love as for the satisfaction of being the master of a European woman; and a certain tang of proud revenge enters into this."[48] He cites Germaine Guex's study of abandonment and passive-aggressive behavior, comparing the man of color to an abandoned child, who tends "to go back over his past and present disappointments, building up in himself a more or less secret area of bitter, disillusioned resentments."[49] Vergani's Boykin, as both an orphaned street child and a member of a subject race, is thus, like Fanon's black arrivant, a man of buried rages, wounded by betrayal.

We have no way to choose between Stol's Louis, confused, boyish, elated, and Vergani's Boykin, a passive recipient of romantic overtures that awake conflicted desires. Siki himself did not leave behind a commentary on his own love life. But we can, at least, take the liberty of recasting Vergani's notion of a black man mesmerized by whiteness. Siki after all said quite the opposite, that he at first had found white skin "loathsome," "disagreeable," and "ridiculous." He added, however, in his letter to *L'Auto*, "I have changed my opinion [now]. My wife, who is Dutch, is white, blonde, and her eyes are blue. I love her very much, she loves me too, and we love each other very much. And now that our little Louis is born, it's even nicer and life is agreeable all around us."[50] We can take the liberty too of revising the scene of Siki's and Lijntje's first kiss, set by Stol under the gawking eyes of an arena crowd after his first-round knockout of Nicol Simpson. In fact, by then Siki had known Lijntje nearly three months. They were well past the stage of pecks on the cheek.

Het Swarte Wonder

Stol implies Lijntje fell in love with a man basking in the adoration of Dutch fans. But in reality, at the moment of the imagined kiss, Dutch fans were hardly enthralled with Siki. In fact, they widely suspected him of a fix in his second bout with English fighter Tom Berry. Berry had won the heavyweight title of the military camps in Holland in 1918. Now, trimmed down, but still outweighing Siki by ten pounds, he hoped to challenge for the light heavyweight crown. When the announcer introduced the two on July 17, 1920, Rotterdam fans gave the Englishman the biggest ovation, though Siki, *"het swarte wonder"* (that black wonder), got warm applause too.[51] *Het Stadion* struggled for words to convey how skillfully that *"ongeslagen neger-bokser"* (successful nigger-boxer) Battling Siki fought that night, cutting off the ring, working angles, slipping or riding punches, baffling Berry. For once he even forsook the clowning he'd at times done against lesser men. "In a word, it was magnificent." Berry, if "a little slow on the attack," was "sublime" on defense. For the first three rounds Siki stormed after him, landing stinging blows to the face. But in the fourth and fifth Berry turned the tables, landing counters. From then on the two men fought evenly, as Berry met Siki's every rush with counters and hooks. Over the final rounds, as Berry faded, Siki piled up points to secure the win. It had been a magnificent bout. The crowd gave the two a standing ovation. Berry demanded a rematch, over fifteen rounds.

The night of the rematch it looked at first as if the fans would get more than their money's worth. Both men boxed exquisitely. Siki showed refinements in attack and defense, said *Het Stadion,* that Rotterdam fans had never before seen. After the tenth, however, the bout took on the look of a setup. All urgency left the men. At one point Siki went down from a tap so gentle it wouldn't have felled a novice.[52] Berry got the decision this time. In the wake of the bout, *Het Stadion* fumed that someone had better investigate. Henri Mionnet had to come clean: What deal had been made? Had the men really fought in good faith? The match had "to such a degree outraged [our] trust in an encounter between two foreign boxers" that there might never be another. If boxing, like professional wrestling, degenerated into Vaudeville, public enthusiasm would be destroyed. The sequel was easy to predict, the columnist jibed: Siki would demand a twenty-round rematch and win a dubious verdict. Then Berry would demand a thirty-round rematch and take his turn at winning. After which maybe they could stage a twenty-four-hour match, then maybe they could camp out somewhere and stage a six-day marathon. Had Siki really thrown the match? *Het Stadion,* founded as *Die Boks Sport,* was Holland's boxing bible, and had many inside contacts. Still, reckless charges of fixes were commonplace. And simple fatigue is a more likely reason for the anemic final rounds. Siki had never before gone fifteen rounds. Besides, we have plain evidence of his ineptness at faking. Against Carpentier two years later, his histrionics were so lame it's hard to believe he'd had prior practice.

Nevertheless, the fix charges stalled Siki's Rotterdam career. In four months he'd fought six times there, but he wouldn't again for a year. He fought in Amsterdam on October 24 (the bout Stol embellishes with his and Lijntje's first kiss) and sought expiation for his showing against Berry by sailing into the English boxer Nicol Simpson from the opening bell, closing his eye with a brutal left hook, then flattening him with a left to his midsection forty seconds into the fight.[53] But distaste for Siki lingered. When Mionnet brought him to Antwerp for a December 4 rematch with Jeff de Paus, *Het Stadion* tossed barbs about the "ape-like goings on" with which the "neger" prefaced each assault, feinting, pulling his punches. Siki seems to have taken de Paus lightly. Instead of his usual fierce assaults, he played cat and mouse while the Belgian held his own "in a rough struggle on the inside." Though Siki won the decision, the Dutch paper wondered if he was on his way out.[54]

The report of Siki's clowning is intriguing. The African American welterweight Aaron Brown, the "Dixie Kid," who'd given Carpentier a humbling public boxing lesson before the war, had turned ring clowning into an art (as later would Muhammad Ali). Brown "was the finest entertainer one could wish to see," Fred Dartnell (Lord Melford) recalled. "He combined the supreme artistry of his science with a grotesque *diablerie* that amused.... He could disguise his great powers with a clumsy antic that would send the crowd shrieking with laughter. When they thought the negro had blundered farcically it was really his opponent who had escaped destruction by a hairbreadth."[55] After the war, weakened by cocaine abuse, Brown returned to France. He fought in Paris on January 30, 1920, against Constant Pluyette, and all over the south of France.[56] It seems very likely that Siki saw Brown during this period and copied his histrionics in the ring.

By 1921 business had dried up for Mionnet. His physical culture school and boxing gym closed in January.[57] The busy schedule of the year before gave place to waiting. Siki had fought most of the best Dutch boxers, and matches between foreigners were suspect after the second Berry fight. The public did, however, remain keen for Siki to fight one boxer, Piet Van der Veer, the handsome idol of the Rotterdam *jongen.*[58] That fight could pay well, but until Mionnet could cut a deal, it made no sense to fight nobodies for a few guilders. Mionnet decided to take Siki's show on the road—to harvest a fresh crop of ethnic heroes elsewhere. He booked Siki to fight a well-paid main event adhering to a familiar script: the black monster versus a blond ethnic champion—"the Carpentier of Germany," Hans Breitensträter. Siki's consistent attitude in the postwar prize ring was that though he was willing to serve as foil for the pale protagonists of Europe's ethnic illusions if the money was right, he wanted, and thought he deserved, a shot at a title. Siki had called out French middleweight champion Ercole Balzac in 1919, and he still had his eye on that title, for both the lucre and the luster it might bring.

Meanwhile, Siki was the all-purpose nemesis, without whom the heroics of sturdy local heroes became boring. He spiced the tepid sameness of the sport. Stol has a scene where children gape through the windows as Siki's train pulls into the Berlin station, shouting, "Look here… a monkey!" He has Siki hide in his hotel room, sick of people trailing him down the street cutting monkey shines, scratching armpits, crying, "Eep! Eeep! Eeeep!"[59] Stol's cliché may well be accurate, for the German public at large did see black men as links to man's primal origins. The year 1920 had witnessed a fierce outcry over *"die schwarze Schande"* (the black shame), General Mangin's alleged effort to humiliate his ex-foes by joining *tirailleur* battalions to his Tenth Army of Occupation in the Rhineland. The press fanned the hysteria, depicting drunken black soldiers marauding German cities.[60] When American newspapers echoed the lurid tales, Woodrow Wilson ordered Ambassador Henry Cabot Lodge to investigate. Lodge curtly reported, "The wholesale atrocities by French Negro colonial troops alleged in the German press, such as the alleged abductions, followed by rape, mutilation, murder, and concealment of the bodies of the victims, are false and intended for political purposes."[61] Yet the "black shame" stayed etched upon German consciousness even after Mangin pulled out his *tirailleurs.*[62]

Seen by the public as "the savage Senegalese," Siki stood suspect of similar barbarity. His appearance in a Berlin ring seemed a provocation, a usurpation of human status by a grotesque trained ape. *Berliner Tageblatt*'s weekly supplement *Ulk* ran a four-panel cartoon on the day of Siki's second German fight, February 25, 1921, airing its fears over Europe's racial future.[63] The first panel, labeled "Europäern 1914," shows a white woman modestly attired in knee-length black dress, flowered hat, pocketbook, handbag, and shawl. The second, "Negerin 1914," shows a black woman, naked but for a handkerchief-sized loin cloth, with cropped hair, giant earrings, and what look like ankle chains. The third, "Negerin 1922," shows the black woman in a light-colored European dress, with high heels, pocketbook, tiny earrings, and a hat shaped vaguely like a crown. The fourth, "Europäern 1922," shows a white woman, turned slightly sideways, in a flared, sheer mini-skirt with a huge bow in the back, hands covering bare breasts. She regards the observer in wide-eyed distress. The caption, *"Kultursortschritte"* (cultural progress) points up the moral: How times have changed! How the social order is overthrown! Hard by notices of Siki's bouts, one finds a shoe store advertisement with a top-hatted, bushy-haired black man in swallowtail coat, striped pants, and spats pulling a bellrope to herald an inventory clearance sale, eyes wide, hat absurdly high (nearly half his body length), lips painted white to imitate a white man imitating a black man.[64]

Both the *Berliner Tageblatt*[65] and *Berliner Lokal Anzeiger*[66] pitched the bouts at Berlin's *Admiralspalast* in racial terms, referring to Siki and stablemate Jimmy Lyggett as "des negers." The *Lokal Anzeiger* called the bout the most intriguing yet staged in Berlin. A win would bring "international renown" for Breitensträter, a towering ex-sailor (Siki's biggest opponent to date) who'd learned to box as a prisoner of war in America. On fight night Siki didn't quite knock out the hulking German, but handed him a bloody fifteen-round beating, breaking his nose, and unmasking him as "manifestly inferior."[67]

You'd think German fans would be sick of seeing black men batter white ones, but the bout proved so popular (*L'Echo des Sports'* correspondent called it "one of the most beautiful boxing matches we've ever seen here")[68] that Berlin promoters offered Siki a bout with Italian heavyweight champ Giuseppe Spalla. The German press was "full of praise for the form of the Senegalese."[69] Siki seemed self-evidently the brute they'd imagined, the very picture of savage cruelty, and they loved him for it.

But the fans' love conceals a darker truth. The greater their ardor the greater their latent wrath. The original purpose of the boxing ring wasn't to keep the boxers in, but the crowd out, not to protect the crowd from the fury inside the ring, but the boxers from the fury outside it. The crowd seethes with a double passion—exulting in its own illusions, yet loathing its self-made icons for the crime of not quite being who they'd imagined them to be. The boxers themselves bring nothing so malignant through the ropes. The ring, for all its gore, is the safest place in the arena. Boxers fight for money, not blood lust.

CHAPTER SEVEN

The Phantom Fighters
at Salle Wagram

Notre Grand Georges National

aymond Manevy, whose "Tales of the People" ran in the communist daily *Le Peuple,* had an odd assignment July 3, 1921: to cover a boxing match. *Le Peuple,* which often railed against the sham of spectator sports, had it in especially for boxing, a bizarre spectacle in which two working-class men beat each other senseless to amuse the crowd, serving the dual aim of enriching capitalists and distracting workers from their real class enemies. But today even *Le Peuple* gave rapt attention to boxing—for this was no ordinary bout. "*Le Grand Soir*" (the Great Evening) would witness the greatest sporting event France had ever known, light heavyweight champion Georges Carpentier's bid to take the heavyweight crown from Jack Dempsey. It wasn't actually Manevy's editor who gave him the assignment—but his *"petit coco adorable"* (adorable little cutie) Julie. "We can't miss this," she bluntly told him. "You'll manage any way you can, but we aren't going to miss this!"[1]

Nobody in Paris wanted to miss the fight. Few could afford to see it in person—for it would unfold 5,838 kilometers away, in Jersey City, New Jersey, where eighty thousand patrons at Boyle's Thirty Acres would pay a gate of $1,789,238.[2] Transatlantic radio didn't yet exist, but Paris would go out *en masse* that evening anyway, intent on sharing the fervor. Parisian and American dailies cut secret deals to share coverage. *Le Petit Parisien* worked quietly for six weeks with the *Chicago Tribune,* arranging special cables to relay minute-by-minute reports from Jersey City to Paris, where the French paper would project them on a giant screen between two pillars before the

Automobile Club of France on Place de la Concorde. During gaps in the news, they'd roll film of the boxers in training. Fifty thousand people could share the excitement almost as it happened.[3]

But Manevy's *adorable coco* had a different plan. She'd heard airplanes flying above Montmartre would fire colored flares to signal Carpentier's victory. She wanted to join the thousands atop *La Butte* sharing the moment of triumph. Julie wrapped a *rôti de veau* and bottles of wine in cloth, filled a shoe box with cherries, and they set out. With the match hours away, people jammed the trams hunting good spots to share the delirium. By 8:00, trapped on a tiny, fenced-in square of grass on rue Saint-Eleuthere, Julie and Raymond idled away the time eating cherries and listening to fans around them recite Carpentier's past triumphs. Paris was in ecstacy. "*Notre Grand Georges*" (our Great Georges) was about to make history, and Paris would live it together. As the plane finally appeared above Montmartre, before the first flare fired, a rash whisper spread: "*Il a gagné!*" He's won! How could he not? He was so perfect a hero, so marked for majesty. The idea Carpentier might lose, on such a night, with the hearts of all Paris singing his fame, was unthinkable. "*Vive la France!*" a man shouted. "*Vive la France! Vive Carpentier!*" burst from thousands of throats. Julie waved her handkerchief. Exultant whoops filled the air. Rejoicing mounted. Then the flare went off and a ghastly silence fell.[4]

Miles away, at Salle Wagram, fans had awaited word while watching a boxing match. Normally it would have headlined the sporting press. But today Carpentier's challenge for the title had pushed even the Tour de France off page one. Salle Wagram was packed all the same. Fans had come early, anxious for a seat—but they hardly even knew who was fighting on the Continental Sporting Club card. Like the crowd atop *La Butte,* they'd come to share another spectacle, one strictly of the imagination, keyed to a real event taking place across the ocean. They jabbered through the preliminary bouts, until the magic hour drew near, 9:30, when first reports would arrive. They hardly even looked at the main event fighters, a brawny white heavyweight and smaller, quicker black man. Who was winning? Who was losing? Who cared? Their eyes kept darting to the ringside telegraph station. The instant word was received, promoters promised, every scrap of news would be passed on. They'd *better* pass the news on quickly—for if Carpentier really beat that brute Dempsey, and the crowd somehow missed the moment, they were capable of demolishing the arena in their eagerness to get to the street. The phantom boxers circled and punched as if in a dream, before a crowd nearly rabid with excitement—but utterly indifferent to their presence.

Georges Carpentier and his wife, Georgette. (Central News Photo.)

Across Paris at Montmartre, when the flare finally burst and was the wrong color, Raymond's *adorable coco* went into such a funk she couldn't swallow another bite of roast veal. "That ruined my appetite," she swore, as a fistfight broke out nearby. "Filthy Dempsey!"

The couple began the long trek home. "By her furrowed brow," Manevy moaned, "I could tell, without doubt, that there was some water in the gas.... The night of the *Grand Soir* we would sleep at the hotel with our backs turned towards each other."[5] At Place de la Concorde and other sites where crowds had awaited word, chaos reigned. *Le Matin* had arranged for green rockets to signal Carpentier's victory, red for defeat. But *Le Petit Parisien* would fire red for victory, green for defeat. Many thought Carpentier had won—only to be disillusioned later. "Paris has celebrated the victory of Carpentier," observed Jules Rivet in *Le Canard Enchaîné*. "Unfortunately the result of the match has come to disturb the celebration."[6]

Men who'd won fortunes wagering against patriotic feeling had to stifle their glee, and furtively pocket their cash. Ecstatic Americans were less wary—and paid the price. Parisian fans forgot the recent sacrifices of Pershing's doughboys and beat up American sailors who too openly exulted. *Le Peuple* found grotesque the spectacle of an entire country caught up in chauvinistic paroxysms. So rabid had been the Carpentier mania that on fight day press and public alike ignored the arrival of Mme. Marie Curie from America bearing a gift of $100,000 worth of cancer-curing radium from a Pittsburgh laboratory.[7] "The terrible punches of Dempsey," mused Jules Rivet in *Le Canard Enchaîné*, ". . . have not failed to profoundly wound us in our national self-esteem and dearest illusions." He squeezed out, drop by satiric drop, each crocodile tear of solace. "We've been beaten," he owned, "but it's by brutal force only! And that's what consoles us. The glory of France does not depend upon a punch!" And again, "We've been beaten, yes, perhaps, but who knows but what we might not have ended up as victors if Dempsey had been willing to accept a second match a few hours later?" Or, hold on a second! Are we sure we really lost? Maybe we should await the return of *"le brave Descamps"* (Carpentier's manager), who will surely find an excuse to say we haven't lost at all.[8]

The lithe black boxer fans had all but ignored at Salle Wagram had been Siki—come back to Paris for good just days before. What a shame, *L'Auto* mused, that the frenzy over Carpentier had so eclipsed his return. He'd achieved miracles on his European jaunts, and that night bested a rival, Gabriel Pionnier, who'd nearly ripped France's national title from Balzac in Casablanca.[9] The Siki / Pionnier bout had sold well enough—everyone in Paris needed a place to go that night, and where better to await news of a boxing match than at a boxing match? But *L'Auto* gave the bout a mere ten-word notice: "Battling Siki beats Pionnier, who abandons in the seventh round."[10] Such is the force of celebrity!

Stol has Louis bring Lijntje to Paris months earlier, in March, devising pretty scenes on the train together and assigning them an apartment on rue du Turenne, in a district of winding streets and little shops, near Place de la République. His Lijntje busies herself cleaning, decorating, admiring the garden court, as Louis looks on, proprietorial, enjoying domestic bliss. A few weeks later, Stol's Lijntje announces she's pregnant. Louis, at first dumbfounded ("the food sticks in his throat"), finds his voice to cry out in joy, "It might well be a son!"[11]

Perhaps Stol has Siki's reaction about right, but he's set it in the wrong city. By July, when he and Lijntje arrived in Paris, her pregnancy was five months along. It perhaps provoked their move. Stol has Lijntje's rift from her parents begin in January, when Siki returned from the Breitensträter bout. He has her mother, Jenneke, anxious to forestall a crisis between Lijntje and her father, invite Louis home to dinner. Siki, in a brown suit and shoes glistening with polish, pleases Mama with a huge bouquet. Lijntje's little brother Carel is thrilled to meet Rotterdam's best-known boxer. Mama watches Louis bolt turnip tops and rice, thinking how different he is from what she's used to. Still, he's "not at all primitive."[12] She feels a spark of motherly affection. Papa, however, glowers his guest into silence. Their brief, strained exchange—about Louis's birth in a stone hut and youthful vagrancy—hardens Papa's resolve: Lijntje should find a decent young chap from the lawyer's office where she works.

Lijntje is steadfast: "We'll go to Paris and get married there," she tells Louis. Louis, Stol suggests, knows he'd get ahead faster alone. He's missing chances for good bouts by lingering in Rotterdam. Still, he answers, "We'll go together to Paris and then we'll make a whole lot of children."[13] Let him go alone, Papa pipes up. When you've had a chance to think things over, you'll realize it's just a romantic incident. But Lijntje is adamant. Stol creates a poignant leave-taking, with Mama Van Appelteer alone tearfully escorting Lijntje to Delftsche Poort station, handing her a neatly wrapped packet of buttered bread.

Actually, Siki stayed in Holland through early spring, traveling to Germany to fight Jugo Budzun in March, to Belgium to fight Jeff de Paus in April. Perhaps he tarried to be near Lijntje, but as Mionnet's woes mounted, Siki's career waned.[14] He'd fought eighteen times in 1920—a busy schedule—but only seven from January to June 1921. In the 1920s boxers fought more frequently than they do now, especially if they were black. Tiger Flowers's extant ring record, which may well be incomplete, lists thirty-one fights for 1925, the year before his title win. Even in the 1950s future lightweight champion Sandy Saddler often fought twice a week.[15] Champions, then as now, fought less often. Jack Dempsey defended his heavyweight crown just six times in the seven years he held it.

Three of Siki's fights in 1921, at least, were memorable bouts, and a fourth began a rivalry that would lure fans to three rematches. Just three days after the Breitensträter bout, Siki met the latest Dutch hero, Herman Sjouwerman. An ex-potato merchant and national wrestling champion, the burly Sjouwerman was no matinee idol,[16] but he had a loyal following and put up stubborn resistance. Siki moved around the ring, *Het Stadion* observed, like a dictator, forcing the pace, piling up points, as Sjouwerman, blocking and parrying, keeping out of trouble, now and again uncovered to unleash haymakers, trying for a one-punch knockout. In the wake of Siki's decision win *Het Stadion* was touting the mobility and virtuosity of the *wonderlijke Senegalese* (marvelous Senegalese).[17] Only Piet van der Veer, the new Rotterdam boxing idol, had a chance to match this dynamo.[18] Fans clamored for that contest.

Instead, Siki remained idle, except for an Amsterdam exhibition against "Terrifying Turk" Sabri Muhir—actually a German (male) whose real name was Sally Mayer.[19] At about this time Siki also took a ten-round decision from journeyman Bertes Ahaus.[20] Afterward, Siki returned to Berlin to satisfy German fans eager to see if he could brutalize Guiseppe Spalla as he had Hans Breitensträter. It turned out he could. At Cirque Busch, February 25, Siki forced the hulking Italian to throw in the towel in the ninth, grumbling about a broken hand.[21] His more evident injury was a broken face. A month later, in Hamburg, Siki knocked out German heavyweight Jugo Budzun. His next scrap, a decision win in a rematch with Jeff de Paus, got a bare one-line notice in *L'Auto* and *L'Echo des Sports.*

Siki's one meaningful bout that spring came against the heavyweight Harry Reeve, a top-ranked English boxer. Bouts with English fighters had symbolic importance. England had created modern prizefighting, framing its Marquis of Queensbury rules. The first non–English-speaker to win a world title, Carpentier, had held his crown only nine months when Siki fought Reeve. A brawler who outweighed Siki by twenty pounds and looked more like a saloon thug than a professional boxer, Reeve had held the prewar British heavyweight crown, but boxed only sporadically during the war. A scandal had tainted his name, a shooting at a British staging base in Etaples, France, in 1917. Harry Mullan retails the version of that event surviving in boxing lore, insisting Reeve, a military policeman, murdered a soldier "for ignoring an order to fasten his tunic button," provoking a mutiny.[22]

Reeve did, in fact, shoot three people with his service revolver on September 9, 1917, but he had no time to check tunic buttons. The shooting occurred during a confrontation with an angry mob trying to force its way over the Etaples bridge, which Reeve's military police unit were guarding to prevent trainees from unsanctioned nights on the town. In mid-broil, Reeve went after an Australian with his fists. When others rushed to the Aussie's aid, Reeve opened fire, wounding several men and a passing Frenchwoman, killing a corporal. Convicted of manslaughter, Reeve spent a year at hard labor.[23] Four years later, the ex-MP remembered as a sadistic goon was set to square off against the Senegalese ex-soldier sporting war medals. Fans came dreaming of a bloodbath, but though Siki stormed after the beefy Reeve in his usual ferocious style, Reeve was too cute for him, wrestling, holding, neutralizing Siki's advantage of speed and power. Siki escaped with a decision win. Reeve demanded a rematch. Eventually, there would be three.

Our Senegalese Siki

Most of Siki's bouts elsewhere got scant Parisian coverage. Still, when he returned after a year's absence, French fans remembered him. The week after the Reeve bout, *L'Auto* wrote:

> Among our rare good boxers exists a redoubtable middleweight, the best in Europe with no fear of contradiction: our Senegalese Siki. He has only one defeat in the last two years, at the hands of Léonard, and we all know that the latter would [now] have not the least chance against him. . . . Nobody wants to meet him, and for good reason.[24]

The writer speaks not of *le nègre Siki,* but *notre Sénégalais Siki,* echoing the popular phrase *"nos braves Sénégalais,"* evocative of the *tirailleurs'* wartime sacrifices. *L'Auto* grumbles, "No-one encourages [Siki] or looks to organize a Siki-Balzac or Siki-Gus Platts match to give him a chance to prove himself." After all, it offered, Siki could bring France a new European champion![25] His return would be "passionately followed by his admirers happy to see him again."[26] Two weeks later, *L'Auto* again shilled for Siki (now reconciled with Eli Lepart), declaring he'd fought fifteen tough fights against top men and never known defeat (ignoring his decision loss to Berry). The rest reads as if from Lepart's dictation:

> Siki, at the moment in excellent shape after serious training, weighs exactly 72 kilos 100 grams; he accepts all fights that might be proposed for him by boxers of any nationality, with weights varying from

72 kilos 700 grams to 85 kilos [roughly 160 to 187 pounds] and particularly throws his challenge to Léonard, Pionnier, and Balzac.[27]

After Pionnier and Siki fought their phantom battle before the Carpentier-obsessed crowd at Salle Wagram neither Léonard nor Balzac was eager to fight him. When the boxing clubs closed for the *vacances* of August, Siki headed south, taking a decision in Marseille from Constant Barrick, who'd secured that tainted draw against him a year and a half before.

By August French boxing fans were sick of hearing the European middleweight champ Erocle Balzac declare that he was out of Siki's league. Balzac had fought many of the fighters Siki had, and he had beaten most. But he'd suffered losses too. The thirty-one-year-old Balzac had scored triumphs over Jules Lenaers and K. O. Marchand (twice) on points in 1918 and 1919, and put together a string of knockouts in 1919 and 1920, winning the European title. But in 1921 he'd lost a decision to Gus Platts and a widely disputed judgment to Willem Westbroek. Balzac hardly had a classic style. He held his left out like a fencer's foil, far in front of his body. He got by on guts, fighting spirit, and a powerful punch. Still, his manager Charlie Hellers insisted that Siki, a crude, unscientific slugger with a concrete skull, didn't belong in the same ring with Balzac. And as for Carpentier, Siki had better not even think of meeting him. Carpentier would make him look foolish. Before fighting such men, let him prove himself first! Let him fight...

But who hadn't Siki fought? A few heavyweights maybe: Piet van der Veer, Marcel Nilles, Paul Journée, Billy Wells. But he'd roughed up every credible middleweight or light-heavyweight in Europe. Still, Hellers put Eli Lepart off all summer.[28] Then finally, on August 25, Anastasie, director of the Continental Sporting Club, dropped by *L'Auto* to announce his club would reopen September 5 with a twenty-round Siki / Balzac main event, backed by a 2,500 francs forfeit if either man failed to make weight. One other little detail would surface later: the fight would be for neither the French nor European title. *L'Auto,* sounding as if it had received promotional fees from both sides, danced furiously around the issue of how a match fought under stipulated championship terms could not be for the title. Pondering a Siki victory, it wrote, "His victory over Balzac would place him in the first group of challengers for the title of champion of France and of Europe."[29] Huh? If Siki beat Balzac he'd be considered one of the leading candidates for a chance to beat Balzac? Lucky him! Finally even *L'Auto* admitted that if Balzac lost, nobody would accept him as champion.[30] Hellers seems belatedly to have realized the same thing and decided to make sure his man won. Two days before the fight, he begged a two-week postponement and fled to a rural training camp.[31] Siki, in contrast, stayed loose and relaxed. A week before the bout, doing roadwork before L'École de Joinville with sparring partners from Guénot's gym on rue Oberkampf, Siki suddenly took it into his head to pop in for tea with the commandant. They even staged an impromptu exhibition.[32]

On fight night both Siki and Balzac went through the cords in superb shape in a hall "full to bursting." *L'Auto*'s front-page story had Balzac primed for a big win. Why not? Though at times guilty of "lapses of form," he hit terribly hard. Many doubted Siki, drained by making weight, would be strong enough to overcome a man widely regarded as second in France only to Carpentier. From the opening bell Siki showed the pundits how wrong they were. Balzac tried to carry the fight, but Siki easily dodged his blows. Within a minute, he reopened an improperly healed cut over Balzac's eye. In the second, trading punches, he tagged Balzac with a left hook to the chin, plunging him to the canvas. Balzac stayed down a few seconds, got to his feet, then turned his back and ambled to his corner. Referee Henry Bernstein had no choice but to pick up the count, tolling Balzac out. Then all hell broke loose! Parisian fans hadn't paid 10 francs 20 to see someone stroll away from battle. The protests, loud and aggrieved, flowed out onto the street and into the Parisian papers. *L'Auto* observed, "We won't comment on the performance of the champion of Europe until better informed; it adds, alas, nothing to his glory."[33] Hellers, quick with excuses, alleged Siki hit Balzac on the break, leaving him dazed. *L'Auto* sniffed, "When one is champion of France and of Europe, one should honor one's titles and show oneself courageous in the ring." Siki had dominated the fight and landed heavily. "But all the same, Balzac was not stunned [literally, "really rung"]. He was hit, sure, but not to the point of so quickly giving up."[34] The referee had no business ruling a knockout.

Not everyone agreed. Letting Balzac recover and resume the fight, one reader wrote, would "have been neither very fair nor very sportsmanlike." Another urged, "Since Balzac had gotten up at the count of four, Bernstein shouldn't have counted and Siki should have continued to box." *L'Auto* criticized the promoters and the *Fédération Française de Boxe* for creating a travesty where a man totally outclassed, in a match meeting the terms for a title defense, kept his title; the FFB should award Siki the title, taking advantage of a new regulation giving them that option. The FFB president Paul Rousseau responded that the new article, specifying a title "can be awarded to the boxer of the weight class which seems to it the best qualified," hadn't yet gone into effect.[35] That quibble might make sense if Article 155 had to do with any matter limited to the conduct of the fight itself. But the injustice of upholding as champion a man who'd been beaten senseless by another in his weight class remained as evident as it had two weeks earlier. The FFB would, in time, strip Balzac of his title—but leave it vacant rather than grant it to Siki.

Actually the mystery isn't that the FFB didn't award Siki the title—but that anyone thought it might. The FFB pretended to be a nationwide association, but it was really Rousseau's one-man show. He didn't want Battling Siki as French and European champion. Period. He and his cronies barely knew Siki, who'd fought in Paris for a few months in 1920, and who had only been back for a few months in 1921. They took him to be self-evidently the simple-minded savage the world said he was—hardly the sort to be elevated to the status of national hero. Were French boys to idolize someone who not long ago had lived in a mud hut? They'd let Siki fight Balzac because the match would pay and because they expected Siki to lose. To hedge their bets, they'd ticketed it as a nontitle affair. They hadn't counted on Siki easily demolishing Europe's best middleweight. Now they had a mess on their hands—a once-popular champion whom the public clamored for them to dethrone and a farcical pretender who suddenly had a right to challenge for the biggest prize of all, the world light-heavyweight title, held by the great Georges Carpentier himself. Siki wasted no time filing his challenge, for good measure also challenging the two ranked just below Carpentier for his European heavyweight title, Paul Journée and Marcel Nilles.

Carpentier had been promising Paris a homecoming bout against a top French boxer for years. He'd battled gallantly against Dempsey, stunning him with a right hand in round two, inspiring shrieks of delight from his ardent (largely female) fans. But Dempsey had ended things abruptly in the fourth, dropping Carpentier for a nine count with a hook to the body, then putting him away for good with a right to the jaw. Carpentier's gameness allowed him to escape with his reputation, and adoring legions of fans, intact. But he hadn't fought a major Paris bout in seven years, not since Joe Jeannette took a decision from him in 1914.[36] As the months dragged by and Carpentier showed no sign of keeping his word, the unthinkable happened: letters doubting his sincerity poured into the press. An open letter to *La Boxe et les Boxeurs* scolded manager François Descamps for everything from preparing Carpentier badly to fight Dempsey to teaching him to value money above all else. It begged for a Paris bout at a cut-rate admission, giving "joy to all the lovers of the Noble Art." Had Carpentier forgotten all he owed his longtime fans?[37] In answer, Descamps began a game of evasion, magnifying Siki's faults, Carpentier's superiority. In answer to *L'Auto*'s claim, "Siki is in fact, at this moment, after Carpentier, the best light-heavyweight in Europe,"[38] Descamps offered to have Carpentier dispose of two proposed rivals, Australian heavyweight George Cook and Siki, within four days of each other.[39]

Siki, meanwhile, was having no easier time finding fights in France than he had in Holland. Light-heavyweights couldn't cope with his power. Bigger men couldn't match his speed—though with them, *L'Auto* observed, "the handicap of weight sometimes made itself felt, and the victories of the Senegalese were more painfully gained."[40] Lepart took Siki to Toulouse one week after his destruction of Balzac, for a homecoming bout against ex-sparring partner Battling Marcot. He won in his usual no-holds-barred style, by technical knockout—then waited for something else to turn up. He was slated to fight exhibitions against a Frenchman named Rouquet and a German named Frey, but on short notice found himself instead in a headline bout against Jean Leroi, whom *L'Auto* styled "a skillful man, who can take a punch, mobile and courageous, but who doesn't hit hard."[41] Though officially Belgium's light-heavyweight champ, Leroi weighed only 74 kilos (163 pounds). Like Siki, he'd twice beaten Jeff de Paus, but in everyone's mind René de Vos, who'd bested Leroi several times, was Belgium's real champion. Nobody thought Leroi could hurt Siki, including Siki—who came out steaming. The fans filling the ancient Magic City arena howled approval as Leroi retreated nimbly, with Siki in pursuit, firing with both hands. In round two Leroi gave up on the idea of fighting back and seemed to be looking for a place to hide. He found it in a corner of the ring, flat on his back. As the referee reached ten, he struggled to his feet—more as a gesture of *élan* than to resume battle. The referee waved one arm and raised Siki's hand with the other. The fans whistled in outrage. What! Another quick count? Like hell! Siki and Leroi made their way to the dressing rooms through showers of derision. The promoter, fearing a riot, darted down to plead with his headliners. Did they want to let down the fans? Did they want to read in the morning papers that people smelled a fix? What if they just went back out and took up where they left off? Why, they'd be heroes! Who'd ever forget such *panache?*[42]

Siki shrugged and said sure, I'll go back out. What did he have to lose? Poor Leroi was in no shape to hurt him. After the last undercard bout, to the delight of the crowd, the main event fighters trudged back into the arena. The announcer heralded an instant *match révanche*. The air was electric. "It's something one has never seen," *L'Auto* mused.[43] This time around, Siki measured his man for a round, then in the second again dropped the Belgian to the mat. Leroi might honorably have stayed down, but he struggled to his feet at nine, and "painfully finished the round." Siki knocked him down again in the third. Again Leroi pushed himself off the mat—this time at eight.

Rubber-limbed, he stuck out the round. He steeled himself to go back in the fourth, to push his display of stupid courage to its limit, but as the bell sounded his corner threw in the sponge. His tenacity, at once inspiring and terrifying, would forever endear him to Parisian fans—but at what cost? If one wanted a perfect prescription for long-term brain damage, two cerebral concussions with a half-hour lapse between them would just about fill the bill.

Siki's double knockout gave him instant notoriety. Who'd ever felled a national champion twice the same night? Fans clamored to see Siki fight Journée, Nilles, or Carpentier. Siki wrote to *L'Auto* repeating his challenge to Journée (furnishing us further proof of his literacy). At about that time he took advantage of his celebrity to write a feature for the Dutch paper *De Boks Sport.* A *L'Auto* filler gives a tantalizing reference: "A new boxing journal, *The Boxing Sport,* has appeared in Holland. We have even found there an article by Battling Siki."[44] In fact, *De Boks Sport* had been founded in January 1919, then expanded in February 1920 to cover other sports, changing its name to *Het Stadion* (The Stadium), using the old masthead for a boxing supplement, which lapsed in March 1920. Sadly, only the Rotterdam City Archive retains a file of either paper, and its holdings end February 9, 1921. Whatever Siki wrote seems lost.

Not so his letter to *L'Auto.* Dated October 27, days after the Leroi match, Siki's epistle mocks Journée's reply to his challenge. Journée, who outweighed Siki by ten kilos (twenty-two pounds), had said sure, I'll fight Siki, but he'd better think twice before he lets himself be so badly overmatched. Siki rejoined, "I'm glad to see Journée take up my challenge," but, "as to the question of weight, it has very little importance: Carpentier has very well encountered [Joe] Beckett to whom he gave away ten kilos. Journée is very kind to give me advice to think things over; let him keep his advice; I don't need it. I will prove it with the gloves (literally *les mitaines,* mittens) on my fists the day when we will be face to face."[45]

Siki's epistle is quite different from his earlier challenge to Jeff Smith. He strikes a cordial note *("Je suis heureux de voir"),* has nothing against this guy, thanks him for giving him a chance, as others were unwilling to do. He calls his rival *"bien aimable"*—and one senses he means it. His one touch of sarcasm is in telling Journée to save his advice for those who need it. In challenging Smith, in contrast, Siki's brazen tone had betrayed self-doubt. He'd told *L'Auto "dites bien"* (say *well*—not simply say) that I can stand up to him. He'd seen the mocking smiles, knew people labeled his effrontery ludicrous. "I'm not afraid of Jeff Smith," he'd insisted. He hadn't said he'd win. But now, against Journée, he was guaranteeing victory.

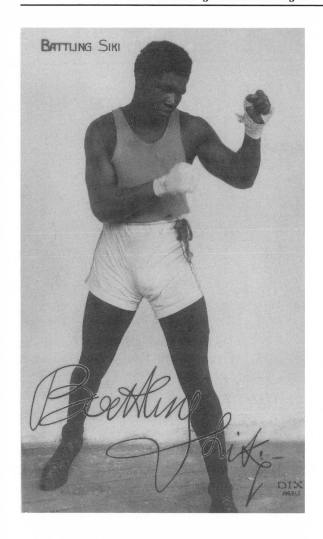

Battling Siki, with
his authentic
signature.
(Author's
collection.)

Not everyone believed him. *L'Auto* said that against soft opponents like Leroi, Siki had a habit of leaving himself uncovered too much. He had to be more careful against the bull-like Journée, who deserved his renown as France's hardest puncher.[46] Jean Auger, in *La Boxe et les Boxeurs,* labeled Siki "a redoubtable puncher, who lands his blows with a speed that one rarely finds among the heavyweights," but "an ordinary enough boxer."[47] Asked to comment, Journée shrugged, "Siki, despite his merits, is too light for me."[48] But a month later (perhaps inspired by a few ducats from Lepart) *L'Auto* was launching paeans of praise for "*L'Homme du Jour: Battling Siki*" (punning on Journée's name), lauding not his ring science but his "elegant figure": "It is even rare among the niggers to see legs so harmonious, and all his body breathes power and tranquility, calm and nonchalance. As soon as one sees him appear, one is impressed, because one senses the formidable power that can let loose from those two fists that do not forgive and that have beaten the very best." Siki's recent string of wins "stupifying French experts" had them ready to declare he'd beat Journée, and even perhaps one day Carpentier. Journée had a dangerous right, but "the nigger is quick, and his last fight has proven to us that [if] he stays always in beautiful shape, he should triumph."[49]

Siki often staged exhibitions with sparring partners, and at times, as Harry Greb did, worked on his speed by fighting much lighter men.[50] Like Greb, he sometimes got frustrated and cuffed them around. Fair tells us Greb's lighter partners sometimes, in requital, ganged up on him and started "a riot in the ring."[51] Leon Sée, who later trained Primo Carnera, retails a yarn of a run-in around this time between Siki and a sparring mate, an abused lightweight who laid for Siki and cracked him over the head with a blackjack, inflicting the sole knockout Siki suffered in his career—outside the ring, not in it.[52]

L'Auto shilled, right up to fight night, for Siki to get a shot at the world title, should he convincingly beat Journée. Finally, on November 25, along-side a cartoon of "Le Faune Battling Siki" (The Satyr Battling Siki), *L'Auto* ran a letter from Descamps saying Carpentier would face Siki in February if Siki won. Descamps had, in fact, little choice if he meant for Carpentier to fight in France. FFB rules blocked him from fighting anyone not ranked in his own *série* or the next lower. Its new ratings listed only three light-heavyweights in the *premier série* behind Carpentier: Siki, Maurice Lefèvre, whom Siki had beaten, and Louis Piochelle, a young Algerian who'd been elevated in rank only months before. Though European champion, Carpentier was *not* French heavyweight champ. He'd won the former title by beating Joe Beckett, but never challenged for the French title. Below the current titlist Marcel Nilles, Journée was listed *hors série*—which made him Nilles's mandatory chal-lenger.[53] If Siki beat Journée, Carpentier could legitimately fight only Siki, Nilles, or Piochelle. The public would whistle any other match to derision. On November 27, a group of promoters headed by C. W. Herring put up 250,000 francs to guarantee a Siki / Carpentier match and Siki formally chal-lenged Carpentier, who accepted. Promoters pledged Carpentier one-third of gate receipts for a bout February 3 at the Vélodrome d'Hiver.[54] Then a hitch developed. Henri Mionnet, Siki's Rotterdam manager, still held a valid contract with Siki. He hadn't complained before, but once the magic name of Carpentier was spoken, he wanted a piece of the action. And so Descamps was off the hook. Until the FFB sorted out Mionnet's protest, no deal could go forward. The American press would later depict Siki as naïvely signing contracts he barely understood. But Siki was not the only French fighter to walk away from a contract in 1921. Following his abysmal loss to Siki, Balzac told Charlie Hellers goodbye. Hellers said fine, see you around.[55]

A huge crowd marked time on December 3 outside "*notre Madison*" (as in "Square Garden"), the Vélodrome d'Hiver (Winter Racetrack), flooding rue Nélaton, near the Eiffel Tower. From six that evening, the boisterous throng besieged the ticket booths, waiting for them to open. Special buses and trains had taken them to the arena. Fashionable Paris was out in force too. The stadium held "the crowd of the great days . . . , the public of dress rehearsals, of the Grand Prix, all those who count as notables habituated to great events."[56] Paris hadn't seen such a turnout since Jack Johnson battled Frank Moran before the war. The card also featured European welterweight champ Piet Hobin against French welterweight champ Francis Charles. Gate receipts set a French record, 192,600 francs.

From the opening bell, both men tried to end things quickly, swinging from the heels with evil intent. Siki aimed for the chin, Journée the body. Siki built up a points lead using his speed to dance out of Journée's reach, boxing with his guard down (à la Muhammad Ali), landing large swings and straight rights that battered Journée. Journée landed straight lefts but kept missing with his right.[57] *L'Auto* felt Siki, despite giving away nearly twenty-five pounds, had clearly settled the issue of superiority, nearly succeeding in sending "the enormous mass" of Journée "sprawl[ing] on the ground for the count, . . . shaking Journée, making him stagger, and completely bewildering him, despite the energetic doping that his handlers inflicted on him."[58] *La Boxe et les Boxeurs* gave Siki less credit, saying once he tired, "his footwork [became] almost nonexistent," and he was forced to "content himself to land some lefts and rights a bit blindly."[59]

Sparrow Robertson of the *Herald*, meanwhile, seems to have watched some other bout. He saw Journée dominate the early going, as if he "meant the contest to be short and sweet," raining punches from all angles, keeping Siki, who "made poor attempts" to retaliate, off balance.[60] Of course, Robertson, intent on heading off a Carpentier / Siki bout at all costs, was saying what he'd been primed to say—both because white America did not want a black challenger to the light-heavyweight title and because Descamps, a power in French boxing, wanted Carpenter to fight Nilles, not his former sparring partner Journée, and certainly not Siki.

Like Robertson, the gang at *La Boxe et les Boxeurs* wanted neither Siki nor Journée to get a shot at Carpentier's titles—but they, at least, were loath to stretch reality too far. Robertson, who had no such qualms, had Journée mounting an assault in the ninth that "had Siki in a very bad way at the bell," though *L'Auto* insisted Siki spent the round dancing around the ring, out of harm's way, and saw "*rien de saillant*" (nothing bloody) in the following round either.[61] *La Boxe et les Boxeurs* said Siki had Journée virtually out on his feet in the twelfth. *L'Auto* said Siki wore himself out over the final rounds slugging at the inert bulk of his rival, who managed only a timid rally at the finish. Even Robertson admitted that in the late rounds "Siki forced the fighting . . . and constantly had [Journée] in dire trouble." After the final bell, Journée's face showed the punishment he'd taken. Siki was doubled over, exhausted. *La Boxe et les Boxeurs,* predictably, called Siki's decision win "honorable, nothing more," inadequate to justify a world title challenge. Robertson characterized the fight as an ungainly back-and-forth free-for-all that proved neither man belonged in the same ring with Carpentier.

The FFB resolved Siki's managerial quandary in Lepart's favor, but by then Descamps could say, *Desolé,* I made another match. Carpentier fought George Cook in London on January 22, a foe fans grumbled was "not worthy of him."[62] Though he knocked Cook out in the fourth, rumors were rife that "*notre grand Georges,*" too busy enjoying celebrity to really train, was ripe for defeat.[63] Meanwhile, as Lepart chased matches in England, Siki was reduced to his old round of bouts against lower-ranked men. He needed the money—for on December 16, he became the father of a robust baby boy he and Lijntje named Louis. They had, by then, moved to rue d'Orléans, near Porte d'Orléans in the fourteenth *arrondissement.* Stol, to explain the move, has Lijntje struggle, in the advanced stages of pregnancy, to mount the narrow stairs at their former digs, and Louis, sweetly solicitous, hire assistants to watch over her. Stol also has him, on advice of a friend, a postal worker, and fight-fan named Senghor (!), journey to Roubaix to hunt up a marabout. The meeting proves disturbing as the marabout, from Siki's home city of Saint-Louis, makes a nebulous prediction: Siki "Senegal shall never again be able to share."[64]

Did Siki really see a marabout when his son was born? Perhaps. Of the 134,000 Africans who served in the war, thirty thousand remained in France.[65] Any Senegalese community would include *marabouts.* For a Wolof *ngente* (baptismal ceremony) the assistance of a Muslim holy man is vital. The *ngente* takes place eight days after the birth (for Siki, that would have been Christmas Eve), giving the mother (the *wasinn wees,* newly delivered) time to recover, and the family time to organize the biggest festival of family life. Usually the *yëgle* (invitation) is sent at once to the family at large (*mbokk*) and friends (*xarit*), but tradition dictates that even casual passers-by may

Siki with his first wife, Lijntje, and their baby, Louis Jr. in 1922; after August 1923 he would never see them again. (Courtesy of Mamadou Niang.)

join the party. Even today in Dakar one sees them, squatting curbside before a house where a baptismal party (*xew*) is going on, a bowl of *laax* (cereal with curdled milk) on their laps, a *beignet* (fried dough ball) in hand. The central ritual, the *tudd,* is held at a mosque, with only the father and a few others present. The father's eldest sister, the *njëkke,* as spiritual sponsor, holds the child. The marabout whispers in his ear the name he'll bear before God. Even the phrase with which one asks another's name (*"Naka la tudu"*) evokes this ceremony.[66]

Did little Louis undergo such a moment of consecration? Did he hear intoned, "In the name of God, the compassionate, the merciful"? Perhaps. After all, when the Louis Fall known as Battling Siki died, friends chanted Muslim prayers. For Stol, the marabout is a fortuneteller, but in fact a marabout is neither a *seer kaat* (diviner) nor *faat kaat* (magical practitioner). A marabout is a spiritual guide, uniting features of both Islamic and animist traditions. He at once asks Allah to bless the child and seeks to link him with the vital forces which quicken all existence—which come not only from God, but all living things. There is no real contradiction, for the *Koran* is silent on such questions. As Alessane Ndaw points out, for an African, place, time, sensible beings (plants, animals), and intelligent beings (man) are not essences impelled by forces, but forces themselves, dynamically moving other forces. In life, *l'être-force* (vital force) grows or wanes. It affects others, bears a "metaphysical dependence" on other forces "which differ in intensity according to the order of primogeniture or ... their place in the hierarchy of being."[67] At the moment of fatherhood, Siki's *être-force,* so irresistible in the prize ring, called into being his son's *être-force* and received an augmented dose of vitality in return. As a father, he was greater, more powerful than he'd been as a childless man.

Stol's imagined augury predicts Siki's physical fate (would he live to return to Africa?) and cultural fate (would he reconnect with his heritage?). What that culture may have already taught him about life, Stol doesn't consider. Did Siki think in terms of monetary success, health, emotional fulfillment and release? Or of that growth of *"la force vitale"* of which Ndaw speaks? Ndaw explains, "All moral codes are founded on this conception: that which is good is that which augments the vital force. That which is bad is that which diminishes it." We hear Siki himself say, in rare interviews, he wanted to triumph, to be a champion—of France, Europe, the world. One is perhaps too quick to assume he meant he wanted the wealth and celebrity a title brings. Perhaps he wanted to win because he wanted to be strong, because strength conveyed itself to those around you, because his strength would pass on to this new son, form his destiny. If Siki asked the marabout anything, perhaps it was this: What kind of force will I transmit to my son, a strong good one or a weak bad one? If the marabout really could read the future, his reply might have made the new father heartsick. Grown to adulthood, the boy would repudiate him.

Pretenders to an Idol's Throne

For the moment, Siki seemed the incarnation of implacable energy. He didn't outsmart foes. He overpowered them. Part of his potency was external: an amazing physical specimen, he blended a welterweight's speed with a heavyweight's punch. But his greatest strength was internal. He knew he *could* win. He felt it. With that sovereign urge to triumph, he hated to fight matches that meant little. In February, he rebelled. Leon Sée related, "Battling Siki is on strike! Everyone knows that, as he has been singing it everywhere."[68] Siki grumbled his manager took too high a cut of purses and wasn't getting him good fights. Lyggett and Teta, Lepart's other fighters, were set to rebel too. Over the next six months Siki would fight ten times, in seven cities, but only once face anyone ranked as high as he, the Algerian Louis Piochelle. He'd twice battle a sturdy Belgian heavyweight, Alphonse Rogiers, twice English nemesis Harry Reeve, and once rugged African American Al Baker. None of these bouts brought him any closer to a title.

Siki soldiered on, wandering around Europe to get fights, sending Lijntje curt telegrams recording triumphs.[69] Siki had attained a level of success that ought to have gotten him banner fights, but seldom did. He kept falling back to the level where he'd begun, fresh out of the army—fighting the local favorite in a grungy arena. In the two years since he'd returned to boxing, he'd outclassed the European middleweight champ, defeated every ranked light-heavyweight in Europe but Carpentier, and beaten most of the best heavyweights. Rousseau spoke of making him prove himself, but in Europe he had little left to prove. Descamps declared Carpentier would fight, by early summer, at the newly built Stade Buffalo. Then he'd take on Dempsey again or a top English rival at Newcastle for 30,000 pounds.[70]

When Descamps, in March, put off the Stade Buffalo bout until September, promoters and managers jockeyed frantically.[71] Somebody was going to lure the European heavyweight and world light-heavyweight champ into a ring. Siki meant it to be him. He was more and more baffled that Lepart was doing so little to win such a prize. He needed someone like Descamps— but who in Europe could match wits with that fast-talking sharper? One top pilot had become available—an insider from Rousseau's crowd, adept at publicity and behind-the-scenes maneuvers: Ercole Balzac's former pilot Charlie Hellers. For now Siki cooled his heels. He'd bickered twice with Rousseau over dumping managers. But in time, if he really wanted to fight Carpentier, he knew he'd have to get rid of Eli Lepart.

For now, he must attend to the business of winning fights that mattered little but could blow his chances. He went in against Rogiers January 17, disappointing fans with an "ugly inside battle." Siki piled up a big point lead, but Rogiers fought back in "a completely unhinged style." The crowd called peevishly for a knockout, muttering against "a battle that was hard, very hard, but truly monotonous."[72] *La Boxe et les Boxeurs* thought Siki, on the verge of a knockout in the third, held back out of pure "fantaisie" (whim). The bout ended with Rogiers battered and bloody, but with the victor, Siki, marked as well.[73] Siki won an equally ugly rematch on points two months later in Rogiers's hometown, drawing a big crowd to the Salle de Trocadéro in Brussels. He also knocked over a couple of tomato cans named Iter and Lenaers that winter (both in round two), at Strassbourg, and again dropped Vige for the count in Rotterdam.

By April, Siki was in against a tough rival, Louis Piochelle, in his hometown, Algiers, before a big crowd. Siki and Piochelle went after each other hard, with Siki landing at will to the head. Piochelle, however, stood up under the hail of blows, working inside, delivering shots under Siki's ribs. The impasse continued round after round, with Siki tagging his green adversary again and again, Piochelle riding out every storm.[74] *La Boxe et les Boxeurs* wondered why Piochelle didn't use his remarkable footwork to sidestep, instead of coming in flat-footed and catching everything Siki threw. At times he seemed to use Piochelle's head like a speed bag. The decision, for Siki, was a foregone conclusion.

Days later, in Barcelona, Siki "amused himself like a cat with a mouse" against Franck Hoche, a *Bitterrois* (resident of Béziers) who somehow held the Spanish heavyweight title.[75] A week later, Siki went twelve tough rounds there against the African American heavyweight Al Baker in a bout *La Boxe et les Boxeurs* called *"la belle boxe"* (beautiful boxing).[76] Sparrow Robertson said the issue was in doubt until the late rounds, when Siki, bloodied and exhausted, stormed back to win a close decision.[77] *L'Echo des Sports,* however, saw Siki's victory as routine, even boring. He'd been content to pile up points against a man too slow to make him "really work hard."[78]

When Siki returned to Paris, he found the French capital enthralled by other things than his distant victories. In late April, the American thug enshrined as heavyweight champ, Jack Dempsey, had arrived with his manager Doc Kearns. Paris watched with hypnotic fascination the man who, a year before, had broken its heart, and emptied pockets. When Dempsey went to the Casino de Paris, eager throngs unhinged the doors. Society reporters chased down the glittering boulevards a man who hardly knew how to button a cufflink or hold a fork. Writers hung on the eighth-grade dropout's every word. The heavyweight champ made a freakish contrast to their own vanquished hero. The American press had called him a "slacker," while their own *"Noble Georges"* had flown into machine-gun bullets in an artillery observation plane at Verdun.[79] Dempsey reminded them with every breath of his origins as a drifter and saloon thug. Kearns, the night of his first public appearance, had blurted out, "Why, you bum, you can't even bow. What kinda upbringing didja have?"[80] Dragged on stage, he was unable even to utter "thanks." The crowd jeered. Someone yanked him off with the long-handled hook reserved for amateur night.

When his train arrived from Calais on April 23, Dempsey said he had no plans to fight. He'd stay a week, then move on to the Côte d'Azur. Within

Siki ready to enter the ring,
probably in Barcelona, Spain,
April or May 1922.
(Author's collection.)

hours he and Kearns were on the town, living it up in a music hall on rue de Clichy. He accepted a medal at a banquet thrown by *L'Echo des Sports,* bounded on stage for a quick turn in the revue *La Grande Star Américaine* at the Casino de Paris, and refereed a boxing match between Balzac and Prunier.

Like Dempsey, Siki had come up from the hard world of the streets, the boxing booths, the dollar-for-the-winner free-for-alls. Dempsey had left those days far behind him now. Paris watched, fascinated, as he and Kearns dropped thousands of francs at the track, in clubs, and in casinos. Siki, meanwhile, was still stuck in the harsh world that Dempsey and Carpentier had escaped. Within days he was off to Amsterdam, for another run-in with Harry Reeve. He escaped with a decision win, but hardly had time to unpack before he was back on a train, headed north to fight the ex-convict again, in another grungy hall, with a less auspicious result.

Carpentier, meanwhile, was in England settling the hash of Ted "Kid" Lewis. World welterweight champion before his loss to Jack Britton in 1919, Lewis (real name Gershon Mendeloff) was one of Europe's roughest in-fighters. He'd campaigned for five years in America and won his title there. At the bell, despite the weight handicap, Lewis crowded inside, tying Carpentier up, hammering his ribs and stomach. Descamps cried foul. The referee cautioned Lewis. He turned to protest. Carpentier's Sunday punch leveled him in mid-protest. "Remember, defend yourself at all times," the standard prefight caution goes. All the same, enraged fans, sick of Descamps's chicanery, rose in a body, slinging bottles.[81]

That left only Siki and Nilles in the picture as potential Carpentier opponents. And although the Parisian boxing fraternity still found it hard to say Siki and "champion" in the same breath, Descamps was running out of excuses. Who besides Jeff Smith and Marcel Nilles hadn't Siki fought? Smith wasn't French, and Carpentier had already beaten him. Nilles and Siki were plainly the best French boxers in their weight classes. Nilles had lost his French heavyweight title to Paul Hams in June 1919, but won it back in a rematch. He bolted around the ring with a nimbleness surprising for so big a man. Strong, fast, adept at in-fighting, always in top condition, Nilles would be a tough rival for a man fifteen pounds lighter.

Descamps finally signed a contract for a September match at the new Stade Buffalo—with, he said, the only European boxer deserving of it: Nilles. In truth, he preferred Nilles for strategic reasons. A loss to Nilles, who couldn't make the light-heavyweight limit, would save Carpentier's world title. The idea of Carpentier defending his European heavyweight title while sitting on his world light-heavyweight title was vaguely comic: Carpentier had ignored his European crown for years. But the FFB agreed to sanction the bout—insisting only that Nilles fight Siki first. If Siki won, Descamps would have to ink Siki's name into the contract.

Sure, sure, said Descamps, who thought little of the Senegalese. The money men began talking turkey—while Siki marked time with out-of-town bistro-fare bouts, and Carpentier went back to making one-reelers and enjoying the pleasures of society. So lightly did Rousseau and his cronies take Siki's claims that a June 14 *La Boxe et les Boxeurs* feature about Nilles's training (1,270 meters above sea level, at the Grand Hotel of Mont-Pilat in the Massif-Central) ignored the bout with Siki, referring to Nilles only as training for the September bout with Carpentier!

Siki's name came up in that issue only in a farcical back section, in a running gag the French media had worn out for years, depicting blackness as an irksome blemish any black man would wash off if he could. A long-running soap advertisement for "Savon la Perdrex, 72% d'huile" (Perdrex Soap, 72% oil) pictured a minstrel-show African with bug eyes and pale sausage-shaped lips washing one arm white with the advertised product.[82] Even serious news reports took up the gag, as did *Le Populaire* of July 26, 1922, whose story about a Bordeaux merchant (Robert Nègre) accused of profiteering on stocks of alcohol amassed for the army at Salonika was titled "*Un nègre qui voudrait être blanchi*" ("A Nigger Who Wanted to Be Bleached"). The far-fetched gag (twisting *blanchi* to mean found innocent of a crime) shows how far writers would go to work their pet wisecrack. Now, with nothing at all to say about Siki's training for the big bout, *La Boxe et les Boxeurs* trotted out a reversal of the skin-bleach gag, urging the merits of a fictitious dye: "Use the dye Nigger Ultra-Plus, the only one that doesn't bleach in the wash. Write: Battling Siki, at Rotterdam."[83] The gag carried a special message for Siki: even if Nilles yielded to Siki's slashing fists, that wouldn't wash away Siki's color—or make France accept him as champion.

While Nilles trained in isolation at his grand hotel, Siki made the rounds of sweaty gyms and rickety arenas. One week after his second bout with Reeve, he headed back to Anvers, where an injury left promoters with no opponent for Harry Reeve in the sold-out Hippodrome. George Platteau, in *La Boxe et les Boxeurs,* doubted the switch had been for the better. Both Siki and Reeve seemed in no mood for combat. The fans whistled to derision the tame goings-on. The referee urged the fighters to "carry their blows all the way through." They answered with brief flurries that were "really beautiful."[84] But *L'Echo des Sports* observed, "Whoever it was who matched Battling Siki and Harry Reeve must have reproached himself a great deal for this exhibition."[85] The hulking Englishman, Platteau thought, perhaps deserved a win, if one could make oneself care. The verdict was for a draw.

The Nilles bout, set for June 23 in the cavernous Velodrome d'Hiver, didn't worry Charlie Hellers, Balzac's former pilot, who by now was handling Siki's career. Though a potent puncher, Nilles would have no answer for Siki's speed. Hellers was so sure of his new *poulain* he bet Nilles's manager, Louis Lerda, 10,000 francs—their entire stake.[86] Hellers and Lerda were old-timers on the European boxing scene. Lerda had been one of a handful of men who'd brought English-style boxing to France. Parisian by birth, he'd returned to his native city to answer a family emergency in 1899, after sixteen years in America, four of them fighting as "Kid Adler" in the welterweight division. Back in France, he set about introducing American-style boxing to French kick-boxing fans. Matched at Salle Wagram against American Dick O'Brien, Lerda won France's first public-admission professional bout. For his pains, he was labeled a savage endorsing a blood sport. Unfazed, he set up a Latin Quarter gymnasium, promoted matches, and publicized the sport. Its popularity in 1922 largely owed to his efforts.[87]

Jean Auger in *La Boxe et les Boxeurs* suggested Siki might be Nilles's toughest opponent yet.[88] *L'Auto* said Siki was following his new manager's orders without a murmur, though he'd at times laughed off others' efforts to reign him in. He'd put on ten kilos since he fought Balzac. He'd face Nilles at his heaviest yet. *L'Auto* mocked Descamps for backing down and agreeing to let Siki, should he win, replace Nilles on the Stade Buffalo card, even though he'd once insisted Nilles was the only French fighter worthy of facing "the great Georges."[89] Auger too favored Nilles. The lantern-jawed heavyweight, a "redoubtable slugger" who hit hard with either hand, fought well in the clinches, but was also a skillful boxer with remarkable footwork. "He leaves far behind him," Auger judged, "the whole lot of European heavyweights and places himself immediately behind Carpentier." Siki was "strong, agile, quick," a man "blessed with great physical abilities" who attacked "like a thunderstorm, raining a hail of blows on the adversary whom he cuts down." But when he failed to floor a rival, he became "much less dangerous," tiring quickly, slow to recover.

L'Auto, in contrast, argued Siki had been far busier than Nilles, with a string of successes over the hardest hitters in France. Nilles, after suffering a broken hand losing a twenty-round decision to Paul Hams two years before, had laid up inactive and fought infrequently. He seemed passive, fragile. Siki might well surprise detractors again. *L'Auto* invoked the indomitable fighting spirit of the *tirailleurs:*

For those who know the courage of the valiant Senegalese race, we are certain that, without having to submit to a handicap of temperature or of weight, he is a fighter of invincible courage who will confront our heavyweight champion next Friday. The past of *Siki the Unbeatable* reveals his success and his victory would surprise only those who don't want to believe in the inexhaustible resources of supreme force and energy hidden within that marvelous statue of ebony.

Nilles often started sluggishly, but Siki came out "like a whirlwind."[90] They put it to Nilles directly: is there a risk Siki will knock you out before you find your legs? "I've seen Siki box," he replied. "I know the nigger is particularly redoubtable in the opening rounds, but I've trained especially for that."[91]

The ancient arena was bursting on fight night. But from the moment the bell rang for the main event nothing went as expected. Siki's tactics startled everyone: instead of pasting Nilles with long-range flurries, he crowded inside. *L'Auto* said he landed a good left in the first and a right in the second, but got caught with a hard left too. In the third, battered on the inside, Siki tried to tag Nilles at long range, but near round's end got caught again by a "beautiful left."[92] Sparrow Robertson said that from the fifth round on, Siki began to dominate with "furious charging tactics" that "smothered his man."[93] By the ninth, the African had his rival "floundering helplessly about the ring." In the eleventh, with Nilles utterly listless, he began dropping his guard, taunting, "provoking with a malicious pleasure the fists of Nilles, who seemed petrified by such a display of audacity."[94] *L'Auto* and *Le Miroir des Sports* said Nilles seemed *"médusé"* (hypnotized).[95] *La Boxe et les Boxeurs* said Nilles did "nothing, nothing at all," except stall, clinch, and hang on. Siki wasn't more skillful, the FFB's official journal whined, only more aggressive, leaping, punching clumsily, but at least punching, landing any way he could. The bout had been a "pitiful exhibition." Nilles seemed like a novice. Siki's punches had been a bit *"à tort et à travers"* (all over the place), "but at least he did something."[96]

Jean Auger moaned, "What a disillusionment for me, who have always lauded Nilles." *L'Auto* called the match "horribly disappointing." So utterly had the boxing world set its heart on Nilles, so little had it considered that he might lose, that like a jilted lover it whined of base ingratitude. Had Nilles forgotten, sniffed *La Boxe et les Boxeurs,* the promised contract for a Carpentier match? With all that riding on the fight, how could he come out so flat? It seemed to slip their minds that Siki too, if he won, was promised a title shot. They vented their spleen on Lerda too (for badly preparing his fighter, letting him grow rusty). Anyone could infer what came next: the FFB and Descamps would declare that Siki's showing didn't justify a challenge to Carpentier. The bout's moral, wrote Auger, was that "in the form that these two men showed Friday night, they would have been rendered *hors de combat* by Carpentier, one after the other, in less than two minutes."[97] But the real moral to the story was that the men who controlled the boxing game in France would do anything they could to keep Siki out of the ring with Carpentier—and when, in spite of them, a few months hence, he did get in the ring with Carpentier, it would only be as a hired extra in a staged farce. Too bad Siki never bothered to learn his role.

CHAPTER EIGHT

"Yes, We Have No Bananas!"

A Fair-Sized Fortune

Ironically, in America in November 1923 Siki still hadn't accepted his role. He still was hoping for a chance to fight Carpentier—for real this time, not in a setup—or McTigue, or Tunney, or Greb, or Gibbons, or any top white light-heavyweight. After his brutal loss to Kid Norfolk, however, Siki was in no shape to fight anyone. His lips, mouth, nose, and eyes were swollen and lacerated. His body was an aching lump. The pain fighters go through after a fight, heavyweight champ Jack Sharkey told Peter Heller, is "never brought out in the press." After his loss to Dempsey, Sharkey had to be hospitalized. "I passed blood there for a long time," he recalled. The low blows, the tension, the body punches all had taken a toll. "You dry out like a lightweight, you're dehydrated, pains that you have, you come home, you soak in a tub full of Epsom salts."[1] Siki suffered also the emotional agony a beaten fighter feels after a big match. Emotional wounds heal yet more slowly. "It's not the blows," King Levinsky once said, "much as they hurt. But it's all them witnesses. Everybody watching you. You split to pieces, like a goddamn plate glass window hitting the sidewalk."[2]

Siki's novice manager, Bob Levy, seems to have had little understanding of what his man had gone through in the ring. In fact, he seems to have written Siki off before the bout began. Gaston-Charles Raymond, the French lightweight who came to America with Siki, said that after Levy (whose name he misconstrues as "Lewis") bought his contract in 1923 he "understood quickly that Siki was in decline; he had to rapidly conclude a match before the black reached the bottom of the slide."[3] After the loss to Norfolk he planned to book as many quick matches as he could and spend the minimum on training. W. O. McGeehan paraphrased Levy: "Battling Siki will never win a championship unless Lady Luck gushes all over him, but he can clean up a fair-sized fortune within the next six months."[4] Rickard offered bouts with Greb or Tunney, but Levy said no thanks. He meant to set up "several matches against less dangerous rivals."[5]

Levy's plan to book less risky opponents made sense, but without a good trainer to teach Siki how to cope with the American style of in-fighting, it might well backfire. Any fighter needs to keep learning, because any fighter can be beaten. A manager's job is to see that his man is ready to win and that he faces men he can beat. Thomas Hauser quotes manager Mickey Duff on his strategy in arranging fights. "Without exception," Duff explains, "quality managers know that boxing is a sport where one or two losses can kill a fighter's career at any time." Duff had, he mused, "managed guys through thirty or forty wins without a loss." It was easier to do so with a "quality fighter," but a good manager could keep even a less-skilled man's record unblemished—at least, until that "moment of truth" arrived "when your guy has to fight a real fight."[6] Managers needed to be realists, to keep their men working hard, honing their skills—and make sure they fought a fight that might become a war only in return for a big payday or a real chance to advance their careers. Siki needed time to recover, to get in shape, and to work on the weak spots in his style, before Levy sent him out to fight another war. But Levy would soon prove to be as inept a manager as he was a cut man.

A few weeks after the Norfolk bout, Siki bumped into matchmaker Lew Raymond, promoter of the Garden's Christmas relief card, and promptly volunteered his services, but Levy had other plans.[7] He'd already set up bouts on December 19 against Joe Lohman in New York and on Christmas Day in Philadelphia against Jack Taylor, who'd sparred with Siki in Summit. He also had bouts set for January 1 in Detroit, January 7 in Buffalo, January 14 in Grand Rapids, January 21 in New Orleans, and January 28 in Havana. Basically, he planned to have Siki fight once a week and to spend most of the rest of his time not in training but in trains. He did finally cancel the Lohman match, when it became evident that Siki was in no shape to fight, but he went ahead with the Taylor bout, less than a week later.[8] Boxing men liked to tell you how the great Harry Greb "fought himself into shape in the ring." Levy must have figured the same thing would work for Siki. But actually Greb trained harder than he let on. He worked out in secret for his July 1925 match with Mickey Walker, for instance, faking a drunken spree the night before, squiring a bevy of females from club to club, tipping waiters to serve him colored water, faking a curbside pratfall—just to inflate the odds on the bout.[9] Fair wrote of Greb's training for the Walker bout, "For all his nocturnal activities he found time to run a few miles on the road and work eight or ten rounds daily, always using good, fast, fresh sparring partners."[10]

If Siki was serious about an American career, he ought to work himself into shape on his own. But few fighters do. Most need help to focus singlemindedly on an upcoming bout. Siki was tough and determined, and he was a hard worker when the spirit moved him. The Rotterdam promoter Theo Huizenaar describes the Siki of old showing off for other fighters by punching a tree trunk until his hands bled.[11] But few boxers have a taste for rigid discipline on a long-term basis. That's why they have trainers. Moreover, what had worked in the ring against Nilles and Journée hadn't against Kid Norfolk, and it wouldn't against Greb, Gibbons, or Tunney either. He needed a new strategy. The furious rushes and wide swings left him open to counters. After his loss to Norfolk, unfortunately, Siki was in no mood to rethink his way of fighting. He wanted a spell of transitory excess. When he'd worn out the pain, the sense of futility, and the money, he'd go back to boxing. The papers might sing his praises as the gamest of fighters, but the Norfolk fight had returned him to his wartime role of the man tied to the post, awaiting the blows of a hammer another wielded. With the money he'd won, he had the means to fuel self-forgetfulness. Perhaps he ought to have resisted that temptation. He didn't.

James Fair describes Siki, at the Greb / Tunney match December 10, sitting up in "Peanut Heaven" (the balcony reserved for blacks), dizzy with alcohol, surrounded by "Harlem admirers" who shouted with pride to have him among them. Called to the ring to be introduced, Siki spent fifteen minutes pushing through the press of well-wishers. Fair says Siki, "smiling toothily like a child contemplating a lollipop," outfitted in "broghans, skintight pants, tails and topper and carrying a cane," bowed theatrically and, leaning out over the ropes, "slipped in a pool of blood from one of the preliminaries and started to tumble out of the ring" before a Jersey City bantamweight "grabbed him and pulled him back in."[12]

Handlers of main-event boxers would hardly have been so careless as to leave puddles of blood in the ring. But never mind. Even if one doubts the by-now-mandatory furnishing of Siki with ill-fitting trousers, top hat, and imbecile grin, he may well have hammed it up for the crowd. Why not? He was in the entertainment business. Fair also claims Siki tried to kiss his proposed future foes, but that little detail escaped ringside reporters. The *Times* blandly noted, "Battling Siki was one of the boxers introduced," before turning to the weighty news that the Manhasset fire department gave Greb a loving cup.[13] The *Evening Journal's* Willie Fitzpatrick saw no blood, no pratfall, no top hat, broghans, or dodged kisses. He did notice the uproar in the back balcony when Siki arrived—and swore Humphries, impatient to get a preliminary underway, yelled, "As soon as Battling Siki finds his seat the show will go on."[14] The *Evening Post* said Siki was dressed in "a dinner coat"—*sans* cane, kisses, pool of blood, top hat or broghans—though it did say he "slapped Mr. Humphreys... cheerfully on the back before leaving the ring."[15]

The fight that night rivaled Siki / Norfolk for sheer blood and brutality. For fifteen rounds Greb bounced around the ring "like a monkey on a string," tossing windmill punches that seemed to come from the floor, the ceiling, and every place in between. Tunney weathered storm after storm, punishing the lighter man with jabs and a grunting body attack. Several times he caught Greb low. Greb paid him back by holding and hitting. Knowing Levy was negotiating bouts with both men, Siki must have wondered: Would a Siki / Tunney bout be Siki / Norfolk all over again? Tunney, as good a counterpuncher as Norfolk, was a slick boxer too. Greb was another story. He won with speed and relentless pressure, as did Siki himself. He didn't hit all that hard, but he cut people up, fouled them, brutalized them, until they wished they were anywhere else than in the ring with him. Siki wasn't ready for either of these guys, and he must have known it. In fact, he wasn't ready for much of anybody.

When Siki finally left town December 18 for last-minute training at Madame Bey's camp, he incited one of the oddest incidents of his American career—one sportswriters cheerfully retailed as proving his "singularity"— though granting Siki's cultural antecedents, there's nothing so very strange about it. He waited at Weehawken's West Shore ferry terminal while Levy made a phone call. A crowd came to gawk. He sang songs to them, just for fun.[16] Then he pulled out a wad of six hundred one-dollar bills and started handing them out, telling recipients "to buy a drink."[17] This wasn't chump change. In 1923 a dollar would buy you three pounds of pork chops, or rent two rooms at Chicago's Hotel Wychmere.[18] Nor was Siki's abrupt liberality out of character. In Paris he'd once promised 10,000 francs to striking seamstresses.[19] He's said to have often left a bigger tip for restaurant waiters than the total of the bill. With a fresh purse in hand, he liked to hand out money to the newsboys around Times Square. Partly his generosity seems to have come from a sense of solidarity with ordinary people. In any case, what African would weep over an act of generosity? As Magel notes, *yewen* (generosity) is one of the cardinal virtues of a Wolof *borom jom* (man of virtue), an outward sign he lacks pettiness or meanness. Its opposites, *sisate* (self-ishness) and *nhere* (greed), are among the worst offenses against propriety, consistently ridiculed in Wolof folk tales.[20] Prominent West Africans, in fact, give gifts to all and sundry to mark special occasions such as baptisms or national holidays. But Siki's impulsive charity, all the same, drew a burst of press mockery, confirming preconceptions about his innocence concerning material value and inability to live in any but the present tense. The story became a basic ingredient in the Battling Siki myth, repeated in obituary notices, boxing encyclopedias, and essay after essay about boxing in the wild 1920s.

More than twenty years later, John Lardner would memorialize the event thus: "Another time, he gave away all the money in his pockets to passengers on a Lackawanna Railroad ferryboat on which he was returning from a fight in New Jersey. Scolded for this by his manager, Siki wept."[21] The weeping occurred in Lardner's imagination. Levy later swore Siki only handed out about thirty dollars, and with it bought "hundreds of dollars of [free] publicity."[22] If reporters took Siki's gesture as an inane caprice, in his culture it signified mastery, power. He had money. He was famous—a champion boxer. It was, for him, neither bizarre nor irrational to give open-handedly. Gratuitous largesse might seem strange in America, but perhaps he partly meant it as a provocation, a gesture accentuating his dominance over weaker, poorer men—who'd been lulled by the illusion of race into thinking themselves superior. Siki certainly didn't mean his liberality the way the press took it, as a childish effort to buy friends, nor the way the police took it—as a threat to public order. They promptly arrested him, demanding a hundred-dollar cash bond for a hearing on December 26.[23]

One more delay. Just what Siki needed! With the Taylor bout in a week, he'd yet to begin training. Blame Siki for his own lapses—but blame Levy too. It was his business to see to it his man was ready for combat. Instead of Siki, Levy should have had to deal with some of the other characters who made a living in the ring. Siki at least, once in camp, did all he was asked and more. Boxing lore abounds in stories of managers driven mad trying to restrain their boxers' worst inclinations. Liebling tells of a fighter who dodged his pilot for weeks, pretending to do roadwork in Central Park but actually sitting on a bench flirting with the nannies wheeling prams. He'd sneak a shower in workout togs and reappear seemingly drenched in sweat. Another manager watched out a hotel window with a shotgun, ready to rekindle his fighter's enthusiasm if he slowed from a run to a walk on frozen Greenwood Lake.[24] Mickey Walker recalls how, training to face heavyweight champ Max Schmeling, he got down to his fighting weight, 158 pounds. His manager, Jack Kearns, worried he might "go stale," gave him a day off. Walker promptly got drunk and cut his eye hopping a fence in a showoff stunt. The bout was postponed three weeks—enough time for Walker to drink and eat himself to 174 pounds.[25] Siki, like Walker, fed on the rapture of big-city nightlife. At times, in Paris, with a gang of boxing pals, his drinking binges lasted days at a time. American newspapers record no such debauches in December 1923, but you don't gain six pounds in four weeks doing road work, sparring, and banging the heavy bag.

A manager leaves nothing to chance. If he wants his boxer to show up in shape on fight night, he watches him train every day—or hires a reliable man to do it for him. In fact, in January Levy owned up that Siki had done no road work "in recent months."[26] Siki reacted to Levy's laxity about as you'd expect. He turned up at the gym sometimes—and more often didn't.

Levy was no fit judge of potential opponents either. Jack Taylor, for instance, might be an ex-sparring partner, but he wasn't quite the "less dangerous rival" Levy imagined. Taylor had had a checkered career, marred by the usual arrangements, non-fights, and mismatches that were the lot of black fighters. But he'd had notable triumphs too. He got started as a fighter when three white men in Seattle tried to bully him into leaving a bar. One threw beer in his face. Taylor "knocked him out with a right-hand punch in the stomach." The others "went out the same way." The next day "news spread that there was a certain shine, Jack Taylor by name, was licking everybody around."[27] George P. Moore, the black manager who exposed boxing's color bar in 1922, took Taylor under his wing. Taylor claimed he beat Kid Norfolk in 1922, but the *Ring Record Book* lists a draw. Still, holding Norfolk to a draw was no mean feat. Norfolk had lost but two bouts in five years—one on a cut from a head butt, the other, many said, on a fix.

Siki weighed 177 1/2 pounds on fight night, his heaviest yet, a sure sign he hadn't trained. Even with no weight limit to make, Siki had always before come in under the light-heavyweight limit. The headline ten-rounder at Philadelphia's Adelphia Arena looked like a poor man's imitation of Siki/Norfolk, with Taylor doing the same imitation of Norfolk's ducking, counterpunching style as he had in Summit. The *Philadelphia Inquirer* (unaware Taylor had been Siki's sparring partner) said he seemed afraid to take risks with an "unknown" opponent. If only! Though Siki "began the fun by tearing into [Taylor],"[28] Taylor remained wary, letting "the shifty Siki get away with too much fancy stuff," but sticking his jab, drawing blood from Siki's nose.[29] When it became evident Siki wasn't in shape, Taylor, dodging "wild lunges," shot "damaging blows" to the body.[30] By the seventh, Siki was bleeding from a cut lip, one eye nearly closed. As the bell ended the eighth, he slipped—and, falling, got caught by a left hook. It was ruled a slip. Both the *New York*

Times and the *New York Evening Journal* said Taylor left the ring with his right eye swollen shut—a fact (if it really was one) the *Inquirer* missed. Taylor won on every card.

It was Siki's worst showing since the war. Through 1922 just one post-war loss had marred his record. Now, in eight months, he'd lost four times—once on a foul, once on a dubious decision, twice in bloody points losses. These setbacks ought to have sent Levy a message. Another loss, however much credit Siki had won for the Norfolk fight, might destroy his drawing power. He had two bouts slated in the next week—in Michigan against the sturdy veteran Joe Lohman and in Buffalo against rising newcomer Tony Stabenau. Siki had to win, if he wasn't to be written off as a fistic oddity with one lucky major win. With all the hours he'd spent on trains, at weigh-ins, at press conferences, in court (on that December 26 "disorderly conduct" charge), upcoming bouts weren't likely to find him in any better shape than the Taylor bout had.

Siki soon had one fewer match to worry about. Michigan athletic commissioner Louis Piles told Grand Rapids promoters "Siki's past performances are such that Michigan can get along without any matches in which he is a principal," abruptly revoking Siki's license. His reasoning is hard to fathom. Apart from giving away money, Siki had done nothing antisocial. Though boxing commissions had wide latitude in deciding what constituted undesirable conduct, if they started weighing misdemeanor offenses in far-away states, the prize ring would empty out quickly. Piles didn't say what "performances" he meant. He insisted, "A Siki match might injure the boxing game in the State." His action, noted the *Times,* "followed a conference between Governor A. J. Groesbeck and Harry B. Jackson, Commissioner of Public Safety," which suggests the politics of racial exclusion rather than Siki's alleged misconduct was behind the ban.[31]

Maybe it was just as well the Lohman bout was shelved. Siki had hardly trained. He and Levy spent the first weeks of 1924 chasing deals, from Chicago to Detroit, then to Cleveland, then Buffalo. The *Cleveland Gazette* reported Siki's visit to the home of Mose Cleveland where he showed himself to be "a very tame creature," shaking hands genially and trying to express himself in English. An exhibition set for East Chicago January 10 and a main event for Peoria January 19 fell through when promoters "could not sign a suitable [read black] opponent."[32] Two days later, "a hitch in the terms" nixed the rescheduled Lohman bout, set for January 19 in Ontario. Levy even fielded an offer for a February bout in Copenhagen.[33]

In the midst of this chaos, Siki and Levy headed for Buffalo, where one fight was still on, with light-heavyweight Tony Stabenau. Though no contender, Stabenau was no palooka. He'd won his last eight fights by knockout and had "put in two weeks of the hardest conditioning of his life" to get ready for the ex-champion.[34] Siki, meanwhile, was lucky to get in some calisthenics at Bert Finch's gym. The fight sold out its ten thousand seats.[35] On fight night, "Darktown was out in force," said Stuart C. Maguire in the *Buffalo Evening News,* "and it was such liberal patronage from William Street and its potential environs that swelled the crowd to its record proportions."[36] *Potential* suggests the volatility of the situation. As black migration swelled, local authorities used every extralegal expedient to exclude African Americans from white neighborhoods. Siki's advent roused white fears. Who knew how many blacks Buffalo would ultimately attract, how many districts Darktown would swallow? Against Norfolk, "the Race" had seen Siki as an intruder. Now, against a white boxer, it was categorically *for* Siki. His Buffalo training exhibition drew better than either Dempsey's or Harry Wills's main events there had.[37] On fight night, "cheered wildly" by the huge crowd, Siki led down the aisle "a retinue that would have been a credit to a Rajah," including "Sam Bliv, a man of importance in local colored circles, and two or three others of Buffalo's most prominent colored citizens." Warmed by the crowd's fervor, Siki grinned and waved.[38] He was, said Maguire, "quite an affable 'wild man,' shaking hands with everyone who cared for the privilege."

When Stabenau ducked through the ropes, "the other side of the house cut loose." If Siki needed a visual emblem for American racial polarity, he had it. Maguire called Siki "the man-ape," but otherwise didn't much work the savage-primitive angle. Weirdly, the *Defender's* Frank Young worked that angle nearly as hard as had Ford Frick:

> Siki, a shiny black figure, marvelously built and showing wonderful physical development and a catlike grace, as menacing as it was beautiful to watch, drew a chorus of "oh's" and "ah's" as he tossed off a dingy purple bath robe and stood revealed as the wild man from Africa. He pirouetted and pranced while the announcements were being made, while Stabeneau, nervously taut and erect in his corner, surveyed him with wonder and alarm.

"Frightened almost to helplessness," Stabeneau betrayed no "glint of determination or confidence" in his "staring eyes."[39] He inched from his corner "like a man who had gone to his doom."[40] Siki, "loping like a hound," hunted his prey like a "black jaguar" with "lashing, stinging, jarring hooks and swings."[41] As Stabenau retreated Siki fired a right hook to the chin and two hard rights to the body that sent him to the canvas as Siki "pranced from one corner to another."[42] Stabenau rose at the count of eight and tried to hold on, but Siki hammered him to the body. By round's end, Stabenau had gone down again for a seven and again for a nine count.[43]

Sensing victory, Siki "pranced back to his corner and leaped up and down, pawing the atmosphere, his features bedecked with a huge grin."[44] The Race side of the house chanted for a knockout. Siki rushed out to oblige them, raining punches on Stabenau, who cowered in a corner. A final body blow sent him down nose first "as if struck at the base of his skull with a poleax." As the referee tolled the count, Siki "danced a jig of joy," shook hands with back-slapping supporters, and rushed to help Stabenau to his feet, planting kisses on both cheeks. "Confused and flushed," Stabenau pushed Siki off with both hands, his first vaguely hostile action all night.

It hadn't been much of a fight, but the gate had been large, the crowd captivated with the persona of "Battling Siki"; promoters spoke of another bout a week later in the same arena. Still, Siki was peeved. Levy had run off chasing further paydays without settling up for this one, leaving him with nothing but pocket change and a train ticket. He purposely missed the train. Why should he fight another bout before he'd been paid for this one? He found his way to Niagara Falls, buying five dollars worth of postcards, mailing many to his wife, Lijntje. Later, cooped in the Little Savoy Hotel, he became increasingly fretful. What was Levy up to? Another pointless bout on no training?

The *Ring Record Book* credits Siki with a win in Los Angeles the next day, January 9—but he could hardly have gotten there so quickly, and the *Los Angeles Times* reveals that the boxer who fought there was "*Young* Siki," a 112-pound novice lightweight borrowing the ex-champion's ring name. The real Siki's next fight would be against a sturdy young heavyweight, who also sported a pilfered ring name, "Young Norfolk"—no relation to Black Thunderbolt William Ward. Siki had other reasons than missing cash to "pace up and down the corridors" of the Little Savoy that night. To fight Young Norfolk he'd have to cross the Mason Dixon line. After all he'd heard about McTigue's bout with Young Stribling, and probably read about black uprisings and Klan lynchings, he must have wondered what possessed Levy to arrange such a match. What would the American South think of a black man married to a blonde?

The *Buffalo Evening News* reporter who broke in on Siki's late-night vigil declared he'd "conducted himself like a gentleman" so far, but "pretty soon the strain may prove too great." He meant the strain of staying on good behavior, but Siki's real worry was quite different. Reporter after reporter describes his evident affection for Levy, and Levy's "fatherly" regard for him. But Levy's fondness was mediated by the politics of race and lure of lucre. His devotion was the kind Lucie Cousturier saw white officers cherishing for the *tirailleurs* during the war. She conveys it in a memorable metaphor of a peasant woman bottle-raising a baby pig, kissing and caressing it as if it were her own child—until the time for the slaughter came, when she herself held the basin to catch the blood from its slit throat, weeping as her "son" squealed in terror, yet crying in ecstacy all the same: "What beautiful blood! Oh, how white the meat will be!"[45]

Were Levy's emotions after the Norfolk fight any different from those of Cousturier's peasant woman? He may have felt real anguish as he watched his young protégé choke on his own blood, his face battered to an unrecognizable lump. But once Levy had a chance to count his share of the purse and calculate what the total would reach if all the other matches he'd booked materialized, he too must have murmured, "What beautiful blood!"

The Best Press-Agented Boxer in Captivity

Siki's train clattered into Memphis on January 11. What happened next depends on how credulous you are. Nat Fleischer, boxing's "gnome guru" (as Ralph Wiley called him) and eternal purveyor of fight stories, had two favorite "Battling Siki" yarns: one set on Broadway, featuring a walking stick, an opera cape, and an obstreperous monkey; another on Beale Street, featuring a bunch of bananas and a popular song. Fleischer claimed he witnessed the former incident. Levy told the latter tale at a boxing writers' dinner. In it, a simple, unlettered black primitive, dazzled by the splendors of celebrity, ignorant of the hostility his antics may provoke, arrives in a strange southern city. He grabs a copy of the local paper, anticipating with childish glee seeing his beaming mug in print. He thumbs through the paper once, twice. He throws it down in disgust exclaiming, *Qu'est que c'est que ça? Ma photo? Il-n'y-a pas?* No photo? None at all? No photo of the biggest celebrity in world? No photo of the great Battling Siki?

His genial manager doesn't tell him that whoever he might be in Paris, in Memphis he's just another . . . *nègre*. He says, Gee, lookit that? No photo! How'd that happen? The shaggy-haired foreigner grunts. He can't have this! He wants to be seen, followed down the street, pointed at. He wants to hear the buzz of startled voices, whispered exclamations. He wants adoration, even mockery—anything but apathy. "Why my name no in zee papers?" Fleischer's "wild man" snarls.[46] Then his simple mind unearths an expedient. He heads to the docks, buys a huge bunch of bananas, hoists them on his shoulder, and saunters up the main avenue, tossing them one by one to a curious throng. As he tosses, he sings a song he's been hearing on the radio—the season's biggest hit: "Yes, we have no bananas, we have no bananas today."

True or apocryphal, the story reveals how Levy looked upon the black man whose notoriety he'd set out to exploit. The publicity stunt, even if it happened as Fleischer says, was less outlandish than many another in that publicity-hungry era. If Jack Kearns had come up with it, who'd have batted an eyelash? Kearns once showed Tim McGrath, heavyweight champ Jack Sharkey's manager, how to overcome press apathy: he hired a guy to throw buckets of water against the "Fighting Gob's" hotel windows while Kearns got on the horn to every writer in town. "It's all due to his old life as a sailor," he declared. "He can't sleep unless he thinks the waves are beating against the portholes." "They bought it too," Kearns mused, "proving my lifelong publicity theory that writers go hook, line, and sinker for anything out of the ordinary."[47]

Clever manager, that Kearns! Cutest in the game! Yet when Siki tried an "out of the ordinary" stunt, who saw *cuteness* in it? Publicity stunts cooked up by men with bushy hair were symptoms of savage simplicity. Neither Levy nor Fleischer, of course, considered another burden of the tale: that Siki had, though imperfectly fluent in English, mastered America's code of race. In prewar Marseille's Old Town a local promoter had caged a local character nicknamed *Gueule de Bois* (Wooden Jaw), fed him raw meat, peanuts, and bananas, and charged admission to view his ersatz savage.[48] Memphis limited its wild men to bananas. Marseille's wild men were aboriginal, Memphis's proto-simian. Both were dangerous outside cages.

By now, Siki knew his *rôle*—hardly an original one. The African American Abe Franklin already had appropriated the *nom du ring* "Human Gorilla." A Memphis middleweight fought as "Gorilla Jones." He'd soon bequeath the name to Memphis teenager William Jones, already haunting local gyms, who'd migrate to Atlanta, work as a handyman for manager Walk Miller, and in time win the middleweight title.[49] For black prizefighters, donning a virtual gorilla suit was a useful gesture of acquiescence to the racial status quo. But Siki actually inverted the racial iconography. After all, he was the one tossing the bananas.

Siki's prank, Fleischer insists, was short-lived. Irate over banana peels littering the streets, two mounted policemen scattered the muscular stranger's "little army," collared the instigator, pulled nightsticks, and threatened him. The crowd, from a safe distance, goaded the flustered cops, who hauled the bushy-haired stranger off to the station. Arraigned before a magistrate for his brazen public display of—what was it exactly, generosity?—Siki ducked his head and faced the music. His account of his actions provoked such riotous laughter that the judge sentenced him to sing the song again for the court. He cheerfully complied.[50] At least, that's what he did if you believe yarns retailed at boxing dinners.

In fact, the *Memphis Commercial Appeal* suggests another version. It's true Siki's picture didn't appear there. About the only black face that did was that of a minstrel-show character, "Hambone," whose addle-pated "meditations," in crude dialect, daily graced a front-page cartoon strip ("Ah ain' gwine buy me no new hat," he muses January 15; "I ain' nevuh use dis heah haid o' mine fuh nothin' en I ain' gwine do nothin' fuh it!!!!"). But though no photo of "one of the darkest representatives of one of the darkest tribes in darkest Africa," Battling Siki, did appear, he'd been the butt of running gags for months.[51] "The best press-agented boxer in captivity," in fact he got more coverage in Memphis than anywhere else on his American junket.[52] The mere news of his signing a contract drew headlines. The *Appeal's* Gerald L. Dearing flogged the usual bromides: that Siki trained on alcohol and left trails of broken skulls in his wake—that, "only a step removed from the jungle where his ancestors were of the tribes not the least easy to subdue," he was "the man to prove that the Darwinian theory is not a myth."[53] The paper even improved upon the Weehawken ferry incident, having Siki donate one hundred dollar bills, "throwing the money into the air and watching the passengers scramble for it."[54] Get your seats early, the paper warned. Even though promoter Billy Haack had upped ticket prices, the bout might sell out.

When Siki and Levy arrived twelve hours ahead of schedule that Friday, at 10:00 P.M., promoter Haack dispatched a "welcoming delegation" to escort Siki to Beale Street and a weary Levy to his whites-only hotel, the Chisca. He'd have been better advised to see his meal ticket to bed. As word spread, gangs of curious revelers trailed Siki. Ultimately they steered him to a theater, where the boxer startled patrons at a midnight show, mounting the stage. Then he went off to bed. End of story. The morning paper made his night out sound tame enough. By Sunday, however, beneath the headline "Siki Cavorts Along Beale Ave," Dearing was enjoining readers,

> Conjure a Mississippi plantation Negro from off a delta farm, black as the shades of night, small-headed, thick-lipped, flat-nosed. Imagine him receiving the adulation of France and of the effete East. Picture him monocled—but clinging to galluses—dressed in the latest extreme style, supplied with money and followed by an admiring crowd of members of his own race. The composite is a sketch of Siki.[55]

Sure. Except that Dearing hadn't laid eyes on him yet. Hearsay had supplied the "triumphal march through the Negro district," a "joyous party" that "gathered recruits along the way," swelling its euphoria until Siki escaped at 3:00 A.M. Though the next morning Siki dutifully skipped rope for two rounds, shadowboxed two more, punched the heavy bag, and sparred two rounds against black lightweight Young Joe Gans, Dearing was soon embroidering Siki's adventures yet further, retailing an escapade in which, chafing at restraint, he'd turned upon two burly handlers sent by Haack to keep him out of trouble, thrashing them. On Sunday Siki supposedly "jumped" and "beat... up" a fresh set of keepers so he might again "parade the avenue."[56] It wasn't until Wednesday that Dearing supplied a final prop, that bunch of bananas so dear to Fleischer's heart—which the savage Battler "donated... to a bewildered but enthusiastic public."[57] Why Siki did so, he didn't speculate. He didn't say a word about Siki being hauled before a facetious judge to sing "Yes, We Have No Bananas."

The writers might structure Siki's sojourn in Memphis as a farce, but it might more appropriately have been framed as social realism. The black boxer's initial dose of sobering reality came on his first night in town, when he discovered that Battling Siki might be a worldwide celebrity but was unfit to sleep in a downtown hotel. Then on fight night, January 14, the evening's entertainment at the Southern Athletic Club began with a "battle royal,"a dozen blindfolded young blacks in the ring at once, throwing haymakers at any sound they heard. Two battered survivors then fought a conventional bout, to a draw.[58] When Siki himself finally appeared, a thunderous ovation from "the Beale Avenue forces" greeted him. He craned his neck to survey the scene. The crowd, Dearing wrote, "filled the arena, seats, aisles and rafters and flowed out through the doorways to a huge gathering on the outside."[59] Fans besieged the arena. More than two thousand held tickets, and another thousand tried to crash the gate, blocking legitimate ducat-holders, forcing Haack to offer refunds.[60] Levy himself "almost came to blows" with one patron, an undertaker, who refused to show his ticket.[61]

Siki's opponent, "Young Norfolk," a left-handed New Orleans heavyweight who outweighed him by twenty-two pounds, had won a major victory in his last Memphis bout, knocking out George Godfrey in the sixth round.[62] In training sessions, Young Norfolk had seemed fast and hard-hitting, but markedly apprehensive. He might have the stuff to beat Siki, but he'd have to make himself believe he did.[63] The New Orleans boxer started warily, keeping his distance from the powerful smaller man. Untutored against southpaws, Siki at first pawed with his jab, looking for an opening for his right. But when the bell rang for the second, he went after Young Norfolk, leading with his right, then launching hooks. By round's end, he'd backed his foe into a corner where he "tore in with lefts and rights and Young Norfolk flopped to the floor." Somehow he struggled to his feet by the count of nine, whereupon Siki strode to his corner, gloves raised, thinking he'd won by knockout. The bell came, Dearing relates, as his "excited manager was making him comprehend that he was to continue."[64] In the third, Young Norfolk fought gamely back, tossing punches at the crouching Siki, who "all but sat on the floor at times," landing one flush atop his skull that pitched Siki to the canvas. The knockdown was disallowed. The fourth ended with Siki battering his foe's head, leaving him "tottering on his feet," hands at his sides. But instead of ending things, Dearing whines, Siki "held him against the ropes and punched him tenderly, with blows that wouldn't have awakened a sleeping babe... All the while Siki was smiling at the crowd and waving one free hand to indicate that he was enjoying himself, or as fresh as he was before— or something." When Siki rushed out in the sixth intent on giving the crowd the knockout they clamored for, Young Norfolk caught him with a right, sending him sprawling again. Siki scrambled to his feet before Referee Haack (yes, the fight's promoter) could count, and tore afer his rival. By round's end Siki was "chasing him about the ring, swinging wildly, but landing hard punches."[65] The decision went to Siki. By the time he'd changed into street clothes, Beale Street's celebration was under way. He went to join the party, a beautiful fair-skinned woman named Lillian on his arm.

With his next fight days away, Siki should have caught the morning train. He didn't. The *Commercial Appeal* said he left on January 16—then recanted, hinting the unruly boxer had run amok. When Dearing ran down Levy, he granted he hadn't seen Siki. But Siki phoned daily. He was hardly "missing." He was just off enjoying himself while Levy tried to finalize deals for fights in Omaha and Ontario. The reporter hinted another bout was in the offing too, in Hot Springs, Arkansas, the vice haven to which New York mobster Owney Madden would later "retire."[66] But Haack wasn't buying Levy's story. Quietly amusing himself, like hell! "For three days" Haack had "lived in fear that the Singular Senegalese might escape, elope, or do something that might prevent the bout Monday night."[67] Wait a minute! "Elope"? Not get himself shot or drink himself to death? "Elope"? For once, they had the story right—as the sequel would show.

By January 18, Siki was on a New Orleans train, to face black heavyweight Battling Owens, erstwhile sparring partner of Dempsey and Harry Wills. In 1920 Owens had fought Jack Johnson inside Fort Levenworth Prison, where Johnson served his term for violation of the Mann Act.[68] At his declared weight of 218, he had a 40-pound edge over Siki. But his real weight was more like 230—and even Siki's 178 was misleading. In top shape, at 170, Siki would have given away 60 pounds. If the Taylor and Young Norfolk matches had seemed ill-advised, this one seemed insane. Owens was a rough customer in the clinches and could wade through Siki's hardest blows.

Siki had other things on his mind. The woman who'd left the Memphis arena on his arm was Lillian Warner (or Werner, as she at times spelled it), the daughter of boardinghouse keeper Ella Warner, at whose establishment Haack's minions had installed Siki in the wee hours January 11. Lillian, a few years older than Siki, with dark hair and eyes that set off her fair skin, accompanied Siki on the train to New Orleans. The wild-man-on-the-loose tales appearing in the papers were almost laughable. Siki hadn't disappeared. He was in his hotel room with Lillian.

Siki did show up at the New Orleans Coliseum for a press conference, training show, and weigh-in. After the exhibition, at Marullo's gym, Levy worked the war hero angle, getting Siki to display shrapnel and saber scars. He rebutted the simple-minded savage nonsense. Siki, gifted at languages, he said, spoke fluent Turkish, German, Spanish, Italian, Sudanese, Dutch, Arabian, Senegalese (*sic*), English, and French. "Siki speaks certain parts of the American language," Dearing observed sardonically, "well, fluently. He can carry on a halting conversation without falling back to the part he speaks fluently."[69] In other words, he cusses like a native. Then Levy told a zinger: Siki had "been confined to his room," except to do road work and go to the gym.[70]

The *Times-Picayune*'s William McG. Keefe thought Siki must have ordered some unique room service. He came into the ring, Keefe wrote, looking "either half drunk or still dizzy from the effects of a 'big night' before." Curiously, though Keefe gave Siki credit for being "a crafty, fast, and danger-ous fighter with as keen and rapidly working a mind as almost any... in the game," his description of Siki in the ring made him sound like an extra from a Tarzan film (six had already appeared, the most recent in 1921). "In much the way his forefathers must have danced to the moon for the satisfaction of some voodoo doctor," Keefe urged, "Battling Siki from Senegal of Africa twisted, squirmed, fought, and grimaced for fifteen rounds."[71] He had Siki coming out of his corner knock-kneed, "doing a body dance," squatting on his haunches, and bobbing like a cork as Owens tried vainly to slug his rubber-limbed rival. Siki spun backward like a top, he said, blocking punches behind his back, tossing "a backhand pivot blow," pirouetting like a dervish, and "jump[ing] up like a cat, swinging a scythe-like left hook."

This was old stuff—recast to fit a new "negrophilia."[72] Siki likely hadn't read *Renseignements sur l'Afrique centrale et sur une nation de Niam-Niam ou 'hommes à queues' qui s'y trouverait, d'après les nègres de Soudan* (Information concerning Central Africa and a nation of Niam-Niam or "men with tails" who are found there, according to the blacks of the Sudan), but he'd suffered many weary jokes about Africans being half monkey, half cannibal, newly descended naked from the palm trees. "First of all," Siki told *L'Auto* in 1922, "I'm not a cannibal. Certain newspapers interview me and have me speaking *petit nègre* [pidgin]. I speak and I write French like the average French person. I am a son of France and proud to be Senegalese, happy to be black."[73] Nor had he likely read Joseph Arthur de Gobineau's *Essai sur l'inégalité des races humaines* (Essay on the inequality of the human races), which labeled the *mélanienne* the most animalistic race, marked by ardent "loins," paltry intellect, and lustfulness of "an often terrible intensity," but he knew what the crowd, with a "terrible intensity" of its own, gawked at him expecting to see.[74] Nor did Siki need to read the comments of a white missionary in 1835, who said attempting Zulu women's dances "would cause a European female to go upon crutches for the remainder of her life" to know people imagined his body to be of India rubber elasticity. Nor did Siki need to read the libels of Lord Baden Powell, founder of the Boy Scouts, about the "stupid inertness of the puzzled Negro," to know people expected him to be half imbecile, half child.[75]

Keefe says Siki came out in round one "strutting out proudly and ducking like a fighting cock." At one point he pretended to point out something in the crowd, then nailed Owens with a hook. As Owens pursued him, Siki "backed or twisted away, blocking well, suddenly stooping in under Owens's leads," firing two-handed counters.[76] In round two, when Owens pushed Siki to the canvas, he jumped up and landed a stunning left-hand swing. Then, presaging Muhammad Ali, he went passive, "blocked, twisted, turned, and danced," trying to lure Owens into punching himself out. In the third, Siki's "whirlwind" attack bloodied his hulking foe. Twice, breaking from clinches, he backhanded Owens (a pet trick of Harry Greb's—nowadays illegal). With the crowd on his side, Siki goaded the hometown boxer into opening up and "cleverly parried" Owens's misses. Keefe describes Siki "dancing about like a monkey,"[77] mocking and confusing his rival[78]—drawing a caution from the referee. Owens answered with "vicious" tactics, holding and hitting as Siki covered up, rabbit-punching his neck. In the late rounds Siki pantomimed the size discrepancy to the crowd, as if to say, I'm doing my best against this elephant, but don't expect too much! In the eleventh, he jumped on Owens "like a wild cat," hurting him so badly that "had [Owens] not been such a giant in physique" he'd have gone down. At the final bell, the crowd cheered the smaller man. His mouth "cut and bleeding," eyes "puffed," he'd matched his equally bloodied rival blow for blow, winning another moral victory—as he lost another decision.

Cash-poor African American papers often lifted out-of-town stories from white papers, spinning the facts to fit their own ends. For this fight, the *Chicago Defender* borrowed virtually every blow, twist, and pirouette from the *Times-Picayune,* yet recast them as suggesting innate superiority, not innate monstrosity. As Miller notes, Africanist discourse has a history of "dual, polarized evaluations."[79] The *Defender* dropped Keefe's "voodoo doctor" lead, linking Owens instead to Jack Johnson, and stressing the weight disparity. It dropped Keefe's tagging of the bout as "clownish," his aspersions to the "grotesque antics of the Senegalese," and his assertion: "Siki, of course, doesn't think he's clowning. It's his way of fighting." One thing it kept, however, was Keefe's avowal, "And he certainly has many tricks, twists, and turns... never before... seen in a New Orleans ring."[80] The *Defender's* editing offers a classic example of how blacks had to make race work in the 1920s. To be included at all in representations of ring heroism, they must recast to their advantage the language of race, giving a different spin to its terms. In this case, Siki's exotic "twists and turns" are played up— but made to suggest natural grace and agility, not grotesque clowning. One day, another black boxer, Muhammad Ali, would teach the world to see taunting, trickery, and dancing as part of his ring craft and personal magic, but that day was far in the future.

If Siki arrived in the arena much the worse for carousing, he left it, Cliff Abbo implied in *Ring Magazine,* for more of the same. The Latin Quarter "had a particular appeal for the wild man from Senegal. He was missing for some five days and reported everywhere but the right place."[81] Soon papers all over the country were headlining "Siki Disappears Again." They might instead have bannered, "Lonely Stranger Falls in Love," for that was what really happened. By July, they'd be headlining exactly that—and adding "with a white woman."

Rings in My Nose, Rings in My Ears

A rigid-faced black man in topcoat, jacket, tie, and homburg squints toward the camera, as a scowling, square-jawed white man, cap low over his eyes, grips his elbow. His mouth half open, the white man seems about to say, "I've got him. Clear a path so I can drag him away." Behind him stands another, in bow tie and felt hat, with lowered brows and a puffy, middle-aged face, like a pre-prohibition saloonkeeper mounting guard over the free lunch. The *Minneapolis Morning Tribune's* caption reads:

> Billy B. Hoke, matchmaker of the Hennepin County Boxing Club, evidently is taking no chances on Battling Siki running out of his fight with Joe Lohman at the Kenwood Armory tonight. The *Tribune* photographer snapped Hoke holding Siki by the arm when the Senegalese pugilist arrived in Minneapolis Wednesday morning. Standing between Hoke and Siki is Tom Gallagher, veteran Minneapolis detective, who

went to the station expecting to see a wild-eyed Negro hop off the rattler.[82]

The ex-champion suffered with resignation being greeted like an escaped felon. He told George A. Barton, an ex-pugilist turned journalist who was slated to referee the bout, "I am not wild and crazy like some of the newspaper men say. I drink some wine and like to play but I am not guilty of many of the things said about me. I am what my manager calls—what—you—call-'em? Oh yes, good copy for the newspapers and the writers have much fun with me."[83] Instead of someone resembling a "half-brother of the 'Wild Man of Borneo' featured for so many years by the late P. T. Barnum," Barton observed, Siki was smiling, soft-spoken, and well mannered.

Hoke had staged his bit of hokum to scare up publicity. To turn a dime he needed to sell out the bandbox arena where Siki would battle Toledo's leading light-heavy. This stunt with the city detective might have been just the ticket. If only the visiting wildman had made as if to take a poke at somebody! Or taken off running, coattails flying, at the sight of the gumshoe. That would make a great photo: "Wild man on the run, keepers in pursuit." Instead, all Hoke's cameraman got was that firm hand grasping a crooked elbow, that stiff-faced look of... was it bewilderment, indignation?

To stir up ticket sales, Siki staged an exhibition at Jimmy Potts's gym, where onlookers gasped as he skipped lightly around the ring, muscles rippling, "lashing out with both fists at an imaginary foe."[84] The "railbirds" expected a "wild-eyed dinge leaping from ringpost to ringpost or flying around the gymnasium on traveling rings," but Siki was neither unschooled nor crazy. Many rushed out to get down bets on him. Once three to two for Lohman, by Thursday the odds were even. "While he isn't a [Tom] Gibbons for speed and cleverness," noted Barton, "yet there is a certain amount of grace in Siki's movements that convinces one that he is not a clown."

It had been the same in Chicago. He'd arrived there with no fanfare, bushy locks hidden under a hat, had strolled Lincoln Park peacefully until a cry had rung out, "Hey! There goes Battling Siki!" and a shouting crowd pursued him. They'd jammed the sidewalks outside Kid Howard's gym in the Loop, where Siki held an exhibition, making a bigger racket than the thrill-seekers outside the courthouse where "boy killers" Richard Loeb and Nathan Leopold were on trial for murder. That night, in the dining room of the Hotel Vincennes, a gang of sportswriters called Siki to their table. A "wild night of pleasure" ensued. For once, the writers telling tsk-tsk tales about his late-night prowl knew what they were talking about. They'd been drinking right alongside him.[85] Siki slept off his folly, ate a late breakfast, and headed over to "the World's Greatest Weekly" on Indiana Avenue. Chicago *Defender* editors were amazed to meet, instead of a preposterous man-beast, a soft-spoken, articulate (in passable English) fellow, quick to smile, patient under abuse. Siki had, Juli Jones wrote, no illusions about his treatment in the United States: "He left his dear home in France to get the needed American experience more than the American dollar. He is paying an awful price for it and he knows it." European boxers usually got "setups" when they first arrived. Instead, promoters had "done all in their power... to get Siki murdered." He'd gone in against Kid Norfolk, "by far the best light heavyweight in the world,"on little training, yet astonished those who expected to see him put "to sleep for a week." Since then he'd been fed a steady diet of huge heavyweights, on scant training.[86]

As he and Siki strolled off to the Howard arcade, Jones heard more candid imputations. "Nobody's fool," he mused, "Siki knows money is being made off his ability as a fighter, but feels he is not getting all that he should out of the earnings." Levy was cutting corners on training expenses, overmatching him. Siki wouldn't put up with it forever: "He... said that he had learned a good deal about our way of fighting; that when he came again, which would be soon, ... he would pay everybody off for thinking him a joke." He condemned the way the newsmen wrote about him. He resented having his identity travestied. He had told one white journalist, "You put rings in my nose, rings in my ears—I give you some news and you write much that is wrong and in the wrong way too." Nor was he slow to draw a political moral: "You got a statue in New York, Liberty you call it—hah. It mean nothing. No freedom here—no, no, no—not for you—me."[87]

Siki said he'd soon return to France, find a new manager, and regroup for a second try at the American prize ring. His broken record had been stuck on "that dear France" for so long American journalists had made it a running joke. But something kept him in America—and it wasn't only the money he was making. He might miss France—but the France he longed for was the one before "*le affaire Siki.*" If it had once accepted him, it had also nearly run him out of boxing. He knew that if he wanted another title shot he'd have to go to school, at age twenty-seven, to master what Kid Norfolk had learned over hundreds of fights—the ins and outs of the "American style of milling." And what Norfolk knew hadn't him gotten anywhere near a title bout—though Norfolk and Battling McCreary were as tough as any top white light-heavyweight. What Siki was living now might be the whole story, the best boxing would ever offer him: a bizarre notoriety that sold tickets, but allowed hucksters to live off the slander of his name, and the public vicariously to feed off a racial pipe dream.

After the interview, Siki posed for a photo with the *Defender* staff. In it, they stand rigid, dazzled by the bright sun, eyes blank, emotions shut down against the intrusion of the camera eye. Siki, however, glares into the camera lens as if into an enemy's viscera. In wool overcoat, white shirt, tie, porkpie hat, the ghost of a smile on his lips, he rests one hand on a beaming five-year-old boy's shoulder. Hips turned, shoulders square, he looks every inch the powerful athlete, even through a heavy coat. He seems intense, wound tight as a spring. Jones had asked Siki if it was true that he could not be managed and Siki had retorted "no, I cannot"—not "from the American way of thinking." He'd never "be managed in that way." He had "been his own man—succeeded in his way." Why should he change now? He'd return to Europe in a few months, see his son, take up his career from there, toughened by the lessons he'd learned in America. After all the "wild, ridiculous stories" written about him, Jones commented, "far beyond the bounds of reason," it was easy to forget how "game" Siki had been against America's best fighters. He ought to get credit for guts and ambition. Instead he endured derision. "One would think," Jones mused, "that the pleasant little Siki was the 'bad man from Borneo' at large."[88]

At least Siki's bad name paid well. At the Minneapolis armory, ticket agents turned away thousands. His opponent for the no-decision bout, Joe Lohman, a rising Toledo light-heavyweight who would ultimately face world champions Battling Lewinsky, Jack Delaney, Tommy Loughran (twice), and Paul Berlenbach, showed no fear of the muscular African. For once Siki's rival was the aggressor, mounting "rushes" that the African turned away with "a fair defense."[89] The *St. Paul Pioneer Press* said Siki fought most of the way in second gear. He had Lohman in trouble more than once with left hooks and right swings, but let him recover. He ignored low blows and rabbit-punches, patting the referee's shoulder as if to say "those little things are apt to happen." The *Cleveland Gazette* felt Siki might have won at any time, but for a strange lethargy. In the tenth, when Lohman slipped and fell, he hauled him to his feet, laughing off the storm of hooks with which his rival reciprocated.[90] "Again," noted the *Pioneer Press*, "his broad grin indicated that everybody was having a fine time and he didn't want Lohman to feel the least bit embarrassed over the incident." The *Pioneer Press* gave Lohman the win.[91] The *Defender* gave it to Siki, ten rounds to six. Referee George Barton, in the *Minneapolis Tribune,* called Siki "the harder puncher," noting "three times during the bout the Senegalese sent his white rival staggering across the ring."[92] Barton, scoring the no-decision bout unofficially for the *Tribune,* had Lohman ahead, but had Siki winning going into the final rounds. Had Siki taken any of the last three rounds, he'd have won on Barton's card.

Charmed by Siki's "ready smile" and "willingness to give and take," the fans cheered him as a "thorough showman." He'd carried the fight and slipped punches well. Lohman's efforts to hurt him brought only "a look of tolerant amusement."[93] Barton praised Siki's "natural fighting ability," yet urged, "The Senegalese boxer's peculiar ring tactics gave the spectators many laughs. At times he would bob almost to the floor, and by means of clever head-slipping would make Lohman miss.... On other occasions he hopped and jumped around the ring for all the world like a huge chimpanzee and while leaping would lash out with both fists."[94] The two-fisted airborne combinations occurred in Barton's imagination. Siki had no talent for levitation.

By Saturday, February 2, his modest purse in his pocket (the fight grossed only $8,000, despite the sellout), Siki was back in Chicago, where he cabled money to Lijntje and Louis Jr. Reporters ran across him at the Dreamland Café, planting a kiss on the flustered owner's cheek. "This is simply a Frenchman's greeting,... the same to them as our handshake," the *Defender* explained.[95] It didn't need to explain what fueled Siki's affection: he was on a bender. He toured South Side clubs minutes ahead of his manager. It became a joke: "Yeah, he was here. Just left." Once inebriated, Siki acted as if he hadn't an enemy on the planet, beaming at everyone who thumped him on the back. He had "plenty of money and gave a good deal away." Reporters found him at the Entertainers, "where he was having a 'lil two-step' with a high brown." Lilian Werner? Maybe. One friend placed her in Chicago with Siki. When someone threw a spotlight on them, Siki, "with a little persuasion, ... did an old-fashioned Senegalese tribal dance." Why not? I'm not ashamed to be an African, he had told the *Defender.*

By morning, Levy had reclaimed his wayward warrior and bundled him aboard a train for Toledo, searching for bouts. Levy also pursued a Chicago bout and one in Canada, but when those schemes failed he took his boxer east—to Rochester, New York, to face Alabama heavyweight Joe White, whose race matched his name.[96] Again a surreal welcome awaited. Promoter Tommy Bresnahan had detectives posted at the station, supposedly to keep Siki from mischief—to trail him everywhere and mount guard at his training site (Nick's gym on North Clinton Avenue) and at his hotel (on Industrial Avenue). Fans, eager to see the "cave man" chased Siki down the street, swarmed the tiny gym, perched on boxes, chairs, radiators, straining for a glimpse.[97] Levy hadn't paid for sparring partners, but one volunteer came forward, black boxer LeRoy Hardin, ironically styled "Tommy Burns' new hope."[98] Siki, "all muscle and bone," with slender legs and brawny shoulders evocative of black marvel Sam Langford, awed onlookers—who goaded Hardin, "Aw come on! He's half your size!"[99]

The same throngs awaited when Siki showed up on Thursday, as Bresnahan stood by counting the quarters he'd extracted at the door. What's up? Siki asked. They don't expect me to work out on the day of the fight, do they? "Day of the fight?" Bresnahan roared. "You fight tomorrow!" Siki stared. "Fish Day!" Bresnahan cried. "Vous Comprendez? Fish Day?"

Siki laughed—and changed into boxing togs. The *Democrat and Chronicle* catalogued his apparel: a watch, bracelets, cane, clothing, perfume bottle—but not, it ruefully noted, "a monocle."[100] Sigh! Wasn't that too part of the advertised spectacle? Their prefight caricature showed a black boxer with a shaggy gorilla head as big as his torso, his long arms encircling a white boxer, planting a kiss on his cheek. The next night, as the prelims wore down, Bresnahan discovered Siki was nowhere in the arena. Levy had no clue where he was. Frantic, he sent someone racing to the hotel—where, sure enough, the boxer patiently awaited a ride to the arena.[101] So much for Bresnahan's detectives!

Though he got there just ten minutes before the bell, Siki stormed out intent on dismembering his strapping rival (White weighed in at 197 to Siki's 177). With barely a minute gone, he drove White to his corner and had him staggering "like a drunken man," battering his face, tumbling him through the twines. White barely climbed back in to beat the count. In the second and third, Siki was all over him again, smashing left swings and hooks, dropping White twice, leaving him "bleeding profusely" from a badly split lip. White stalled through the middle rounds, grabbing Siki with one hand, swinging hooks with the other. Siki grinned and waved off the fouls. In the tenth, White took another pasting. Siki easily got the decision.[102]

He'd proved, the Rochester paper said, he knew "more about the fighting game than he has been given credit for." Yet it added, "Siki's peculiar fighting stance, his monkeylike crouches and his tigerlike springs quickly found favor with the crowd. He drew numerous laughs." The radical crouch and leaping blows, in fact, were more Carpentier's style than Siki's. Yet no one wrote of Carpentier, "And the Orchid Man's odd monkeylike crouches and tigerlike springs drew numerous laughs." The *Defender,* despite hearing Siki, a week before, vent his spleen at America's distortion of his identity, played changes on the same tired tune, copying the Rochester paper verbatim, even the "monkeylike crouches" and "tigerlike springs."[103] Why not? Readers loved it.

By Tuesday, February 12, Siki was headed to Columbus, where he'd face another heavyweight, Dempsey sparring partner Tut Jackson. Harry Wills had knocked him out in April 1922. In 1923, John Lester Johnson, Kid Norfolk, Carl Morris, and Bill Tate had floored him. He'd lost decisions too. What black fighter hadn't? But Jackson had rung up six knockouts in 1923, and over his career had knocked out some of the best, including ex-middleweight champ Frank Mantel, uncrowned champ Jeff Smith, Joe Lohman, Battling Owens, even the great Sam Langford. Columbus went fight-mad. Fans thronged Mike O'Rourke's gym an hour before Siki's arrival, shoving through doors, jamming hallways, harassing employees who "strove to maintain order." A squad of police charged to clear a path for Siki to the door. Once inside, catching sight of his rival, he smiled, extended his hands, and said, "'Good luck, Keed."[104]

Luck may not have been strictly necessary. The *Columbus Dispatch* said Siki visited "several sporting centers" (speakeasies) on the eve of the bout, attired like "a native boulevardier of Paris," surprising patrons by conversing "quite well in broken English."[105] Levy must have asked Jackson to "ease up," for he did little more than stick his jab, only rarely uncorking his powerful right, as Siki, his swings missing by "feet," moved at half-speed, clinching, holding. Babe Adams of the *Dispatch* described him as "slow and deliberate," stooping low to look Tut over, searching an opening. At first, the sell-out crowd at Fort Hays Arena "stayed in a talkative, keenly interested mood."[106] By the eighth round, however, they were lustily booing—until finally Jackson stepped up the pace, showing enough pugnacity to gain the newspaper decision.

Afterward, his reputation further tarnished, Siki boarded a train for a tryst with a rangy, Bible-thumping white heavyweight from Michigan who outweighed him by fifteen pounds. Homer Smith had fought ninety-four matches, losing only six (with forty-five no-decision bouts). He'd scored thirty-five knockouts and only been counted out twice, by the two top heavyweights of the era, Jack Dempsey and Harry Wills. When he faced Dempsey in 1918, the year Dempsey won the title, the two were "rated about equal."[107]

Levy had tried to set up the bout for Buffalo or Toronto, but towns willing to host potential racial carnage were scarcer than politicians ready to denounce the Ku Klux Klan (that year neither political convention did). City after city turned it down. In the wake of Jack Johnson's tumultuous career, the nation was wary of interracial contests. That very week wealthy summer residents in Newport, Rhode Island, had petitioned their aldermen to block a bout between Dempsey and Wills. If even the pious, innocuous Wills had a hard time getting bouts with whites, how much more reluctant might local officials be to risk the scandalous, outspoken Siki? Levy at last decided to take his bout clear off the North American continent—to Cuba.

CHAPTER NINE

"I No Fight"

I'm Tired of His Nonsense

On February 21, 1924, as they had for days now, a jostling throng jammed the Havana dock, craning necks to scan the railings of the one-stack ferry *Governor Cobb* arriving from Key West. *La Discussion* had run a banner headline: "The Boxer Battling Siki Arrives Today at Four."[1] But though N. B. Forest, Grand Dragon of the Ku Klux Klan, had already descended the gangway, the freakish fighter who'd savaged Carpentier hadn't yet appeared, to the *fanáticos*' profound regret. Havana was in the mood for things grotesque. On Sunday, *Grito de Baire* revelers would jam the streets.[2] *Carnivale* would follow a week later. Boxing shows played big parts in both, as did freak shows. The *Havana Post,* for example, promoted the season opening of Havana Park with a photo of its chief attraction, the "Seal-Woman," a poodle-haired lady flaunting arms withered to stumps, hands twisted into flippers.[3] With Siki, the public got double satisfaction—a bloodbath and a freak show at once.

The *fanáticos* thought they had picked Siki out leaning over the ornate railings of the upper deck beside a blonde woman. They watched American tourists, surprised at the fanfare, lug hand grips down the ramp. Just a hundred miles from Key West, the resort city tempted many to enjoy a single night's revelry and slip back the next day. The smart set had been steaming over for the last ten years, ever since the engineering miracle of the railroad bridge spanning open ocean had linked Key West to the mainland. Down the ramp came Habañeros, too, prominent citizens like José Pérez Hernández and Ana Pérez Abreu. The crowd waited impatiently for them to clear out and make room for the man they really wanted to see, the savage Senegalese who'd conquered Carpentier.[4]

Havana was passionate about boxing as about little else. Bouts involving Cuban light-heavyweight champ Santiago Esparraguera, middleweight Felio Rodriguez, or featherweights Angel Diaz and Carlos Fraga drew full-page coverage. Boxing mania had begun nine years before when Jack Johnson, a fugitive from America's racial apartheid, had lost his heavyweight crown in twenty-six broiling rounds to Jess Willard at Havana's Oriente Race Track. Now Havana would host another mixed-race spectacle—not a title fight, alas—but Battling Siki brought his own brand of drama. His intended foe, Homer Smith, hadn't yet arrived. He was busy fighting Johnson in Montreal. In the meantime, *fanáticos* dreamed of a Cuban fighter getting a shot at international fame. They'd followed with passionate fervor the Latin hero Luis Angel Firpo's battle with Dempsey the summer before, and now rumors were flying that Esparraguera would fight Battling Siki.

On the ferry dock, they cross-examined disembarking American passengers. Yes, they'd heard Siki was aboard, but he had never appeared on deck. They too longed for a glimpse of him. They'd heard he was ill. Then all at once down the gangway, arm in arm, came smiling manager Bob Levy and slick promoter George Lawrence, trailed by a small Latin man, a stocky black man with close-cropped hair, and a shaggy-haired black man arm-in-arm with a smiling blonde. Newsmen ditched cigarettes, pulled out notebooks, and lobbed questions. Mostly they were of the what-mayhem-has-your-wild-man-been-up-to-lately variety. Lawrence had an answer primed: What's he been up to? Why, if we told you, you wouldn't believe it. He got arrested again. How? Why, he was walking along, by the Key West ferry dock—when what did he see but a couple of guys in ragged clothes—blacker than himself. He's so good-hearted, he grabs those guys and drags them up the street. Couldn't stand to see them looking down in the mouth! Went looking for the nearest tailor shop. And meantime, folks of his own color were running after him. The shouting crowd got bigger and bigger. Soon it begins to look like a riot. Somebody calls a paddy wagon. They collar Siki, who's trying to explain. But of course he can hardly speak English. The cops arrest him. Meanwhile, Bob and I are running all over town looking for him. Finally Bob has the idea to check the police station And sure enough, that's where he is—but by the time we spring him, we've missed our boat.[5]

Great stuff! "Battling Siki's Generous Whim Again Landed Him Behind Bars," the *New York Times* headline cackled the next day. He had "missed a previous boat by reason of getting in jail on charges of creating a disturbance," the story related.[6] The *Times* didn't bother to check its facts. Battling

Siki tales, like all legends, are true by definition. And so the lie comes down to us, mixed with other tales of Siki the wayward *naif.* Of course, it only comes down to us at all because Lawrence couldn't think up anything more original—which for him was rare. Lawrence, Ray Arcel tells us, had a gift for saying whatever it took to turn a buck, and his specialty was conning people to invest in illusory boxing promotions in South American climes.[7]

What, if anything, did happen? If we scan the *Key West Citizen,* we find just two Siki blurbs, both on February 20, one noting, "Battling Siki, who wrested the world light-heavyweight championship from Georges Carpentier, accompanied by his manager and trainer, is in the city for a short stay," and the other, in a column devoted to doings at a chic resort, adding, "Geo. Lawrence and Robert Levy, both of New York City, manager and press agent respectively of Battling Siki, are guests at the Casa Marina." Siki himself stayed in a colored boardinghouse.[8] The *Citizen* noticed no boisterous parade of black men down the street, heard no sirens, saw no club-wielding cops disperse mobs, heard of no former world champion clamped behind bars. Were the *Citizen*'s city desk reporters so inept? No. Battling Siki may have bought somebody a suit. But the rest of the story never occurred— except in the fertile fancy of George Lawrence.

Key West was booming in 1924. It had its canning factory, naval base, fishing fleet, and famous turtle kraal. It had semi-pro baseball, jazz clubs, speakeasies—and nearly full employment, for blacks and whites. Its fight club ran weekend cards matching young men who worked all day in the turtle soup factory or on the shark boats. Its one troubling change had been the advent of the Ku Klux Klan, whose Grand Wizard, N. B. Forrest, that very week hosted a firelit rally. If Siki had felt inclined to lead troops of unruly blacks down the streets, Forrest's visit might have deterred him. But something else would, too. He was sick. He arrived in Cuba suffering from "a cold" that would later prove to be pneumonia.[9]

Two days later, a huge crowd, itchy with anticipation, turned up at Arena Colón, where Santiago Esparraguera, the "idol of the fans," would fight Sergeant Ray Thompson—with Siki in attendance to challenge the winner. The crowd, mistaking light-heavyweight Battling Thomas for Siki, cheered so loud and long that Thomas finally gave up and stood and waved his hat.[10] Siki himself never showed. He was flat on his back, sick with pneumonia.

The *New York Times* insisted he'd tumbled down his boardinghouse steps, glassy-eyed and incoherent with alcohol, staggering to the street, where passing cops caught him and hauled him to bed. Other papers improved the tale, saying he'd fallen from a window or balcony. Days later, the *Times* divulged Siki was suffering not from alcohol poisoning but "pleurisy."[11] Eventually Levy too set the record straight. Siki hadn't fallen from any balcony. He'd simply collapsed from fever.[12] Siki's doctor, Benigno Sousa, labeled his condition "serious."[13] A *Havana Post* reporter saw him carried out on a stretcher like a dying man from his boardinghouse at 34 Zulueta Street, whispering Levy's name as a crowd gaped. *La Discussion* said Siki's health worsened the following days.[14]

One struggles to fathom how Levy, holed up at the Pasaje Hotel, could allow his meal ticket to arrive at death's door. The *Post* explains Levy's negligence by saying he got an urgent wire saying his wife, in New York, was gravely ill. Though a "business transaction" had made him miss the boat the day before, he'd catch the one on February 28—but his wife must have gotten better (or may never have been ill in the first place), for a week later he was still in Havana. Levy, the *Post* urged, had "spared no expense" to put Siki in a private clinic as he faced the crisis that would come "within the next few days."[15] But why wait so long? Siki had been deathly ill for six days. Where, for that matter, was Lillian Warner? Her friend, Mrs. George Kinelle, later said she went with Siki to Havana.

On Friday, February 29, "not much improved," Siki was "delirious most of the time," but by March 2, as carnival rhythms filled the streets, he'd won his walking papers.[16] Promoters had canceled his bout with Esparraguera, who, on March 8, instead faced Battling Thomas. Though Levy and Lawrence insisted Siki wouldn't be out of the hospital for two weeks, in fact he and a gang of pals turned up to see Thomas get knocked out in the fifth.[17] Again and again, Siki "rose to his feet responding to the incessant shouts of 'Hooray for Siki.'"[18] By morning, caught up in the glee of carnival, he was riding around in a touring car, arms full of roses, waving a French flag. He booked a taxi for the night and, on a happy whim, joined the parade from Central Park to the Malecon along the Prado. To take part, you just wedged your car into the procession.[19] He threw so much money around that he wound up short when the time came to pay the eighteen-dollar taxi fare—a stunt that earned a thirty-one-dollar fine.[20] Cubans showered Siki with attention while he gave Levy and Lawrence "the cold shoulder," going around with "unscrupulous parties"—which probably meant gamblers. By 1924 Havana was already a haven for American gangsters.[21]

He also had new cauliflower pals. He'd started training at the Stadium de Marina, in the center of town, delighting *fanáticos* who paid forty centavos admission by going six fast rounds against Black Bill, a lightweight. The next day he went six rounds with a pair of light-heavyweights.[22] Levy, nervous about Siki's new pals, shifted his training to the Cuban Lawn Tennis Club, outside town (where Firpo and Johnson had trained). Siki, far from ready for a bout, was content to survive on admission fees from training sessions—which rankled Lawrence and Levy, who wanted to rush him into a headline match.[23] He put them off. On March 25, he went to the Stadium de Marina to second a fighter in the first preliminary—but was kicked out of the ring.[24] Cuba was strict about insisting that cornermen hold official commission licenses.

Then, two nights later, at a late-night dive, Siki said the wrong thing to a stevedore and chose a bad moment to turn his head. Twenty-six-year-old Miguel Chacon Sariol promptly cracked open the back of his skull with a sugar bowl. Six stitches closed the gash.[25] The American papers played up the episode as another of Siki's irrational rages, but the row may have been political. Within days dockers would close down the port of Havana in a massive general strike. Cuban papers ignored the incident. They'd seen worse brawls between outsiders and Cubans. Weeks before in Santiago de Cuba drunken American marines, after "creating scandals in the hotels and parks," had attacked the chief of police himself and had to be dispersed by pistol-wielding soldiers.[26]

If Siki had any idea of getting back in shape quickly, those stitches settled the issue. They were the last straw for Papa Bob Levy, too. He kept eyeing the *Post*'s baseball columns and the ferry schedule to Key West. His beloved Giants were barnstorming the American South with the White Sox. On March 31 they'd play in Orlando. On April 1, they'd be in Jacksonville, on April 2 in Augusta. The man who'd brag, up to his death, that he'd never missed opening day at the Polo Grounds had a chance to see his heroes two weeks early. Besides, with the dock strike looming, if he lingered too long, he might miss opening day itself. Lawrence, it seems, had different dreams. The *Post* reported his departure for New York with new protégés in tow: Mexican featherweight Angel Diaz, Spanish heavyweight Andres Balsa, and dancer Miss Sarita Watle, whom he'd promised a place in the Schubert theatricals.[27]

The day Siki got clunked on the head, *La Discussion* said promoter Eddie Roberts had offered Mike McTigue $75,000 to give Siki a title shot in July or August. Paddy Mullins, McTigue's new manager, sweating out a no-decision title defense against Young Stribling in Newark, had said sure, we'll work out details later.[28] But after the Stribling bout, Mullins wanted no part of another tough rival. McTigue had at first fought his standard fight, dodging and skipping away, but then abruptly turned aggressive—and nearly gotten himself killed. Stribling knocked him through the ropes, and though McTigue climbed back in and somehow made it to the final bell, retaining his title, even he admitted he'd really lost.[29]

Bob Levy, meanwhile, was burning up cash with little reward. On April 1, Jack Taylor, who'd beaten Siki at Christmas, arrived to substitute for him against Esparraguera. Levy tried to talk Siki into leaving. Siki said "maybe tomorrow." Finally Levi gave up and left on the twelfth on the liner *Siboney,* tossing a final barb, "I'm tired of his nonsense, and I'm going home. I don't care what becomes of him."[30] Back in New York, Levy found the press in an uproar of delight over Ringling Brothers Barnum and Bailey's latest wonder, a domesticated gorilla from the Gabon jungles named Sultan, pampered by his English mistress in their room at the Hotel McAlpin. Reporters jotted down his every grunt, sketched his every caper, particularly his alleged fascination with pretty females' toes. Levy must have shaken his head over the irony. His own star attraction, from "the jungles of Senegal," had vanished from public view. Yet here they were making a huge fuss about a monkey. Sultan would soon be ringing in the ducats at Madison Square Garden, while Siki languished in Havana. Meanwhile, Frederick W. Wells, a black law student at Columbia University, was trying to face down a boycott by white students and anonymous death threats.[31] Was it any wonder Siki was in no hurry to return?

He showed up for the Taylor / Esparraguera bout in madcap humor, leaping to shout encouragement as his old sparring mate, his cut eye spurting blood, weathered a fierce assault from the Cuban. As Siki gesticulated to Taylor to throw his left the exuberant gesture caught a neighbor in the gut, doubling him up. Cuban police marched Siki away. When he slipped back to his seat, he was again told to leave, or so the *Post* alleged.[32] *La Discussion* saw no such incident. Six days later, the *Post* said Siki, down to his last centavos, cabled Levy to beg forgiveness.[33] When Levy wired money, Siki booked passage on the *Siboney*—in steerage.

He disembarked on Monday, April 28, hoping to slip unrecognized into New York City. Immigration had other ideas. The country, at that moment, was hardening its heart against foreigners. The House had just passed, over bitter Japanese protests, an immigrant exclusion bill aimed at barring non-whites.[34] Ellis Island officials halted Siki at the gates: the country had all the penniless pugilists it needed. Unless this specimen could prove he wasn't "liable to become a public charge," he could go back where he came from. Levy was either preoccupied or inclined to teach his mercurial charge a lesson. Two days passed while Siki cooled his heels in a holding room. Finally, as deportation loomed, Levy turned up with an affidavit vouching for Siki's solvency ($3,000 deposited to his credit in a savings account).[35] Levy drove a stiff bargain, however. He wanted Siki back in the ring immediately. If a gorilla who played with ladies' toes could enrich his handler, so could Siki.

A bout was set for Lexington, Kentucky, May 9, Siki told the special board of inquiry. They signed for his readmission on a six-month visa.

Somehow, he didn't wind up in Kentucky but in Omaha, Nebraska, and not in a boxing ring but a wreck beside the road. An oil truck had smashed into Levy's red roadster. Siki's companions climbed from the car little the worse for wear. They included Levy, who'd been driving; Jose Lombardo, imported from Cuba a few weeks before; Pierre Nicolas, who'd given Siki two of his toughest fights in the south of France in 1913 and 1914; and Ted Derwetter, an erstwhile training partner and factotum. Siki, less lucky than his fellows, lay groaning in pain from broken ribs.[36] He sued Nicholas Oil Company for $75,000, for lost income, costs, and lost opportunities. His tort specified five broken ribs. Two months later they still hadn't healed.[37]

Levy by then was taking his cut from a string of boxers—Davey Abad ("flyweight champion of South America"), Lombardo ("featherweight champion of Panama"), Nicolas ("former French middleweight champion"), and Derwetter (a.k.a. Ted Zegwaard, "light-heavyweight champion of Holland")—but Battling Siki was his real draw.[38] The mishap with the oil truck sidetracked Levy's plans. He had to wait two months before he could work his publicity magic again in Bellaire, Ohio, across the river from Wheeling, West Virginia.

Siki's opponent there, heavyweight Ray Bennett, a handsome, doe-eyed fellow with a receding hairline, spent the early rounds taunting him in unprintable phrases, as Siki, astonished, replied, "Ex-kuse me?" Despite the expletives, Bennett, who outweighed the ex-champ by twenty-seven pounds, dared do no more than gingerly stick out his long left, like a man poking a rowboat away from a pier, keeping his right clamped to his chin, except when he used it to clinch. Siki, meanwhile, exhorted by the fight's promoter (doubling as referee), put on occasional bursts of punching "fast as forked lightning," but seemed to the local paper to pull his punches. Seven thousand fans paid to see the show, the "biggest crowd that ever saw a boxing bout" in the region. Two thousand cars jammed an adjacent parking lot and stretched for miles down two highways, blocking the local streetcar line.[39] The charade drew black fans from all over the region.

One week later, in Manchester, New Hampshire, Siki fought an even more implausible foe, African American heavyweight "Blacksmith" Russell. When Russell doffed his robe, the crowd gasped. He was, said the *Union Leader,* "hog fat." In no mood to hang around in punching range, Russell, whenever Siki tried to open up, skipped inside, pawing and grabbing, once in a while trying to club Siki below the belt (the only evidence he meant to punch at all). Siki, meanwhile, gasping for breath, a "roll of fat around his middle," struggled to pry his arms free from his beefy rival and make this travesty look like a boxing match. Finally, in the seventh, he uncorked a swing that sent Russell flopping like a flounder (had it connected, the *Union Leader* mused, or had air turbulence sucked the blacksmith down?).[40]

As the ex-champion's seconds pulled off his gloves, the crowd was on its feet roaring, glad they'd come, showing no displeasure at the sorry mis-match.[41] You could go out with busted ribs and put on a stinker, against a guy who ought to stick to pounding horseshoes—or throwing them. The fans didn't care. They'd come for a freak show, not a boxing match.

Small and Very Fair

As they waited out the run-up to perhaps the last big match of *notre grand Georges's* splendid career, the French writers had a familiar problem: The reporter must have something to say! Something other than the daily banalities of road work, sit-ups, sparring sessions, lineament rubs, and made-for-publicity avowals. He's in the best shape of his life... he's devel-oped a brand-new punch . . . we've studied our opponent and found a secret weakness.

Besides, to witness the daily banalities you had to take a train to Jamaica, Queens, then switch for Manhasset, Long Island—just to dutifully scribble "best shape of life... new punch... secret weakness"—if you didn't give up and doodle. American papers had been full of tales of the "Orchid Man"—dancing with socialites at the Manhasset Country Club, sparring on Jack Curley's Great Neck estate before starlets and rich men's daughters who'd arrived in chauffeured automobiles. But who in Paris had heard of Mary Eaton, Jane Cowl, or Mrs. Oscar Hammerstein II? Then someone had an idea: *Et Siki?* What about him? He's always good for a story! They piled into a taxi and headed uptown to Grupp's gym. There they found... exactly the scene they'd fled: another sweaty gym, more calisthenics, sparring. The only things missing were the fake "tips" to be fed to the press. But then Bob Levy wasn't there to hand them out.

Siki himself said he was in excellent condition and meant to get serious now: "I want again to become a great champion." They wrote it all down. "Siki Takes Resolutions," "Resumes Training At Last," ran the item in *L'Auto.*[42] Yawn!

But if they'd hung around a while they might have had a real story. Within days, Battling Siki's smiling mug would beam at them from every front page on New York newsstands.

We shift now to the city room of the *New York Sun,* where the news breaks of that other story. Even the reporters must have been cynical at first. You can imagine the dialogue:

"Hey, get a load of this! Battling Siki's gone and gotten married."

"Aw, come on! Who'd marry that gorilla? Besides, ain't he already married?"

"Beats me—but somebody did—and she's white, too!"

"Aw for crying out loud! What do they see in that ape?"

"You don't know? Think about it. What do you get if you add *l-u-s* to the end of his name?"

"Add *l-u-s* to Siki? Beats me. Sikilus?"

"No, not to Siki—to his real name. To Phal. If you add *l-u-s* to Phal."[43]

The city desk editor sends a reporter off at a run. That ugly ape married to a white girl! And for Christ's sake, he already had a kid by another one! It's late to make the final edition, but if they do they'll scoop every paper in town. Nobody will walk past a newsboy without whistling, "This I gotta see! Here, gimme a copy." The *Sun* reporter races to the Municipal Building—where he finds the deputy city clerk John J. McCormack, who performed the ceremony, as well as several who witnessed it. At first nobody recognized the "coal black face" of the groom, in evening coat, waistband, and sash, as he inked his name to a paper asserting he'd never before been married, but when a spark of recognition flared, fifty couples rushed to get a glimpse of the boxer and his bride.[44] Clerks ran to shut the doors before the office was mobbed. As Siki led his lady, in a cloche hat, with an armload of long-stemmed roses, to the deputy clerk's office for the no-frills ritual, word raced ahead: Battling Siki's here! Getting married! To a white girl! Clerks bolted from desks, people gave up places in line to scurry over to gawk.

The *Sun* reporter got his hands on the license and found she was Lillian Warner, thirty years old, of Memphis, Tennessee, and did indeed list her race as "white." "Offering a striking contrast in color," he scribbled, "on account of the Warner woman's fairness."[45] Sweet God, what a story! If only he could beat the deadline! In his hurry, he messed up a few details, giving the bride's father's name as Olie (it appears to be "Ove"), and breaking the curious news (later repeated in nearly every daily) that both bride and groom gave their occupation as "artist" (actually, the form doesn't ask the bride's vocation—and since the handwriting is hers, not his, she may, in all the fuss, have accidentally put her calling down where his should go).

The story did wind up on page one of the Late Edition, competing for the city's attention with another pugilistic scandal, the Argentine colossus Luis Firpo's desertion of his paramour Miss Bianca Lourdes, whom Ellis Island immigration agents were detaining while they checked out her avowal that she was his "stenographer" and had needed a stateroom adjoining his on shipboard to take his frequent "dictation."[46] But by morning, even the Firpo-abandons-mistress tale had paled in interest, as all eleven dailies

Siki and Lillian Warner (on his right) on their wedding day, New York City, July 24, 1924. (P. and A. photo.)

chased follow-ups to the *Sun*'s wild-man-takes-white-wife scoop. From the marriage license they had gotten the bride and groom's address, 470 West Twenty-third Street, and the witnesses' names: Mrs. George Kinelle, Mme. Landie. Then they scrutinized the detail that mattered most: sure enough, the bride had listed her race as "white." Beside the racial designation they noticed a scrawled "Ok." What did that mean?

They roared off to 470 West Twenty-third, and found . . . the Adelphi Hotel. "Sorry," said the clerk. "Mr. Siki has checked out."[47] They spun off to Levy's office at 138 West Twenty-fifth—but he wasn't around. Then off they rolled to 251 West Thirty-ninth to look for Mrs. Kinelle. Why, this was nearly as good as when Dempsey's ex-wife, Maxine, testified at his trial for draft dodging that she'd once supported him from her earnings as a prostitute.

Mr. and Mrs. George Kinelle turned out to be Belgian friends of the bride and groom. The husband, an ex-professional wrestler, said he was Siki's trainer. The news-hounds fired questions: Say, what's she look like? I heard she's a blonde with blue eyes. What's this about them being artists? Is Siki quitting the ring to make movies? Get up a song-and-dance act? Say, where's the loving couple now? Where's she from, how did they meet? Did he tell her he's already married and has a kid—or did that minor detail slip his mind?

The Belgian couple remained loyal. Yes, Miss Warner was fair-skinned—but as for her racial origins, it hadn't occurred to them to ask. Where did she live? Why here, with them. She'd been their boarder for months. Lillian met Louis in... was it Chicago? She'd fallen so head over heels in love, Mrs. Kinelle enthused, that she'd followed the dear boy to New York:

> Siki is so funny. He met Lillian, who is a handsome young woman with big black eyes and black hair, when he was fighting in Chicago seven months ago. Lillian traveled all over the country to see his fights. She even went to Havana. But I was afraid that jealous ones would cause Siki to be sent out of the country. For the last few days men who said they were immigration police were here and made such terrible accusations. I made them get married.[48]

Now the loving couple were off somewhere in the city enjoying their felicity away from prying eyes. Mrs. Kinelle didn't know where. She hadn't asked. They had so little time for a honeymoon. Louis had a fight in ten days. Why, yesterday, he went straight from the ceremony to Grupp's Gym to train. The gentlemen of the press, no doubt, would understand and let them decently alone.

Fat chance! The gentlemen of the press hustled off to Grupp's—but they already had all the dope they'd get that day. "Siki Married to White Girl" blazoned the *American*. "His First Time, He Says," a subhead trumpeted. "Wife of Pugilist's Trainer Was Matchmaker and Proud of It; Lauds Honeymooners." "Siki Takes Southern White Girl," marveled the *New York Mirror*. "Battling Siki... White Woman...," bannered the *Times*, stressing that the groom was "charcoal black," the bride "small and very fair." "Paris Friends of Senegalese Say Prizefighter Is Already Married to Dutch Girl," a subhead divulged, setting up an inevitable follow-up.[49] The editors cabled Memphis: Look for the bride's parents. Ella Warner and... what was the father's name? Olie? A Paris correspondent grilled Lijntje's friends, who insisted, "Why, of course they're married." Mrs. Siki lived in Vanves, in a cottage he rented for her a year ago last November. She was working in a shop to support herself and Louis Jr. The boxer had sent her money for a while, but lately the remittances had dried up.[50]

The *World* ran a front-page photo of Siki decked in flowers, with Lijntje and Louis Jr. in Amsterdam in 1922. "Siki Takes White Woman, 7 Years Older

Than He, as Bride," the headline shrilled. A side-lit photo of Siki, brow furrowed, eyes shadowed, made the *Daily News*'s back cover. The *Daily Mirror* rushed to press a garbled story giving the groom's age as thirty-three, having the couple honeymooning in "a rooming house at No. 470 West 23rd St." But for all its errors, the article found the story's true angle: fear of racial carnage. "What effect another mixed marriage will have on the pugilistic world would be conjecture," it warned. "Jack Johnson stirred up race wars and tremendous feeling by marrying two white women. His first wife, [a] one-time New York beauty, committed suicide in a room over Johnson's gilded café in Chicago."[51] The image of Johnson's wife as a "beauty" exacerbates his sin, as does the new Mrs. Siki's being "small and very fair." Johnson's wife's fate, of course, suggests what Mrs. Siki's may well be.

The *Telegram and Evening Mail* faced the quandary of how to brazen out a story that lifted every fact from rival papers. It decided to hide behind an irreverent, slangy voice. "Siki Makes Denial of Double Marriage," it clamored, as if citing a spectral interview. Siki may well one day wish he'd "stuck to his lions and red, white, and green chimpanzees, instead of taking onto himself a wife in this country." He already had "one hale and hearty spouse" in France—and "incidentally, she is taking in back stairs and sidewalks to scrub until he does come back." Siki, it dead-panned, "who seems to be a glutton for punishment, says he never was married before. Removing the minute black derby which has been his constant companion since the gendarmes divorced him from his lion, Siki said he was a 'one time gen'man' and that he never did 'two-time nobody.'" Nice try, but the accent's a bit off! The poor sap couldn't even plagiarize right: he gave the *bride*'s name as Olie.[52] The writer did offer one real revelation: though the groom was "by several dippings the blackest gent ever married" at City Hall, his "fair-skinned" bride also qualified, by America's racial logic, as "Negro." Levy had set the record straight on that. The new Mrs. Siki had only passed for white because "out of feminine vanity" she'd bleached her hair.[53] Her mother was "quite dark."[54]

The news-beagles caught on quick. Now the story wasn't Siki's new white wife, but his old one. Some deal for the old Mrs. Siki! Not only did her hubby ditch her for someone else, but the someone else wasn't even white. The pursuit became frantic. Wire service writers grabbed suburban trains to Vanves, pestering the old "Mrs. Battling Siki" to tell them what she thought of the new one. Lijntje was first aghast, then sick. The reporters were lying. Her Louis wouldn't do such a thing. He loved her. It was all a mistake. Why must people whisper and gossip? Would her poor Louis never be free of calumny?

The reporters showed her wires from New York. Look, they said, it's true. They goaded her: Your "husband" is telling everyone you aren't even married. Did you know that? Do you have any proof that you are—a marriage certificate? Something official?

She pointed to the child, "That's all the marriage certificate I need."

Yeah? A reporter said. Did you know your "husband" has been saying the child isn't his?

She went into her nearly bare apartment and wept. She'd not had a word, or a *sou,* from Louis in months. She'd had to pawn the furniture and beg friends for help.[55]

She had been from the outset a curious accessory to Battling Siki's persona, their life together luridly open yet discretely veiled. With her golden hair, blue eyes, buxom figure, she'd been hard for the public to forget. A familiar image fixed her: in a flower-garlanded carriage, holding her baby, about to be pulled through the Amsterdam streets in triumph beside the new light-heavyweight champion. To a white American psyche embittered by the humiliation of Jack Johnson's white mistresses and wives, Lijntje van Appelteer looked like a sexual trophy.

An unwritten law in France protected public figures' private lives. But months after Siki's victory over Carpentier a French journalist had defied convention, visiting their home in Vanves. A flustered maid had opened the gate to the garden court, accepting the scribe's excuse that he'd come to deliver a cable. He warily made his way past Siki's two Great Danes—beasts who let none come near but his wife, the little boy, and Siki. The maid escorted him to a dining room where, "in a family atmosphere unknown, certainly, to all those for whom Siki is nothing but a savage," sat the fighter, his manager, a friend, and two of Siki's "brothers" from Senegal.[56] The house was nothing like what he'd expected. It was simple, even bourgeois, its interior "clean, . . . modest, . . . well taken care of": "Above the fireplace a splendid spray of roses exhales its delicious perfume; two little busts flank them; the mother, who beckons to her naked arms her cute little infant, does not clash at all with the high chair in which Siki junior yesterday babbled the 'mama' and 'dada' that remain his only language."

Siki's absent wife and child seemed to fill the room. He'd sent them to a country retreat, safe from the storm of publicity, while he lingered to pack a valise, stow a trunk, pay the gas bill (13 fr. 85). Asked about his money woes, his charge that the Carpentier bout had been fixed, and the loss of his boxing license, Siki said he longed to forget all that and rejoin his wife and newly arrived Senegalese kinfolk who, as soon as they'd heard he'd won the title, had grabbed the next boat to France. He denied a story, run in all the papers, alleging he'd "disappeared" while his manager hunted him everywhere. He was leaving Paris to escape the lies and innuendo—not to mention the bad influence of riotous friends. "I want to live in tranquility," he urged:

They make me say too many things. They make me commit too many ugly acts, but [I do them]...with the guys I train with who do exactly the same things I do. And I haven't done that sort of thing as often as people say. To the whole world, I am a savage. I sometimes let them believe that. But, gentlemen, it's not at all true. Yesterday, once again, they were saying that I had disappeared. I was right here, where you see me now, with some friends and the grandchildren of a friend, and, mister, if you have a home like this, you probably did yesterday the same thing I did....But people always have it that I'm away from home somewhere, even though the neighbors could tell you that I have been more often at my home than in the places where others sometimes make me go, where in any case I have not been so often as people say.[57]

In his letter to *L'Auto* a few months earlier he'd written in much the same vein: "I don't want to change anything of my modest life style. Later, when my turn comes to take off my gloves, I will go with my little wife to a little place in the countryside of this great France, to live there in tranquility, in the midst of my own family members, who, I hope, will be numerous."[58] He drank too much. Okay! So did his carousing pals Bob Scanlon, Jack Walker, Ercole Balzac, and so did Eugene Stuber, whose column in *La Boxe et les Boxeurs* ran a cartoon showing Siki trailed by a gang of ring buddies, with Scanlon chugging a pint of beer.[59] Nobody had written wild-man-on-the-rampage stuff in Toulouse or Paris in 1920, or Amsterdam in 1921. Where had it all come from? He hardly knew. But he was heartily sick of it.

Now New York was worse. Nothing was sacred here. Tabloid reporters chased the newlyweds down sidewalks, shouting questions, dodging past Mrs. Kinelle, who waved them away like a farm wife shooing hens. A *Daily News* photographer settled for a shot of her advancing in a low-waisted dress, arm up, beads dangling, hair bobbed, scowling, while behind her Siki, in straw boater and high-waisted jacket, cane over his arm, scratched his chin in perplexity. How had he stirred up this ant nest? The *News* ran two other photos: one of Siki's son, another of Leon Pleysir, who claimed he held a contract to manage Siki and peddled himself as Lijntje's spokesman, describing pitiful letters begging him to get her husband to send money. By afternoon, many papers were running an Associated Press interview with Lijntje (whose name the AP, in its haste, made into "Gertrude Amphler") and a heart-wrenching photo of baby Louis: eyes-wide, chest thrust out, lips pursed, a necklace askew across his jersey, long hair tangled. "Where's Daddy?" captioned the *Chicago Defender*[60]—and it seems the little boy really had cut into his mother's colloquy with newsmen to pipe up, "Where is my father? When is my papa, the champion, coming home? You know him. I want some chocolate."[61]

In France, the few reports were brief, focused on the plight of Siki's real wife (as French common law made her), Lijntje, and her two-and-a-half-year-old son. *L'Echo des Sports* tacked its notice of the marriage onto a filler about Siki's recovery from his injury in the auto accident. "The sole conclusion to make," it mused, "is that the 'Black Pearl' wasn't yet in the situation of a spouse, as we had thought."[62] One wonders what Siki's old friends in Paris did think. This time he'd done something really cruel—and to his own family. Bob Levy might urge, "Nine tenths of the pranks held at his door originated in the fertile brains of newspapermen," but no writer had made this up.[63] Mrs. Kinelle even denied Siki's paternity: "Oh, he is so good natured. He just stood for a picture holding that baby."[64]

Perhaps the explanation is found in a little detail Mrs. Kinelle let slip. Siki's hasty marriage was partly out of desperation. The wolf had appeared at his door in July, in the form of two snide immigration cops, who'd returned several times making "terrible accusations," these "jealous ones" who wanted "Siki to be sent out of the country." To save him, Mrs. Kinelle had taken a hand. What were those "terrible accusations"? Mrs. Kinelle hints at the answer when she says she told Louis to get married. They'd menaced him with deportation for moral turpitude—living openly, and traveling all over the country, with a woman not his wife. Jack Johnson had been thrown in jail for just such a sin. Without Lillian's aid, criminal prosecution was unlikely (federal agents had set up Johnson by pressuring Belle Schreiber to testify against him). But Siki's visa would expire October 1. All they had to do was build a file of evidence and say, "Sorry! Denied!" Mrs. Kinelle had given Siki the right advice: if, despite telling all and sundry he didn't, Siki really wished to stay in America, he'd better marry Lillian right away.

Siki had been telling people ever since his return from Cuba in May that he didn't care. If the Americans didn't want him around, fine. This was no country for a black man anyway. But confronted with summary exclusion he felt differently. Siki knew Levy was a mediocre manager. But if Siki returned to France on his own, he'd arrive as he'd arrived in America from Cuba, as a pauper begging to be let in. Siki refused to justify himself to the press, but it seems he married Lillian to avoid deportation. Not that he didn't love her. But he'd loved Lijntje, too—and he had a child with her. He'd gotten used to the money in America. He hoped the cards would turn his way again. But his life had begun drifting in a way that boded ill.

On August 1, 1924, sporting a saber, resplendent in a black uniform trimmed in gold and caravel-shaped black admiral's hat with red and gold feathers, the President General of the African Republic, flanked by others in red, gold, and black, sat in summer sunshine watching from a reviewing stand on 135th Street thirty-five hundred black men, women, and children troop by—among them regiments of the African Legion from New York, New Jersey, Ohio, Pennsylvania, and some southern states—not to mention companies from Panama, Barbados, Antigua, and British Guyana. Mounted police, ranks of black nurses, Boy and Girl Scouts swept by, as did floats featuring huge paintings of a black Jesus and Madonna, along with *tableux-vivants* enacting "The Ladies of the Royal Court of Ethiopia" and "The Pleading of Africa's Cause at the League of Nations." Later, the President General led a file of luminaries to 138th Street's Liberty Hall to open the Negro Improvement Association convention.[65]

That afternoon Siki was on a train to Providence to fight Jack Lynch. But perhaps the night before he had joined the two thousand members of the association, many in evening dress, at the Carnegie Hall opening gala, where President Marcus Garvey, despite federal charges he'd bilked followers of hundreds of thousands of dollars, drew thunderous ovations. If so, Siki, who'd himself snarled that America offered no liberty to a black man, might well have vaulted to his feet to join the "roar of applause" when the second assistant president William L. Sherrill raged, "I'm kicked by the same man as you are, the same man who puts a rope around my neck, and the time has come to stop this thing." But he'd perhaps have smiled a wry half smile as Garvey urged the colonial powers to cede him Abyssinia, Sierra Leone, Liberia, and Germany's ex-colonies to create a "United States of Africa."[66] Private Fall had learned too well the Great War's reality principle, the heavy artillery shell. Nor could he have missed the irony that Garvey's legions longed to leave at the moment he himself schemed to stay.

Why he did so is not entirely clear. His fortunes were drifting steadily downhill. He was fighting in worse shape, for smaller purses, battering inferior foes, then stalling through fights he should have won. He might clamor to meet top fighters, but Levy would do him no favors setting up such bouts—unless he found a good trainer and gave Siki time to work himself into shape. Instead, over the next ten days Siki was set to fight three main events—the first with a tough top-echelon light-heavyweight, the second a journeyman light-heavyweight, the third the tough heavyweight he'd gone to Havana to fight. If that didn't give him pause, it should have.

He'd seen his first scheduled opponent, Jack Lynch, give Larry Estridge and future light-heavyweight champion Jimmy Slattery rough battles in New York.[67] At Woonsocket's Clinton Oval, on August 2, as they waited for Siki and Lynch, fifteen hundred fans craned their necks to study a blonde at ringside. The *Providence Journal* had reassured them: she "is not white, never was white, and has no intention of becoming white." Haw, haw, haw! White

America accepted as an article of faith that nobody would be black by choice. Hadn't Siki himself, a year and a half before, delighted American reporters in Paris by saying he would gladly pay 50,000 francs for the chance to bleach himself white?[68] The *Journal's* reference to the old story lent piquancy to the present scene, reassuring the crowd: this childlike brute, this Battling Siki, was no threat to the racial status quo. The Woonsocket crowd didn't know Siki had said he wanted to be white only because he wished to wash away the power differential that skin color symbolized. As a white he could fight whomever he wanted and be paid the real going rate to do so. Siki was disgusted not with his own color but with the racial status quo. His take on racial reality was not really substantially different from that of William L. Sherrill, Marcus Garvey's second assistant president, though Sherrill, just the day before, in Harlem, in contradiction of Siki's famous remark, had roared, "If I could, by the use of some chemical, suddenly change my color to white, I would not do it!"[69]

The bout itself was another stinker, with Lynch mixing a "harmless yet tantalizing" jab with sporadic rights, and Siki, so flabby his crouch exposed "rows of fat around the waist," trying to force the action, with little success. The sole flash of drama came in the fifth when Siki "darted out of his corner like a panther," got nailed with a hard right, but kept coming, landing heavily to Lynch's ribs, before accidentally butting him. As the fight dragged into the late rounds, "the financially alert Mr. Levy" began shouting for Siki to "go and make a finish of it." Maybe he had a few ducats down with local book-ies. If so, he had to pay up. A Siki rally in the ninth fell short, as "three vicious smashes" that "might have sent Lynch into the Blackstone River" landed high. Neither man had done much to hurt the other, but Lynch got the decision.[70]

The Battling Siki sideshow quickly headed back on the road—in Levy's seven-passenger red touring car—to Allentown, Pennsylvania, where a little set-to awaited, so the program read, with "the Dixie Kid." But this Dixie Kid wasn't the ex-welterweight champ. He was a "strapping big fellow" from Panama who came closer to glory this night, during his brief period erect, than he ever would. In round one he caught an astonished Siki with a right flush to the jaw, which the ex-champion shook off. In the second Siki landed a right to the pit of the stomach that his rival whined was low. In the third Siki launched a flurry in the Panamanian's corner, ending with a vicious swing to the back of the neck (an illegal blow) that dropped him for good.[71] It had been an ugly fight, but at least it was over.

If this had been January, you'd expect Siki to ride into Buffalo thinking, "I can lick this guy." Homer Smith had an edge in reach and weight, but Siki had done well in the past against long-armed, stand-up punchers, such as Breitenstraeter and Nilles. Ringsiders had thought Siki dominated Joe Lohman—and Lohman had battled Smith evenly in three no-decision bouts before Smith won an encounter on points. Still, this wasn't the Siki who'd fought Breitenstraeter, Nilles, or Lohman. He was out of shape and injured. Moreover, he was becoming his own worst enemy, his taste for wine and "play" progressing from sporadic release to a self-destructive spiral. "Siki has forsaken the bright lights, late hours, and glowing wine," Levy said, but he was blowing smoke.[72] Siki's only real training came in the bouts themselves. Otherwise, free to amuse himself, he spent more time setting up rounds than sparring them. In Buffalo, Siki worked out just twice, at Bert Finch's gym, August 9 and 10, while Smith, a quiet man who didn't drink, smoke, or keep late hours, showed up as religiously at the gym as at Bible class.

The contrast showed in the ring. In round one, said Jack Laing of the *Buffalo Evening News,* Smith, awed by the "man-ape's" notoriety, was content to "maul around in the clinches" while Siki "danced in and around, shooting his left over now and then, each time with plenty of steam behind it." But in round two a left counter caught Siki in the face, bloodying his mouth. By the third both men were loading up, looking to land decisive blows. Siki snuck in an uppercut to the gut, but Smith returned his own, muscled Siki to the ropes, and "whaled away with both hands," catching Siki to the jaw. Over the next three rounds Siki twice cleverly caught Smith with looping lefts as he slipped from clinches, but Smith was using his size to wear Siki down. By the seventh, Levy was shouting for a desperation rally. Though in no shape for miracles, Siki tore after Smith with his "famous swings," landing several, just missing a vicious uppercut that, "had it landed square, might have ended hostilities." His rally spent, Siki dragged himself through round eight, as Smith stabbed an efficient jab. As the ninth began, reflexes shot, arms weighted, Siki put on a last rush. Smith met it with a right that sent Siki "sprawling on his haunches." He bounced to his feet with no count, but Smith swarmed him, as the fans shrieked. Bleeding profusely, one gashed eye swollen shut, Siki stayed erect, pawing, grabbing, holding. He won what he valued least: the crowd's favor for his tenacity. Smith got the decision. Were you surprised? asked the *Times.* Siki shook his head. "I hurt my right hand," he groused.[73] Until then, he'd stuck by the code that initiated Wolof boys into manhood: a *borom jom,* no matter what, masters himself before others. But a *borom jom* is a human being, and if he controls his emotions that doesn't mean he has none.

A little over a week later, in a small city on Lake Erie, west of Cleveland, the bushy-haired boxer, seconds into a break between rounds, jumps from his stool, exclaiming, "I want to speak to the public." Corner men grab and remonstrate—"Louis, listen! Wait!" He lashes out, twists away, strides to the center of the ring, holds up his arms. The crowd snorts in derision. Hey, he wants to say something. This ought to be rich. For eight rounds, they've taunted and jeered, calling him every name they can think of, and now and then, just to be sure they've gotten through the language barrier, screeching out ape calls. For some reason, the crowd is in a surly mood, having a fine time riding the black man gracing the charity card at Krohn Field.[74]

Hey, the boys are just having a little fun! After all, hasn't everyone gotten used to the idea that a Siki fight isn't an athletic contest but a traveling carnival, where hooting and jeering are part of the spectacle? It's not like the poor savage can be hurt by anything you hoot. Doesn't he come warranted to have a skull as thick as a hydrant and a mentality to match? Didn't the hilarity begin when this guy who wore a grass skirt a few years back showed up "dressed in a classy suit with a white vest, white gloves, and carrying a cane"? All the same, silence spreads to the fringes of the crowd, two or three thousand deep, the biggest to see a boxing match here in many years, despite the recent disaster that leveled this ship-building town. The black man in the center of the ring spreads his arms. One eye is swollen shut (re-injured from the bout nine days before). The other surveys the crowd with a look not quite defiant, but unabashed. The boxer's manager, head bent, palm flat against bald forehead, mutters, "Louis, please! Don't do this."

Alone in the center of the ring, the boxer ignores him. "I want to talk to public," he says. "I get nothing for fight. I no fight." Hoots and catcalls crescendo. His wife climbs onto the apron. Handlers nod over him. "Louis, listen...." "Louis, please...!" He stalks to his corner. The bell sounds. He stays put. His hulking white rival stands stock still at the center of the ring, turmoil boiling around him. The referee raises his arm. "The winner, by technical knockout!"

The black man ducks through the ropes, enraged, and pushes into the crowd, surging against him in its wrath.[75] A National Guard platoon with fixed bayonets wedges him through the mob. The boxer, despite his anger, feels far from vindicated. He's violated his own code—let them get to him, see that they can hurt him. Some "charity" show! Too bad they forgot to bring any of that article with them through the turnstiles.

He's no doubt seen the two-mile wide swath of shattered glass, broken brick, twisted steel left in the tornado's wake in downtown Lorain—the telephone poles snapped like match sticks, the collapsed theater where hundreds of children died. He's heard of the thousands living in tents in refugee camps, the bodies in makeshift morgues, the twelve hundred national guardsmen posted to halt looting.[76] Maybe that explains the crowd's temper.

Maybe they brought that spirit of random anarchy with them. The *Times-Herald* says Siki, feinting, sidestepping, taunting, sliding along the ropes, twisting behind his rival to cuff him beside the head, had had Rochester heavyweight Mike Conroy so befuddled he landed only "a few light blows." Preferring honest mayhem, it labels the bout a display of "How Rotten a Fighter Can Be and Still Get Paid."

Paid? Who got paid? Not me, Siki said—despite Levy's avowals that he *had* been—and that he had given 25 percent of his purse for relief of tornado victims. The promoters swore Siki had gotten half his promised purse, nine hundred dollars, and that they'd lost five hundred dollars on the card.[77] But with thirty-five hundred fannies in the makeshift seats,[78] somebody must have made money.

Siki was to fight aging warhorse Joe Borell in Fairview, New Jersey, August 26, and days later Mexican Joe Lawson in Youngstown, Ohio, but Levy canceled both bouts. He'd had it. He had other boxers in his stable. They weren't big draws, but they didn't incite riots. Besides, Siki was pursuing a lifestyle not likely to get him ready for serious boxing anytime this century. Why, a week before he'd ridden around Harlem and New Jersey all night in a cab, come up with a case of the shorts, staggered to his suite at the Adelphi looking for thirty-nine dollars to pay the fare, and passed out on his bed. The irate driver sent for the police, who hauled Siki off to the West Thirtieth Street Station and kept him there until a friend, proprietor of a nearby restaurant, stood him the cash.[79] Siki then borrowed an extra dollar to tip the cabbie![80]

Three weeks later, Siki's retinue turned up to see towering Harry Wills fight yet more massive Luis Firpo at the huge Jersey City amphitheater where Carpentier had fought Dempsey, Boyle's Thirty Acres. They got no farther than the police barriers where ten thousand ducatless fans shouted and shoved, straining to glimpse the dignitaries who were to attend: Jack Dempsey, James J. Corbett, Al Jolson, Albert Edward Prince of Wales. Eighty thousand ticketholders streamed toward the gates as Siki, rather the worse for prefight lubrication, tugged the elbow of a cop in no mood to listen to a slick, well-dressed black man with a French accent and a pushy attitude. Usually ex-champions got in free and sat at ringside to be introduced to the crowd—especially black ex-champions at a bout featuring a black pretender to the heavyweight title. But Boss Hague's minion was having none of it. Make like a hoop and roll away, he said.

When the "belligerent" African persisted, the cop threatened arrest.[81] He swore the gatecrasher was drunk and disorderly—but in fact the word was out. Battling Siki, the wise guy who thought he could grab the world by its lapel and give it a shake, was due for a comeuppance. Months would pass before he'd climb through the ropes again—and then it would not be because the boxing bosses loved or had forgiven him. They were just desperate for a last-minute stand-in for one of the year's biggest bouts. And you'd better believe they wouldn't have let Siki in a prize ring even then if they hadn't expected to see him get his head beat in.

CHAPTER TEN

Apes and Peacocks

What if . . . ?

The round-bellied, bald gnome in the business suit waves an arm toward a lithe black figure hammering, bare-fisted, a leather teardrop the size of a human head, dancing eyeball-high on a ball-bearing swivel screwed under a circular wooden surface. Thunketa, thunketa, thunketa goes the leather tear, beating an uneven drumroll, back to front, against the wood.

"You're surprised, boys, huh?" says the round-bellied gnome. "You didn't expect to see Louis in such great shape? You figured he'd been training on bottles of red wine?"

"Why don't he wear gloves? Say, why should I waste money on things he don't need? His hands are like rhino hide. Why . . ." He waves behind them. "He could punch that wall an hour . . . would too, if I said so. Does what I say, no questions asked. Don't believe the baloney in the papers. He's just an average guy, no different than anybody else. No better, no worse. I'm not saying he's an angel—nothing of the sort—just a regular guy, like anybody. He's not up to half the stunts you read about. He's just—what do you boys call it?—'good copy'? He's colorful. Laughing all the time. Friendly. People just naturally warm up to him. He kids the reporters along. Next thing I know, I pick up the paper and read about some wild prank he supposedly pulled, but damned if I know a thing about it—and I'm with him all the time. Look for yourselves. If he was up to half the stunts people say, would he be in this kind of shape?"[1]

The out-of-town reporters gawk at the superbly defined pectorals and biceps of the lean, quick boxer. "We heard he was on the skids," a *Passaic*

Daily News scribe risks. He sure doesn't look it. The man battering the speed bag looks as if he could flay and dismember the clumsy Patterson heavyweight promoter Mike Donohue, standing there with jaws unhinged, has matched against him. It's not just that he's trim and muscular, but he moves quickly from side to side, on the heavy bag in the Harlem gym, as if sidestepping a foe, and thuds home blows that make the men's ears ring. "All the ease and agility of a tiger, ready to pounce on the prey," the *Passaic Daily Herald*'s Bob Irwin bangs out on his typewriter later.[2] Only Bobby Neilly, Patterson's "live wire sporting man-about-town," demurs. Siki looks tough, okay, but young Roscoe hits hard too, he thinks, and Roscoe is hardly unskilled.[3]

Siki is up next to spar, but the Passaic boys have trains to catch, deadlines to meet. Another boxer is in there now, skittering about, quick as a crab, flicking a jab. For a while they watch the wasp-thin, pale light-heavyweight champion as he sidesteps and slips punches. He makes a radical contrast to the black dynamo with the concussive fists. They have a question in mind, but before they can ask it the black fighter comes, gripping hands, saying (in English!), "Hi, I'm Siki. How you do?" He drags over a black sparring mate. "Say, what's it like sparring with him?" someone asks. "Make it pretty rough on you?"[4]

"Naw. He's good, but I hold my own," Al Campbell pipes up. "Say, Louis, you gonna let me work your next fight?" Siki, misconstruing, mutters something in his crony's ear.

When Bob Irwin asks what he said, Siki explains (as Irwin has it), "Me tell him me can't be his manager because me need 'im manager myself." The Passaic boys laugh. "You'd make some manager," Bob Levy mutters.[5]

Suddenly a small, energetic female bustles in. "Boys," Bob Levy heralds. "Let me present Mrs. Battling Siki." Lillian has fetched fresh ring togs. For the fight, she'll outfit Louis in home-made purple silk tights.

You gonna knock him out? someone asks Siki. Sure, Siki says. He's ready to fight any man in the country. This guy? This Roscoe? Sure, he'll knock him out. Why not?[6]

The newsmen haven't even seen Siki spar, but they've made up their minds: he'll murder the Patterson heavyweight. For that matter, watching Mike McTigue in there sparring, they have to wonder if he really did beat Siki. Bob Levy has been hinting pretty broadly to anyone who'll listen that he didn't. An hour before, when the door swung open and McTigue appeared, he'd glowered at Levy, fists clenched, snarling, "What's this nonsense you've been spreading? Saying I only won the title because some goons at ringside said they'd kill Siki if he won?" Levy begged off, denied he'd ever said such a thing. Then Siki had rushed over, calling, "Mike, hey Mike!" Grinning ear-to-ear, he threw an arm over his ex-rival's shoulder. "To Siki the world seems to go around the same whether it rains, snows, or is sun-shiny," Bob Irwin scribbled.[7]

You're tempted to wonder: Why was Siki so wearyingly genial? Why couldn't he, just once, thumb somebody in the eye, like vicious trickster Harry Greb, cold cock someone from behind as he crawled to his knees, like mask of malice Jack Dempsey, sucker punch a guy taking off his coat, like wise little mug Mickey Walker, or con a rival into dropping his guard, like slick social climber Georges Carpentier? For Christ's sake, the scrawny rooster across the room stole his title, and since then he's not only not given *Siki* a rematch, he's given *nobody* a fair shot.

But Siki was just following the code of his sport. Its first principle is to hurt the other guy any way you can. The crowd protests whenever the mayhem inside the ropes fails to supply sufficient pain. But the fighters fight for money, not out of rage or spite, as heavyweight champion Jack Sharkey once said.[8] Sure, Mickey Walker and Harry Greb re-fought their brutal 1925 bout hours later on the sidewalk, but before they did they spent hours buying each other drinks, laughing at each other's jokes.[9] The guy across the ring is a boxer's only real friend, the only one who knows what he goes through.

One is tempted by imaginary *denouements,* resolutions. "What if...?" you can't help but wonder. What if Siki and McTigue had fought again? The chance encounter at Grupp's seems to promise such a turn in the tale. You itch to have them go after each other tossing punches—to have reporters gleefully pounding keys, telling a tale that seems to write itself. You itch for a public outcry to force them back together in the ring, for a wiser, better-trained Siki to catch his adversary with a crisp left hook. But you're alone in such projections. No writer imagined that destiny. And destines must be imagined to occur. In fact, the writers had "written off" Battling Siki, tagged as his destiny "gets what he's got coming."

Gerald Early says Siki played an urgent role for white America, which, "far from wishing to kill [him], would have loved to have kept him alive forever." His status as "a socially dead yet culturally prominent figure" was "reassuring," validating "their assumptions about the world."[10] To fulfill that role, Siki must be eternally dangerous yet flawed. And how better to do so than by fixing himself in the public mind via a final, indelible failure. In the year he had left of life, he'd fight eleven bouts. He'd fight sometimes well, sometimes badly. Neither mattered. When his final tragedy took place, on a dirty Hell's Kitchen street, the public, white and black, found the same self-congratulatory solace in his death as it had in his life.

No, the chance meeting changed nothing. McTigue held the world title, but he wasn't the best fighter Siki had faced, Norfolk was. Siki would soon fight two men tougher than McTigue: an ex-Olympic wrestler from Astoria, Queens, and a lanky New Orleans middleweight moving up in class. Of Siki's five toughest rivals—René de Vos, Carpentier, Kid Norfolk, Paul Berlenbach, and Tony Marullo—three (two he beat, one he didn't) were behind him. Two were ahead—and one of them would soon win a world title. If the boxing crowd had been asked to bet on which of Siki's rivals would win a title, they'd have picked Marullo. Berlenbach had run up a string of knockouts, but mostly over nobodies. Marullo had stiffed nine men in a row and had taken a decision from the Klan's darling Young Stribling, losing a rematch on a badly split lip, though ahead on points and "perfectly sound otherwise."[11]

McTigue, meanwhile, was milking the title for all it was worth, squirreling away every nickel against a coming winter that would nevertheless destroy him. He'd hang onto his crown past the second anniversary of his Dublin triumph, investing heavily in the stock market—only to lose it all in the 1929 crash. The setback would crack his will, provoking a nervous collapse, leading to years in mental hospitals, up to his death in 1966.[12] Nor were financial reverses the whole story. After sixteen years in the ring, McTigue may well have suffered from *dementia pugilistica*. In 145 bouts, he'd be knocked out ten times and weather scores of fifteen- or twenty-round ordeals. Siki, in his 90 fights, would only once fail to go the distance, but would survive many marathon combats. In a way, that's the inevitability linking them. Had he lived long enough, Siki too might have suffered the form of dementia caused by a life of getting your skull hammered. Fans might dream of a bout to blab about for decades, a defining moment of escape from unheroic lives, but fighters just want to get to the final bell in one piece, get paid, and for a while to forget the grim, uncertain way they earn a living.

Partisans of the "Patterson brown panther" jammed the Passaic Arena to the rafters, "a mixed crowd of color" hoping to see Young Roscoe's powerful right and concrete chin upset Siki.[13] After all, wasn't the Passaic heavyweight's trainer the legendary black heavyweight Joe Jeannette? But when Siki and Roscoe stood side by side for prefight photos, the fans lost heart. Siki looked in superb shape. The fight began with Siki dodging Roscoe's lunges. Then all at once in the fifth, as Roscoe plunged in to throw a left, Siki nailed him with a short right and he went down as though pole-axed. He crawled erect at seven, tossed a wild haymaker, and, still addled, went sprawling. Siki repaired to a corner, nodding to Levy "as if to say 'Gosh, I didn't have to knock him out. He did it for me.'" Staggering upright, Roscoe got caught flush and "flopped" again.[14] Though everyone expected him to stay down, he made it again to his feet. Siki rushed him to the ropes, nailed him on the chin, and dropped him a fourth time. Despite Jeannette's energetic protest, the referee waved a halt. "You were toying with him, right?" a reporter asked Siki. "You could have knocked him out any time."

No, no, Siki said. "He did the best he could and so did I." He put on an affable face. "I received every consideration in your city. I was treated royally and I enjoyed my brief stay."[15] He hoped to be invited back. Papa Bob, unfortunately, had other ideas.

At that moment the light-heavyweight division was overstocked with talent. If he weren't clinging so grimly to the title, McTigue, in fact, would barely have made most experts' top ten lists. In addition to seasoned veterans both black and white—Gene Tunney, Kid Norfolk, Georges Carpentier, Battling McCreary, Tommy Gibbons, Jack Taylor—a rising generation was coming along that included Young Stribling, Tony Marullo, Tommy Loughran, Jack Delaney, Jimmy Slattery, and Paul Berlenbach. That's without even considering two lighter men who would challenge for the light-heavyweight title, Harry Greb and Mickey Walker. Ten of these guys would hold world titles, and three who didn't hold the title, Norfolk, McCreary, and Stribling, might have been the toughest of the lot.[16] It's doubtful there ever was a moment in boxing history when the division possessed so much talent at once. With the public getting more and more impatient with no-decision defenses, McTigue's days seemed clearly numbered.

Meanwhile, managers of the other top light-heavyweights were trying to maneuver their men into position for the main chance, when it finally came. They circled the scene of each big boxing card like sharks, anxious to get their man in, but ready with excuses in case the promoter proposed somebody who might kill his chance to fight for the title. For Siki, this sort of thing was tailor made. He'd been disparaged so much lately in the press, and really had fought the summer before in such atrocious shape, that to some managers, who hadn't heard much of him lately, he seemed a safe risk. And despite the humbling reverses of the past few months, he remained paradoxically a good draw. Suddenly, in mid-November 1924, Levy was appearing on nearly a daily basis with word of big fights Siki could have for the asking—and with white fighters! Part of the breakthrough had to do with the fact that the New York State commission had finally jettisoned Muldoon—and with him the silent conspiracy against interracial bouts.[17]

When Siki got back from Passaic, the talk among boxing people was of how manager Dan Hickey had stiffed the town's biggest promoter, Tex Rickard, pulling his young attraction, Paul Berlenbach, out of his bout with Tony Marullo on an injury. Of course, nobody much believed the injury was for real. It was about as easy to injure the "Astoria Assassin" as it was a charging rhino. Berlenbach had taken up boxing just two years before, when he'd walked into the boxing room at the New York Athletic Club and Dan Hickey, the trainer there, had let the muscle-bound ex-Olympic wrestler lace on gloves just to show him up.[18] But Berlenbach wasn't only as burly as an ox, he was as stubborn as one, too. Scarlet fever had cost him his hearing and speech as a child and he'd been ridiculed as "the dummy" by other kids. Finally, at fifteen, he'd recovered his hearing via a freak accident and took up wrestling at the Turnverein, Astoria's German-American social club. When Hickey let him spar, Berlenbach turned out to be as ungainly as he looked, but he caught Hickey once, to the belly, with a punch so powerful that Hickey sagged to the canvas. Hickey took to training the brawny, silent neophyte full time.[19] Adopting the sport as late as he did, he'd never be a clever boxer like Jack Delaney, but with that powerful left hook, even if he only learned to do a few things well, he'd beat a lot of boxers.[20] As it happened, that brutal left hook turned out to be nearly the only thing Berlenbach did well, so his style consisted of throwing a vicious left hook, then throwing another one, and then throwing another one. He knocked out his first nine opponents before getting knocked out himself by Jack Delaney. By November 1924 he'd had twenty-one professional bouts, losing just one. Still, to most people the loss to Delaney proved he wasn't ready for Marullo.

Marullo, a New Orleans fighter, like Siki had started out as a middle-weight—even though he was over six feet tall. The January 1925 *Ring* magazine, already on newsstands in November 1924, named him the world's most promising light-heavyweight, ahead of Tunney, Berlenbach, Jack Delaney, and Young Stribling. Word was out among Eastern managers, Cliff Abbo said: Marullo was "a killer."[21] McTigue had spurned an offer of $10,000 to fight him.

But when Levy bustled over to tell Siki he had a fight for him—at the Garden, in a main event—and against a white guy—he didn't have to ask Siki twice. Promoter Tex Rickard had offered eight others the chance to replace Berlenbach against Marullo before he approached Levy. All eight had said no thanks. Siki, in contrast, took the fight on two days' notice![22] It would be the first mixed-race bout at the Garden in five years. Levy tried to get Harry Greb for Siki, too, casually proposing an evening of gouged eyeballs, barked shins, and elbows in the teeth. Frank Flournoy wanted to stage that bout, as did Tex Rickard. One would like to believe Levy chose Marullo instead to save Siki from an evening of filthy tricks. But in fact it was Greb who backed out at the last minute.[23] On the face of it, Siki should have backed out, too, on Marullo and Greb both. He'd fought exactly five rounds for real since August—and the one time in the last nine months he'd faced a rival of Marullo's caliber, Homer Smith, he'd lost badly.

Paul Berlenbach.
(Author's
collection.)

The scribes played Siki / Marullo as a lark, with Siki half clown, half freak. "The last purse that Siki won in this neck of the woods," Jack Lawrence jibed, "he gave away to amazed strangers in trolley cars, subways, and ferryboats. One of his most recent stunts was taking a dive out of a fourth story window of a hotel in Havana. He landed on his head and consequently was uninjured." A year ago they might have been picking him to win back his title, yet now Harry Newman would only venture, "If they can keep the old boy right side up on his conduct long enough . . . , the customers . . . are in for some fun." Siki was "a riot in every show."[24]

The match was a huge letdown for Rickard, who griped about unreliable fighters spoiling his show. Fewer than five thousand fans graced the pews of the huge arena, paying just $12,160. Siki's purse alone for the Norfolk bout the year before had topped $15,000.[25] With no time to train, against a boxer who, despite his bony frame and stork's wingspan, hit hard, Siki began cautiously, crouching, bobbing, weaving, covering up. For three rounds the crowd sat grimly through a one-sided display. They wondered: Had the money men made Siki fight "under wraps,"—as they often did black fighters? But as the fourth round began Siki unleashed a torrent of hooks and swings. Marullo, ducking and slipping, got caught with "whistling drives" that had him reeling.[26] In the fifth, Siki seemed about to "carry Marullo's head off."[27] He kept sticking jabs and swatting hooks that "shook up the New Orleans scrapper" through round six.[28] By the seventh, however, Siki, exhausted, was back into his defensive shell, fending off all but that long jab and a few routine pokes to the ribs. The crowd amused itself with speculation about the bout's surprises. Aw, Tony hurt his paw, urged some (including the *Times* and Mercer of the *Evening Journal*). Come on, insisted others (including Newman of the *Daily News*), it's in the bag for Marullo. When the judges gave Marullo the nod, boos cascaded down. Siki, unmarked at fight's end, had landed all the heavy blows.

"The Frenchman clowned a great deal," noted the *New York Age,* "but when in the mood . . . he outboxed the New Orleans fighter." In several rounds he'd "made Marullo look like a mug." Despite the verdict, Siki had triumphed. He'd taken a fight nobody wanted, on two days' notice, and outfought one of the best light-heavyweights in the world. The *New York Age* called it his "best fight since coming to this country."[29] Even sullen Sid Mercer admitted, "Siki was spectacular."[30] Others spun things differently. Siki, they said, could have won, should have won—if only, like Marullo, he'd "stuck to his knitting."[31] Instead, he "clown[ed] away" chances.[32] Thus did they write Siki's skillful effort out of existence—as another caprice of the man Nat Fleischer called "boxing's harlequin." In fact Mercer makes it seem the man guilty of "clowning" (a word suggesting fake aggression instead of a real effort to do harm) wasn't Siki but Marullo, who "slapped with his open gloves, jabbed with his left hand lightly," and generally did nothing "vicious."[33]

If the Marullo verdict was dubious, the decision in Siki's next bout was preposterous. Two weeks later, in Syracuse, he faced young Utica light-heavyweight Frank Kearns. Levy did his best to stir up interest, resurrecting the gambit of having armed guards meet Siki at the station. The local scribes dutifully turned out the usual tripe, calling Siki "one of the most eccentric performers in the ring,"[34] a purely instinctual primitive who just "stands up and whales away, jumps around the ring like a jumping jack and fights by no set rule or custom."[35] Great! Siki could expect a houseful of fans primed to see a freak: half vicious animal, half human pogo stick. What would they make of the man who stepped in the ring instead, in good trim (trained for more than a month), with solid defensive skills, and no especially outlandish stylistic quirks?

They saw, said the *Syracuse Post-Standard,* a man with a flat nose and "a crop of hair like an amateur minstrel man's wig," making for the wrong corner—a mistake that, though "done regularly" by others, cracked up the "dollar boys" in the cheap seats.[36] When both men grabbed and held through the first round, the crowd jeered, goading the referee into issuing Siki (alone!) a warning to be more aggressive. By the second, Siki had "broadcast the fact that he has a mighty good left hook of which Kearns took immediate and painful notice."[37] The *Post-Standard* thought he could have knocked Kearns out any time he felt like it. Kearns, Charles J. Kinney wrote in the *Herald Journal,* "didn't land a clean punch in the first five rounds and not so many thereafter."[38] In the fourth, a Siki hook spilled Kearns to his knees and left him "wander[ing] around ... like a new tenant in an apartment house trying to find his bunk in the dark." Kearns opened the sixth aggressively and walked into a hook. Siki chased him to the ropes, battered his body, and seemed about to "drape Kearns on the canvas."[39] The late rounds were slower and more even. When the announcer proclaimed a draw, Siki hardly grumbled. He'd gotten used to America. He knew he had to beat rivals senseless to win. Scoring a prizefight is a wayward exercise—especially in that Neverland that the legendary trainer Whitey Bimstein called "out-a-town." But in Europe, after the war, fighting the best men in the top three weight classes, Siki had knocked out 44 percent of his rivals and won nearly 80 percent of decisions (11 percent were draws). A 44 percent knockout rate was above par for top black fighters of that era. Jack Johnson knocked out 40 percent of his foes, Sam Langford 39 percent, Joe Jeannette 36 percent, Sam McVey 41 percent.[40] Kid Norfolk knocked out just 34 percent of opponents up to 1923,[41] while Tiger Flowers, the next black world's champion, knocked out 40 percent through 1924.[42]

During Siki's American sojourn, his knockout rate dropped to 24 percent. The drop makes sense. He fought sick, injured, and out of shape, with no trainer and an inept manager. He also faced tougher competition. Circumstances might explain a similar drop in his rate of decision wins. But Siki went from winning nearly 80 percent of his European decisions to just under 17 percent in America. He fought twelve times to a decision, winning only twice. His knockout rate dropped by 45 percent. A similar drop in his rate of decision wins would have had him winning five or six

American decisions, bringing his victory total overall to about two-thirds of his American bouts. The two decisions Siki did win in America came early in his stay. After January 1924, he'd never win again except by knockout. Had Siki figured that out? Probably. In fight after fight, he stormed out in the early and middle rounds trying for a knockout, and if he didn't get one, he eased off. Why pile up points the judges wouldn't score?

It was the same deal in Brooklyn against the Irish-American heavyweight Jack Burke, a Dempsey sparring partner who'd fought well in losses to Greb and Tunney. As usual, prefight features played up the ravening-savage-on-the-loose angle. The *New York Sun* risked the well-worn opinion that Siki "might be a great fighter" were it not that he "mixes fun with fighting," which might be amusing for the fans but got him nowhere in the standings. Still, if Burke could "rouse the Battler to a fury," fans might count on "excitement in large quantities."[43] Come see the fight, boys, they seemed to say. If you don't see a bloodbath, you're sure to see a circus. Only the *Brooklyn Daily Times* bothered to ask Siki his opinion. He told them he wanted "to make a name for himself as a scrapper and not a ring clown."[44]

The bout, lamentably, Vincent Clabby groused, turned out to be "strictly a boxing match the entire route."[45] Burke jabbed Siki's "game left eye" (injured in training), walked into clinches, and held on until the referee called "break."[46] He wasn't above fouling either—grinding the laces of his glove into Siki's eye. Fifteen pounds lighter than Burke, Siki fought so lethargically he barely mussed his rival's plastered-down hair.[47] The decision went to the white boxer. "The boy from Senegal," the *Daily Eagle* taunted, had "jumped around, stamped his feet, made faces," done everything but fight. Burke, for his part, "frightened from the start," had "fought only in spots."[48]

Healthy and in shape, Siki had finally gotten his wish to fight white fighters—but he faced a new reality: if his rival went the distance, Siki didn't need to wait for the verdict. He'd lost. For that matter, he may well have been told to "carry" opponents, to back off and not try for a knockout.[49] After the three disappointing losses, Siki quit training. Days before Christmas, due to leave on the morrow with Lillian for Memphis, he went on a racket in Harlem, taking along a new pet, a tiny West African monkey. He staggered from a taxi at 135th and Lenox, by the Commonwealth Sporting Club, as fans streamed from a Friday night fight card. Across the street, by "John Connor's soda water emporium," Siki passed the driver his nearly empty jug of wine and gestured for the dregs to be poured down his throat. The crowd shrieked, the monkey on Siki's shoulder chattered, the cabbie grinned. A cop growled, "Break it up!" Siki tottered off. But before he got to the speakeasy's door, he took offense at a wisecrack and dropped the offend-

ing party, one William Walker, thirty-eight, of 197 Edgecombe Avenue, with a
hook to the ribs. Walker went off groaning. The next day, as Siki boarded his
train, Walker called an ambulance to take him to Harlem Hospital—and
called a lawyer to press charges. Why not? Wasn't Siki throwing away money
left and right anyhow?[50]

Boxing's Harlequin and Miscreant

Backs twist, heads crane back past shoulders. Chairs scrape, eyebrows
arch. Mouths gape in affront. The only sound is an in-drawing of breath. In
the center of a circle of twisted torsos, half-turned chairs, three forms lean
together across a tablecloth and candle—two men and a woman. They're
out for a quiet family evening on the town, the week before Christmas, but
they've chosen a strange place for it. The man in the center stares across
the table at a waiter who stands, tray pressed against his stomach. His
rounded eyes, arched eyebrows suggest a puzzling question. Instead he mutters an explanation, a refusal. The two other people at the table gaze at the
set face of the man sitting between them. His compatriots are fair-skinned,
straight-haired. Both could "pass"—and have. The man in the center can't—
not with his raven skin, bushy hair, thick lips, wide nostrils.[51]

I'm sorry, the waiter whispers, as if confessing a shameful secret. But
you'll have to leave. We only serve whites. White patrons, twisted side-
saddle, strain to hear.

No, the black man declares. He won't leave. Why should he? He's eaten
in better joints than this—in Paris, Amsterdam, New York. Why should he
meekly slip into the night because a timid little man in a nondescript café
says to go? The waiter scurries off.

Herbert Allyn's Café on Dunlap Avenue in Memphis makes no pretense
to *haute cuisine*. It's too modest a joint to have much call to refuse anyone
service. The waiter peeks around the corner to see if the intruders have left.
But the dark-skinned man stays put. Finally the owner picks up the phone.
The waiter murmurs, as if announcing the soup, that they've phoned the
police. The three wait numbly. They hadn't expected this. America's system
of apartheid has its odd exceptions. "Foreigners," in theory, are exempt.
Years later, the Louisville teenager Cassius Clay will dress in flowing robes
and pretend to speak "foreign English" so he can crash whites-only theaters
and eating places.[52] The light-skinned man, no foreigner, is Beverly Warner,
a truck driver for Corlis-Seabrock Paint Company. If he needed reminding of
how dangerous a gesture this is, he might have read the story in the
December 19 *Memphis Commercial Appeal* about how two hundred whites

beat up a Charleston, Missouri, sheriff, grabbed a twenty-year-old black man named Roosevelt Grigsby, dragged him "screaming for mercy and protesting his innocence" (of molesting a white girl) to a tree in the town square, hanged him, fired bullets into the corpse, doused it with gas, burned it, tied the charred remains to a car, and dragged them through town, firing in the air and bawling threats, before finally tying the corpse to a post in front of a grocery.[53]

The light-skinned woman at Herbert Allyn's Café, Beverly Warner's sister Lillian, might not be up on local news, but her year away hasn't made her forget Memphis's style of racial intimidation, either. Still, she holds her ground, as defiant as her husband Louis. The *Commercial Appeal* will later insist that she, not he, balked at leaving, sassing restaurant personnel—that the dark-skinned stranger merely misconstrued "Southern customs," his offense "more due to unfamiliarity... than belligerency." Finally two cops, officers Littlejohn and Bryant, arrive to escort the outlaws from racial propriety out the door. Before the desk sergeant, Lillian does "most of the talking" and "very uncomplimentary" [sic] abuses "the hospitality of the South." Though all three are booked, only Siki spends a night in jail. He alone faces a fifty-dollar fine for "drunkenness and disorderly conduct." The idea he might, stone sober, defy a repressive social order is treated as laughable. "Testimony in court developed the fact," the *Commercial Appeal* claims, "that Siki, battle-scarred veteran of a hundred police courts, entered the premises of Mr. Allyn, looked in the mirror, saw triple, and sat down by the other three negroes."[54] Lillian, it insists, had "passed for white several times in the East," implying that if he was befuddled with drink, she was beguiled by exposure to a misguided social system.

Apparently not all of white Memphis proved so hostile, for during another night on the town Siki made a brand-new pal, a young fellow named Ben Bluestein, who got him to sign a contract and quickly lined up a headline bout in Atlanta.[55] To exacerbate his perfidy, Siki, once he got there, staged Levy's familiar publicity stunt of having detectives follow him around town, meanwhile protesting how the media misrepresented and "misunderstood" him, swearing he was "not guilty of many of the escapades with which he [had] been charged" while others had been "greatly exaggerated."[56] He told a story to illustrate his maltreatment: "Once I was introduced to a man as Battling Siki. He laughed and said, 'You are not Battling Siki.' I asked him why he didn't believe it and he said, 'Why you haven't got rings in your nose and ears.'"

"Misunderstood" or not, Siki was savvy enough to know how to work his ill fame for a profit. That same day, according to the *Atlanta Constitution,* rumors that the Senegalese wild man would be giving things away on a downtown street corner drew throngs of eager supplicants dreaming of free cash, or tailored suits—whom Siki rewarded instead with a single banana each. Well, why not? A similar gambit had drummed up customers a year before in Memphis. But just hours before his scheduled headline bout against local club fighter Happy Hunter at the city auditorium, where a segregated section had been reserved for persons of color, Siki learned that the state boxing commission, which the fight's promoter had believed to be defunct, had hastily called itself into session for the express purpose of banning the fight.[57] The commissioners gave as their rationale that they hadn't been paid their fee or given two weeks' notice of the bout and that the combatants were "far from being of the first-class type"—a ludicrous excuse since Siki was a former world champion and Hunter had fought and won in Atlanta days before.[58]

Aware of the real reasons for the ban (its effect on the fans in the segregated section for persons of color), Siki accepted the inevitable. He'd hoped to lure into an Atlanta ring future world middleweight champion Tiger Flowers. That wouldn't happen now. Then a final twist developed to the story. Tipped off by someone of his fighter's whereabouts, Bob Levy arrived by train from New York, waving his contract. Bluestein obligingly renounced his rights—whereupon Levy amiably offered to cut in his new rival, as "southern representative," on any fights he could line up below the Mason Dixon line.[59] Nonetheless, however genial he was with Bluestein, Levy must not have been too pleased with the fugitive fighter—for it would be months before Siki again stepped through the ropes of a professional prize ring.

While Siki was off chasing fleeting opportunities elsewhere, he missed one of the biggest fights of the New York / New Jersey winter season and one that said a lot about his own status in the boxing game. Mike McTigue had defended his title against one of the hardest punchers in boxing. His manager had stuck to his no-decision stipulation and for good measure dipped down two weight classes to find an opponent. Not much risk there, you'd think—facing a man from a class whose weight limit was twenty-five pounds below yours. But McTigue was really a middleweight himself—and the man he faced, welterweight champ Mickey Walker, was struggling lately to make the welterweight limit. Besides, Walker hit like a heavyweight.[60] A pug-nosed wise guy with a taste for the high life, he bragged he'd take McTigue out early, and on fight night, good as his word, came out firing, bulling inside, banging away, as McTigue went into a shell, ducking and covering up. Battered and bruised, McTigue rode out Walker's furious combinations.[61]

Then, his bolt shot, from round eight on, Walker showed only flashes of pug-nacity as the crowd booed and stamped its feet. Siki, had he been around to witness the bout, couldn't have missed the irony: Walker / McTigue precisely mirrored Siki / McTigue of nearly two years before. As in Dublin, McTigue waited until the late rounds, when his rival was lead-limbed, to skip into range and snap off counters. But this time his belated pugnacity impressed no one. The writers unanimously awarded Walker the newspaper decision and would have handed him the title too, had it been theirs to give. Since it wasn't, they gave him a silver loving cup, inscribed: "Mickey Walker wins light-heavyweight title by defeating Mike McTigue in Newark... January 7, 1925."[62] Siki had chased McTigue for twenty rounds, not twelve—and if he too ran out of gas, unlike Walker he came back four more times to try to put McTigue down under a barrage of blows. Against Siki, McTigue waited six-teen rounds, not ten, before he fought back. Why hadn't it occurred to the gang of writers in Dublin to pitch in for a silver loving cup for Siki? Because they had a rigid rule where Battling Siki was concerned: if he didn't knock his rival out, he was "just clowning... not really trying."

On the outs with Levy, and sick of the boxing game, Siki was absent from the professional ring for a full three months, the longest hiatus of his career. He missed the entire lucrative winter season. A new edge came into nocturnal rampages, too, a dangerous abandon sports writers spun into invidious legend. In a memoir written fifteen years later, Nat Fleischer fash-ioned an image that would become an abiding element in the myth of the "Singular Senegalese." His tale places Siki in the middle of Forty-second Street, in evening clothes, silk hat, red gloves, red satin-lined cape, and gray suede shoes, directing traffic with a walking stick. A crowd gathered, chaos loomed, a policeman approached. Siki "politely bowed, doffed his hat and extended his hand in greeting. The droll bluecoat lifted his cap and extended his hand, whereupon from under Siki's cape leaped a monkey. He landed on the head of the officer, who almost fainted with fright while the crowd and Siki roared with laughter." This version of the tale ends with Siki gliding far-cically away, as the cop hurls imprecations.[63]

If the clothing is standard-issue Siki-the-savage-freak, the monkey, at least, was real. So was the period of self-forgetful abandon. Fleischer tells the tale to illustrate his notion that Siki, "more than merely different," was "fan-tastic, incredible."[64] But one can take it otherwise—as a lost soul's gesture of repudiation. Flaunting icons of wealth and status, he feigns a sign of mas-tery, making Broadway his orchestra. Then along comes an emblem of the reality principle, in zookeeper-blue, to assert order. Lit with wine, Siki ges-tures acquiescence. The monkey simultaneously loses his hold and leaps for a more secure perch. The cop recoils, cursing to cover panic. Siki moves away to seek solace elsewhere. Fleisher retold the tale fifteen years later, giving the cop an identity ("big Pat McDonald, the Olympic-hammer thrower"), setting it soon after Siki's arrival in America (before he actually bought the monkey). In the evolved version, rather than shaking hands, "the fantastic Negro, Siki, took off his high silk topper, [and] bowed in ceremonial French style." Rather than cursing Siki's retreating form, big Pat "caught Siki by the collar, bustling him away."[65]

The monkey story came with a companion piece at boxing dinners, a tale Fleischer sets on the day Siki returned to the ring in March 1925. The two versions match better this time. In *Black Dynamite* Siki saunters down an avenue near his home, monkey on arm, followed by a curious crowd. He comes upon three women chatting, "sneak[s] up behind them, chatter[s] something in his native tongue to the monkey, and, in a jiffy, the little simian [is] climbing the back of the woman nearest him." In "his native tongue"? Wolof? Did Siki say, "*Gis na, golo. Jigeen jii rafet lool*"? "Look, monkey. What a beautiful lady"? In Fleischer's tale, the woman collapses in hysterics and Siki flees—straight into the arms of a cop, who growls, "What are you doing with that scarecrow around here? You come along with me." He collars the miscreant and marches him off to face the music, urging the women to press charges, until Siki declares, "Eet is not my fault, gendarme; eet is my monkey. He likes charming ladies." Flattered, they relent.[66]

In Fleischer's *Fifty Years at Ringside,* Siki, a provocative exhibitionist in a "playful mood," "strutting like a peacock," is delighted that a crowd follows him. This time he speaks not "his native tongue" but French (or did Fleischer think Siki's native tongue *was* French?). The woman on whose back the monkey leaps is part of the curious crowd this time. Again she shrieks and faints, while Siki "stood grinning like an ape" and "the crowd began to murmur angrily." This time the cop ends his speech "you're taking too many liberties" as he pulls out his billy. Siki again wins a reprieve. This time we get gratuitous animal analogies: Siki as ape, Siki as peacock—creatures embodying rage, lust, sexual display.[67] This time the incident is not a chance encounter but willful provocation. Like an ape or a peacock, the savage, captivated by his own indecent panoply, wants the world to share his self-love. And when they won't, he sics his monkey on them. The monkey is a euphemism, a latent sign for a breach of taboo. The leap on the woman's back suggests sexual violation, for which liberty black men were lynched in 1925.

Actually, the only monkey tale involving Siki that appeared in the daily papers that year occurred a few months later, when Siki's pet, startled by the crowd surging out of the Coney Island BMT, leaped from his lap, bolted through the closing doors, and led police and waiting passengers a merry chase before it disappeared beneath the Thirty-fourth Street platform. The *New York Times,* trying its best to build the tale up into a saleable farce, had precious little to work with. But then it was handicapped by writing too soon after the fact. It didn't dare add shrieking female victims or cops rushing to strong-arm savage miscreants. It was stuck relating that Siki, who'd been on his way to the Johnny Dundee / Sid Terris lightweight bout, calmly switched trains and returned to the station. But by then the monkey was nowhere to be found.[68]

"I sat at ringside and saw . . . ," Fleischer begins another tale, validating it via a linguistic code. "In the eighth round, Paul worked the negro against the ropes just in front of me, and bombarded him with paralyzing rights and lefts to the head." Fleischer thus marks the moment as etched indelibly in memory, as plain physical fact, unmediated, free of interpretation. He employs the same verb at the end: "I have seldom seen. . . ." Thus does Fleischer, like a perjurer with his hand on the Bible, solemnly witness as pure fact what is, in fact, pure fiction. He tells of a "primitive" African, "only half human," who "rolled his eyes and snorted" in the early rounds of his final match, as if to "terrify" the German-American punching machine circling an arm's length away, an African who, by the seventh, "had taken so much punishment that his eyes rolled in agony."[69] Fleischer loads his tale with clues as to how it's to be read. Siki is "boxing's harlequin," an "imitation King Kong" in a "flowing French cape lined with purple satin," wearing "bright red gloves and grey suede shoes."[70] Civilization has failed to remold his "primitive nature," leaving him "three quarters savage." Dissipating money and brutal energy with equal abandon, he is "in fact more than merely different," he's "fantastic, incredible."[71] But in fact, Battling Siki is "incredible" only as a bad imitation of a white man.[72] As a racial stereotype, he's perfect, a flawless incarnation of the code of race. Fleischer foretells a self-evident destiny: "With his unleashed passions given full sway and amply provided for by his ring earnings, he was bound to come to grief eventually."[73]

Poor misguided Siki! With "only the crudest idea of defense" (matching his faulty notions of civilization), he made it to round ten, says Fleischer, on stupid obstinacy. Then his white rival, "punching with lightning speed, shot home a bone-crushing right to the jaw." The half-man / half-ape "fell forward on his face as if a bullet had struck him and was counted out" in "his last fight in the ring."[74] Fleischer's image is so memorable you think perhaps you witnessed it yourself—saw Siki tumble face-first, arms splayed, legs flopping, as if gunned down by a gangster on a darkened street, saw him lie face down, inert as a rag doll.

So real do Fleischer's images seem you're surprised to find, when you check his own *Ring Record Book*, that the bout ended not with Siki dropping senseless to the canvas but with the referee leaping between the two men, waving his arms, shouting, "That's it, boys! It's over!"—declaring a "technical knockout,"a ruling that one boxer is no longer "making a contest of it" and might be permanently injured if allowed to go on. When one looks for the real bout that took place in Madison Square Garden, on March 13, 1925, spinning stress-worn microfilm at New York Public Library, one keeps finding the same thing: the bout was halted at 1:12 of the tenth. A knockout? Siki wasn't once even knocked *down*. "Slugger Batters Senegalese, But Unable to Score Knockdown," the *Herald Tribune* headlines.[75]

One spins the reel and wonders: where did Fleischer get it from, his image of a black man falling face-forward, as if shot? Then suddenly there it is, in the *New York American*—in plain photo-offset. Five photographs line up in a seeming series, like a cartoon strip. In the first, a lunging white man misses a right hand aimed at the head of a black man, who has turned his body sideways, tucking an elbow to protect his ribs. In the second, a white man, back bowed, puts his back into a left hook that also misses, disappearing behind the torso of a black man who paws at the white's face with a feeble hook. In the third, a black man, bent forward, exhausted, drapes an arm over the shoulder of a brawny, bolt-upright white. In the fourth, a black man, bent from the waist, flips a feeble hook, as a white man, legs clumsily crossed, blocks it with an open glove. The final image seems a consequence of the others. A white man, back to the camera, leans forward, shoulders hunched, right arm in mid-follow-through, as a black man tumbles face first, feet comically flopping in the air above his torso, arms flailing, like a clown acrobat at the circus. He looks exactly like the man Fleischer describes in *Fifty Years at Ringside.* The only trouble is he isn't Siki. He's Harlem middleweight Larry Estridge, and the white boxer decking him is Frankie Schoell, not Paul Berlenbach. Berlenbach and Siki are, in fact, the fighters in the first four photos, but this last photo is of an undercard ten-rounder fought the same night.

The next reel discovers another set of photos, beginning again with four from the Siki / Berlenbach bout, ending again with a shot of Schoell hovering over the fallen Estridge, this time from the opposite side, taken seconds later.[76] Again a casual observer could misread the series, mistaking Estridge for Siki. But how could a seasoned boxing writer such as Fleischer make such a bizarre mistake? Estridge, by the way, wasn't knocked out, either. Saved by the (first-round) bell, he got up and fought on to a close decision loss. Was Fleischer absent that night? (Is his "I sat at ringside and saw" a lie?) Did he skim the headlines the next day, glance at the photos, and fix in memory a misreading? Sid Mercer in the *Journal* might have confused him too by flubbing his lead, insisting Siki "was the victim of a technical knockout in the tenth round, but he was soon on his feet groping for Berlenbach, half blinded and blood streaming from lacerated lips."[77] "Soon on his feet"? He never left them.

"It was his last fight," Fleischer insists—though in fact Siki fought on for the rest of the year, contesting five more bouts. Fleischer has the excuse of a thirty-year time lapse—but why didn't he check his own *Ring Record Book?* The error almost seems deliberate—as if, from a safe vantage beyond Siki's grave, he wants to finish the job of writing Siki out of existence. What impelled him thus to memorialize this black man's comic, bellyflop tumble from eminence? Why, racial progressive that he was, did Fleischer need to tag Siki with a final *commedia del'arte* pratfall, stripping him of every other virtue than a courage which, if "undying," also bordered, for Fleischer, on the grotesque or absurd?

In fact, badly out of shape, struggling to outlive the worst night of his career, Siki battled bravely that night against a brutally strong rival who had his number from the opening bell. Jack Kofoed in the *New York Evening Post* offers a contrary moral to the tale:

> There may have been men in the history of the prize ring who have stood up more courageously than the Senegalese but it is doubtful indeed. It did not seem possible that any human could be capable of withstanding such hammering. But, though the Astoria Assassin placed every ounce of power behind his blows, and he must have landed several hundred of them, Battling Siki never appeared to be in danger of being knocked out.[78]

The real story was as grim as waiting out an artillery barrage in a fetid trench, an analogy the *American*'s W. S. Farnsworth explicitly made.[79] Siki had no illusions. His notoriety had gotten him the bout, despite his utter unreadiness, and put nearly twelve thousand patrons, paying almost $44,000, into the seats. George Underwood, in the *Telegram,* said Joe Humphries gave "the Senegalese Adonis" a florid introduction, to boisterous applause, which Siki recognized by strolling over to plant a kiss atop Humphries's bald skull.[80] Through the early rounds Siki waved to pals, bantered with strangers in the diamond-stick-pin seats. Prefight features described him as surprising critics with his "speed and improved boxing ability and stamina,"[81] but in fact he'd arrived at Madame Bey's Summit training camp just four days before the bout, for his first real workout in three months.[82] In the *Daily Mirror* weigh-in photo, a pudgy Siki bends to peer at the scales. His muscular rival stands bolt upright beside him. Odds were dead even Siki would be knocked out. Most expected the bout to go only a few rounds. Still, who knew? The *Telegram* ran an Ed Hughes cartoon of Siki's head as a goggle-eyed speed bag (with sausage-shaped white lips) that bounds back to smack "Punching Paul" between the eyes. Hughes captioned, "Paul expects to have a lot of fun tonight, but you can't always tell about these imported punching bags."[83]

Mercer in the *Journal* said Berlenbach, confused by Siki's defensive crouch, "could not do much with him for three rounds."[84] But Lawrence in the *Herald Tribune* saw "fierce" blows to the head and body that seemed to have Siki "on the way to the rosin"[85] and W. S. Farnsworth in the *American* said a left hook that landed "very low" in round two had Siki "ready to flop."[86] Three papers saw Siki launch his own assault. The *Herald Tribune* swore he "swept Paul across the ring and made him realize that Mr. Siki was no bargain." Some say Siki stuck out his chin to taunt Berlenbach in the third. One claimed that he turned his head to wave to friends and got clocked with a Berlenbach left. In his corner Siki was spitting blood from split lips and dripping gore from his nose. Even so, rapt in banter with ringside cronies, he had to be pushed onto his stool.[87]

Farnsworth saw Siki just miss a right swing in the fourth that "would have ended the festivities had it landed." Hype Igoe in the *World* saw Berlenbach thud home a half-dozen body blows that "shook Siki to his socks," but saw Siki in turn send Berlenbach "floundering" with a right to the head.[88] As the round ended, Siki protested low blows, "wav[ing] his glove… and walk[ing] to his corner shaking his head."[89] Underwood calls Berlenbach's attack "lumbering," his blows "ponderous," his style "awkward," but he kept working his uppercut, slashing a cut above Siki's left eye that sprayed blood over the "belting beauty's" chest and trunks.[90] In the sixth Siki rallied fiercely, landing to the body, only to be dealt a half-dozen uppercuts in return. He caught Berlenbach with a right breaking from a clinch, courting retaliation to his bloody lips.

Exhausted, Siki was standing up gallantly to a left hook that Hype Igoe said landed harder than any in boxing history.[91] Reporters saw Siki wince and heard him "groan" or "gasp" when body shots landed.[92] Between rounds, Levy braced him with jolts of whiskey.[93] He had six rounds to go—and little to throw at Berlenbach to slow him down. From here on, the fight became that unsettling spectacle, a one-sided bloodbath. Writers might smugly put "fight" in quotation marks, or label the bout "nauseating," but admitted to "the shadow of a thrill."[94] Siki's era, after all, made a cardinal virtue of "gameness," the ability to absorb unheard-of pain. It "looked more and more," Underwood wrote, "as if Berlenbach simply was practicing in the gymnasium against the heavy sand bag."[95]

The crowd, however, clung to the notion of Siki as a wounded beast, grand in his instincts, dangerous in extremity. In the seventh, Siki essayed "a few shimmy steps" that set them howling, but Berlenbach reached him with hooks that had him hanging onto the ropes.[96] Igoe thought Berlenbach's power had begun to fade from sheer fatigue. Siki came "hobbling" out for the eighth, an ear shattered, an eye nearly closed, his mouth "a bloody smear." Even so, he went toe to toe, and "gave as good as he got at close quarters."[97] Then, legs shaky, he went into a turtle defense, as Berlenbach poked at him with uppercuts. By round's end, fans began to stamp their feet. Referee Eddie Purdy warned Siki he'd halt the bout unless he fought more aggressively.

When Siki made a "brave attempt to slug it out" in the ninth, Berlenbach caught him with a "terrific left hook to the body" that "shook [him] from head to foot," followed by a flurry of lefts and rights.[98] "Nobody would have blamed Siki," Mercer said, "if he failed to come out for the tenth," but at the bell he rushed across the ring as if he, not his rival, were on the verge of triumph.[99] The referee's warning had been an ultimatum: quit trying to stick it out. The fans want a knockout. Siki nearly obliged them, walking into a left hook to the chin. Dazed, he "slid along the ropes" as Berlenbach pursued, clubbing him to the body and head, leaving him "spitting blood like a wounded bear and bent almost double in his own corner."[100] Purdy wedged himself between the fighters, waving his arms to end the bout. Siki protested through torn lips that he could have weathered the two minutes left in the round, the eight left in the fight. Igoe thought he might have, but "it wouldn't have been nice to look at." Underwood and Mercer doubted Siki had won a single round. Mercer spoke of "the twilight of his career."[101] Levy must have drawn a similar inference, for when Siki turned to look for someone to cut off his gloves, Levy had vanished.[102] "You're on your own kid," the gesture seemed to say. Siki took it at face value, heading straight from the arena into the alcoholic obscurity from which, a week earlier, he'd emerged.

I'll Take Care of Him Myself

Since 5:00 P.M., the last Saturday of May, fans had been filing into the stands at Jake Ruppert's Yankee Stadium. Eventually, forty-five thousand people would jam the new palace of baseball—and not to see the "Sultan of Swat," Babe Ruth. Earlier that day, the last-place (!) Yankees had lost to the Athletics in Philadelphia—with Ruth absent, mending from surgery for an "intestinal abscess" newsmen privately hinted was venereal disease. No, the crowd had come to witness the first big boxing card of the outdoor season, light-heavyweight champion Mike McTigue defending his crown—to a decision! Six of the best light-heavies in the world graced the undercard.

McTigue was lucky. At the last moment promoters told Jack Delaney, an artful boxer with a "rapier-like jab" and a knockout punch, "Listen, we're making a switch. Berlenbach gets the title shot before you."[103] Delaney had dumped Berlenbach on his ass in four rounds the year before, but Berlenbach boasted hosts of local fans. A McTigue / Berlenbach clash would sell. With a gangster for a manager, Delaney knew how to take orders. He'd fight in the semifinal against Tony Marullo. Jimmy Slattery would face Jack Burke to fill out the card. Delaney might not know it, but both Marullo and Slattery would get title shots before he did. And Siki? Had anyone thought to include him?

Hardly! He'd dropped from sight. His wife, Lillian, would later say they loved to listen to the radio play-by-play of big bouts, and "hug each other when his man was winning."[104] Listening to WNYC's pioneering broadcast, Siki must undoubtedly have predicted Berlenbach's fierce pursuit in the early rounds of the elusive Irishman, who hardly risked a return blow. But he must have been startled in the sixth when McTigue changed tactics, cutting off Berlenbach's rushes and stinging him with counters. From the seventh to the ninth, the red-headed wraith kept beating the ungainly Berlenbach to the punch, slipping his hooks and slashing him with rights. The fans cheered his reckless abandon, but manager Doc Bagley no doubt moaned, "Mike! What are you doing?" Then, arm weary, rubber-legged, McTigue tried to hang on as the Astoria strongman pounded his ribs and head with that lethal hook. By fight's end, he wore Siki's precise stigmata: an eye swollen closed, lacerated lips, a bloody nose. "Punching Paul" got the decision.

Berlenbach didn't give Delaney his promised title shot right away, but in the year he held it Berlenbach took on eight title challengers, fighting brilliantly at times. Once he lost his crown to Jack Delaney, he fell into a profound depression and was never the same. When he returned to the ring after a five-month absence in 1927, McTigue knocked him out.

When Siki returned to the ring in June his options were few. Levy's best contact was promoter Ben Bliven, who'd run cards at the Buffalo Velodrome, where Siki had flattened Tony Stabenau and lost to Homer Smith. Lately Bliven had found his way to North Jersey, staging bouts at West New York Playgrounds, in gang-riddled Hudson County. Hoods such as Big Red Donovan, Larry Coyle, Herman Black, Pete Reilly, and Henry and Frederick Werther took advantage of political corruption there and a tolerant climate

for "wets," to openly run breweries, divert industrial alcohol, and land bootleg whiskey like cordage. Bronx gang boss Dutch Schultz got his beer from
Union City's Frankie Dunn.[105] Manhattan rumrunner Waxey Gordon peddled
Jersey beer, too, and eventually, when Gotham got too hot for him, would
retreat to Boss Hague's domain for good.[106] In 1926, a few miles upriver, federal agents would uncover a scheme running illicit hooch from an Edgewater
boatyard that enriched the mayor and police chief by sixty thousand dollars.
Manhattan mobsters Frank Costello and Joe Adonis would also eventually
flee across the Hudson, bribing local officials to look the other way as they
set up a gambling den in Cliffside Park known as the "Big Hall."[107] Ben Bliven
could not have moved down from Buffalo to Hudson County without local
mob sanction. Buffalo's mob boss, Stefano Magaddino, born in Brooklyn, may
have been his go-between. He maintained links to New York City gangsters.

Siki himself lived in a stretch of decaying real estate where every
second tenement housed a clip joint, gang social club, gambling den,
speakeasy, or whorehouse. Maybe Levy gave it to him straight: I got you
some fights that will pay, against white guys, but you'll have to fight under
wraps—and no funny stuff. They won't be amused if you pull a fast one. In
late June Siki faced twenty-year-old Utica middleweight Art Weigand, who
would in time fight three other world champs, beating one—Owney
Madden's house light-heavyweight Maxie Rosenbloom. Siki and Weigand
fought half-heartedly, doing just enough to keep patrons from throwing
things. The *Buffalo Evening News* noted, "Occasionally Siki would show a
flash of aggressiveness and cut over a few nasty right wallops to the head.
Weigand played largely for the body but with no great effectiveness."[108]
Weigand got the decision—naturally. On July 10, in boxing-mad Rockaway's
new beach-front arena, Siki faced last-minute fill-in Chief Halbran, an ersatz
Iroquois whom he "hammer[ed] from one end of the ring to the other,"
knocking him out in round three.[109]

Two weeks later, near craggy Hudson River bluffs in West New York,
Siki faced a boxer who'd also flattened the "Hoboken Iroquois," Union City
Italian-American Jimmy Francis—who boasted, said the *Jersey Journal,* a
strong jaw, rugged physique, and surly disposition.[110] A 1915 Independence
Day program reveals the fight's setting: a board-flat, bare-dirt tract, devoid
of trees, bordered by brick apartments and undulating waste ground. A
ragged file of onlookers circles an unfenced ballfield, screening busy teeter-
totters and swings behind center field. By 1925, the landfill had expanded
and bleachers hedged the field. West New York Playgrounds seems a strange
locale for a big prizefight, but it had hosted McTigue's 1923 title defense
against Tommy Loughran, and flyweight champ Pancho Villa's against Henry

Catena in 1924. Siki / Francis very nearly outdrew both. Jimmy Francis, though he won no special renown himself, shows up on the records of several champions. The top men he faced had two things in common: they were all secretly owned by the same mob bigshot, Hell's Kitchen native son Owney Madden, and Francis did surprisingly well against them, going the distance every time. He faced the future heavyweight champion Jimmy Braddock, managed by Madden stooge Joe Gould, three times in no-decision bouts. Braddock would, in the early 1930s, lose decisions to so many mediocre fighters that he would drop out of the sport, work for a time as a longshoreman on the Jersey waterfront, even sign up for relief. When Gould finally beckoned him back to the ring, he was rewarded (despite having fought just three times in two years!) with a title fight against heavyweight champion Max Baer—which, despite being a massive underdog, Braddock won—earning him the nickname "the Cinderella man." Of course, that nickname was handed him by Damon Runyon, whose own fairy godfather was the same Owney Madden.[111]

The title "Cinderella man" might equally well fit Francis, for he did seem to have a godfather looking out for him. Though the most ordinary of boxers, in addition to Braddock, he also faced future light-heavyweight champ and mob-protégé "Slapsie" Maxie Rosenbloom—as did (three separate times) Joe Silvani, a fighter Siki openly mocked in the ring for his novice ineptitude (see page 223). Yet Silvani, like Francis, would go the distance against Rosenbloom (twice) and once hold him to a draw. Art Weigand, who had benefited from that ill-smelling decision against Siki in Buffalo in June, would have similar good fortune against Rosenbloom.

Who was Bliven's contact in Hudson County? The answer isn't far to seek. When Siki fought another West New York bout a month later, he posed for a prefight photo with his opponent (Billy Vidabeck), the referee, Levy, Bliven, and Charlie Doessereck, a promoter who doubled as Vidabeck's manager. Though his office was on Forty-second Street in New York, Doessereck had run fights out of the Bayonne Athletic Association for years and gotten Gene Tunney his earliest bouts. Both Tunney and his later manager Billy Gibson had mob links. Dempsey was so leery of Tunney's ties to Philadelphia racketeer "Boo Boo" Hoff that he wrote the heavyweight champion an open letter in 1929, before the famous "long-count" bout, demanding Tunney acknowledge them.[112] Jimmy Francis would go on boxing until 1938, when he'd fight his last bout in Hot Springs, Arkansas—a favorite mob resort, where Owney Madden ran the rackets after New York got too hot for him. In light of what would happen to Battling Siki just days after the Francis bout, these factors add up to one thing: somebody bet a lot of money on the

Siki / Francis fight. And that somebody was very upset with how it turned out. That somebody had strong enough links to the Hell's Kitchen mob to order Siki's murder in the heart of their turf.

Hudson County was Jersey City boss Frank Hague's domain, as Hell's Kitchen was ward fixer Jimmy Hines's. Anything went in either realm— including murder. Huge breweries ran with impunity straight through prohibition in both districts. In North Jersey, top bosses Willie Moretti of Cliffside Park and Longy Zwillman of Newark turned the numbers racket, loan sharking, and gambling into local industries. Nicholas Delmore, Union County's biggest bookmaker, took any sports action that offered—cutting in boss Hague, who'd once managed a boxer himself and had close ties with Zwillman and Moretti.[113] Westbrook Pegler would later charge that Hague's realm hosted "the greatest gambling industry in the United States and perhaps, by volume, in the world."[114] A week after Siki's second West New York bout (against Billy Vidabeck), a Jersey City judge warned seven Hell's Kitchen hoods (caught with concealed pistols) to keep out of Hudson County.[115] Boss Hague frowned on outsiders invading his turf. Hague's cops once even beat up the Bronx gangster Dutch Schultz for having the temerity to cross through the Hudson Tunnel without prior sanction. Moretti and Zwillman were less parochial; they formed an alliance with Manhattan mobsters Owney Madden, Meyer Lansky, Arnold Rothstein, Frank Costello, Joe Adonis, and Lucky Luciano that came to dominate the entire metropolitan region.[116]

Bliven worked hard selling out the Siki / Francis bout, playing up a familiar angle, racial conflict. Bliven swore his ferocious "Union City lad" had "ripped up sparring partner after sparring partner... over a dozen the past week alone, all of them blacks... for Jimmy as he puts it, 'wants to get used to the color.'" Hudson County papers routinely exploited racial phobias, casting every possible story from a racial angle. "Cops Gun Down Two Negroes" blazoned an article on an aborted burglary. "Negro Forfeits $1000 Bond" shrilled a blurb about a chauffeur's nonappearance on a drunk-driving charge.

As Helene Stapinski points out in her memoir of growing up in Jersey City, gambling was an everyday fact of life in Boss Hague's domain that seemed to involve virtually every citizen. As Donald Trump has noted, boxing, because of its physical intensity, more than any other sport lures fans to gamble.[117] Siki's star was fading, but the strange allure of his name still filled arenas. With a local hero involved, a lot of money must have been bet, and whoever was holding the book seems to have felt obliged to protect his investment by ordering Siki to carry his white rival. Bliven told reporters of a junket he made across the river to track down Levy at his shirtwaist factory and of five or six hours he spent outside Siki's Hell's Kitchen lair, mounting guard to make sure Siki didn't disappear before fight night. Siki had never once, in fact, missed a bout, but Bliven swore he "nabbed" Siki when he finally emerged and "rushed" him across the river.[118] Bliven's vigil may have been just a publicity stunt, but it may have had other motives, too. Bliven may have made his pilgrimage to ask Levy, "Are you sure Siki will carry our boy the way he promised?" And if he did, Levy must have answered, "Hell, with Louis who knows? Why don't you go ask him yourself?" If Bliven did camp out in front of Siki's apartment on West Forty-second Street, it was probably to make sure he understood the deal—and knew he'd better keep his end.

The fans crowding the West New York Playgrounds must have wondered if the Union City fighter hadn't gotten too "used to the color," for when the main event began under bug-clotted lights, he was hardly ferocious. Neither was Siki. By the second round, the crowd stopped twitching with every feint, expecting every second that the "jungle fighter" was about to pounce on the "pride and idol of Union City"and tear his head from his shoulders.[119] Perhaps Siki came intending to play along with the fix, but something must have soured him on the Italian kid from Union City. Maybe Francis said the wrong thing in the clinches. Or maybe Siki expected his money up front and didn't get it. For whatever reason, as Francis faltered in a corner, Siki let loose a fusillade that pitched him through the ropes. Like Dempsey against Firpo, Francis tumbled onto the heads of ringside reporters and only beat the count because they pushed him back into the ring. Siki went after him again like a threshing machine, jerking him side to side with a left hook and right cross, draping him by the neck over the middle rope, head lolling, limbs flaccid. As referee Sailor Fritz's count reached eight, Francis pitched sideways onto the canvas with a sickening thunk. Fritz could have counted to thirty if he felt like.[120] The stunned crowd didn't even murmur for three full minutes, gazing at the "gleaming, glistening figure of the jungleman as he stood there supreme."[121]

Four days later a *New York Evening Journal* reporter came to French Hospital on West Thirty-fourth Street to check out a rumor: an ex-champion boxer was bleeding to death. These days, bleeding to death would be about his only hope to get his name in a New York newspaper. He was great copy once, but lately public curiosity about the "Singular Senegalese" had gone stale. Dying, however, was different. If he could arrange that, he'd get all the ink he wanted, especially if he did it in some picturesque way. And it looked as if Siki had done just that. He'd found a downright original way to croak. Murmurs of disbelief had greeted the call to the city room. But when the reporter arrived at Siki's bedside, hoping Siki might expire in his arms with an eccentric word of farewell, he found him instead sporting ugly gashes across his face and neck but otherwise alert (he'd refused anesthesia) and dangerous. He glared at his wife, Lillian, who had the temerity to refuse to fetch him clean clothes and to insist he stay in the hospital as ordered. He threw off the bedclothes and charged after her, but then, seeing the reporter, he grabbed his arm, frog-marching him down the corridor and out the front door.[122]

At the curb, the boxer found a taxi whose driver knew him from all-night prowls and who didn't bat an eyelash at seeing Siki in his nightclothes, swollen face cross-stitched with surgical thread. Into the cab he hopped, as the bewildered reporter recovered his dignity and flipped open his pad. He hadn't gotten a deathbed declaration, or even Siki's version of what happened, but fleeing from a hospital in pajamas was pretty good. He'd make a story out of that.

The dailies offered readers their pick of versions of how Siki got knifed in the wee hours Sunday, several originating from Siki himself. At first Siki said he'd broken up a street brawl and one guy had turned on him.[123] Then he said three men gabbing on a corner attacked him for no apparent reason.[124] Then he said he was going out to buy cigarettes when three men, two of whom he "knew slightly," fell into step with him, jumped him, and tried to slit his throat. "They got me from behind," Siki told the *Times*. "I would not care if they were four if they would fight fair."[125] Meanwhile, the cops had nabbed one Joseph Hanrahan, twenty-five years old, of West Thirty-eighth Street, caught sniffing around the crime scene, at Forty-first and Ninth, after Siki, unconscious from loss of blood, had been carted away. The police scrambled across tenement roofs to catch Hanrahan, who had bolted at the sight of them and now blithely declared he'd just heard a guy got stabbed and came to see the fun.[126]

Confronted with a suspect, Siki's memory began playing tricks. No, he didn't know this guy—didn't really remember what had happened. At Jefferson Market Court, before Judge Jesse Silbermann, Siki let Hanrahan off the hook, confiding later that he feared for his wife's safety. "I don't want to send him to jail," Siki added. "I'll take care of him myself." "Friends of the arrested man," noted the *Times*, ". . . urged Siki not to prosecute."[127]

"Take care of" a Hell's Kitchen thug? Did Siki have any idea what he was getting into? Even the cops knew better than to nose around that foul quarter. Owney Madden's gopher gang ruled the turf between Forty-second and

Fourteenth, west of Eighth. When riot squads had raided their dens a few years back, the gophers had showered them with bricks from upper-story windows. Lone patrolmen still turned up murdered.[128] Nowadays Madden had gone big-time, allying himself with Jewish and Italian hoods on both sides of the river. Maybe Siki thought himself too tough for street thugs— but if he did, he hadn't been reading the papers. Bill Brennan, a heavyweight who'd nearly taken Dempsey's title in 1920 (ahead on points, he got careless late in the fight and got knocked out), had thought he was tough, too. He'd had the nerve to give two gangsters the bum's rush from his Tia Juana Club, at 171st and Broadway. They came back to empty a revolver into his chest.[129]

The attempt on Siki's life could have been a simple mugging. He'd come back three days before flush from his Jersey payday. But in Hell's Kitchen a man who didn't dare press charges after getting his throat slit probably wasn't mugged. Both Siki's contradictory explanations of the attack and a conversation Bénac overheard years later about a failed fix make gang revenge the likely explanation. Zwillman or Moretti could easily have ordered a hit across the river. Moretti was pals with Frank Costello, and both men had ties to Owney Madden. Madden himself, for that matter, could have sent Hanrahan to slit Siki's throat. Having served one term for murder, "Owney the Killer" no longer did his own killing. Whoever ordered Siki murdered had to have Madden's okay. And whoever ordered Siki murdered would try again, once the heat was off. Gang enforcers were patient. They'd wait months if necessary.

The black fighter disputing the headline bout on the Saturday night card at Harlem's rickety Commonwealth Club seems, to a reporter from Harlem's *New York Age,* to be acting as if downright deranged—as if the stab wound to his face thirteen days before had affected his brain. He's sticking out his chin, taunting his white opponent, a husky teenager from Greenwich Village named Joe Silvani, daring him to hit it if he thinks he can. When Silvani tries to take Siki's head off, Siki spins him and pats his back: nice try, kid! He banters with ringsiders, waves a gloved hand at friends in mid-round, Charlestons in his corner between rounds. The Greenwich Village teenager keeps swinging murderous haymakers—looking more and more inept.[130] Years later, his younger brother Al, a leading trainer, would say Joe had gained a local reputation before he had the ability to back it up, making up in reckless pugnacity what he lacked in skill. Before the year was out, Joe Silvani, age nineteen, would retire from boxing for good, with a severe brain injury. Joe's brother Al Silvani would manage his first fighter chiefly to keep him out of the hands of men like those who'd ruined his brother.[131]

Did Siki guess what was in store for Joe Silvani? Probably. It's hard to hide deficient skills from a man with ninety professional bouts. His antics said, "What the hell is this kid even doing out here?" That half-healed knife wound didn't make him feel especially belligerent anyhow. He treated the bout as a lark. Referee Andy Griffin didn't see it that way. All at once, in the eighth, he handed Silvani a disqualification win. Siki acted as if a bucket of ice water had been thrown in his face, pawing past Levy to get at Silvani, as if he thought flattening the teenager might undo the ruling. Two policemen jumped into the ring to head him off.

By Monday August 10 Levy was furiously chasing down boxing commissioners before their regular Tuesday meeting. A disqualification could lead to a suspension. Siki would leave in a few days anyway to fight in Buenos Aires, he pleaded, so a suspension would be an empty gesture.[132] So what, the commissioners insisted, we've got reciprocal agreements with all of South America and most of Europe. If we ban him, he can't fight anywhere. Levy wasn't buying that. Foreign commissions would honor a New York suspension only if it didn't cost them money. Besides, everyone knew that lately, with all the paranoia over thrown fights, boxing boards had become suspension-happy. Dave Rosenberg had lost his license for pulling out of a fight with Siki in July. Even Harry Greb and Mickey Walker were suspended for performances deemed inadequate. After his first title defense, a no-decision bout before twelve thousand Newark fans on July 13, light-heavyweight champ Paul Berlenbach too had been suspended for an effort judged too tame, along with challenger Tony Marullo. By September, Berlenbach, reinstated, was defending his crown in New York against Jimmy Slattery. Battling Siki was another story though. The commission made special rules where he was concerned.

The federal immigration commisioner Henry H. Curran backed up the boxing board, threatening deportation proceedings. Only Levy's promise that Siki would leave willingly headed him off.[133] The bureau had only let Siki into the country in 1923, Curran insisted, on a one-month visa. Despite Siki's marriage to an American, he was unwelcome. But Curran may have been grandstanding, like the Jersey governor who swore, the summer before, he'd ban the bout between Harry Wills and Luis Firpo. Eleventh-hour anti-boxing crusades played well in the press.

Thursday the thirteenth found Levy, Siki, and Lillian again on a ferry-boat, under pelting rain, headed to West New York. They made the 3:00 weigh-in at the ballfield, then waited out a deluge with axe-faced promoter Ben Bliven, in baggy gray suit and straw boater. The field became a quagmire. Reporters killed time quizzing Levy, as Siki, sporting a bright bow tie and Jimmy Walker campaign button, listened. Levy had helped Walker wage a crusade to legalize Sunday baseball. The dapper state senator, ex-songwriter, show-biz wanna-be, dipsomaniac adulterer, and all-around grafter, had fathered the law legalizing boxing and sponsored another to force the Ku Klux Klan to reveal its secret membership rolls. The writers didn't ask Siki why he liked Walker (his stand on the Klan would win him the black vote, and ward-healer Jimmy Hines's support would win Hell's Kitchen), calling out instead, "Hey, champ, that was some knockout you put over on Francis last month. Looks like a washout today though."

"I don't care," Siki said. "The rain's good luck for Vidabeck. But Tuesday night, this right hand will knock him dead anyway. Then, when I finish Joe Borell [his next scheduled opponent], I'll go to Canada and have some fun, and afterwards maybe Levy will take me to South America to fight Luis Firpo. Huh, Papa Levy?"[134]

They turned to Levy. What about the deportation? Was it on the level?

"Aw," he answered. "They didn't issue deportation papers—and they won't. We were ready to leave anyway. It's just Ben's bouts that are keeping us. Then it's off to Buenos Aires."

"Yeah? You really gonna fight Firpo?"

Levy hesitated. "Yeah," he said. "First we fight Ferrara. Then Luis Firpo."

Wow! The Wild Bull of the Pampas! This little guy with the bow tie was going to fight the huge Argentine who'd knocked Dempsey out of the ring! They turned to Siki. What about it, champ? Can you beat Firpo?

"Sure," Siki answered. "I can take him."

The writers shrugged. Nobody thought much of his chances. "What about this stunt of sneaking out of the hospital in your pajamas?" someone asked.

Levy cut in, "Aw, listen, I wasn't even around. I was in Philadelphia for a match with another one of my boys, Jose Lombardo, when I saw the headline: 'Siki Escapes from Hospital Wearing Pajamas!' I didn't read another word. I knew that story was fake. Siki couldn't escape from a hospital wearing pajamas because he has no pajamas. He wears a night-gown!"

Everyone had a good laugh, including Siki. But the writers served another high hard one: What about this fight up in Harlem with Silvani? Why was Siki clowning around?

Siki cut in, "I'll tell you why. Before I fought Silvani, I fought Jimmy Francis, and before I fought him I fought Chief Halbran. I knocked out Halbran in three rounds and Francis in two, and I thought I needed a little workout with Silvani so I took it easy. Then when I was ready to knock him flat, the referee threw me out. He must be a taxi driver! But never mind. He's a good fellow anyway. Only he didn't give me a chance!"[135]

Finally, Bliven gave up. That's it, he said. I'm postponing the bout until Tuesday.

But on Monday two immigration agents turned up at West Forty-second Street to haul Siki off to an Ellis Island cell, leaving Levy scrambling to find one thousand dollars bail. Somehow, Levy got his cashier's check down in time, for the following evening found Siki, Lillian, and Levy back in Jersey. Most of the sparse crowd at the West New York Playgrounds was Slavic this time—like the ethnic hero of the moment, a lad from Bayonne just out of his teens whose ring name was Billy Vidabeck but whose real name was William Veydovec. Life didn't look so rosy for the blond, blue-eyed hero of the Bayonne faithful. Siki, after all, had abjectly thrashed Jimmy Francis—and Francis had knocked Vidabeck out. But four rounds passed with no hint of mayhem. The *Hudson Dispatch* gives a slangy description: "Stab! A long, lean left shoots itself into Battling Siki's face. Another swish—another stab! And again Billy Vidabeck's elongated left lunch hook is floating all over Battling Siki's dusky map."[136] The rounds ticked off hypnotically as the patrons at the dirt-packed ballfield waited. Then in the fifth, with the two in close, banging away, Siki abruptly straightened up. Blood ran from an eye. "He butt me mit head," the *Dispatch* has him bawling. The referee ignored him. The Bayonne faithful yelled, "Hold him when ya can't hit him, Billy! Don't slug with him, Billy! Box him!" Billy was all discretion. Siki chased him from ring post to ring post, the *Dispatch* related. "But when they got in close Vidabeck slapped over a left jab, fell into a clinch—and the poor Battler had to start all over again." So it went for five more rounds—a scant five miles from where Berlenbach and Marullo were kicked out of the ring for a similar lack of belligerence.

The next morning the Associated Press gave Vidabeck a narrow edge,[137] but the *New York Evening Journal* swore, "The battling one was in earnest and really turned in a meritorious performance." Vidabeck had only gone the distance "by dint of holding on tactics."[138] The *Jersey Journal* crowed that Vidabeck had handed the ex-champ "one of the worst ring losses" he'd "ever suffered," making the Bayonne fighter's jab out to be a jackhammer, Siki's accidental cut a bloodbath.[139] It seems likely that Siki carried the local favorite. But even if he hadn't the local kid had done nothing to merit orchid bouquets.

Siki had his pay packet at least—and other things to worry about. Levy found a lawyer, who filed a deposition with Curran urging that "no offense warranting deportation" had been reported during Siki's two-year stay.[140] Refusing to take seriously a mismatch at a Saturday smoker was hardly a federal crime. But boxing wanted no more of Battling Siki. New York went ahead with its ban. Within months, New Jersey would follow suit.[141] Siki would be left with hardly a state willing to let him into the ring. Though he didn't know it, he'd fought his last fight in New York or New Jersey.[142] In fact, though just turned twenty-eight, he'd appear only once more in his life in a boxing ring.

CHAPTER ELEVEN

"Trop de Cinéma"

Here Goes Nothing

At 7:00 P.M., December 14, 1925, a clear, cloudless day struggling past freezing, Lillian Fall bumped into her husband, Louis, coming in the front door at 361 West Forty-second Street as she adjusted her hat bustling out. "I'm going after some fish," she said. "You like fish. I'll be back and cook it for dinner."[1]

Fish with rice, *cebu jen,* was Senegal's national dish, cooked with broken rice to give it just the right texture—with perhaps a nice *capitaine* (barracuda), cabbage, carrots, onion, eggplant, pumpkin, turnip, and diakhatou, topped by a flaming pepper, as gnarled as a boxer's swollen ear. Senegalese housewives deliberately seared the rice until it caked against the cast-iron pan, making a brittle crust. How long was it since his teeth had crunched down on the crust of a good *cebu jen?* Nearly twenty years?

Fish would be fine, he said. He was "going out to see some of the boys," but he'd be back.[2] He smiled, walked off. She stood a moment on the stoop of their building, a five-story brick walk-up with two flats on each floor (theirs faced the street), then set off herself, headed not toward the Ninth Avenue markets, but east, toward the theaters. She'd get the fish later. She wanted to look at the posters for new movies, even though she couldn't afford to go in. They were so broke these days! The money from Louis's last fight, in Baltimore, had vanished so fast.

She'd gone there with him, of course. Her Louis was a sweet guy, but impulsive. He meant just to go out, enjoy the lights and sights, relax, talk, forget the world's prejudices. But before you knew it, with a few drinks under his belt, Louis was on his way, throwing money at his troubles, pouring solace down his throat. When they first married, Lillian had tagged along every time Louis went out the door. She went to fights, contract signings, weigh-ins, even workouts at the gym. About the only thing he did alone was road work—but Louis hardly ever did that. She'd loosed the leash since then, stopped grabbing her hat every time Louis headed for the door. But she still *never* missed a road trip. Their own love affair, after all, had begun on one. In Baltimore, she'd met the promoter, witnessed the weigh-in, then ridden with Louis to the arena and settled into a ringside seat. Louis had gone down there full of expectation, hoping if he put on a good show he'd get back in the good graces of the boxing bosses—who'd had it in for him ever since he'd hammed it up against Joe Silvani in Harlem. And in any case, once he got his purse at least they'd have two nickels to rub together for a while.

As the undercard wore down, in the drafty 104th Medical Regiment Armory, the tiers of bare seats remained unbroken by any but a few knots of mostly black faces. It began to be clear: the bout had sold badly. This was bad news. You signed a contract for a set sum—but try to collect it if the joint was empty! "Boys," the promoter would say. "I can't pay what I said! I'd lose my shirt!" Louis had been stalling creditors for a month with the promise of cash from this fight. His opponent, a light-skinned African American from Arizona named Lee Anderson, came down the aisle under the gaze of only fifteen hundred pairs of eyes. Once again Levy had set Siki up with a rugged rival, after months of idleness, and no tuneup. Anderson had beaten both Kid Norfolk and Tiger Flowers. But Louis had little choice. New York had suspended him. Michigan and Massachusetts barred him. New Jersey had followed suit on November 5. Maryland soon would, too. Levy had rushed him down here with no fanfare, promoting the fight only in the African American paper, aiming for a quick payday.

Waiting in the center of the ring in their robes (Anderson's dull brown, Louis's brilliant garnet), the boxers paced slowly, heads down, as if waiting for a train. At the bell they glided over the canvas, in that familiar series of circling movements—and right away something was missing. The tension of the opening seconds of a real fight wasn't there. They were fighting under wraps. Anderson landed a low blow—and apologized. Siki grinned and said, "Forget it." When they clinched, they waited for the referee to push them apart. The crowd booed. The referee warned them for stalling. The fans began calling, "Make 'em fight . . . ! Put 'em out!"[3]

The *Baltimore American*'s Ernest A. Bowersox said Siki staged bursts of speed, mixed with liberal doses of vaudeville: "Catlike, he displayed a marvelous ducking ability and an offensive that was, indeed, varied. He would cast his eyes away from his antagonist for a second or so and then . . . surprise him with a whirlwind two-handed barrage. He kidded with his rival, talked to seconds in his corner, and went through all sorts of gyrations with his arms."[4] Then, abruptly, the show was over. Siki and Anderson clanked down to a "creepy, don't-care pace," now and again tossing punches that "harmed nothing but the atmosphere." The referee gave Anderson the decision, though many in the crowd, Bowersox said, shouted for a draw. At least Louis had gotten through the bout without incident. Now if only he'd been paid his whole purse!

He hadn't. He got just three hundred dollars, enough to settle the rent and pay the grocer—if Louis didn't throw it away first.[5] But of course he did—and now creditors were getting ugly. A few days ago they'd bumped into a bootlegger who demanded twenty dollars Louis owed him.[6] Louis had put him off with a laugh and a promise—as he had one Mr. Ritter from Pacific Finance, who came demanding cash or the keys to Louis's car. When he bought it, Louis had paid four hundred dollars down, more than half the sticker price. Now he'd decided he'd been cheated and wouldn't pay another dime. Ritter could wave the contract all he liked. If he wanted the keys, he could give Louis back his four hundred dollars. The agent sputtered, "Where's the car? Pay up, or I'll repossess." Finally the guy hauled Louis off to court, charging "criminally secreting mortgaged property."[7]

Lillian sauntered past the glittering rank of movie palaces, whose lurid and misleading posters promoted stars like Pola Negri, Rudolf Valentino, Harold Lloyd, Lon Chaney, Gloria Swanson, Charlie Chaplin, and Tom Mix. George Jessel was appearing live in *The Jazz Singer* at the Cort Theater a few blocks north, but Lillian would hardly go to a Broadway show alone. Then suddenly there it was, the movie she'd been dreaming of seeing.[8] If she bought a ticket, she wouldn't have enough left for fish, but what the hell! Louis was probably gone for the evening anyway. She pulled out her purse. Louis had his realm of oblivion, she had hers.

The next day every paper in town would mention Lillian's ill-timed impulse of celluloid escape, but none would name the film. At Forty-second and Broadway Harold Lloyd's *Now or Never* and Gloria Swanson's *Stage Struck* were playing—but the former was a revival, the latter in its final week. Had she strolled a block south, she'd have found Blanche Sweet in *The Sea Woman,* but it too had been around awhile. Was the film that so struck her fancy the new Paula Negri two-reeler up on Forty-ninth at the Rivoli, *Woman of the World?* Edwin Carewe's *Joanna the Million-Dollar Girl* at the Mark Strand on Forty-seventh? Or *The Cobra,* starring heart-throb Rudolf Valentino and

Nita Naldi, at Broadway and Forty-fifth? The new film nearest at hand, at the Rialto on Broadway and Forty-second, was a farce about a wisecracking woman burglar caught creeping down a hallway in a rich man's mansion—Zukor and Lasky's *The Splendid Crime.* "Say?" jibed the sassy burglar, played by Jack Dempsey's one-time lover Bebe Daniels, "Don't you birds ever go to bed?"[9] One would like to place Lillian there, glowing with delight at the heroine's immunity to fate and fiscal confusion. But we have no way of knowing which film so enthralled her that she forgot her promise to Louis.

In the morning she and Louis were to rise early to catch a train to Washington where he had a Vaudeville engagement. He'd work a familiar routine, leaving patrons gasping over a display of what they took to be savage elasticity: shadowboxing like a dervish, spinning Indian clubs like blades on an electric fan, snapping a jump rope in a seamless whirr, pumping piston-fast calisthenics. Then, poised on a stool, he'd tell, for the hundredth time, how he'd thrashed the great Georges Carpentier. Afterward, they'd take in the sights in D.C., shop, and reach Memphis by Christmas. Levy had sworn he'd get Louis a personal introduction to President Coolidge.[10] Wouldn't that be something! Then she remembered Louis and hurried home.

Louis was sweet and attentive. He did much of the cooking, most of the cleaning, she would tell reporters a few days later. He even helped with the wash.[11] She pushed open the door and found no one home but their monkey, two big dogs, two kittens, and several squawky parrots. So he'd gone out after all. At 11:00 P.M. she brushed her teeth, got in bed, and slept the sleep... if not of the just, at least of the unarraigned—until 6:30 A.M., when a pounding at the door roused her, and her life changed forever.

Maybe Louis had strolled up to Broadway, too. Maybe he, too, took in a film, perhaps *The Sea Woman,* which was followed by both a vaudeville show and the newsreel of the Berlenbach / Delaney title fight. Gang-ridden Hell's Kitchen was tight-lipped in the morning. Even innocuous information could turn out to be dangerous. But several people, the *Times* said, saw Siki "unsteady on his pins" around midnight in Times Square, so he must have been in the neighborhood. One report placed him at the Comet Restaurant on West 41st.[12]

Perhaps he also stopped by the little French restaurant on Forty-seventh where he was a regular—just to see who was there, maybe get Villepontoux, the owner, to advance him the price of a bottle of *pinard.* Eduardo Arroyo, Al Brown's biographer, says Villepontoux, an ex-champion motorcycle racer and trainer, had come to America after the war dreaming of making his fortune, but had been reduced instead to running a dank bistro in the old West Side French quarter, struggling to make ends meet feeding a mixed clientele of expatriates, Vaudeville entertainers, showgirls down on their luck, and prizefighters awaiting their next purse. Villepontoux didn't mind feeding Siki on credit. Eventually he'd have more money coming in. Besides, his patronage attracted others. For a time, Arroyo tells us, the clan at Villepontoux's centered around Siki, soaking up his reflected glory, and, when he was flush, his cash.[13]

The circle that surrounded Siki at Villepontoux's, Arroyo says, included at various times Gaston-Charles Raymond, Levy, promoter Eddie MacMahon, and various stablemates. Notable among them was future bantamweight champ Al Brown, a Panamanian who'd come to New York in 1923 hoping to put the arm on an old crony from Colon, Kid Norfolk. By the time Siki crawled from his steerage berth on the Havana steamer in 1924, Brown was a rising attraction. In three years, he'd won all but two of thirty-two bouts. A superb boxer, despite a freakish build (at six feet tall, 120 pounds, he was so skeletal you could count every rib), Brown was popular with New York fans. Not that being a fan favorite got him anywhere near a title match. Brown and Siki soon became pals—perhaps through a shared cynicism about ring exploitation and a penchant for periodic alcoholic debauch. Ocania Chalk (interviewed by Niek Koppen) places them together the night of December 14, 1925, but Arroyo mentions no such meeting. Brown had fought in the city three days before and wouldn't leave for his final bout of the year, in Albany against Johnny Forbes, until days later—so the meeting is at least plausible.

If they did meet that night, you can guess what they must have been talking about: the brand-new Mecca of boxing, Madison Square Garden, just opened for business (with Tex Rickard's cash) a few blocks to the north, and the bout just staged there for the title Siki once held, between Paul Berlenbach and Jack Delaney. Delaney, a fighter whose career was handled by trainer Pete Reilly and mobster Bill Duffy, had boxed so slickly he'd had Berlenbach lumbering after him like a drunken bear. But Berlenbach had kept coming and somehow taken the decision. Perhaps Siki was still reassuring himself he'd go home and eat Lillian's fish—once he got a drink. He had reason to need one. Tomorrow would be the fourth birthday of the son he'd abandoned, Louis Jr. Perhaps, too, he remembered December 15 three years before, when, as champion of the world, he'd been in the vortex of a huge scandal, with the Parisian dailies sneering at his refusal to appear before the French Boxing Federation's tribunal investigating his charges that he'd won the title by overturning a fix. Perhaps his mind drifted back as well to September 24, 1922, the day of that fight itself.

He had stood in the ring, that warm, overcast afternoon in 1922 in white shorts with a green sash, under flecks of rain, in a huge stadium still tacky with new paint. Nearby, bored, blasé, had stood the man he'd dreamed for so long of facing. At the weigh-in, bashful as a schoolboy, he'd gravely said, *"Bonjour, Monsieur Carpentier,"* loath to address too familiarly the idol of French sport. It became a joke among men like Henri Desgranges and Victor Breyer: *"ce nègre"* Siki, terrified of Carpentier's very name! How would he dare face the man himself in the ring?

But Siki wasn't afraid of Carpentier. In the ring, he looked oddly fragile, his muscles small, his frame slender. Not that it mattered. This wasn't a real fight. It was *"du cinéma."* The fix had been on for weeks. Siki must play his role on cue—that was all. He had to go down for a quick count in the first round—reassuring the gamblers, who'd double their bets—then take another quick tumble in the second, another in the third, for a nine count, then a real dive in the fourth. Descamps even said that as he was counted out he must stretch out his arms in the form of a cross.[14] Siki hated the whole idea, but if he hadn't agreed to go through with it, there would have been no bout. So even though the ring gave off all the familiar smells—of rosin, sweat, lineament—it might more properly have smelled of greasepaint. For this wasn't a prizefight, it was only *du cinéma.* His movie-star rival stood draped in a robe, a towel around his neck, hair slicked back. As a second taped his hands, hurrying since the match was late, Carpentier frowned, "That's the first time I've had my hands wrapped this fast. Come on, let's get going, it's going to rain."[15]

The fans had hooted through the finale of a tourney of class-C heavyweights. They hadn't come to see elephants in boxing trunks, but to witness "the return of the prodigal son," *"notre grand Georges national,"* whose name "resounds in our hearts like a military trumpet," as crucial to "the veritable religion that is sport" as "the name of Joffre is to the victory of the Marne, and that of Foch is to the great victory."[16] And Siki? Well, he was a good enough fighter in his way. But you could get any odds you wanted to bet on him to win. Sparrow Robertson said one American bet 10,000 francs against 1,000 that Siki would lose, 5,000 against 1,000 he would not last a round.[17] The poor guy didn't know the fix was on. He'd soon be out 4,000 francs.

Or would he? Siki still hated the whole idea of a fix. He later admitted, "Inside my heart I kept repeating, I will knock him dead if I can."[18]

"Come on, let's get going, it's going to rain." Carpentier would wish for fifty years he'd never uttered those words. The fans would pillory him for them. The haste with which they turned on him would astonish him. He'd risen too high, he'd later muse, become too rich, too happy—outstripping their petty imaginations.[19] Even as his corner man finished wrapping his hands, ringsiders jeered, "Hey, Carpentier! What's up? Too much cinema?"[20] You could see it! He wasn't the same man who'd fought Jeff Smith or even Dick Smith. He looked like an actor stepping into the ring for a lark.

Fifteen days before, Hellers had sprung the news: the bout Siki had fought so hard to get must be a setup. Descamps had said flatly Siki had to throw the fight. He promised them Carpentier's share of the purse, 200,000 francs, the biggest ever for a fight in France. Carpentier would make do with Siki's share, plus newsreel royalties. That was the deal, take it or leave it— and they'd better take it or Descamps would back out, no matter what people said. He'd already pushed the fight back three weeks, to try to coax Carpentier into doing some real training. He finally set up camp miles away, at La Guerche, where he ran a cheese processing plant.

Siki himself had been engaged in brutal sparring sessions for weeks. Bob Scanlon, who'd been Siki's sparring mate in a makeshift gym under a tent in Paris's Luna Park skating rink, said (in his inimitable style) that Siki seemed "a big hearty boy, strong and very quick, but did not know very much about the noble art, so I said to him, come on, let's have a round or two and I'll show you how to hit straight; but after a few days it got to be very uncomfortable for me as he was very young and strong and very brutal so I suffered a great deal."[21]

When Scanlon couldn't take any more of Siki's punishment, Carpentier's trainer Gus Wilson called him to La Guerche. For three days he and two other sparring mates, Jack Walker and René de Vos, worked out together, awaiting Carpentier. When Carpentier finally turned up, he did a little road work, calisthenics, shadowboxing—then went hunting. Scanlon adds, "This was three weeks before the fight, and after those days of work I never saw Georges, only rarely.... He said, I'll beat him, I'll knock his black head off. So I said, No, Georges, he's very strong and has plenty of speed and wind and can hit, and is tough, so what more does a man need?" But Carpentier preferred to take off in his car to go fishing or hunting rather than to train. "So I tried to scare him," Scanlon says, "by telling him of Siki's measurements, his big arms, and that he never gets tired, but brave Georges said that he cared nothing for those big arms and speed as his right to the jaw would put a stop to all that nonsense."[22]

If Siki's big arms didn't worry Carpentier, they did Descamps. He didn't like to take risks where money was concerned. Siki wanted nothing to do with a fix. But he was broke and had been counting on this purse. If he was going to lose out anyway, he might as well swallow his pride and take Carpentier's 200,000 francs. It was a lot of money, nearly the price of two

Rolls Royces.[23] Still, Siki had dreamed for so long of winning a world title that something inside said no even as Hellers said yes. At Luna Park, Hellers kept taking him aside, saying "slow down." He was still getting up at dawn to run along the city wall, still doing calisthenics, still battering sparring partners. It was as if the fix hadn't registered on his brain. Why did he need road work and sparring sessions to take a dive? But Hellers couldn't very well call off Siki's training. He might as well announce the fix was on.

Siki clung to the idea that some turn of fate might give him back his chance. He'd always been lucky. Nearly every man he'd enlisted with had died in the war. Yet he'd survived. Descamps's *cinema* might just surprise him by turning real. Siki wanted to be ready. Just in case. After nightfall, however, Siki's resolution faded. Sparrow Robertson found him more than once at his favorite haunts in Montmartre.

On fight night, a *"garde noire"* (black entourage) had ushered Siki into the new stadium, beyond Porte d'Orleans. He'd smiled amiably, left and right. The *Garde Républicaine* band had played martial airs as ladies in stylish dresses strained to see movie-star ringman Carpentier—and to shudder at the ugly African. As Carpentier climbed into the ring, a deafening roar epupted and a stunt flier fell into a death spiral, missing the top tiers of seats by scant meters, panicking fans. Friends and admirers, crowding ringside seats, called out *"bonne chance!"*[24] Carpentier smiled like a man bored with the party who's trying not to glance at his watch. Newsmen at ringside thought they saw disdain in his eyes—and would later mock him for it. He wished, he would later admit, he were anywhere but at this irksome bout. A parade of notables crossed the ring—not just boxers, but luminaries of every sort, including Jean Brunier, who'd just won the French hundred-kilometer bicycle title, and Finnish track star Paavo Nurmi, whose teammates shrieked as he climbed into the ring. It was quite a show! The vast, restless throng, the largest ever to witness a European boxing match, even included scattered clusters of black and brown faces representing every far-flung corner of empire.[25]

When the bell rang, Siki crouched low, moving as if his legs had fallen asleep, trying hard not to betray the fix. How do you seem to fight without truly fighting? He had to get knocked down by round's end. But how could he make it look real? Carpentier pranced nimbly about, a veteran actor carrying a stage-struck amateur, circling the ebony statue in mid-ring, weaving, feinting, punching air. Siki's acting was so bad that months later, when he revealed the fix, ringsiders swore he was lying: they were sure they'd seen fear in Siki's eyes, seen his limbs tremble, knees buckle. They'd read stage fright as terror. *L'Echo des Sports* called him "paralyzed." *Petit Parisien* said

Carpentier hardly bothered to mount a guard, that Siki was "hypnotized" by his "sharp stare." *L'Echo de Paris* said Siki showed "a tendency to hide his head in the chest of his adversary"—which made him sound downright puerile. *Le Populaire* said Carpentier "seem[ed] to play with Siki who hid behind his gloves."[26]

The grainy newsreel shows Carpentier firing his signature right, Siki instinctively ducking, letting it pass over his shoulder. He'd missed his cue to take a tumble. Oops! But then Siki went on with the script anyway, bobbing down on one knee like an altar boy at mass. *Le Petit Parisien* spoke the plain truth: "He let himself... go down without having been touched." And there Siki stuck, chin upturned, gazing at the referee as if awaiting the Eucharist, as cries of *"chiqué!"* and *"cinéma!"* floated from the grandstands. Pudgy referee Henry Bernstein whispered, "Come on, get up, Siki! You weren't even hit!"

What else could he say? "For Christ's sake, don't you know how to take a dive?" He was in on the fix. He'd already awarded one of Descamps's boxers victory on a foul, another a win on a disqualification for "not fighting." He'd do his best to keep this in the bag. Siki sheepishly rose. Carpentier tossed two rights, one of which really landed. The crowd whistled. Some thought the bout was fixed, others that Siki had come unglued. Siki felt degraded, Carpentier enraged. *"Ce sale nègre"* seemed bent on turning his homecoming into a farce.

He hoped his absurd rival would snap out of it in round two. No such luck! Frank Withers, reporting for the *Chicago Defender*, admitted Siki "never returned a blow."[27] As the crowd grew more derisive, Carpentier, exasperated, tried single-handedly to save the show, throwing punches with malign intent. *Le Matin* says when Siki tried to tie Carpentier up he jerked free, firing a nasty combination. Siki got caught with rights to the ear and face.[28] Though scripted to go down again, he instinctively fired a left. Withers saw the champion counter with "a terrific blow" to Siki's jaw, but Siki merely grinned, and dug hooks to the body. Both reports imply an abrupt break in the tenor of the bout. On the newsreel the punches seem genuine—especially that hard right of Carpentier's. But the fight still wasn't entirely for real—not yet. Siki ended the round dancing and feinting, lifting his feet like a drum major at a halftime show.

The day after the bout, at *L'Echo des Sports'* offices, Siki swore Carpentier really had at first hypnotized him with his crisp counters, so different from the wide swings he was used to. In round one, said Siki, "He landed a punch and I went to the ground; but that didn't last long. That went away and I got up right away. And also his punches aren't like mine; they come very fast, like this." He mimicked a rapid shift and short hook. "He lifts an elbow and they're there right away; I expect them [from] far away."[29] Months later, Siki admitted he'd faked the early knockdowns, saying he'd spent these rounds "in a trance, saying to myself, 'Will I quit or will I fight?'" Carpentier, he added, "hit me on the jaw with two hard rights, but did not hurt me."[30]

In the third round Carpentier, intent on saving appearances, kept putting real sting into his blows. Later, shooting a film in Germany, Siki told a friendly cameraman that Carpentier had brought about his own downfall by not pulling his punches.[31] Carpentier looked, to ringsiders, "still very calm. . . very sure of himself," playing cat and mouse, feinting, snapping back Siki's head with jabs.[32] Then abruptly the newsreel shows him land a leaping overhand right, a bit high, at arm's length. Siki bobs down—and bounces right back up. Carpentier lunges after him, firing a hook, an uppercut, losing his footing on a wet spot and spilling to his knees. Back on his feet he fires hooks and uppercuts. Siki squats to the floor, rubbing his eyes, as if blinded by rosin. Carpentier, ice-skating on the wet canvas, misses, then lands a right to the jaw, a left hook, a right to the head. He lurches after Siki, shoving him across the ring. "Then, pow!" trills *Le Matin*. "Left, right, Carpentier this time has landed to the back of the head." This knockdown appears genuine, but *L'Echo de Paris* sneers, "Siki withstands well the rare blows his adversary lands, which doesn't at all prevent him from again dropping to the ground."[33]

L'Echo de Paris was dead right. The knockdown was a phoney. "Going out for the third," Siki later explained. "I fully decided to take another of the agreed counts. The round went over two minutes before Georges hit me hard enough to give me a chance to go down. A right swing then hit me high on the face and I said, 'Here goes nothing.' I dropped to one knee, fully resolved to stay there."[34] As Siki kneeled at his feet, Carpentier, arms resting on the ropes, must have breathed easy. One more round of *la comédie*, then a quick tussle in the middle of the ring and Siki would pitch to the canvas. We pick up the story in Siki's own words:

> Me I was nothing before the fight, isn't that true? I was nothing but an ordinary boxer, without reputation and without money. Hellers said to me: "By fighting Carpentier, you might get a lot of money, but you'd better go along." I came to the ring with the intention of going down as they ordered me to. In the first round, in the second, in the third, I went along, but in the fourth round [he misidentifies the round], when I was on my knees, in front of fifty thousand people, I thought like this: "Look at you, Siki, you've never gone down before any man, you've never been on your knees in public the way you find yourself at this moment," and my blood only circulated once before I was on

Action in an early
round in the Siki /
Carpentier bout,
September 24, 1922.
(A. Beagles and Co.)

my feet and I was punching. I hit with far more force and energy than
the punches Carpentier threw at me, which I didn't even feel.[35]

Siki's ex-sparring partner Bob Scanlon supplies yet another wrinkle:

So when the fighters was going to the ring, a featherweight by the
name of George Gayer ask me if Carpentier was in good shape, and I
not knowing, thinking him a friend of Carpentier's, I said naturally, No,
he has not trained. So he said, Thanks, I'll get my revenge because I
have a grievance against Descamps, since my match with Paul
Fritsch, so I am going in Siki's corner. So he did, and he told Siki: now
is your chance to become champion of the world . . .—just look at . . .
the cars you will own and all the houses you can buy with the money

you will make, everybody will be crying Siki, the President will invite you to dinner.... So Siki seen nothing but dough.[36]

Passevant corrects the spelling of the featherweight's name to Georges Gaillard, and says that he was working Siki's corner as a second. Originally scheduled to fight, Gaillard had been bumped from the card, replaced by Descamps's own boxer Paul Fritsch.[37] *Le Populaire,* too, repeats rumors of an unnamed boxer persuading Siki to overturn the fix.[38] Sénégalese deputy Blaise Diagne's version leaves out the spiteful featherweight but confirms Siki's change of heart:

> In his corner, resting, the manager reminded him of the arrangement he'd made, the sure money that was there for him to gain, and it was at that moment that two psychological phenomena intervened.... Siki concluded that although he would gain a lot of money to let himself be beaten, he'd gain a lot more if he was the winner... thoughts of lucre, but who could blame him?... A second [notion], also psychological, marked with physical force, came into the brain of Siki. He sensed he was stronger. The sentiment of a greater physical vigor entered brutally in his brain.... He didn't go down. He fought and he won. And in his corner, during each rest, the objurgations were yet more pressing, up until the moment when Siki, sure of himself and forgetting obligations in which he had not been involved, cried, "I've had it with this shit."[39]

If Siki saw "nothing but dough" he was in for a shock. Descamps had offered 200,000 francs for an artistic bellyflop. Reneging, Siki wouldn't even get the 55,000 francs originally promised.

Whether pride or lucre brought him to his feet, at the count of seven Siki was up, stalking forward, looking at last like a fighter. On the newsreel you see him shake his head, blinking tears, eyes still stinging. He tosses an uppercut, gets caught with a hook, then twists his torso and launches in succession a short hard right, a left hook, and another crunching right, sending Carpentier tumbling like a café sign on a windy day. On all fours, Carpentier wipes blood from his mouth, crawling erect at the count of three, still wobbly. Apart from the hecklers who'd cried *"trop de cinéma"* at the start, the *grande foule* had until now lustily cheered their hero, but now fifty thousand throats let out a roar of triumph—and for the rest of the fight the faithful were on their feet howling for the throat of their former idol.

Carpentier tossed wobbly punches, then grabbed and held on, snarling in the clinches, "Bastard! Bastard! Go down now! Go down!" After the bell, Siki got it good from Hellers: "Are you going to act like an idiot? Did you forget what was arranged?"[40] Siki said nothing. Hellers assumed he'd squared him around. Every onlooker, said *La Boxe et les Boxeurs,* shared a single thought: Carpentier would come back. He'd been badly hurt in other bouts and rallied to win.

Siki came out for the fourth determined to put his rival away for good. Still shaky, Carpentier tied him up, leaning on the ropes, as Siki banged away. "I began to feel sorry for him," Siki relates, "and whispered to him to quit. His blows lacked sting and he was not strong."[41] Before the round was a minute old, Siki tagged Carpentier with vicious shots to the eye and mouth. Carpentier stayed grimly vertical, at one point hazarding a quick flurry of his own—but Siki hammered the dazed champion's ribs, tagged him with uppercuts and short rights. His face bloodied, one eye closed, Carpentier seemed ready to go down for good. As fifty-five thousand pairs of eyes focused on the ugly drama in the ring, Descamps slipped from his place at Carpentier's corner. The newsreel shows his head bobbing above the ring margin, like a target in a shooting gallery, nearing Hellers's kewpie-doll head, jabbering fiercely. Then Descamps circles back, in time to leap up at the bell to minister to his mutilated *poulain.* What message had he delivered? The same one Carpentier had snarled at Siki.

Everyone in the arena expected Descamps to throw in the towel. But he wasn't out of ideas even yet. He knew he could count on Referee Bernstein to wink an eye. Round five offered a sad spectacle. The newsreel shows the two fighters locked together, bent low, like rugby players in a scrum. Siki clubs Carpentier's ribs, whacks at his head. Carpentier suddenly dips his head and charges like a country bull baited by boys playing matador. His skull bangs into Siki's, driving him across the ring. Siki, on the ropes, spreads his arms in protest. They touch gloves, but Carpentier promptly butts Siki again. Bernstein warns *both* men. Siki lands a quick combination. Carpentier again aims his skull at Siki's face, sending him sprawling on the seat of his pants. Siki protests, then seeks reprisal with his fists. Carpentier covers up, bent over—then again tries to butt Siki, slipping to his knees on the wet canvas.

Siki bends down, wraps his arms around his fallen rival, and lifts him to his feet—which favor Carpentier returns by twisting free and tagging him with a hook. Seconds later, after the bell, a *London Illustrated News* photo catches Siki, eyes wide, jaw slack, holding a glove to his cheek, like a guy whose goodnight kiss has been answered by a slap.[42] "That settled it," he later said. "I was now out to knock him out, and I went after him right and left. The crowd was cheering and this further encouraged me."[43] His punches were twice as hard as any he'd hit Nilles or Journée with, wrote *L'Echo des Sports,* raising ugly welts on Carpentier's torso. Reeling, dripping blood, blinded, the champion couldn't escape. The only issue left in doubt was how long he'd stand up to the beating. Only one person in the arena thought he might still win—scraggle-toothed, flop-haired ex-gymnastics coach, ex-prestidigitator François Descamps.

I Had No Choice—It's His Fault

Between rounds, the boxers sat on café chairs. This was France, after all. But a stool would have been handier, for as the bell rang, distracted by Hellers's ministrations, Siki had barely begun to rise when the Carpentier came running toward him, sending the chair spinning, firing punches that, had Carpentier been less enfeebled, might have stolen the fight. The crowd, sick of perfidy, intoxicated by the smell of blood, howled for Siki to finish the champion. Flailing blindly, missing by feet, Carpentier walked into fierce combinations. Siki went after him like God from his whirlwind assaulting Job, with an abandon that would fuel the myth of Siki the wild beast. He wasn't inspired by blood lust, just the exhilaration of mastery. His destined moment had come. He caught Carpentier with hooks, body blows, pole-axe swings. Finally, in a corner, he drove a left to the body, right to the head. Barely conscious, Carpentier hung on, as Siki, struggling to break free and twist his torso to throw a hook, lost his balance and jerked a leg in the air. Carpentier pitched forward as Siki landed a vicious hook to his ribs, flopping him to the canvas. The champion lay on his side, a leg upraised, gasping in agony.

As Siki raised his arms, giving a whoop of triumph, referee Bernstein stood stock still, making no move to start a count. A second leaped to the ring apron. Bernstein waved him away. Another ducked through the ropes and hunched the limp form of Carpentier onto a chair, where he slouched forward as Descamps leaped through the ropes. An announcer in a dark suit carrying a megaphone half as big as he waited to relay the verdict. A dozen figures, all talking at once, crowded the ring, including ring physician Dr. Sauphar. The jabbering went on a full minute. Then the announcer bawled, "Siki disqualified for tripping. Winner Carpentier." The crowd erupted, "Siki's the winner! Siki's the winner! Fix! Fix!" They surged toward the ring, scattering temporary seats. Descamps fled to a knot of gendarmes. "It's the revolution . . . ," *Le Populaire* exulted. "One senses it would take very little for everything to be entirely demolished in the arena."[44] As tumult raged, Carpentier was carted up the aisle, piggy-back behind a handler, arms around his neck, legs dangling, "face swollen, his gaze, fixedly vague, expressing anxiety and suffering, . . . like a wounded soldier in

Siki knocks out Carpentier, September 24, 1922. (Author's collection.)

wartime." Siki, leaving the ring, turned left and right to proclaim, "But I did nothing! Nothing! Absolutely nothing!"[45]

Meanwhile, judges Ben Bennison, Emmanuel Pujol, and *Echo des Sports'* editor Victor Breyer, along with FFB boss Henri Rousseau, debated how to save the situation. Finally Breyer climbed into the ring to declare that Bernstein had ruled improperly. His verdict was set aside pending review. They'd give their decision after the last bout. Breyer's avowal was rubbish: only a referee has authority to disqualify a boxer for a foul. But never mind. Mollified, the crowd returned to their seats. Rousseau and the judges repaired to a nearby hotel to ruminate.[46]

And Siki? He waited beneath soaring tiers of seats, wondering if this travesty would stand. Rousseau, who ran French boxing like a cottage industry, wasn't a man to stand for anything so slipshod. Subordinates grumbled that he loomed incessantly at their elbows, checking every detail, re-tabulating figures. He'd been that way ever since he founded *L'Auto* years before. Pujol and Bennison would do as Rousseau told them, and Breyer had a venerable feud going with Desgrange, Siki's early booster.[47] Could Descamps brazenly steal back the title? Would Rousseau and his gang give the crowd time to calm down, then march back and put off a decision until the morning (when they could uphold Bernstein's disqualification without facing an angry mob)?

When they came back into the arena and announced instead that Siki had won, they presented Hellers with a strange quandary. He was now manager of a world champion. But he and Siki had broken their word. How could he ask for Siki's purse? What would he say to Descamps, to Carpentier? They owned shares in the stadium and had been co-promoters of the bout. When Siki and Hellers returned to the Hotel Floreal, where Siki, Lijntje, and the baby awaited, they didn't go up to Siki's room. Siki, Hellers, his corner men, and a few friends crowded into the owner's office—everyone standing silent—as if they'd lost.

The scene found a witness in a casual gate-crasher, a guy who'd plunked down money on Siki to win, on a tip from a cousin of Blaise Diagne's, but who'd been too jumpy to go to Stade Buffalo to watch. Now, beside himself with anxiety, he'd come nosing around looking for the cousin. He stood there attentive to the smallest detail, perplexed by the group's subdued air:

> Siki allowed the proprietor to kiss him and then ordered champagne. On that subject, Hellers said, "No, white wine would be a better idea." A doctor who was with us in turn gave his advice: "It would be better to give him something hot." As I found myself in the first row, I couldn't stop myself from saying, "What about giving him some

tea?" Siki leaped up, seized his chair in two hands, and cried loudly, "No! No! No tea! No tea!"[48]

Finally they settled on white wine. Fifteen people jammed together in an office three meters square, with Siki and Hellers poised on chairs, the doctor on the desk. Siki said, "He hit hard all the same, he hit hard, but that was rotten."[49] The observer thought Siki was voicing chagrin at Carpentier's sucker punch. But actually, he was exculpating himself—to the only person in the room who grasped his reason for doing so, Hellers. He meant, "I had no choice—it's his fault, not mine. He double-crossed me first." To the edgy gambler, the phrase hinted Siki had lost, despite the champagne and his unmarked face.

Hellers answer seemed yet stranger: *"Bah! t'en fais pas, va, ... le cinéma est là, tu seras bien vengé"* (Bah! Forget about it, go on, the cinema is there, you'll be well revenged). The poor gambler was beside himself. Revenged *for what?* Perhaps Hellers's allusion to "le cinéma" meant the newsreel would show Siki hadn't tripped Carpentier. But had the gambler heard Hellers correctly, or did Hellers make some other allusion to *"le cinéma"*—perhaps mocking Carpentier's life of pleasure, as ringsiders had before the fight? Did he say, "you'll be well revenged" or "you've had your revenge"? Did Siki's *c'est vache* mean "that was rotten" (hinting victimization by a third party) or (as it equally might) "what a shame" (implying an ugly situation that was no one's fault).

By morning Siki had awoken to a world at once glittering and pernicious. If in round six at Montrouge, Siki had been like God assailing Job out of a whirlwind, by morning he himself was caught in a whirlwind. From his hotel balcony he saw a cheering crowd blocking the street. They threw bouquets, sent up champagne. He bowed, waved. When he went out, they sent up a shout: "There he is! It's him! It's Siki!" Paris fell in love with him—for a time. He could hardly walk for the people throwing themselves in his path, draping an arm over his shoulder, both arms around his neck, kissing him, dragging him by an elbow into cafés for a celebratory glass. To their surprise, this man they'd heard liked to "train on *pinard*" turned them down. No, no, he exclaimed. He meant to be a real champion, to honor the eminence he'd attained. He was through with the drinking, the escapades in the demi-monde of Montmartre. He'd make France proud of him.[50] Siki walked himself off his feet with a band of pals, black and white, then hired a taxi with a black driver to cruise Montmartre, causing horrific traffic jams.[51]

It was comical how men like Desgrange of *L'Auto* and Breyer of *L'Echo des Sports* tried to wriggle onto his good side, droll to read the letters that poured in: from women offering themselves to him, a businessman wanting

Siki celebrates with a gang of ring cronies, including his manager Hellers (with cane, *center*, his left arm through Siki's), Paris, 1922. (*L'Actualité Sportive.*)

him to endorse a new pill, a director wanting to cast him in the film version of René Maran's *Bataoula,* a music hall soprano wanting to teach him to dance and put him on stage.[52] The director's offer seemed especially ironic. If he'd had any acting talent would he have shammed so ineptly in the first two rounds against Carpentier?

Soon the sideshow turned ugly. Siki told *Le Miroir des Sports* he longed to turn off the spotlight and shoo away the crowds.[53] René Herbert of *L'Echo des Sports,* meanwhile, found Carpentier on rue Magellan, near the Champs Elysées, lying forgotten, in a bathrobe on a couch in a dismal office smelling like a hospital. He studied his visitor through his one eye still partially open, twisting his mouth into a smile that looked more like a scowl, his face "puffed up, swollen, bruised, the nose without form, the eyes two miserable lumps, the lips enormous, lacking any shape." Carpentier tried to make plausible excuses. Why hadn't he tried to knock Siki out in the third when he had him at his mercy? "They aren't made like we are," he sniffed, his hands plunged in steaming water (the worst possible therapy if they really were broken)—and besides four-ounce gloves were "awful... for heavyweights." Herbert couldn't resist musing, "Those fists that have dropped so many victims at the feet of he who was the glory of France couldn't accomplish their pitiless task. 'They' aren't made like us."[54]

Thirty years later Carpentier hadn't forgotten those days in the shadows, tormented by one thought: "I've been beaten by Siki. I, Carpentier, have let myself be beaten by this nigger I could have stretched out at my feet... after one or two minutes of combat." He brooded over the outrages of his ex-idolaters: "Yes, they insulted me, and there were even those who spit in my face as I came down from the ring. And also those who grabbed hold of my automobile as I was leaving Stade Buffalo to lash out at me with one final abuse."[55] Descamps, who'd led him from the stadium before the judges' ruling, did his best to keep his protégé in ignorance of the final result, excluding visitors, banning papers, steering conversation away from the fight. Carpentier's wife, unwilling to undergo a long train ride, had skipped the bout, staying in Biarritz. *"Notre grand Georges national"* had only Descamps to solace him.

The long-haired gnome who'd discovered, trained, and protected Carpentier since he was a Lenz schoolboy was busy as a parimutuel clerk as the horses go to the post, bustling about, justifying, pleading, citing every *wherefore* in the rule book. There really had been a *croc-en-jambe*. The newsreel would show it. Carpentier had twisted his ankle, torn a tendon. The ring physician would swear it. This absurd *nègre* hadn't beaten the great Carpentier. He'd broken his hand against the freak's skull. X-rays would prove it. The fight really hadn't been for the title, nor was it even an official bout. The longer the ex-illusionist talked, the more you wondered: would he succeed in making defeat dissolve into thin air? But fifty-five thousand people saw what Carpentier looked like as he was carried out that night. Why did Siki need to trip him? *L'Eclair* commented, "The one who fought elegantly, forgiving the most doubtful punches of his opponent, was Siki, yet he was the one who got disqualified!"[56]

On the twenty-fifth of September, Siki ran into Descamps at the offices of *L'Echo des Sports,* whose editor Henri Breyer, the fight's promoter, popped open champagne. They shook hands as affably as if Descamps weren't bending heaven and earth to fleece him. "I'm really distressed," Siki said, "that you have so much pain."[57] That night, he turned up at the showing of the newsreel, a stormy affair with Hellers and Descamps roaring at each other: Look! He did trip him... Aw, he did not. He just lost his balance—and anyway he was already on his way down! Siki arrived after the film had run through twice, looking "uncomfortable,... put out by the animated discussions."[58] He stayed "nailed to his seat like a well-behaved child," saying not a word until he went out into the corridor, where, to friends, he protested his innocence.[59]

Days later, again at *L'Echo des Sports,* Siki ran into referee Bernstein and after an awkward moment proffered his hand. Breyer told Siki to forget nasty gossip. He could see he was well liked here, and anyway, "Black or white, friends or adversaries would be equal for us before a balanced criticism." Siki stood balancing his head to one side, then seized Breyer's small hand in his big callused one and kissed it. As they walked out, Siki declined an offer of a drink and Bernstein roared he must pay a forfeit "to the boy who opened the door for you." The assertion was bizarre, but Siki handed over a five-franc note anyhow.[60]

By the weekend, resolutions forgotten, Siki was making nonstop rounds of bars, buying drinks for anyone who cared to say "congratulations champ," and many who didn't. Americans, said Withers, were "stunned" by Carpentier's defeat: "In the cafes and the American bars, in the Casino de Paris, the Café Americain and in front of the American Express office they congregate, these Southern hounds, and whisper while all France is in a state of enjoyment, evidently glad to see a champion uncrowned."[61] Groups of resentful white Americans provoked nightly pitched battles in Montmartre with exultant persons of color. Most galling of all was the fact that often enough they found Siki's partisans in the arms of pretty French women:

> Objecting American whites have precipitated quarrels and in many cases free-for-all battles have taken place with unpleasant results for the white Americans. The Paris Race colony . . . is carrying its chest and its head high, while the French women's color blindness . . . is increasing, even to the embarrassment of many of the Race themselves, who find themselves hunted by French women of all types and stations in life.[62]

The *Canard Enchaîné* ran a cartoon, headed "Disgrace," depicting a shaggy-haired black man, his head shapeless as a dumpling, gazing saucer-eyed upon a curly-haired blonde who looks at him in twinkle-eyed admiration as his hand squeezes her bare shoulder. "And so Georges," mocked the caption, "after all, is not such a pretty boy as this." A headline taunted, "You know, Siki . . . maybe he isn't such a nigger [*nègre*] after all."[63]

Americans seemed bent on treating Siki as a skunk at their private Parisian lawn party. When he turned up at bars and ordered drinks for the house, many marched out in a huff.[64] Soon they were touting a "white hope" to reclaim the title, 215-pound ex-Dartmouth football player Malcolm Waite.[65] Descamps's fable that Carpentier had broken his knuckles on the skull of a freak of natural selection played well even in relatively tolerant France. Shirt-sleeve racial theorists nodded sagely: "Never hit a nigger on the head." In London, George Bernard Shaw said it plainly for attribution in the *Sunday Chronicle,* swapping "negro" for "nigger."[66]

French papers stressed Carpentier's scant training and overconfidence, giving Siki credit for speed, strength, "an agility, an astuteness,... an apelike vigor." Sparrow Robertson evoked the image of "an African tribesman, not far removed from savagery [who] call[ed] upon the cunning, courage and skill of an uncivilized hunter of the jungle and beat by sheer force one of the greatest exponents of scientific boxing that the ring has produced."[67] The *New York Times* insisted "the black man, like a wild beast, battered the champion," depicting Siki as "made of leather," with a "physical makeup... like that of a great leopard," moving in "great leaps" as his "muscles play fascinatingly under a dark skin."[68] The *London Daily Mail's* Trevor Wignall said the final rounds suggested a modern human lured into combat with an aboriginal ancestor: "No boxing. It was the kind of thing that must have been popular when men settled their disputes with stone hatchets.... Siki was in his glory... drunk with the prospect of victory..."[69]

Besieged by reporters eager for his take on the bout, George Bernard Shaw said he hadn't been there, but it sounded as if Carpentier had thrown away his title on a cat-and-mouse game. Not that it mattered. "Don't be alarmed," he jibed, "civilization with survive the shock." America had survived Jack Johnson, after all. "Siki will not assume the title of Emperor of Senegal and march on Paris."[70] Once he'd seen the newsreel, he added,

> I think that Carpentier does not know how to fight a Negro.... Siki made nothing of Carpentier's long shots, which dazed Beckett and made even Dempsey look serious. Siki not only understands the art of getting away and being hit by a spent bullet only, but, like all negroes, he does what no white man dare do—meets a straight lead by dropping his head neatly and taking the shock on the ridge of his eyebrow, where it makes about as much impression as a mushroom on a Minotaur.[71]

One photo seized public fancy. Shot level with the canvas, it showed a fallen Carpentier twisted sideways, a leg hoisted in the air, like a stunned steer, as a scowling Siki, fists clenched, loomed over him, held back by the referee, as if eager to dismember his foe. Thus was a legend born: Siki, beast of the jungle. The *Herald* ran side-by-side a studio publicity shot of matinee-idol Carpentier and a curbside candid of Siki in an ill-fitting, tightly buttoned suit. The cuffs of his high-water pants dangle six inches above his shoes. He clutches a fragile cane in white-gloved mitts. That photo, too, led a charmed life, resurfacing to remind readers that the "Singular Senegalese" wore civilization like a cheap suit. "Georges looked like a Greek idol," mused the *Times*. Siki was "ugly, ungainly, and awkward."[72]

Soon, Siki's conduct began to match his suit. As his emotions swung from euphoria to dejection, he began dosing himself abundantly with absinthe and wine. Drunk and unruly much of the time, he played celebrity for its one advantage: that it led authorities to look the other way when he raised hell. Bob Scanlon tells of finding Siki in the street firing a pistol in the air, urging his Great Danes to do tricks, to the delight of a rowdy crowd, as police officers stood by wondering what excuse to use not to arrest him. Scanlon talked Siki into a taxi and spirited him to the *Chope du Nègre* (Nigger's Tankard), a Montmartre café. After a few drinks, he tried to steer Siki homeward, but Siki insisted on going to Luna Park. When they stopped en route to buy hats, Siki refused to sit inside with Scanlon and the dogs, perching instead beside the driver. At Porte Maillot a pedestrian shouted, "Look at that drunkard Battling Siki who beat Carpentier, drunk as a lord." Siki leveled his revolver and threatened, "Repeat that and I'll blow your head off." Police halted the taxi. Siki refused at first to surrender the pistol. Finally they marched him off to the station house, to face the police commissioner. Scanlon takes up the tale:

> So he said, What, a man like you with a revolver, and you who beat Carpentier want to kill a poor working man? Siki said, No I was only kidding him. But lucky for him it was a very small revolver and he only had blanks in it. The police chief said, I am going to send you to jail, and winked at me and told the policemen to search him. Siki said, Oh Monsieur, don't do that as I have a rendezvous with my wife to go to the cinema.... He had 18,000 francs on him. So Siki said to the workman, Here, pal, and handed him 400 francs. So he put it in his pocket and flew down the stairs, crying out, I am finished with the affair, bonsoir Siki camarade, tomorrow I hope.[73]

The ending comically reassures us: no one's out for blood. Siki's abuser will take cash in lieu of civilized decorum. But disputes over Siki's triumph weren't always so benign. The owner of a *débit* on rue Boinod in Montmartre, *Le Populaire* tells us, was debating the Siki / Carpentier bout with his son, a soldier, when suddenly a black man at the bar pulled a revolver, shot up the place, and fled.[74] Siki was in Rotterdam at that moment, so he wasn't the shooter. Furnished with a real pistol, the second shooter is hardly comic or reassuring, reminding us that Siki's victory produced real rancor on both sides of the rift created by the word *race*.

Before Siki's triumph, his challenge to Carpentier had briefly created a vogue for interracial bouts. In September, Stade Anastasie had run a whole program of them, featuring one pugilist who fought as *Têta le Nègre* (literally "sucked the nigger").[75] But no one had expected Siki to win. Now, racial rancor brought a backlash against the new champion. In working-class Belleville, the socialist counselor Luquet urged the police prefect to ban boxing, insisting, "Such matches constitute . . . spectacles where either sport has little to do with it, or the race has very little to gain, which can do nothing but develop instincts of brutality tending towards bestiality." The municipal council endorsed his petition nearly unanimously.[76] Within weeks, the British Home Office banned a Siki / Beckett bout, declaring, "In contests between men of color and white men, the temperaments of the contestants are not comparable and moreover all sorts of passions are aroused." With so many persons of color in the British empire, "such contests are considered against the national interests and they tend to arouse passions which it is inadvisable to stimulate."[77] In December Rotterdam police stopped a match at the last moment between Bob Scanlon and Daan Holtkamp, proclaiming a ban on all future interracial bouts.[78]

The Dutch at first had greeted Siki's victory with race-blind glee. An AP wire photo of his October return to Rotterdam shows Lijntje peeking out from under a wide-brimmed hat as a grinning Siki, in natty evening dress, draped with flowers like the winning horse at Longchamps, holds his infant son. U.S. editors re-ran the photo every time a new Siki story broke. The Dutch revels both galled and intrigued Americans. Cheering Rotterdammers had mobbed the station, blocking the streets, as the mayor waited at the town hall to welcome Lijntje and her now-famous husband. They pushed through a guard of honor, hoisted Mr. and Mrs. Louis Fall in the air, and carried them to a waiting carriage filled with roses, with blooded horses in the traces. They unhitched the horses and themselves pulled the Falls through the streets. That night at *Het Stadion's* welcome party Siki thanked his hosts "in a charming manner."[79] He wrote Desgrange:

> The reception that they gave me was incredible. . . . At the Rotterdam station military music awaited me. They put me in a superb four horse coupe and, like the nigger king of Malicoco, I paraded through the streets while all around me people cried "Long live France!" and nearer by others threw bouquets of flowers in my car. I was very moved by that welcome and will always keep a strong memory of it.[80]

The dinner menu featured *Potage à la Sikinoise, Poisson Battling, Pommes de Georges, Beurre Bernstein,* and *Gâteau Negro.*[81] Sipping his "Siki Soup," Siki must have laughed. Just two years before he had cooped in a bare room and eaten at dockside dives. He told *L'Auto* any title defenses were Hellers's affair. He'd go on an exhibition tour in Eastern Europe, and then he wanted to stay in Holland. Paris? He had friends there, but it was "too tiring for a champion."[82]

Ernest Hemingway, who'd been away covering Greco-Turkish warfare for the *Toronto Star,* returned to Paris on October 21 to find Americans there with their noses out of joint. Before his trip, he'd watched the Carpentier / Siki bout with his pregnant wife (from ringside, one critic claims),[83] and would recreate its feeling in *The Sun Also Rises,* which has Bill Gorton tell of a prize-fight in Vienna between a local hero and a "wonderful nigger" imported to carry the white stalwart and obligingly lose a decision. Bill's "awful noble-looking nigger" ("like Tiger Flowers—only four times as big"), flubs the fix, floors his white rival, and afterward tries desperately to exculpate himself. Bill tells us, "Nigger put up his glove. Wanted to make a speech."[84]

"I didn't do nothing in there for forty minutes but try and make him stay," the "splendid nigger" moans to Bill. "That white boy musta ruptured himself swinging at me. I never did hit him." But as the boxer signals for the crowd's indulgence, the "local white boy," like Carpentier at Montrouge, sucker punches him. In reprisal, the black fighter knocks him out cold—and gets showered with chairs and abuse for his pains. Left high and dry, watch stolen, purse withheld, the black boxer is relieved when Bill offers to bail him out.[85]

Hemingway's parable played well once, implying a hard-won stoicism. Now it seems an effort to scratch sand over the rising stink of racial cant in 1922 in Paris. The black man, in this version, knows his place and keeps it, raising a hand to beg, presumably, as Siki really did, "It wasn't my fault! I tried to go along!" Like Siki, Bill's black boxer overturns a fix. Like Siki, he's robbed of his purse. Siki, too, will soon have chairs thrown at him by an irate crowd. Siki too will beg in vain to be heard. Bill's "wonderful nigger" ducks his head under the abuse, and settles for . . . a handout! When the door of the cage of race pops open, he's complacent enough to pull it shut in his own face. Siki wasn't so "wonderful."

Hemingway's story "Fifty Grand" also borrows elements from Siki / Carpentier (as well as Benny Léonard's 1922 loss to Jack Britton). Jack Brennan, a fighter with little chance to win a title defense, bets against him-self to raise a stake for his daughters' private-school tuition, but his rival, who's also secretly bet against himself, double crosses Brennan, deliberately fouling him (to the groin) in hopes of a disqualification loss. Brennan, a sour cheapskate with a grudge against the world, has one redeeming grace: he faces up to the reality that the fix is always on. He waves off the low blow, "holding his body in where it was busted," and uncorks a nasty foul of his own.[86] Thus does he triumph in losing—walking off with the cash by sheer force of will. Brennan, who's Irish, struggles to find the right ethnic slur to pin on rival Jimmy Walcott, sneering as they touch gloves, "What do you call yourself 'Walcott' for? Didn't you know he was a nigger?" and later taunting him for being Danish or Bohemian.[87]

Hemingway's tale, however, comes up lame alongside the spectacle at Stade Buffalo. Holding it in and fouling back would have done Siki no good against Carpentier. A real foul would just have given Bernstein a credible excuse, despite Carpentier's head butts, sucker punches, and low blows, to take away Siki's chance of a lifetime. In 1922, referees at times saw visions more miraculous than those at Lourdes. After the Siki / Carpentier bout, boxing touts (Shaw among them) swore they saw Siki trip Carpentier. Weeks later they'd swear they saw him throw a punch at manager Fernand Cuny that Cuny himself said never happened. In the end, like Jack Brennan from "Fifty Grand," Siki would learn the life lesson that the fix is always on, and like Brennan he'd try to settle accounts his own way. Doing so wouldn't get him fifty thousand dollars or get his child into private school. Eventually, in fact, it would get him murdered.

The Heart of a Senegalese

For the Carpentier fight, even though he won, Siki got the loser's share, 35,000 francs (a little over $3,000). Carpentier got 200,000 francs, as if he'd won. In America Rickard said he'd match Siki with Harry Greb, Tom Gibbons, even Dempsey. But Commissioner Muldoon insisted that he had to prove himself first. Prove himself? He was light-heavyweight champion of the world! Then Rickard stopped talking about Greb or Dempsey. All he'd talk about was Kid Norfolk, which was strange, because if Norfolk won, a black man would still be world champion. Siki told the reporters: I wish I could get a chemical to turn my skin white. I'd pay 50,000 francs. If you're white, you can fight whoever you want, where you want.

Meanwhile, he was running out of money fast. When you were world champion, Siki discovered, everywhere you went people expected you to buy drinks, cigars. You had to take taxis. If you walked down the street, people mobbed you. The 35,000 francs was gone before he knew it, and he was back to giving exhibitions in dirty little arenas. Hellers, in the meantime, had taken to playing up Siki's new image as a savage. In one interview he went so far as to compare his fighter to a gorilla, declaring, "Siki has something in him which is not human. A long time ago I used to think that if one could find an intelligent gorilla and teach him to box one would have the world's champion. Well, that's what I found in Siki." Siki had "the gorilla's tricks, the gorilla's skill and manners." A "living illusion," he was "just a little bit crazy, judged by human standards."[88]

Intent on setting up a bout with British heavyweight champ Joe Beckett, Hellers counseled caution, telling Siki to wait until his calumniators calmed down, but Siki was sick of short rations and inaction. *L'Auto* gossiped he meant to dump Hellers at the end of October when their contract lapsed.[89] One day in *L'Echo*'s offices Siki bumped into Hellers, who was in the process of swearing on the graves of near relatives that he and Siki were getting along fine. Sure, Siki agreed. "He's more than my manager. He's my guardian angel."[90] Breyer blithely printed Siki's words, sneering at *L'Auto* for getting its facts wrong. Siki wrote Breyer:

> To end once and for all the ill-intentioned uproar regarding me, where it is said that I am about to quit my friend and devoted manager, Charley Hellers, who conducted me to the championship of the world, I say that people who circulate such rumors don't know very well the heart of a Senegalese. I said in the magazine that Hellers was my guardian angel, and I stick by that. As long as I continue to box, he who made me champion of the world will always be my friend and devoted manager.[91]

Siki's words didn't tell the whole tale. He really didn't trust Hellers—or anyone else. He could feel the boxing crowd closing in, shutting off his options. They called him a drunk, a thug, an embarrassment to the sport—anything to slander him.

Soon they'd find the excuse they needed to take away his right to earn a living, his French and European titles, even his visa. All it took was one little shove, in front of a few thousand witnesses, in a Paris ring. And Siki wasn't even in boxing togs at the time. The next day French papers ignored the incident between Siki and Fernand Cuny, the manager of Maurice Prunier, following Prunier's bout with Ercole Balzac. *L'Echo de Paris* gave the bout's bare result, an eleventh-round knockout, nothing more.[92] Siki had been working the corner of his pal Balzac, who seemed on his way to a successful defense of his French middleweight title, until he clutched his groin and sank to the canvas, moaning in pain. The referee began a count, as Balzac's handlers leapt up, screaming, "Foul! Foul!" At ten, they spilled into the ring, Siki at their head. He ran straight at Cuny, shoving him across the ring. When gendarmes led Siki from the hall, fans mobbed him, shouting insults. Cuny would later say he hadn't been hit or hurt, hadn't felt especially menaced, didn't believe Siki meant him harm. Siki told anyone who cared to listen he "deplore[d] a gesture due to the frustration of seeing his stable mate beaten, but denie[d] that he had for an instant dreamed of hitting Cuny."[93] But Rousseau's boxing federation stuck its nose in the affair and within days a medley of Parisian journals were screaming scandal, demanding Siki be stripped of his titles.[94]

They knew they were talking nonsense, and *L'Eclair* even said so. Who'd have made a fuss if Siki were white? White boxers and managers, including Descamps, had done worse things in moments of indignation without rousing an outcry.[95] Still, the FFB, on whose board Descamps sat, said Siki must be punished. He'd struck a rival manager, disgracing French sport: "He is only happy in scandals and excesses and already many escapades have given him problems with the police. In short, Battling Siki, champion of France, Europe, and the world, does not honor his profession."[96] But I didn't hit him, Siki protested. No, he didn't, Cuny confirmed. It didn't matter. Hellers moaned, "300,000 francs [the Siki / Beckett purse] fall in the water."[97] Siki was suspended, then stripped of his French and European titles. Rousseau had no authority to take away Siki's world title, at least.

Paper after paper lined up to vilify Siki, reviving tales of erratic stunts—drastically revised in retelling. The tale of Siki and his dogs resurfaced, set now in a "grand café of the boulevards" where Siki "to amuse himself" gave them "great kicks, wishing to prove in that fashion the evident superiority of man over animal." Siki was portrayed as threatening to shoot (with his starter pistol!) one dog that bared its teeth.[98] What's the fun of being champion, *Le Miroir* mocked, "if one isn't free to beat up [or annoy?—*d'assommer* suggests either] one's neighbors at the hotel, to box with news vendors, to undertake firearms practice in the bars, to put on exhibitions in the cafes that have nothing to do with those of the ring, and to sell, under one's overcoat, products that, more agreeably and more slowly than the fist, send victims to the land of dreams?" Before an FFB tribunal, Siki mused, "When I was just the nigger Siki nobody bothered with my jokes, or [they] laughed at them; now that I'm champion, they get angry!"[99]

When Siki turned out to celebrate Armistice Day in an embroidered Senegalese *bou-bou,* he was arrested, on the grounds he had no right, despite his war medals, to wear what the police styled a colonial military uniform.[100] French papers spread libelous tales, whose essence evaporated in the light of day—of Siki selling cocaine in Montmartre, of an *"outrage à la pudeur"* (offense against shame) toward an underage girl, which turned out to mean merely that he'd flirted with (*"faisait la cour"*—which doesn't necessarily suggest advances that were crude or sexual) an eighteen-year-old woman, walking at that moment with her twelve-year-old sister.[101] Hellers, out of his depth in the flood of innuendo, forsook Siki, remarking, "Ask me to make Siki a boxer, but not a gentleman."[102]

CHAPTER TWELVE

———————————

Tagged

You Told Me to Take a Dive

It's after midnight now in Hell's Kitchen, and Siki's pals have drifted off to warm beds. But he has a bit of the devil left. He's hell bent on Harlem, where life, noise, distraction from the dismal prospect of duns and back-alley hoods await. In Times Square, bleary-eyed, shamble-footed, he hails a taxi, telling the driver he wants to hire him for the night. The driver answers with a mocking smile. What cabbie hasn't heard of Battling Siki, who makes hack-drivers chug-a-lug from his demijohn of wine, challenges them to fight him for the fare, then either tips them a week's wages or stiffs them altogether. Thanks, but no thanks! It's late, he's tired, he doesn't feel adventurous just now. Siki remonstrates. Soon they're shouting.

The cabbie calls Siki a barfly. Siki invites him to climb out of his cab. The cabbie guns his engine, spins his tires. Siki, to the merriment of onlookers (who repeat the tale to reporters in the morning), spins on his heels, enraged. The cabbie has a point. Siki has no money to pay for a cab. But who thinks about such little details late at night under a load of cheap wine? He ambles off. If he can't get to Harlem, he might as well go home.[1]

Diagne had said, three years before, "If, at 23, he goes out to amuse himself in the bars, it's just that he's gotten used to your civilization. We don't point the finger at whites who do the same."[2] France's first black deputy had never backed down from his insistence that men of color who bled for France be given the same rights as whites. Tall, angular, elegant, a stickler for ceremony, though his father had only been a cook, Diagne's superficial aplomb hid a stubborn pugnacity. In his first run for office, he'd provoked a riot in

Dakar when he confronted a white colonialist who'd mocked him by naming his dog Blaise.[3] Three years before, in the hallway outside the Chamber of Deputies, Siki had strained to hear Diagne's speech protesting Siki's treatment by the French boxing league.[4] Footsteps had pounded, clerks and messengers jabbered, "Look! It's him, Siki!"—as the bell-like clarity of Diagne's voice intoned, "I don't come here either to put on a show for you or to make electoral propaganda. I come only as a representative of the colonies. If I demand a reduction of the credit [for sports], it's because I want the men charged with distributing the funds... to be impartial. But they are not. The incident of Siki proves it."[5] As the African deputy took his symbolic stand, disputing a routine budget item, the deputies listened intently, interrupting only to laugh, shout assent, or murmur protests. He wasn't enamored of the power of his compatriot's fists, Diagne insisted. He had no passion for boxing, no taste for displays of brute force.[6] Siki had heard Diagne's set speech on the subject before. He'd soon mimic it himself in interviews, face stiff, biting off each word, no longer the exuberant young man of October.

Inside the chamber Diagne held nothing back, including his opinion of fallen idol Carpentier. The crowd around Carpentier, Diagne insisted, had connived against Siki even before the match, and later stolen his title and boxing license through a series of shabby ploys.[7] "Why have we ousted Siki?" he cried. "Because he's a person of color, there you have the real reason."[8] What's more, when Siki had not, as agreed, taken a fall in the fourth round, he'd inspired "the hatred of 'sportsmen' from the boxing federation," for whom Carpentier was not merely a *"belluaire"* (gladiator), but "an industry." The "interests of those who wanted to live off [Carpentier] were hurt."[9] Few papers would repeat Diagne's accusation of a fix, though he'd made the rounds the day before to reassure them Siki could prove it.

Diagne made no bones about why Siki now came forward. He'd been driven out of boxing. He wanted revenge. "Siki won," Diagne exclaimed. "Immediately we denounce him as a drunk, a drug seller, as having committed an outrage against shame in a bar, at an hour when those who frequent such establishments no longer have any notion of common feeling."[10] A roar of laughter erupted as Diagne looked pointedly at André Maginot, the hulking defense minister whose amorous liaisons, despite a crippled leg suffered in the war, were the stuff of popular legend. He added, "We reproach Siki for lacking distinction! Have you ever heard of men of the world entering the ring?" Would anyone hurl such abuse at Carpentier? Could one imagine his private life exposed in print?[11]

The next day the dailies gave most of their space not to Diagne but to the responses of Maginot and Henri Paté, the high commissioner for sport.

Paté promised an inquiry; Maginot declared, "I only know one thing, as Minister of War, that during the hostilities Siki was an admirable soldier."[12] Both insisted the Chamber of Deputies couldn't waste its time debating the fate of one boxer. That was between Siki and the boxing federation. By a vote of 408 to136, the Chamber of Deputies killed Diagne's motion.[14]

Until now, Rousseau and the FFB had kept silent. But when Diagne went to the press, swearing he'd sue the boxing fedaration for conspiring against Siki, the FFB announced that Marmouget, Piochelle, and three less credible pretenders would fight an elimination tourney to choose Siki's successor as French light-heavyweight champ.[14] Rousseau wasn't looking to provoke "a racial confrontation," he insisted, just holding Siki to "the rigors of our regulations" as judged by a board of "dispassionate men."[15] His "dispassionate men" then voted to call for Diagne to be stripped of parliamentary immunity so Rousseau could sue him for libel.

At his apartment, Diagne exhibited a silk *bou-bou* he'd worn to receive a group of Senegalese notables. You see! he said. Our traditional costume! This is what Siki wore when he was arrested on Armistice Day, not a *tirailleur* uniform.[16] He flatly denied to *L'Eclair* that Siki had assaulted Cuny.[17] "One must not exaggerate the importance" of that or other "clumsy acts" imputed to Siki. He had a point. In fact, some of Siki's more notorious stunts, from today's perspective, seem more worthy of applause than censure. Senegalese friends would later tell of a chic Parisian podiatrist who disdained touching a black man's foot—whereupon Siki dragged the doctor's furniture into the street, closed the shutters, and roared, "The place is now closed, by order of Siki."[18]

Rousseau might pretend to be aloof, but Diagne had hit a nerve by invoking "the blood spilled among France and her colonies." Hellers phoned Diagne to say, "Don't you think it would perhaps be good not to bother any more about the Siki affair? If we continue to make noise . . . , don't you think we'll put ourselves on bad terms with the boxing federation?" If that's all you have to say, Diagne shot back, stop right there. As for the FFB's threat to sue, they'd do well to learn the law before "amusing themselves" with such avowals.[19]

Siki, meanwhile, though he'd had no signed contract for the Carpentier bout, hired lawyer Alcide Delmont to sue for the balance of his purse, the difference between the 200,000 francs advertised as the winner's share and the 35,000 he'd actually received. Carpentier was nearly apoplectic at this impudent black clown's "repulsive tales." He told *L'Auto,* "I don't understand why the press publishes all the declarations of the Senegalese who, in order to revenge himself for his disqualifications, amuses himself by demolishing the sport of boxing."[20] Menaced with a countersuit, Siki fumed, "I have been too good. I wanted to be too honest. Why didn't people leave me alone? This is a lesson for me. I am through with so-called friends."[21]

At *L'Auto*'s offices he declared to Hellers's face, "It was a fix: Hellers knows very well."[22] "No! I always said you could take him," Hellers protested, calling the scribes to witness. They pitied poor Charlie, who "found pathetic accents, cries coming from his heart." As for Siki, "through phrases cut with digressions, with parentheses," he stuck to his guns. *L'Auto* had it exactly backward, of course. The heartfelt cry was Siki's, the evasions Hellers's. "Don't you remember that time at Luna Park when I said ... ?" Hellers began.

"Oh sure," Siki replied, "but you told me that in front of everyone. You weren't going to say the truth in front of everyone." He laid it on the line: "You told me to take a dive."

"Listen ... ," Hellers interrupted.

Siki cut him short: "I avenge myself. They disqualified me by inventing lies. They deprived me of my living. I have a wife, I have a kid, and me, I was too good to the French, and it's the French who've attacked me. I avenge myself, but I don't want to [do it] against you Hellers, and if they hadn't attacked me, I would have kept your secret." Then he laid out the whole frame-up, as Hellers lamely quibbled with details.[23]

The gang at *L'Auto* might declare Siki's story preposterous, but in fact people had talked of a fix all along. André Glarner recalled waiting for news of the fight in Geneva at La Régence, a cozy café in les Rues Basses, near the Rhone Bridge, jammed with men eager for tidings. When news of the early knockdowns came, unaware how stagey and implausible they'd been, he ordered another *bleu* and muttered, "It won't last much longer!" The next phone call brought news of two more knockdowns—one by Carpentier, one by Siki! Suddenly, the joint was buzzing. It had to be a mistake! Then came the stunner: Carpentier knocked out in the sixth. "What?" everyone screamed with one voice, *"Chiqué! Chiqué!"* (Fix! Fix![24]) By morning, many Parisians were singing the same tune. Then Italy's *Gazzetta dello Sport* said the rumors had it exactly backward—the fight had been fixed okay, but for Carpentier to win by knockout. Siki had double-crossed him. Two French writers crashed a boxing federation meeting to vent their suspicions. A manager went to *L'Echo des Sports* to push the same theme. He and two trainers who hung out at *La Chope du Nègre,* the boxing crowd's favorite café, said they had proof. But when they were called before the boxing federation, their story died on their lips.[25]

Still, rumors persisted. Boxing fans tried to swallow the rationales offered: *"visiblement terrifié"* for Siki, *"trop de cinéma"* for Carpentier. But the

more they thought about them, the less sense they made. Siki had flaws in
the ring: he didn't always train seriously, and at times fell in love with that
right swing of his. But who'd ever seen him show fear? He'd fought at
Gallipoli, the Somme, Champagne. Was a punch in the nose going to terrify
him? Even before the bout, rumors had swirled of a fix, but Hellers insisted
he'd had "no propositions . . . to have Siki lie down," adding with strange
prescience—or reckless candor: "If any are made . . . , I, of course, will have
to accept them in order to get Carpentier into the ring against my black man,
but I will double-cross them."[26] Soon people began to wonder: had Siki,
rather than being terrified, just been a lousy actor, and then, on a sudden
whim, quit faking and returned to what he knew best, fighting? It made
sense. Siki was like that, wasn't he? Impulsive? Capricious?

As doubts about Carpentier grew, so did sympathy for Siki. The tennis
star Suzanne Lenglen said no champion should lose a title because of anything done outside the ring.[27] Colonel Girod, the deputy from Doubs, proposed a bill tacking a 50 percent tax on boxing—a measure that, if adopted,
would kill professional boxing in France.[28] At first inclined to distance himself from the scandal, Desgrange of *L'Auto* began voicing sympathy for Siki:
"It's only because Siki is a nigger [*nègre*] that Carpentier wants to climb back
into the ring. If Nilles had come out the winner at the arena at Montrouge,
Carpentier would have retired without fanfare." France had "asked during
the war of the niggers to whom we have given the imprint of the French
spirit" to come to its defense. "The nigger did it: he helped us preserve the
little things that we cherish. It is therefore logical that he has the right to sit
at the same table with his white compatriots. Whether Siki is black or white,
what's the difference? He's a magnificent French athlete who's proved himself better than Georges Carpentier. And that's all."[29] *L'Auto* was soon printing a storm of letters, including one bristling, "When we don't want to
declare a nigger the winner, we eliminate him. It's the FFB that's 'fixed.'"[30]
The FFB finally launched an inquiry, led by its own advisory council, on
which Descamps sat! The panel dutifully took testimony. Everyone involved
swore on twenty Bibles there'd been no fix. Ah, *le cinéma!*

And what of that other cinéma, the one showing Descamps jumping
from his seat and slinking over to scream at Hellers? The FFB went so far as
to hire lip readers—who swore they weren't sure what Descamps had said.
It looked like he was shouting *"Ta Gueule"* ("your mug," a French equivalent
of "shut up"), but others thought he'd said *"T'es fou?"* ("Are you crazy?").
Descamps swore he'd only run over to shriek at his fighter from a better
angle.[31] Meanwhile, a bicycle firm offered to stage a rematch, giving every
sou of profit to the scientific laboratories. "A return match without a purse

for the boxers. That's very nice!" one reader wrote *L'Auto*. "For Carpentier who is a millionaire.... But Siki's kid will perhaps get to eat nothing but glory." Carpentier and Descamps owned shares in the arena that would host the fight.[32]

Most thought Siki would duck a quick rematch. New champions usually do. They prefer to exploit the title by making a few easy defenses first. But Siki accepted, setting terms: the bout must be within ten weeks, his earlier purse must be paid in full, his license reinstated. Since Carpentier had already accepted, "at the risk of being disqualified himself," the FFB ought to pull strings to arrange the bout.[33] If they didn't, Siki wrote, the bicycle boss would do it on his own:

> If you pretend to subordinate the match to my making a *"mea culpa"* as regards your demanding my appearance before my requalification, you will narrow the debate and bring it down to a petty question of pride. You ought to understand that there are in France men who are inspired by other considerations, and who, tomorrow, if you don't permit it, will organize the fight without you ... for the profit of our laboratories.[34]

The effort of a black man to speak up in his own defense struck some Parisians as ludicrous. A *Canard Enchaîné* cartoon, under the heading "Siki writes letters well," featured a minstrel-show black man sitting at a table, the intense effort to find words contorting his face, as a top-hatted, stoop-shouldered black man with a sorrowful mug (Diagne) bends over him, and a brawny white, hands upraised (Delmont?), looks on. "And the poor sap has again passed a sleepless night" (literally *nuit blanche,* "white night"), the caption read.[35] *Nuit blanche* suggests both a night of worry and a night of playing at being a white.

When the FFB finally called Siki to testify—refusing at the same time to reconsider his suspension or look into the money withheld from his purse—he refused. "I don't understand your insistence on wanting to hear me," he wrote, "after your commission has behaved the way it has, declaring me stripped of my title as champion, taking away my license, depriving me of my way of earning a living, all that without having heard me, and yet a simple explanation from me would have established the inanity of the grievances and inventions formulated to my ruin." He'd answer written questions, he said, or give a written deposition—nothing more.[36]

By late December, with no bout in sight, Siki was reduced to giving shows in a music hall on rue de Clinchy bordering Montmartre. Meanwhile, the Théâtre de la Fourmi (Ant Theater) on boulevard Barbès, hosted a public forum on the boxing scandal. The debate at the packed hall was fiery but inconclusive. Siki, Carpentier, Descamps, and Brouillet, all invited, kept away.[37] Siki knew in time the FFB would have to return his license. But when? People laughed when he decided to fight in Dublin on Saint Patrick's Day, but if he'd fought Carpentier in Paris, Greb in New York, or Beckett in London, would he have gotten a better shake? Besides, he'd been banned in all of those places.

It's after midnight now, in the early hours of December 16, 1925. Suddenly, out of the shadows of the Ninth Avenue El a policeman emerges whom Siki knows from the Thirtieth Street station. "Hello," he calls. "I'm on my way home."

Patrolman John J. Meehan eyes the unsteady boxer. He'd first met Siki back in July, after Siki had been stabbed just around the corner from here. He's warned Siki more than once since then to stay away from brawls. He figures in his present shape Siki might well get embroiled in another one. He jokes with him about his monkey, then warns him again about picking fights. "You'd better keep going in that direction," he cautions.

"Don't worry," Siki reassures him, moving on. "I will."[38]

The cop shakes his head. That Siki! He'll kill himself one of these days! Just a few weeks before, he'd suddenly appeared at the Thirtieth Street Police Station, trailed by a sputtering taxi driver who kept carefully out of range of those hard fists. "Here I am again boys," the thick-tongued miscreant said. "Money, I have not got it. I owe this poor taxi driver. I want a nice clean cell. I understand. I've been like this before. I just want a nice clean cell."

It was the damdest thing, the driver, Brooklynite John Dick, told them. Siki had said, "I'm Battling Siki. Take me up to Harlem." He drove Siki to nearly every cabaret in Harlem, dropping him at his door as the sun rose. "It costs you $10.80," he said. But when Siki pulled out his wallet all he had was three bucks. He gave a poor-mouth look, said, "I know. I'm going to jail. I know how. Drive me to the West Thirtieth Street Station. I have friends there."[39]

At Jefferson Market Court, next morning, nobody felt like giving Siki a hard time. All the boys liked him. One clerk emptied his wallet and slipped him seven bucks—which the hack driver pocketed, snorting "close enough." The cops laughed and shook their heads. That Siki sure could get into scrapes![40]

I Know Who Shot Him! I Know Who Did It!

A young man dashes down the street in the early morning darkness, a .32 welded to his fist. He flings the pistol to the opposite curb and picks up speed, sprinting uphill toward Eighth Avenue. At the corner he turns and slows to a walk, a hundred yards from the man he's shot but hasn't killed, a black man with far too belligerent a way of talking, far too obnoxious a habit of waving his fist in other men's faces. Tonight those fists did him no good. You can't punch a bullet—especially when you get it from behind. The gunman peers up the avenue. Not a soul around. Except for that poor sap lying face down in the gutter in a pool of blood.

The instant the pistol fired the first time, one of his two accomplices had taken off like a purse snatcher, his tan overcoat fluttering moth-like down Forty-first Street toward the river. But he and the other man had waited, and watched their victim stagger down the street for nearly fifty yards, coughing blood. He didn't go down easily. Berlenbach hadn't put him down. Neither did those guys who tried to slit his throat around the corner from here four months ago. The rounds were low-caliber. At the front, where most of the bullets had been thirty caliber, wounded men time and again had crawled back across no-man's land at night with one, two, even three such slugs in them. The gunman pumped another bullet in his victim's back, sending him spinning, spraying the street with blood. Even then he lurched onward, intent on making it home. He only had a block to go to reach his front door. He got another twenty yards before he pitched to the tarmac, blood bubbling from his nose and mouth, lung collapsing, and lost consciousness for good. Then the two assassins fled.[41]

Lillian is still in bed, though outside it's nearly full light, when the pounding at the door awakens her. She unbolts the door to two stony-faced men waving badges, Detectives McNamara and Sheehan. "Mrs. Siki?"

Yes, she answers. She's Battling Siki's wife. What is it? What's he done this time?

They don't answer, just tell her to get dressed and come down to the station. They want to question her first before they tell her about her husband.[42] Standard procedure.

When they take her to identify the body, she gives a wordless cry of horror, loses control of her legs, collapses. When words come, she shrieks, "I know who shot him. I know who did it." They'd run into a bootlegger on Ninth Avenue, a "scrawny" fellow named Jimmy whom Louis "could beat with one hand" and who liked to hang around at 331 West Thirty-first Street. He said if Louis didn't pay the twenty dollars he owed he'd get him. It had to be him. He must be the killer. But when the cops go looking for him, Jimmy is nowhere to be found.[43]

When she calms down, she succumbs to an urge to exonerate, prove somehow Louis's murder wasn't his own fault. "He was a good boy," she whimpers. "He was just a little too mischievous, but he'd never harm anybody."[44] Then she remembers. There was another man, a guy who stole Louis's overcoat in a lunchroom the day before. Louis said he knew where to find him and was going to get the coat back. Maybe that's it. Maybe he found that guy and beat him up. Maybe the guy went out afterward to get a gun.[45]

The cops figure by nightfall they'll have the killer. They already have a witness, a porter for the *New York Telegram* who was heading up Forty-first to work when he heard a gunshot and saw a man in a light-colored coat come flying down the street.[46] But another witness, one Oscar Bilbern, garage watchman at 346 West Forty-first, near where the murder weapon was found, swears that though he saw Siki walk down the street he heard no gunfire, saw no shooting.[47] The cops reckon Siki must have been up to his old stunts, drunk, bullying some stranger with a fuse even shorter than his. An inspector tells reporters, "Ninth Avenue is no place for a man to push another off the sidewalk, and that was a favorite trick of Siki's."[48]

Funny thing, though—Siki had looked as if he hadn't an enemy in the world when Patrolman Meehan came upon him after midnight, lumbering

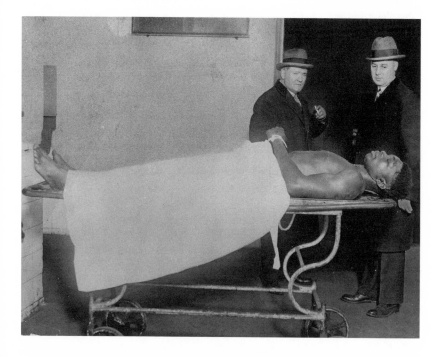

Siki's corpse in the police morgue, with two police detectives, December 1925.
(Courtesy of Mamadou Niang.)

unsteadily toward home. At 4:30 A.M., when Meehan saw the inert form stretched out face-down in the gutter in front of 354 West Forty-first Street, he'd at first taken it for a drunk, passed out. Then he rolled the body over, saw who it was, felt for a pulse, and called an ambulance. The bullet holes, he saw, were only in the back, which suggested Siki had been ambushed, not shot in a fight. Soon Detectives McNamara and Sheehan had turned up, scouring sidewalks and front stoops on Forty-first Street for evidence. In front of 346 they found more blood, and at 333 a small, rusty revolver, missing two rounds. They imagined the rest: a fight in a speakeasy, a sore loser waiting for Siki to leave, shadowing him down the murky street. One bullet, the autopsy would reveal, penetrated a lung, the other a kidney. One was ordinary lead, the other steel-jacketed to fragment on impact, tearing up interior tissue. The pathologist found hardly a drop of blood left in Siki's heart. He found something stranger, too: adhesions from pleurisy in the lungs—perhaps from a gas attack in the war.[49] None of the papers would draw one ancillary inference: that Siki had been fighting fifteen, twenty rounders for years on damaged lungs.

Siki's body was found too late for the early editions, but the murder soon made the front pages. Most papers, filling gaps in the story with detectives' conjecture, borrowed liberally from the iconography of Siki-the-savage-child. The *Times* linked the murder to a spurious version of the July knife assault: "He had attempted to wreck a so-called night club on that occasion, and when he left had been trailed. The police believe that Siki tried to repeat his exploit early yesterday and paid for the effort with his life."[50] Though Siki had sworn the earlier incident had nothing to do with a brawl in a speakeasy, newspapers worldwide peddled as fact the *Times'* conjecture. Why not? Didn't it set up a lovely transition to a final kicker ringing with certitude?

"That which had to happen has happened," wrote *Paris-Soir*,

> Siki is dead, and dead in circumstances that the whole world foresaw. Victim of a brawl, he was found in a New York street, struck by blows of a razor [!] and revolver. The same sort of adventure had happened to him many times before. . . . This time he is good and dead, and despite all of the caprices he has staged during his life, it is to be doubted that, in death, he will find a way to manage to escape from his coffin."[51]

Damon Runyon, who likely knew the real story (a few years later he would zealously guard the secret of who killed the racketeer Arnold Rothstein), wrote, "Folks have long been thinking that the strange monkey-man of Fistiana might go that way, what with drinking, and brawling, and carrying on in dubious resorts."[52] *Le Matin* mused, "One supposes that having visited many night clubs of the district, he was caught up in a quarrel leaving one of those joints."[53] Weirdly, that version of Siki's death evolved into one where an assassin waited, with cool brutality, to time each (of seven!) pistol shots to coincide with the din of passing Ninth Avenue elevated trains.[54]

The writers blamed Siki for his own demise. "Battling Siki," sneered *Le Soir,* "by turns boxer, [lion] trainer, singer, emigrant, but always a nigger, has gone and gotten himself murdered in an infamous neighborhood of New York."[55] The *New York Age* mused, "Gifted with a marvelous body, indomitable courage, and a childlike mind, Siki was a prey for sharpers, grafters, and leeches of all kinds. He was playing and clowning even in the hardest of fights and the police are about ready to embrace the theory that perhaps one of his capers led to his end."[56] Carpentier, too, had a pharisaic epigram ready: "It seems a pity that an athlete of such magnificent gifts should have met with this end. The time has passed when boxers can indulge in drinking and carousing and be champions."[57]

The *Evening Journal* ran a Hal Coffman cartoon envisioning the downfall of "poor deluded Siki." In the first box, Siki, in overcoat and fedora, smiles as he leaves a speakeasy, as a man with tousled hair, tie and collar ajar, fists cocked, glares at his back. In the next, the man, collar up, hat brim low, grips a pistol. In the next, Siki sprawls under a table, beside a spilled coffee cup and broken saucer, above the caption: "On his way home he stopped to get a cup of coffee, but fell off the chair while trying to drink it."[58] *Le Petit Journal* ran a cover illustration showing patrons peering out the door of a brightly lit club, watching a sidewalk free-for-all where a black man lands a straight right to the face of a burly white. Another lies stretched at his feet. A third crawls erect, hand to bleeding mouth.[59] In fact, no one had seen Siki in a fight that night. The last three times Siki had been seen he was arguing with a taxi driver, then ambling peaceably homeward, then falling-down drunk in a coffeeshop, but disturbing no one. Nevertheless, for more than eighty years the story of a barroom brawl has persisted.

Soon European papers would push another theory: an overturned fix, like the one with Carpentier, and a gangster determined to settle the score. Bénac said years later that he got a friend to trick Siki's former manager (whose name he misheard as "Lewis") into revealing the truth about the murder, as Bénac eavesdropped nearby. Yes, there'd been a fix, Levy / Lewis said. Siki, too much in the habit of forgetting promises, had overturned it. A French cook whose place he frequented (Villeponteux?) had told him plainly, "Count on it, Siki. By double-crossing people left and right, you'll come to harm. I've already heard conversations that are at least disturbing."[60] Siki, laughing, replied, "Forget about it, I'm the stronger. I've seen plenty of others like them. They don't have my [thick] skin, I tell you. It's too tough for them."[61]

The third time he pulled this stunt, swearing to carry a fighter but "forgetting," the rival was managed by *"un gangster d'occasion"* (a second-rate gangster) who "took it very badly." Then Siki pulled the same stunt a fourth time:

> The Senegalese had just, as was his habit, played around with a novice who was very much promoted by the gang of the night clubs of Broadway. The fight should have gone the distance and been very equal to justify a draw and launch the career of the new heavyweight, but Siki had stretched him out for the count of ten, during the first round, laughing as he did so, "Here's what I do, me Siki, to your hopes!"[62]

Who had Siki knocked out lately that he might have promised to carry? He'd lost to Lee Anderson and lost a newspaper decision to Billy Vidabeck. He'd knocked out Chief Halbran, but who would bet on that shopworn pug? What about Jimmy Francis? Police had first found Siki in a pool of blood just four days after the Francis bout.

Jersey mobsters Pete Reilly, Longy Zwillman, and Willie Moretti all knew their way across the river. Reilly palled with Manhattan mobster Big Bill Duffy, and Moretti with Frank Costello. Zwillman was allied with Manhattan mobsters Meyer Lansky, Arnold Rothstein, Joe Adonis, Costello, and Lucky Luciano.[63] Any one of them could have had Siki shot as payback. Within a year of his murder, three former world champs would die in dubious circumstances. Harry Greb, Tiger Flowers, and Pancho Villa all died on operating tables of overdoses of ether. Anesthesia was an imperfect science then. But three world champions, two known to have been involved in fixes, all dead within two years from the same "accident"? Not much later, Flowers's manager, Walk Miller, was bludgeoned and shot to death by an unknown assailant.[64] Heavyweight Bill Brennan, reportedly gunned down by an unruly patron who'd gotten crude with a lady in his uptown bar, had in fact been shot because he welched on the fee for a load of bootleg whiskey. Babe Pioli, the thug Legs Diamond sent to collect, overstepped instructions.[65] Siki lived in Manhattan's most gang-infested corner, on the same block where Madden had lived for years. He was last seen alive on the corner of Forty-first and Eighth, where Madden murdered rival Patsy Doyle, outside Nash's Café.[66] You could bet if Siki was killed by the mob, the killer wouldn't come to trial. Doyle's killer never did.

Okay, Bénac gets facts wrong. He can't even keep straight the city's basic geography (Siki was murdered, he says, "near the corner of 12th St. and 10th Ave."). He names the murderer "Harris," insisting that *"petit bonhomme"* hid out later near the crime scene, was caught by police, and confessed his crime—confusing the July knife attack with the December murder, Harris with Hanrahan.[67] But he did get one thing right: Louis M'barick Fall was killed by a gangster. Otherwise, the man who fired the pistol would have been found.

Siki's death inspired reams of philosophical discourse. Now that he was gone the writers missed him—or rather missed the icon they'd made of him. Perhaps the oddest elegy, the *New York World*'s, began by telling over Siki's outrages against decorum, then fetched up with the outlandish assertion that he "could speak nine languages, and his total vocabulary in all, it was said, was 157 words, counting profane expletives."[68] Yet Siki was hardly inarticulate. The *New York Age* wondered if Siki's detractors hadn't perhaps disparaged his linguistic abilities because they spoke no foreign tongues themselves. Entranced with its own illusions, the *World* conjured visions of "hairy and horrific" missing links. Siki, "just such an ancestor as we would wish," was said to have been "given to moody fits not comprehensible to us who have not lived in primordial ages," including "berserk rages" and "strange humors and whimsies." The *World* furnished him with the standard accouterments: yellow gloves, tan shoes, chattering monkeys, leashed lions. Somehow it ended with contradictory sweeping judgments, tagging Siki with "the mentality of a backward toad," yet "the soul of a god." It linked him with mythic heroes: Achilles, Beowulf, Siegfried. His wanton violence and moody sulks were styled classic virtue.

Westbrook Pegler's *Daily News* editorial left just as indelible a mark, marring nearly every recasting of Siki's legacy down to Gerald Early's in 1994. Pegler, who Gilbert Seldes says defended lynching in his first Scripps-Howard editorial, and who was a close friend of gangster Owney Madden, made his Siki a simpleton with a grin as wide as a satchel lined in red, who slobbered wet kisses on his manager and had the personality of an Airedale who licks his master's face with chicken feathers stuck to his muzzle.[69] His Siki was a bewildered naif whose homeland was a place "where they make no great boast of their civilization." Pegler's Siki was amazed to discover that civilization let him exercise with impunity his worst impulses. "Siki," Pegler wrote, "went to nightclubs and to the weird squealing of the woodwinds and the muffled thump of tom-toms, the music of civilization, he saw half-naked black-and-tans wiggling and squirming in the dances of an enlightened tribe. He fought in the ring and when blood showed the civilized crowds came up from their chairs roaring. So from what he saw of it, Siki frankly didn't get the plot of this business called civilization. The whole thing was too much for the simple mind of a primitive African, who got a late start at the racket."[70] In short, Pegler blamed not Siki, the berserk animal who'd wreaked havoc in the china shop of civilization—but the keepers who'd set him loose there.

If it isn't surprising Pegler would write such things, it's surprising that seventy years later Gerald Early would echo them. Early plays, one must note, a subtle game with semantics, voicing representations he at times explicitly repudiates, at times leaves lying on the table. For instance, he seems to buy Pegler's notion of Siki as a cultural innocent bewildered by modernity. He calls Siki "the most fantastic and incredible innocent American racism has ever slaughtered."[71] He adds, "Siki was, in all respects, a deracinated colonial, an absolute marginal man." He calls him "never even quite a man but rather a being who approached being a man," as if such assaults on another's selfhood can be justified in the name of probing the mass psyche.[72]

Early muses over the *World* editorial, which he has only in an *Amsterdam News* reprint (leaving out the "backward-toad" bit), and thus he sees it as a contrast between white and black readings of primitive innocence. If he echoes the *World* a bit artlessly, it's in order to use Siki to formulate a rhetoric of race, exposing its self-contradictions. But in doing so he accedes to the notion that there may once have been such a fantastic, voiceless, crudely visceral, absurdly misplaced fellow as Pegler's Siki or the *World*'s. He doesn't see that getting Siki wrong was the point all along. When the *World* piece ends, "We have had a walking image of our beginnings among us and didn't know it," Early wonders whether "we" refers to blacks or humanity—but maybe the issue is whether such an image ever "walked" anywhere but in our own imaginations.[73] Since Siki's death, the *World*'s has become the enduring portrait of Siki. The "backward-toad" line has resurfaced again and again, as has the reflection that civilization, not a gangster with a grudge, killed Siki. Such is the power of myth!

Adam Clayton Powell, pastor of Abyssinian Baptist Church in Harlem, hammered the last nails into the lid of Siki's posthumous repute at the Effie A. Miller funeral chapel at 64 West 127th Street. "A lack of preparation and a noble purpose were the two dreadful mistakes of his life," declared Reverend Powell. "Our civilization is, perhaps, more to blame for these mistakes than he was." Lillian softly, relentlessly, wept. Could you blame her?

Her husband's body lay there, cold meat cut open by strangers. His heart, lungs, liver, brain had been pulled out and weighed in a pan. His merry eyes were opaque as marbles. And this preacher had nothing more to say about his brutal murder than that he'd brought it on himself. Pressing his theme, Powell reflected upon the flaws of American civilization. As thousands of curious Harlemites stood outside in the cold, waiting to catch a glimpse of a black celebrity's coffin, he delivered a final crushing rebuke: "Emerging from the jungles . . . , charged with the energy of a Grecian mythological god, he could have been molded into a tremendous force for good, but allowed to run wild, like uncontrolled and undirected lightning, he left scars upon the body of civilized mankind of which we should all be ashamed."[74] Lillian listened in the front rank as Powell tagged her husband with a last debasing epithet, as if he wished to revive the custom of spitting on unhallowed dead. The last two days had been ghastly. At the wake, young African friends had sworn they'd go door to door to track down the killers and take revenge. One rose to his feet to act it out, raging, "On the spot where Siki fell there should fall a hundred whites." A lone voice warned, "Brother, those things may not be said." She'd had to fight to get them to put poor Louis in a casket. They wanted to lay his body in bare earth, as they did at home in Africa, to cover it with soil dropped by their own hands, the left covering him below the waist, the right above. She'd insisted on a Christian homily. He'd lived a life of Christian charity, she said, even if he could never believe in any religious faith after the butchery of the trenches.[75]

As the Harmonic Four sang "Nearer My God to Thee," she broke down in sobs, crumpling to the carpet, to be restored, not for the first time, by smelling salts. She wasn't alone in her unbridled grief. A white man wept from the start of the service to the end. "Who are you?" an *Amsterdam News* reporter asked. He replied, "Never mind . . . he was my pal, that's all." Among eight floral bouquets was one from the Newsboys' Association. Siki had made a habit of handing out cash to street arabs when he came back flush from a bout.

His pallbearers wore fezzes, the badge of ex-*tirailleurs*. They watched as the lid of the gray-silver box was screwed shut, as if their friend were goods to be delivered, his soul an animal to be caged. How would his spirit break free of that box to find its home among the ancestors? At home, his body would have been purified, wrapped tight in a white shroud, lowered into the ground without a coffin.[76] Outside the chapel, the bearers set their burden down and recited a Muslim prayer. Perhaps it was a *Thaná* of praise: "Glory to Alláh, and praise be to you and blessed is your name and exalted is your majesty and glorious is your praise and there is none worthy to worship besides you." Perhaps they intoned "Alláhu Akbar," then silently recited the Darud: "O Alláh, exalt Muhammad and the followers of Muhammad as thou has exalted Ibráhìm and the followers of Ibráhìm. Thou surely art praise magnified." Perhaps finally a Du'á, asking Alláh to pardon dead and living, present and absent, young and old, man and woman, begging all be brought to live and die in observance of Islam, the leader turning right, then left, wishing the departed soul peace: *"As-salámu-Alaikum Wa-Rahmatulláh."*[77] They hauled the casket to the hearse, taking their places in a line of cars winding to Flushing Cemetery, where the remains of this victim of blind retribution were buried. And though Louis M'barick Fall's body was exhumed and returned to Senegal in 1993, something of him remains there still, imprisoned in the box of words screwed tightly shut upon his corpse in 1925.

The Bulls Are Wise to Who Killed Siki

He's jumpy as hell, this teenager cupping his hand over a payphone's mouthpiece in the dancehall at Tenth and Fortieth. You can see from the way his eyes dart around, his voice drops to a murmur, then rises so you can hear it even over the orchestra. An undercover cop strolls over, just to see what this kid's so jumpy about. With his loud suit and slicked-back hair, the cop looks like a hood himself. The cop is close enough now to hear, and luckily the kid is lost in conversation, forgetting he's chosen about the worst place he could to nearly shout, "The bulls are wise to who killed Siki. They're close on our trail. But what can I do? I can't get out of town. I've got no money!"[78] The cop freezes, hardly trusting his luck. The punk is so stupid he doesn't know any better than to stand there in a dance hall bragging about killing a man! Suddenly he sees the cop, jams down the receiver without even a "so long," and slinks off. But the cop learns his name: Martin Maroney. Just eighteen, he lives a few hundred yards down West Forty-first from where they found Siki's body—in the direction the man in the light-colored coat fled the night of the murder. For two weeks, undercover cops Walter Clancey and Michael McNamara tail Maroney, hoping he'll lead them to his accomplices. No such luck!

Then they get wind of a plan for all three to get out of town and on March 8 they collar Maroney. He gives his occupation as "laborer," swears he knows nothing about the murder. If he clams up, he'll beat this rap. But he's dumb as hell, and if they scare him, get him to think they've got more on him than they do, he might panic and spill the beans.

Or he might not. Whoever put him up to this has no doubt made sure he knows what will happen if he squeals. Hell's Kitchen is a law unto itself.

And who's going to testify against him when all he did was murder a black man? But three hours later, right on cue, he does crack, this pathetic little fellow who bragged he exterminated a boxing champion. He was there, he admits, with Siki moments before his death. But he didn't kill him. He had nothing to do with that. He was ... just there, that's all—at the Coffee Pot, at Forty-first and Eighth, at 4:00 A.M., when suddenly Siki came in "and threatened to kill every white American in the place, shouting that they had given him a rough deal and that he had no use for them." "A fight followed," swore Maroney, "and Siki was knocked down and a table fell on him." Then "several other" blacks arrived and "took Siki away with them."[79] Soon afterward he heard gunfire in the street.

The detective jots it all down, trying not to laugh. He has other witnesses, people who saw Siki at the little late-night café with "The Coffee Pot" in flowing script on the door, below street level on the northeast corner of Eighth and Fortieth. He knows Siki came in alone and did nothing more belligerent than trip and land on the floor, taking his chair and coffee with him. The witnesses say Siki left that night with none other than this very Martin Maroney.

Little Martin is arraigned before Magistrate Gordon in Homicide Court, on a first-degree murder rap, and remanded to the Tombs. Cops pound the pavements, looking for tips. They keep after Maroney, wanting to know what really happened, mocking his cock-and-bull story about Siki leaving with a bunch of blacks. They have him scared to death. He admits he lured Siki down Forty-first Street, promising to buy him a drink. He admits two other men, by design, fell into step with them, that one pulled a .32 and fired it twice into Siki's back.[80] Yeah? the cops ask. And why did he do that? But little Martin pleads ignorance, insists he hasn't a clue.

Little by little the case fades from public interest. Murders are routine in Hell's Kitchen, witnesses scarce, especially when mobsters are involved. Owney Madden once killed a man in a trolley car, calmly rang the bell, and got off at the next stop, as a carload of riders slipped away. Gangs have allies in city hall, the courts, the police. Racketeers such as Costello, Madden, Luciano, and Zwillman use illicit profits from alcohol, gambling, prostitution, and drugs to buy political control and immunity from justice. Costello would have gambler Frank Erickson approach Congressman Michael J. Kennedy at a prizefight in 1949 to offer to fix Kennedy's election as boss of the Tammany Hall political machine. A 1943 FBI telephone wiretap would overhear Judge Thomas Aurelio thank Costello for fixing his nomination to the state supreme court, to which Costello replied, "When I tell you something is in the bag, you can rest assured." In response Aurelio pledged "undying loyalty" to the mob boss. In 1949 Costello would host a charity benefit at the Copacabana Club at which a rogues gallery of hoodlums turned up, along with the Tammany Hall boss, Bronx Borough president, five New York State Supreme Court justices, four other judges, the election commissioner, and a member of Congress. An FBI internal memorandum stated that prosecutors strongly suspected members of the jury in Costello's 1926 trial on bootlegging charges had been bribed or strong-armed into voting for acquittal. U.S. Coast Guardsmen who had pleaded guilty to taking payoffs from Costello, and even confessed to piloting his rum runners, were never sentenced.[81] Ultimately the very files of the case would disappear—from both the district attorney's office and the Alcohol Tax Unit. In Chicago, between 1926 and 1927, not one of its 130 gangland murders would be legally punished. One of Al Capone's enforcers, gunned down himself, was found with a jury roll and list of prosecution witnesses in his pocket.[82]

For seven months, Martin Maroney cooled his heels in a dank lockup. Then inexplicably, the first week of October, he was out on the street. The prosecutor, despite Maroney's confession of involvement in a murder conspiracy, said he lacked sufficient evidence. The real killer, said Maroney's lawyer, had skipped town.[83] A few dailies gave his release a line in their criminal court column. Most ignored it. They'd unearthed Siki's real killer ten months before: Siki himself. The police had persisted in their investigation longer than you'd expect. Twenty-five years later Ward Greene mused, "Wine drunkard, brawler, cop-fighter, [Siki] was mourned by none the night two bullets in his back laid him dead in a gutter."[84] Gerald Early echoed, "Nobody knows who killed Siki and ... nobody really cared very much."[85] Well, maybe they were right. Who did care? By 1926 Siki's name was already fading into the oblivion so sedulously prepared for it.

And Louis M'barick Fall himself? Watching from the shadow kingdom of ancestors, waiting for the impulse to seize him to seek in the next cycle of rebirth the turbulence and desire of the world of humans, would he not perhaps have preferred to lose any cheap immortality that attached itself to the name "Battling Siki"? But perhaps there's one reason to retell the tale. If it's too late to recover a sense of outrage, to resurrect Louis M'barick Fall from the name he's been tagged with, perhaps it isn't too late to reflect upon how perniciously such labels tag us all.

Afterword

Who Murdered Siki?

Key to this question are Levy's words overheard by Gaston Bénac—*"un gangster d'occasion,"* and *"un novice qui était très poussé par le gang des boîtes de nuit de Broadway"*—"a second-hand [or 'part-time'] gangster" and "a novice boxer who was being very much promoted by the gang of the Broadway nightclubs." Many gangsters frequented Broadway. Several, including Owney Madden and Big Bill Duffy, both heavily involved in boxing, owned Broadway nightclubs. Times Square had been a center of New York nightlife since 1898 when Oscar Hammerstein spent $2 million to build his block-long Olympia theater on what had been a center of the harness trade. By 1925, Times Square had most of the city's theaters and many chic hotels and nightclubs. Tex Rickard's new Madison Square Garden had just sprung up a block away.[1] Boxing people had already begun to call a stretch of sidewalk at Broadway and Forty-ninth Streets "Jacob's Beach," because so many managers, trainers, and boxers loitered there, like sea lions waiting to be tossed a fish by Mike Jacobs, Rickard's behind-the-scenes deal maker.

In 1925 Broadway was also the hub of an illicit industry. Interviewed by FBI agent A. P. Kitchin in November 1938, New Jersey gang boss Longy Zwillman said the cartel that ran New York's illegal liquor trade in the 1920s, styled "the Big Six" or "Broadway Gang" by outsiders, had a string of "headquarters" in Broadway hotels, leasing suites, even whole floors.[2] It is to this group, undoubtedly, that Levy was referring as Bénac eavesdropped. Who were the "Broadway Gang"? They were, Zwillman said, himself, Lepke Buchalter, Jacob "Gurrah" Shapiro, Frank Costello, Charles "Lucky" Luciano, and Benjamin "Bugsy" Siegel (other FBI reports substitute Meyer Lansky for Luciano).[3] Costello was especially close to Zwillman's partner in running the New Jersey rackets, Willie Moretti—and to Hell's Kitchen mob boss Owney Madden. In fact, the "Big Six" were often referred to as the "Big Seven," with Madden the extra member. Broadway was so widely known as the hub of illegal sports betting that a cartoon captioned "the wise bets" in the *New York Leader,* predicting Rocky Kansas would defeat Jack Bernstein in their 1923 fight, had a man lugging a sack of cash muttering "me for B'Way."[4] The *Washington Herald* would note in 1935 that a mob crony of Frank Costello,

Albert J. Contento, who was "one of the country's most powerful gamblers" (he even dictated the odds at major racetracks), had "an elaborate office on Broadway and is said to have led a charmed life insofar as his ability to evade arrest and conviction is concerned." Costello, too, was "one of the city's 'untouchables.'"[5]

Mob enforcer Lepke Buchalter, ally of Shapiro and Siegel, was Zwillman's closest New York contact. He often sent emissaries to Newark, Zwillman told Kitchin, including Henry "Dutch" Goldberg. "Every time Goldberg appeared in Newark," Zwillman said, "he was looking for favors for somebody, and it appeared that he was trying to 'front' for everybody in New York City." Zwillman "would not have hesitated to do any favor no matter what the request might have been for Siegel."[6] One "favor" gangsters did for each other was to kill people. In fact, Buchalter would later head a gang of mob assassins, styled "Murder, Inc." by the press. The FBI noted Zwillman had "placed his candidates in important political associations, using Siegel and Lansky to help him kill off rivals such as [brewery owners] Max Hassell and Max Greenberg."[7] Agents would hear persistent rumors Zwillman had arranged the murder of James La Capra to repay the Kansas City mob for a favor it did the "Big Six" by arranging the 1935 murder of the Bronx mobster Dutch Schultz. Another service Zwillman did them was to hide "Kansas City Massacre" fugitive Verne Miller, one of three assassins who had gunned down an FBI agent, three policemen, and (accidentally) prisoner Frank Nash.[8] So great was Frank Costello's authority over Buchalter that he was able to force him to turn himself in when he was wanted for the murder of Joseph Rosen. Costello promised Buchalter he'd only stand trial on a lesser narcotics charge. When District Attorney Thomas E. Dewey succeeded in pressing the murder charge and Buchalter went to the electric chair his last words reputedly were, "Frank Costello made me surrender."[9]

Most of the "Broadway Gang" were involved in gambling in one form or another. In New York, the most famous gambler was Arnold Rothstein, notorious for having conspired, along with boxer Abe Attel, to fix baseball's 1919 World Series. Buchalter, Luciano, Lansky, and Costello were all Rothstein protégés. Lansky had gotten his start in a Lower East Side gambling parlor run by Fat Al Levy and would in time run casinos everywhere from Saratoga to Havana.[10] Joseph "Hoboken Joe" Stassi was another big New York bookmaker, New Jersey mob boss Longy Zwillman told the FBI.[11] Zwillman had gotten his start in the policy (numbers) racket. His partner Willie Moretti ran roadhouses that featured both gambling and illegal alcohol. Zwillman had a hand in the Jersey City boss Frank Hague's huge, immensely profitable "Horse Bourse," along with the gambling czar Nicholas Delmore, who took other sports action as well.[12] He also was associated, through Costello, with gambler Frank Erickson. Costello and Guiseppi Doto, "Joe Adonis," would eventually join Zwillman and Moretti in running Jersey gambling. By the 1940s the "Big Six" ran a nationwide syndicate with a "share and share alike" split of Las Vegas gambling and interstate sports betting.[13]

Bénac insists Siki had promised the "Broadway Gang" three times before to "carry" fighters, and each time let them down. What three bouts, before Siki knocked out Jimmy Francis, might have irritated the mob by being genuine? Bénac's no stickler for details. He flubs numbers as readily as names. But Siki had in fact fought well at the end of 1924 against Tony Marullo and Frank Kearns, only to get handed questionable decisions. He fought well against Art Weigand in 1925 and got the short end of that verdict, too. If the mob had bet against Siki, they may well have hedged their bets by reaching the referee (as, in fact, their favorite writer, Damon Runyon, has a gambler do in his boxing story "Bred for Battle"). Even if Siki didn't cost them money, they would have been angry that he tried to. Mickey Walker tells how Madden called him and manager Doc Kearns on the carpet after he let Madden down by doing so well against Leo Lomski that he won the decision. Madden only let them live because Walker begged forgiveness for his "mistake," and Kearns promised to make up the lost cash on a future bout.[14] One wonders what similar scene transpired involving Siki and Levy—though Madden isn't the only candidate for the affronted gangster. One of Madden's lieutenants, George Mullins, who'd taken over Tanner Smith's old Gopher gang, actually lived in West New York, at 411 Park Avenue.[15] Rothstein, Costello, or Buchalter might equally have covered a few big bets and wanted to tilt the odds their way. Buchalter ran the "protection" (labor extortion) racket in the Garment District, where Levy ran his shirtwaist factory. For that matter, since Jimmy Francis's fans were from across the river, the injunction to have Siki carry Francis may well have come from Zwillman himself.

When Siki didn't do as he'd agreed, it's clear what happened next: someone went to Madden and asked him to arrange to have Siki's throat slit. When that didn't work out as planned, Madden, a careful man who liked to keep his murders discreet, said wait until the heat is off and then do the job right. Based on the glaring coincidences in his boxing record, it's likely Jimmy Francis was a mob fighter. But the local mob might have taken a proprietorial interest even if he wasn't—if they had bets riding on him. Perhaps they told Siki to carry both Francis and Billy Vidabeck, or maybe the second time he fought in West New York Siki just decided on his own to make discretion the better part of valor, hoping if he carried Vidabeck whoever had tried to kill him would be satisfied with only having half killed him. In any case, when the second set of mob hit men finished the job that had been botched in July the accomplice the police caught was an Irish teenager who lived in the heart of Hell's Kitchen. He could only have been taking his orders from Madden. No mob outsider would have dared hire a killer from Madden's own ethic group on his own ethnic turf. The only real question is whether Madden was taking his own revenge or doing someone else a favor, and that we'll never know.

Siki's Legacy

In 1949, John Lardner, son of one of the original authors of the Siki myth, revived the tale of his murder long enough to replay its mysterious sequel, the capture of Martin Maroney, and his release months later without trial. But Lardner did little to set to rest the real question about Siki's death—who paid his killers. For in truth lots of people in New York City must have heard rumors he wasn't killed by a sore loser in a barroom brawl. In the years since then, the image of Siki the belligerent drunk dying as a result of his own folly has persisted, along with other features of the Siki legend. Siki has turned up again and again in boxing histories (for instance, Fleischer and Andre's) tagged with the same crisp epitaph: the "boy of the jungle," bewildered by the splendors of civilization, who won the championship in a fluke outburst of fury against a ring immortal and then, distracted by celebrity, threw it away on a stupid caprice—fighting "an Irish fighter, in Dublin, on St. Patrick's Day." He has, in short, been dismissed as a bizarre curiosity in a sport with more than its share of such. He came across that way in a 1929 Italian novel loosely based on his life, Orio Vergani's *Io, povero negro;* in an HBO special in the late eighties—"Not So Great Moments in Sports"; in a chapter in Nigel Collins's 1990 book *Boxing Babylon;* and in a strange 2002 compilation of sports legend, Jay Lovinger's *The Gospel According to ESPN: Saints, Saviors, and Sinners.*

But a counter-representation has also taken shape. All along, where black fighters trained, Siki's name continued to be repeated with respect. Sugar Ray Robinson, who trained at Grupp's Gym in Harlem, could, after all, hear about Siki from someone who faced him for twenty rounds in one of the most furious battles two black headliners ever staged in the old Madison Square Garden. Kid Norfolk was for years a fixture at Grupp's, working with young fighters, Robinson among them. Muhammad Ali speaks, in *The Greatest,* of hearing, as a young man training in a gym, Siki's name held up as a hero among other tough old-time black fighters.[16] When Mamadou Niang disinterred Siki's body in 1992 to return it to Senegal, he was astonished to see how many black boxers turned up for the ceremony, many of whom had heard of Siki much as Ali had. His name echoed in other odd ways. Several boxers, including two in Battling Siki's day, another in ours, took it for their ring names. Several wrestlers did as well, including one in Siki's era and a well-known one in the 1960s. A celebrated baseball player from the 1930s heyday of the Cuban Negro leagues called himself Roque Siki; one of Che Guevara's lieutenants, Fernández Mell, waging guerilla war in Africa in the mid-1960s, took the *nom de guerre* "Siki." Yet more recently, and bizarrely, a savage character on the American television show "Xena: Warrior Princess" appropriated the name "Battling Siki."

By the 1970s, Ocania Chalk, in his history of black athletes, was portraying Siki not as a clown or a joke but as a heroic "warrior." On the eve of the first world's championship to be disputed in Africa, the Ali / Foreman fight in Zaire, Dan Shocket, in *World Boxing,* called into question the Siki legend, wondering if it wasn't time to reassess the career of the first black man to win the light-heavyweight title, the only African to win any title until the Nigerian Hogan Bassey won the featherweight crown in 1957. But Shocket, though disputing what the world had made of Siki, had no recourse but to fill out his story from a store of venerable misrepresentations and errors (he failed even to note that the 1922 championship fight had been set up for a fix, and he gave Siki's real name as "Baye Pahl") coming up with nothing much to offer in place of the hoary tale of the boxer as a hopeless lush and "irresponsible wildman."[17] He did, at least, quote Siki in his own defense, and point out that he could "read English, Dutch, and French with fair comprehension," concluding that, though not "overly bright," he was "far from simple."[18]

More recently, an American cultural critic, a Dutch director, a Dutch biographer, a Swedish novelist, two African musicians, a French television producer, and a French multimedia artist have all sought to resurrect the legend of the African boxer who stunned the world on September 24, 1922. Albert Stol's fictionalized biography is short on facts for some periods, gets others wrong, and is at times facile in its projections of Siki's inner emotional drama, but it offers an important alternative to the eighty-year-old slander perpetrated after Siki shocked the white world. Niek Koppen's version of Siki's story, in a Dutch television special, nicely balances images of Siki in Holland, France, America, and Senegal. Koppen commissioned the Senegalese artist Yousou Ndour to write a song to accompany his documentary, which again celebrated Siki as a hero. More recently another song celebrating Siki's legend has become popular in Europe and Africa, by the Burundian artist Khadja Nin. Mamadou Niang, who produces news reports for French television, has worked tirelessly to save Siki's legacy for the coming generation of African children who might otherwise lose sight of his courage and historical importance. He too put together a short film clip about Siki, and he undertook single-handedly the bureaucratic nightmare of getting permission to repatriate Siki's remains from Flushing Cemetery in Queens, New York, to the city of his birth, Saint-Louis in Senegal.[19] More recently, in Dakar, Jean Michel Bruyère has created a filmed montage of dance, music, song, boxing, and theater reenacting Siki's story.

Something continues to spur later generations to imagine Siki's story. That alone gives one faith that common humanity and the force of a passionately lived existence can redeem us from racialist fable and resurrect Battling Siki from the garbage dump of history.

Latter-Day Sikis: Liston, Tyson, Ali

The boxers of our day are still living down Siki's legacy. Mike Tyson once told Mamadou Niang he'd watched old fight films of Siki and copied his hook. But it's not Siki's style in the ring that is his greatest legacy. Siki's style didn't revolutionize the sport the way Jack Johnson's did. Actually, the fighter today who most reminds one of Siki is former welterweight champion Ricardo Mayorga, who like Siki hardly has a classic style. He throws wide punches, eats too much leather, and brags he likes to drink alcohol and smoke cigarettes. Like Siki, Mayorga makes up for his flaws with an indomitable will, a rock-hard chin, and a headlong, whirlwind assault. No, it's not Siki's style that outlives him, but his aura.

Like Tyson, and before him Sonny Liston, Siki brought into the ring an uncanny air of menace. In a way hardly equaled until Liston won the heavyweight crown by flattening Floyd Patterson in two minutes in 1962, Siki's annihilation of Capentier, and rumors of his savage origins, made him seem monstrous, unearthly. Tyson's original managers, Bill Cayton and Jimmy Jacobs, deliberately created a similar image for "Iron Mike," playing up his ghetto origins, mailing television reporters video compilations of one-round knockouts of inept foes. Liston came by his notoriety naturally. He did time in the Missouri State Penitentiary for a string of armed robberies, worked as a mob enforcer, and was repeatedly accused of sexual assault.[20] Tyson, too, was jailed as a juvenile for robbery, and he served three years in prison for raping a teenage beauty pageant contestant. He has admitted, moreover, to getting a charge out of mugging people, a pleasant pastime he indulged in even after he was earning a living as a professional boxer. A criminal accomplice described how Tyson, not content merely to choke a robbery victim, repeatedly slammed him face-first into an elevator wall.[21] Siki's punch outs of patrons in bars pale in comparison. As with Siki, however, the frenzy of the press over each new Tyson atrocity at times outran the facts of the case. Tyson actually tried to walk away from a notorious 1988 altercation with Mitch Green outside a Harlem clothing store, for instance, and his alleged "suicide attempt" months later was in reality just a minor traffic accident.

Boxing, as it had with Siki, tried to squeeze every nickel it could from Tyson's notoriety, and like Siki, Tyson was perplexed by the pleasure the public took in its image of him as a deranged brute. Both boxers even shared an affection for pet big cats. Siki kept lions, Tyson a white tiger. Tyson and Siki, moreover, both continued to rivet the public's attention long after they began losing. Siki made more money after he lost his title than while he held it—$100,000 in just two years, $18,000 for one memorable night's work alone, against Kid Norfolk.[22] In 1995, even with no title at stake, after four years of inactivity, Tyson still so fascinated the public that they were willing to pay $25 million to see him punch out a white undercard fighter with an absurdly inflated record.[23] Later, after Tyson's two one-sided losses to Evander Holyfield, it would cough up $20 million to watch him serve as a hapless punching bag for Lennox Lewis. Both Siki and Tyson, finally, were as adept at spending money as winning it—though no boxer has ever matched Tyson's flair for burning up cash. Despite the $300 million he earned in the ring, Tyson filed for bankruptcy. In a 1988 legal deposition he swore he didn't know what became of a check for $10 million he'd been handed for his bout with Michael Spinks.[24] For years he dutifully took the short end of purses Don King skimmed to pay for everything from maid service for King's apartments to lawyers to fight King's lawsuits with other boxers.[25] Siki, in contrast, in 1922 had the awareness to organize stablemates to go on strike when he felt manager Eli Lepart was short-changing them.

Johnson, Siki, and Tyson drew fans by negative appeal. Years would pass before a black boxer, Joe Louis, would be rewarded for a positive image— and only after he was schooled carefully not to smile in the ring, lest white patrons take his smile for mockery of beaten white rivals—lest, that is, he remind them of Johnson's gold-toothed grin of exultation, Siki's reputed gleam of innate savagery.[26] Yet Siki was hardly, like Tyson, given to fits of surly hostility. Far from being the sort who'd bite off a rival's ear (as Tyson did Evander Holyfield's), he answered Carpentier's attempts to foul him by helping Carpentier to his feet after a slip. Tyson reveled in his identity as "Iron Mike," borrowing the old-time fighters' low-rent ring attire, Liston's baleful scowl, Louis's cold-eyed fatality. But Siki chafed under his image as "the Singular Senegalese." Unlike Tyson, whose best-known line was lifted from the hero of a karate film ("How dare they challenge me with their primitive skills?"),[27] Siki detested being turned into a caricature and spoke up boldly against racial injustice.

In fact, in many ways, the boxer Siki most reminds one of isn't Liston or Tyson but Muhammad Ali. Like Ali, Siki at times hammed it up in the ring, strolling over before bouts to plant a kiss on a rival's cheek, smiling and gesturing to the crowd during rounds, dancing the Charleston in his corner. Both men were sold to the public as idiot savants—cheerful oddballs who could hardly repress their eccentricity. Both were portrayed as eternal adolescents (Ali with his wide-eyed rants outside the ring, his "clowning" inside it; Siki with his supposedly unwitting parody of swank attire, his fondness for exotic pets—lions, leopards, monkeys, parrots). The scribes who coined "Gaseous Cassius" and "the Louisville Lip" to mock Ali (then called Cassius Clay) were linear progeny of the writers of Siki's day, who were unrivaled adepts at coining colorful nicknames and making them stick. Bill McGeehan tagged Siki "the Singular Senegalese," Damon Runyon styled Dempsey the "Mannasa Mauler" and Jim Braddock "the Cinderella Man," while another New York writer dubbed Carpentier "the Orchid Man," a name he detested. Ali, in fact, was the first fighter to beat the writers at their own game, brushing aside their nicknames for him, naming himself "The Greatest," and sticking rivals with monikers they never lived down ("the big ugly bear" for Liston; "the rabbit" for Patterson; "the gorilla," or worse, for Joe Frazier). Both Ali and Siki inherited a racial persona that first saw the light of day in nineteenth-century minstrel shows and Harriet Beecher Stowe's *Uncle Tom's Cabin*. Like Ali, with his nursery-rhyme taunts and knockout predictions (he'd later admit he'd gotten his "I'm so pretty!" routine from the wrestler "Gorgeous George"),[28] Siki was heir to an image shared with Stowe's "Topsy," of the simple-minded innocent given to larks and fits of eccentricity.

Like Siki, Ali was famous for his open-handed generosity. Siki shared his purses with street Arabs who hawked newspapers around Times Square and strangers on a ferry. Ali, seeing a television report of a bankrupt Jewish community center, brought them his check for $100,000.[29] Like Siki with his stunt with the bananas, Ali had a bit of the con man or huckster about him. He duped a photographer into believing he trained underwater (*Life Magazine* actually ran photos of him shadowboxing in a swimming pool!).[30] He conned the public into paying a small fortune for the sadly overmatched "Lion of Flanders," Jean-Pierre Coopman, and suckered them into taking seriously even his bout with Japanese wrestler Antonio Inoki, who spent most of it lying on his back, kicking Ali in the shins. Only Ali's challenge to America's moral order, at a moment when it most stuck in the nation's craw, and the world's memory, saved him from the dubious legacy of oddball hustler, recasting him as a heroic figure of global proportions (witness how thousands, despite Ali's cannibal jokes, chanted his name in the streets in Zaire). Siki had a bit of the hustler to him, too, conning the public into taking seriously fights he fought in abysmal condition, or against a man who outweighed him by forty pounds, or a rugged world champion on a mere five days' training. He conned Descamps, Carpentier, and Hellers in 1922 into believing he would play along with their demeaning fix, then paid them back by leaving Carpentier curled on his side, face swollen, one leg in the air, groaning in pain. He tried to play the same hustle in New York in 1925, though he knew what the consequences might be in that murderous time and place. Siki's political awareness wasn't mixed with a dose of credulity, however, as Ali's was. In the deluge of adulation recently showered on Ali, it's easy to forget that he once held as an article of faith that a huge spaceship was circling the earth, ready to launch fifteen hundred aircraft to annihilate white civilization, or that his jokes about newsmen being stuffed into stew pots and eaten by cannibals so offended the government of Zaire that their foreign minister phoned to ask him to desist.[31]

Both Ali and Siki, finally, showed remarkable courage. Ali fought off Ken Norton for ten rounds in 1973 with a broken jaw, swallowing his blood to hide the injury. Siki, beaten bloody by Kid Norfolk, "never took a backward step," Sid Mercer said. Against Berlenbach, he kept surging forward to the bitter end, spitting blood, swinging from the heels, trying for a knockout. Ali faced jail for his refusal to fight in Vietnam. Siki went to jail, and risked lynching, to challenge segregation in the American South. Nor did he have anyone (as Ali had Elijah Muhammad) to prompt his action. He did it on his own— while the press dismissed his act of conscience as another erratic stunt. Like Ali, Siki was a man of genuine good will, and might have become not merely a press agent's dream but a social symbol—if his challenge to America's moribund social conscience hadn't come at a time when it was in no mood for a dark-skinned gadfly to show up its racial double-dealing.

One would like to say that since Siki's day boxing has reformed, devoted itself to protecting fighters rather than exploiting them, inspired fans with the real drama of sport, rather than selling them back their own illusions. These days, Siki would be amazed to learn, boxing's most successful promoter is a black man, Don King. Black managers and trainers flourish as well. But boxing is as exploitative as ever of the men whose blood and pain make it pay, who can't cut deals on their own terms with the pay-per-view and network bosses. It still betrays, humiliates, and abandons its fleeting heroes. Look how hastily in the 1980s it forsook King's "lost generation" heavyweights (as Tim Witherspoon called them): Tony Tubbs, James "Quick" Tillis, Greg Page, Tony Tucker, Michael "Dynamite" Dokes, Trevor Berbick, Pinklon Thomas, and Witherspoon himself.[32] Fighters still succumb to frustration and despair—or lose themselves in easy, self-destructive pleasures. Mickey Walker's and Siki's drunken binges in the 1920s were matched by Leon Spinks's celebrated penchant for "swooping" in the late 1970s.[33] Siki's abrupt refusal to fight in Lorraine, Ohio, finds a painful parallel in Oliver McCall's sudden emotional meltdown in 1995, when he dissolved into tears in the ring, unable so much as to raise a glove to defend himself against Lennox Lewis.[34]

Boxing in Siki's day was a commercial free-for-all, a carnival of greed run under few rules except that the weak went to the wall, and those with cash, connections, and a flair for shaping salable illusions gained fortunes. It still is. But these days more raw cash is at stake. Siki made more money in the ring than any previous black boxer except Jack Johnson, whom Rickard paid $60,000 to fight Jeffries in 1908, but Tunney made $990,445 for fighting Dempsey in 1927, which translates to nearly ten million in today's dollars.[35] By 1934 even Johnson was reduced to earning a living by stints in Herbert's Dime Museum on Forty-second Street, letting fans gawk at him, alongside fat ladies, sword swallowers, and a flea circus, as he sat on a stool spinning yarns about his days as champion.[36] These days, some black fighters salt away enough winnings to double as promoters (as Roy Jones Jr. has). But white fighters still at times get big paydays just because they're white. Witness the travesty of the challenger Gerry Cooney getting millions more than the heavyweight champ Larry Holmes in their 1982 bout.[37]

Then as now, promoters and managers flourish in one of the few virtually unregulated fields of sport, where contracts mean little, where boxers sign blank sheets of paper with purses and opponents to be inked in later, or sign one "for show," another, with a huge manager's cut, for real—as King had Foreman, Witherspoon, and Tyson, and as Kearns had Dempsey do,[38] or hear with head-shaking incredulity of sums they reportedly received for a fight, knowing only a fraction actually would find its way to their pockets (as happened to Earnie Shavers in 1973, whom King paid only $3,000, not the $75,000 he was supposed to get, for fighting Jerry Quarry[39]; and to Siki in 1922, who got only 35,000 francs for defeating Carpentier, not the 200,000 advertised as the winner's purse). Now, as then, promoters moonlight as managers, or match men from their own stable (as King did Page and Witherspoon in 1984, and Pete Reilly did Battling Battalino and Freddie Miller in 1932).[40] They still call on mob connections (as King did when he staged the Ali / Wepner bout with a stake put up by Cleveland racketeers).[41] They still pay reporters to supply adulatory copy (as Rickard did in the twenties, King in 1977),[42] or supply their own referee (as King tried to do for Ali / Frazier III in 1976; and Joe Jacobs did for McTigue / Young Stribling in 1923). Boxers are still sent out to battle who have no business in the ring— as Ali was in 1980 against Larry Holmes, despite early signs of slurred speech and a brain scan showing a fissure typical of progressive brain damage, and Siki was against Berlenbach.[43] Now as then, fighters rebel, welch on contracts, try to cut their own deal, or find vindication through the press. Now as then, hostage to the vagaries of their calling, they live high, wide, and ugly off cash advances, prompted to spend liberally by managers who swear they'll always be "taken care of." Another windfall will come along. In an atmosphere of instant gratification, like Sugar Ray Robinson, Joe Louis, and Mike Tyson, fighters lose touch with fiscal reality. The men who direct their careers want them to. They need them hungry for that next big purse.

In short, boxing is what it always was, a carnival of greed, cruelty, and cynical manipulation of the public psyche. At times ennobled by the sheer guts and craft of its competitors, it is both gifted and cursed by the slick entrepreneurs who fabricate its sham illusions—and who have, despite themselves, a few times this century, assembled the elements of an epic drama that transcends the ring. Out of the travesty of Don King's boxing empire came Ali / Foreman in Zaire in 1974, Ali / Frazier in Manilla in 1975. And out of Tex Rickard's boxing sideshow in the 1920s came the forgotten tragicomedy of a boxer who captivated the world as utterly as Ali, overawed it as profoundly as Tyson—the "Singular Senegalese," Battling Siki.

Notes

Chapter 1: The Savage Battler and Clever Little Mike

1. January 1924, 58.
2. *Irish Times*, March 6, 1923, 5.
3. *Irish Times*, March 8, 1923, 7.
4. *Irish Times*, March 12, 1923, 7.
5. *London Times*, March 16, 1923, 8.
6. *Le Petit Parisien*, March 18, 1923, 1.
7. *New York Herald*, Paris, March 10, 1923, 6.
8. *London Times*, March 17, 1923, 10.
9. *New York World*, March 18, 1923, 1.
10. *New York Herald*, Paris, March 13, 1923, 8; *Petit Parisien*, March 7, 1923, 1.
11. *Irish Times*, March 6, 1923, 6.
12. *Irish Times*, March 5, 1923, 5; March 6, 1923, 6.
13. Sam Andre and Nat Fleischer, *A Pictorial History of Boxing*, rev. ed. (Secaucus, N.J.: Citadel, 1959), 33–34; Harry Carpenter, *Boxing: An Illustrated History* (New York: Crescent Books, 1982), 17–18; Elliott J. Gorn, *The Manly Art: Bare-Knuckle Prize Fighting in America* (Ithaca, N.Y.: Cornell University Press, 1986), 42.
14. *Irish Times*, March 7, 1923, 8; March 9, 1923, 8; March 10, 1923, 5; March 14, 1923, 8.
15. *Le Peuple*, January 16, 1923, 1; *Le Populaire*, January 16, 1923, 1; *Le Temps*, January 17, 1923, 4.
16. *New York Herald*, Paris, January 16, 1923, 1, 8.
17. *Le Populaire*, January 17, 1923, 4.
18. *Le Populaire*, February 18, 1923, 3; *Cleveland Gazette*, February 17, 1923, 3.
19. *New York Herald*, March 7, 1923, 6.
20. *New York Times*, November 10, 1922, 21; *L'Echo*, November 10, 1922, 1; *Le Populaire*, November 10, 1922, 3.
21. *L'Auto*, October 7, 1922, 3.
22. *New York Times*, November 11, 1922, 10.
23. John Lardner, "The Battling Siki Murder," *New Yorker*, November 19, 1949. Rpt. *Negro Digest* 8, 6 (April 1950): 54.
24. Benny Green, *Shaw's Champions: George Bernard Shaw and Prizefighting, from Cashel Byron to Gene Tunney* (London: Elm Tree, 1978), 134–35.
25. Lardner, "The Battling Siki Murder," 54.
26. Nat Fleischer, *Black Dynamite: The Story of the Negro in the Prize Ring from 1782 to 1938* (New York: Ring Athletic Library, n.d. [1938–1947]), vol. 3, 84.
27. *Irish Times*, March 13, 1923, 8.

28. Maurice Golsworthy, *Encyclopedia of Boxing*, 8th ed. (London: Robert Hale, 1988), 185.

29. Welterweight and middleweight champion Mickey Walker identifies Jacobs as one of the managers controlled by mobster Owney Madden. Mickey Walker and Joe Reichler, *Mickey Walker: The Toy Bulldog and His Times* (New York: Random House, 1961), 67.

30. Peter Heller, *"In This Corner . . . !": Forty-two World Champions Tell Their Stories* (New York: Da Capo Press, 1994), 124.

31. Bill Stern, *Bill Stern's Favorite Boxing Stories* (New York: Pocket Books, 1948), 206, 218.

32. *New York Herald,* Paris, March 12, 1923, 6; March 17, 1923, 6.

33. Bénac insists it was Louis Anastasie, the promoter at the Continental Sporting Club, though in fact Anastasie wouldn't begin managing Siki's affairs until he returned from Ireland. Gaston Bénac, *Champions dans la coulisse* (Toulouse: L'Actualité Sportive, 1944), 109–10.

34. Bénac seems here to mean Lucien Defrémont, the manager who would later take Siki to America. Bénac, *Champions dans la coulisse.*

35. *Newark Evening News,* March 16, 1923, 12.

36. *Seconds Out!* (London: T. Werner Laurie, n.d. [1924]), 178–79.

37. *Chicago Defender,* September 29, 1923, 1.

38. *New York Times,* March 18, 1923, 1; *London Times,* March 19, 1923, 6.

39. *Ring Magazine,* January 1924, 58.

40. *Irish Times,* March 18, 1923, 4.

41. *New York Times,* March 18, 1923, 21.

42. Such as Petrine Arche-Straw, *Negrophilia: Avant-Garde Paris and Black Culture in the 1920s* (London: Thames and Hudson, 2000).

43. William B. Cohen, *The French Encounter with Africans: White Response to Blacks, 1530–1880* (Bloomington: Indiana University Press, 1980), 217–18.

44. Dan Shocket, "Battling Siki—the Man They Turned into a Joke," *World Boxing,* September 1974, 58; "Battling Siki: The Pride and the Tragedy," *World Boxing,* May 1980, 32.

45. Irving Wallace, *The Fabulous Showman: The Life and Times of P. T. Barnum* (New York: Alfred A. Knopf, 1959), 288.

46. March 18, 1923, 1.

47. Carpenter, *Boxing: An Illustrated History,* 17; Andre and Fleischer, *A Pictorial History of Boxing,* 27–28; Gorn, *The Manly Art,* 19–21.

48. Arthur R. Ashe, *A Hard Road to Glory: Boxing* (New York: Amistad, 1988), 10.

49. Al-Tony Gilmore, *Bad Nigger! The National Impact of Jack Johnson* (Port Washington, N.Y.: Kennikat Press, 1975), 19, 66.

50. Roger Kahn, *A Flame of Pure Fire: Jack Dempsey and the Roaring Twenties* (New York: Harcourt, Brace, Jovanovich, 1999), 226, 269.

51. See Gilmore, *Bid Nigger,* 14–17.

52. See John W. Thomason, *Fix Bayonets* (New York: Scribner's, 1926), 108. Frantz Fanon asked over five hundred of his white patients what words they associated with *tirailleur Sénégalais.* The most frequent answers were "dreadful, bloody, tough, strong." Fanon, *Black Skin, White Masks,* trans. Charles Lam Markman (New York: Grove Press, 1967), 166; when Siki won the title, the *New*

York Times explicitly compared him to the *tirailleurs. New York Times,*
September 25, 1922, 1.

53. *Literary Digest,* October 14, 1922, 62.

54. Louis Chevalier, *Montmartre du plaisir et du crime* (Paris: Éditions
Robert Laffont, 1980), 323.

55. Boxing manager Bill Cayton and his assistant Steve Lott were kind
enough to allow me to use their nearly crystal-clear copy in the offices of Big
Fights, Inc., in New York City.

56. Paris ed., March 18, 1923, 1.

57. March 18, 1923, 4.

58. March 18, 1923, 3.

59. March 18, 1923, 4.

60. March 19, 1923, 6.

61. March 31, 1923, 2.

62. March 18, 1923, 21.

63. Nat Fleischer, *How to Judge and How to Referee a Fight* (New York: Ring
Athletic Library, 1933), 24.

64. Fleischer, *How to Judge and How to Referee a Fight,* 24, 29.

65. Fleischer, *How to Judge and How to Referee a Fight,* 25, 28.

66. "Some Tough Ones for the Referee," *National Police Gazette,* November 8,
1924, 7. These days, for televised fights, we have "CompuBox," with two key-
boards and two observers taking the place of the Coney Island referee's
mechanical counters—but the principle is the same. No observer can see
for sure which blow lands hard, which merely grazes. No observer has access
to an electrode in the fighter's brain registering each spasm of pain.

67. "Some Tough Ones for the Referee," *National Police Gazette,*
November 8, 1924, 7.

68. Heller, *"In This Corner . . . ,"* 27.

69. *New York Times,* March 18, 1923, 23.

70. March 18, 1923, 1.

71. *Irish Times,* March 18, 1923, 4.

72. March 24, 1923, 1. In fact, English authorities had stamped his passport,
"It is permitted to Siki to pass through Queenstown on condition that he not
enter into the United Kingdom"–*L'Auto,* April 5, 1923, 1.

73. See, for instance, the *New York Times,* April 5, 1923, 15.

74. *Cleveland Gazette*, April 14, 1923, 2.

75. *L'Auto,* April 5, 1923, 1.

76. *L'Auto,* June 14, 1923, 1.

77. *L'Auto,* April 5, 1923, 1.

Chapter 2: "The Wild Man of the Boulevards"

1. In the *New York Times*—for instance, April 6, 1923, 13; April 8, 1923, 10;
April 10, 1923, 17.

2. *L'Humanité,* June 20, 1923, 1; *New York Times,* June 20, 1923, 16.

3. The anachronism here is deliberate. In fact, King Kong was the culmina-
tion of a series of representations of racial primitives that began with
Barnum's Wild Man of Borneo, passed through Edgar Rice Burrough's Tarzan,

then through Siki, and culminated in Cooper and Schoedsack's 1933 cinematic giant ape. Elmo Lincoln appeared in the first Tarzan film in 1918. The first film crew to attempt location shooting for a filmmaker-hunts-jungle-missing-link thriller in the Kong mode assembled in Singapore in 1925, the year of Siki's death. Gerald Peary, "Missing Links: The Jungle Origins of King Kong," March 7, 2003. www.geraldpeary.com /essays/jkl/kingkong-1.html.

4. Fleischer, *Black Dynamite*, vol. 3, 89; Nat Fleischer, *Fifty Years at Ringside* (New York: Fleet Publishing, 1958), 90, 92.

5. *L'Humanité*, May 11, 1923, 4; *New York Herald*, Paris, July 12, 1923, 8.

6. *Le Populaire*, July 18, 1923, 6; *New York Times*, July 17, 1923, 16.

7. *A Neutral Corner* (New York: Farrar, Straus, and Giroux, 1990), 18–19.

8. Stern, *Bill Stern's Favorite Boxing Stories*, 59.

9. Nat Fleischer, *Jack Dempsey, the Idol of Fistiana: An Intimate Narrative* (New York: Ring Athletic Library, 1929), 65.

10. *L'Auto*, April 5, 1923, 4; April 19, 1923, 3.

11. Bénac, *Champions dans la coulisse*, 103.

12. May 14, 1923, 13.

13. *L'Auto*, July 18, 1923, 4. Bénac, who seems to confuse the victim and circumstances of this incident, insists that suit wasn't finally settled until eleven years later, and in the end not Siki, but Marcel the animal trainer wound up paying damages. Bénac, *Champions dans la coulisse*, 103.

14. May 4, 1923, 4.

15. May 17, 1923, 3.

16. *New York Times*, May 17, 1923, 16.

17. May 17, 1923, 14.

18. *New York Times*, July 8, 1923, 24.

19. *New York Times*, June 13, 1923, 15.

20. Bénac, *Champions dans la coulisse*, 102.

21. *New York Times*, June 13, 1923, 15.

22. June 14, 1923, 3.

23. As *L'Auto* pointed out, June 16, 1923, 1.

24. Bénac, *Champions dans la coulisse*, 104.

25. August 4, 1923, 4.

26. *New York Herald*, Paris, June 17, 1923, 6.

27. June 19, 1923, 4.

28. I watched Bill Cayton's copy at Big Fights, Inc., in New York, through the good offices of Steve Lott.

29. *New York Times*, July 9, 1923, 10; *New York Herald*, Paris, July 9, 1923, 6; *L'Auto*, July 9, 1923, 1; *L'Humanité*, July 9, 1923, 1.

30. July 9, 1923, 6.

31. Heller, *"In This Corner . . . , "* 89.

32. *New York Times*, June 15, 1923, 17.

33. See, for example, the *Chicago Defender*, September 30, 1922, 1; October 7, 1922, 1.

34. *Chicago Defender*, July 14, 1923, 9.

35. *Chicago Defender*, August 11, 1923, 1.

36. *Cleveland Gazette*, July 14, 1923, 1.

37. *Le Populaire*, August 7, 1923, 2.

38. August 8, 1923, 2.
39. August 7, 1923, 2.
40. *Chicago Defender,* August 11, 1923, 1.
41. See, for instance, *La Dépêche du Midi,* July 30, 1919.
42. January 1, 1923, 1.
43. *La Dépêche,* October 8, 1919, 1.
44. *New York Herald,* Paris, July 11, 1923, 6.
45. *New York Times,* July 23, 1923, 10.
46. *L'Auto,* July 8, 1923, 4; July 22, 1923, 4; *New York Herald,* Paris, July 8, 1923, 6; *Newark Evening News,* August 24, 1923, 15.
47. *L'Auto,* August 4, 1923, 4; August 6, 1923, 4; *New York Herald,* Paris, August 6, 1923, 6.
48. *New York Herald,* Paris, July 10, 1923, 6.
49. Bits and pieces of information in various stories seem to hint at a split between the two of them, since she is described as having returned to her native Holland, taking with her many belongings, and another woman apparently turned up at the departure dock with Siki. *New York Times,* July 17, 1923, 16; *Newark Evening News,* August 24, 1923, 15; *New York Herald,* Paris, August 26, 1923, 8.
50. *New York Times,* August 25, 1923, 9.
51. *New York Herald,* Paris, August 26, 1923, 8.
52. *New York Herald,* Paris, August 23, 1923, 6.
53. See, for instance, the *Newark Evening News,* August 25, 1923, 15.
54. See, for instance, the *New York Times,* July 9, 1923, 10; September 2, 1923, 16.
55. American papers, sight unseen, often called Siki "huge" or "giant." See, for instance, the *Newark Evening News,* September 1, 1923, 14.
56. *New York Times,* September 2, 1923, 16.
57. *New York Times,* September 2, 1923, 16.
58. *New York Call,* September 1, 1923, 2.
59. September 29, 1923, 1.
60. *Cleveland Gazette,* October 13, 1923, 2.
61. *Chicago Defender,* September 29, 1923, 1.
62. *Amsterdam News,* September 19, 1923, 5; September 26, 1923, 1.
63. Maurice Golesworthy, *Encyclopedia of Boxing,* 8th ed. (London: Robert Hale, 1988), 185.
64. *New York Times,* September 22, 1923, 8; *Newark Evening News,* September 20, 1923, 6; *Chicago Defender,* September 29, 1923, 1.
65. Michael T. Isenberg, *John L. Sullivan and His America* (Urbana and Chicago: University of Illinois Press, 1988), 265–66.
66. Jack Dempsey, Bob Considine, and Bill Slocum, *Dempsey: By the Man Himself* (New York: Simon and Schuster, 1960), 180, 182–83.
67. *Jack Dempsey, the Idol of Fistiana: An Intimate Narrative,* 54–55.
68. *Cleveland Gazette,* March 10, 1923; Fleischer, *Black Dynamite,* vol. 5, 95.
69. *New York Times,* September 2, 1923, 16; September 18, 1923, 18; September 26, 1923, 6; *Cleveland Gazette,* September 15, 1923, 1; *Amsterdam News,* September 19, 1923, 5.
70. Not to be confused with leading heavyweight George Godfrey of thirty

years earlier who had fruitlessly pursued John L. Sullivan in hopes of challenging for his title.

71. Fleischer, *Black Dynamite,* vol. 5, 94–95.

72. *Amsterdam News,* June 20, 1923, 4; Dempsey, Considine, and Slocum, *Dempsey,* 146.

73. *Montreal Herald,* October 1, 1923, 6; October 3, 1923, 6.

74. *Montreal Herald,* October 2, 1923, 6; *Montreal Gazette,* October 2, 1923, 17.

75. October 3, 1923, 6.

76. Distaillon had returned to the ring after the war despite bearing a scar from a bullet wound in his head and having part of his side torn away by shrapnel; his record boasted a knockout win over world champion Eugene Criqui—*Montreal Herald,* October 4, 1923, 6.

77. *Montreal Herald,* October 4, 1923, 6; *Montreal Gazette,* October 4, 1923, 16.

78. *Montreal Herald,* October 1, 1923, 6; *Cleveland Gazette,* October 6, 1923, 2.

79. *Montreal Gazette,* October 5, 1923, 18.

80. The *Montreal Herald* places the figure paid the two fighters for the tour as a whole at $5,900. October 4, 1923, 6.

81. *New York Times,* October 24, 1923, 17.

82. October 5, 1923, 1; October 8, 1923, 3.

83. *Montreal Herald,* October 11, 1923, 6; October 12, 1923, 6.

Chapter 3: The Leopard . . . his Spots, the Ethiopian . . . his Skin

1. *New York Times,* October 24, 1923, 17; October 28, 1923, sec. 1, 5.

2. Walker and Reichler, *Mickey Walker,* 201–2.

3. Dempsey, Considine, and Slocum, *Dempsey,* 126–29.

4. *New York Times,* January 25, 1924, 17; *New York Call,* August 31, 1923, 5.

5. *New York Times,* October 28, 1923, sec. 1, 5.

6. *Cleveland Gazette,* March 10, 1923; Fleischer, *Black Dynamite,* vol. 5, 95.

7. September 23, 1922, 2.

8. *New York Tribune,* November 6, 1923, 2.

9. *Chicago Defender,* September 23, 1922, 1–2.

10. *New York Times,* October 24, 1923, 17.

11. October 26, 1923, 22.

12. Heller, *"In This Corner . . . ,"* 82.

13. Desverney was a lieutenant in Harlem's celebrated Fifteenth Regiment, the "Harlem Hell Fighters," whose valor in the Meuse-Argonne offensive had won them, as a unit, the French Legion of Honor—and a parade up New York's Fifth Avenue.

14. *Amsterdam News,* October 31, 1923, 1.

15. *Federal Writers Program: Negroes of New York* (New York: Schomburg Center typescript, 1939).

16. *Amsterdam News,* November 7, 1923, 1.

17. Walker and Reichler, *Mickey Walker,* 188–89.

18. Walker and Reichler, *Mickey Walker,* 99–100.

19. James R. Fair, *Give Him to the Angels: The Story of Harry Greb* (New York: Smith and Durrell, 1946), 13–14.

20. Dempsey, Considine, and Slocum, *Dempsey,* 35–36, 113–14.

21. Kahn, *A Flame of Pure Fire,* 108–9.

22. *New York Times,* January 22, 1922, 1; Kahn, *A Flame of Pure Fire,* 271–74.

23. Fair, *Give Him to the Angels,* 5, 280–81; Nigel Collins, *Boxing Babylon* (New York: Citadel Press, 1990), 50.

24. Fair, *Give Him to the Angels,* 180–81.

25. Carpenter, *Boxing: An Illustrated History,* 71.

26. October 31, 1923, 4.

27. *New York Evening Telegram,* November 3, 1923, 8.

28. Kenneth T. Jackson, *The Ku Klux Klan in the City* (Oxford: Oxford University Press, 1967), 176–77.

29. October 20, 1923, 3.

30. Jackson, *The Ku Klux Klan in the City,* 176.

31. John Mack Faragher, Mari Jo Buhle, Daniel Czitrom, and Susan H. Armitage, *Out of Many: A History of the American People,* vol. 2 (Englewood Cliffs, N.J.: Prentice Hall, 1994), 741.

32. *New York World,* October 25, 1923, 15.

33. *Time Magazine,* November 5, 1923.

34. *New York Leader,* October 8, 1923, 6.

35. Stern, *Bill Stern's Favorite Boxing Stories,* 218.

36. *New York Leader,* October 8, 1923, 6.

37. *Time Magazine,* April 28, 1923.

38. Feragher et al., *Out of Many,* vol. 2, 741; *Time Magazine,* September 24; October 1; and November 5, 1923.

39. *New York Evening Post,* December 11, 1923, 4.

40. *New York Evening Telegram,* November 7, 1923, 11.

41. *New York Tribune,* November 8, 1923, 15.

42. Heller, *"In This Corner . . . ,"* 68, 70.

43. Peter Walsh, *Men of Steel: The Lives and Times of Boxing's Middleweight Champions* (London: Robson Books, 1993), 72.

44. Walker and Reichler, *Mickey Walker,* 66–67.

45. Mark. A. Stuart, *Gangster # 2: Longy Zwillman, the Man Who Invented Organized Crime* (Secaucus, N.J.: Lyle Stuart, 1985), 194.

46. In 1945 the *New York Times* would call Costello, Joe Adonis, and Frank Erickson "the three individuals in control of big-time gambling in New York City." On one occasion Costello would accidentally leave $27,200 in a taxicab, apparently a single day's take from his bookmaking operation. Federal Bureau of Investigation. Frank Costello file. Freedom of Information Act. Bu file nos. 62–76543 Sub A; 92–2869 Section 1;

47 Heller, *"In This Corner . . . ,"* 147.

48. Gangster Frank Costello also made frequent trips to Hot Springs to golf with Madden. Graham Nown, *The English Godfather* (London: Ward Lock, 1987), 9; Robert H. Prall, "Costello Got Rich on Rum," *New York World Telegram and Sun,* May 11, 1957—clipping in Federal Bureau of Investigation Frank Costello file. Freedom of Information Act. Bu file no. 62–76543 Sub. A.

49. Nown, *The English Godfather,* 51.

50. Luc Sante, *Low Life* (New York: Random House, 1992), 18–20, 107, 113, 198.

51. Nat Fleischer, *Léonard the Magnificent: Life Story of the Man Who Made Himself King of the Lightweights* (Norwalk, Conn.: O'Brien Suburban Press, 1947), 22, 25, 34.

52. November 6, 1923, 7.

53. Sante, *Low Life*, 173–74.

54. Ruby Goldstein and Frank Graham, *Third Man in the Ring* (Westport, Conn.: Greenwood Press, 1972), 35.

55. Goldstein and Graham, *Third Man in the Ring,* 54–55; *Summit Herald and Summit Record,* November 13, 1923, 6.

56. *New York Times,* November 13, 1923, 18; *New York Herald,* November 13, 1923, 14.

57. Fair, *Give Him to the Angels,* 37.

58. *New York Times,* November 13, 1923, 18.

59. *New York Tribune,* November 19, 1923, 13.

60. *New York World,* November 13, 1923, 6.

61. Personal interview. Manchester, Conn. July 24, 1997.

62. Heller, *"In This Corner . . . ,"* 78.

63. Ferdie Pacheco, M.D., *Fight Doctor* (New York: Simon and Schuster, 1976), 27.

64. One source, the *New York Herald,* has him starting to spar ten days before the bout. November 13, 1923, 14.

65. Kahn, *A Flame of Pure Fire,* 370.

66. November 12, 1923, 12.

67. November 13, 1923 12.

68. *New York World,* November 13, 1923, 6; *New York Evening Telegram,* November 14, 1923, 6.

69. *New York Herald,* November 13, 1923, 14.

70. Summit had its share of bathtub vendors—as the police reports in the *Summit Herald and Summit Record* show. November 2, 1923, 1.

71. *New York Herald,* November 13, 1923, 14.

72. *New York Evening Journal,* November 19, 1923, 20.

73. *New York Evening Telegram,* November 14, 1923, 11.

74. Kevin Smith, "The Black Thunderbolt—Kid Norfolk." Cyber Boxing Zone. Internet (April 20, 1999) www:http://cyberboxingzone.com/boxing/norfolk.htm.

75. November 14, 1923, 24.

76. *New York Herald,* November 15, 1923, 15; *New York Daily News,* November 15, 1923, 24.

77. A. J. Liebling, *Back Where I Came From* (San Francisco: North Point Press, 1990), 92–93.

78. Dempsey, Considine, and Slocum, *Dempsey,* 43.

79. *New York Tribune,* November 19, 1923, 13.

80. *New York Evening Journal,* November 19, 1923, 20.

81. Jean Auger, *La boxe anglaise* (Paris: Librairie Garnier Frères, 1923), 41.

82. Marcel Petit, *Boxe: Technique—Entraînement* (Paris: Éditions Amphora, 1972), 48.

83. C. Rose, *Boxing Taught through the Slow-Motion Film* (London: Athletic Publications, n.d. [1924]), 59.

84. Petit, *Boxe: Technique—Entraînement,* 48.

85. Nat Fleischer, *How to Box* (New York: Ring Athletic Library, n.d. [1929–1932]), 93.

86. *New York Evening Journal,* November 17, 1923, 4; the reference is to *Jeremiah* 13:23, a biblical verse much loved by racial apologists: Kipling borrowed it for "How the Leopard Got his Spots" in his *Just So Stories,* and Thomas Dixon, whose 1905 novel *The Clansman* (later turned into a film), had inspired the Ku Klux Klan's revival, named his 1902 polemic *The Leopard's Spots: A Romance of the White Man's Burden.*

87. Michel Malherbe and Cheikh Sall, *Parlons Wolof: langue et culture* (Paris: Editions L'Harmattan, 1989), 85–90.

88. Gerald Early, "Battling Siki," *The Culture of Bruising: Essays on Prize-fighting, Literature, and Modern American Culture* (Hopewell, N.J.: Ecco Press, 1994), 29.

89. Umberto Eco, *Semiotics and the Philosophy of Language* (Bloomington: Indiana University Press, 1986), 217–18.

90. *New York Evening Journal,* November 17, 1923, 4.

91. *Summit Herald and Summit Record,* October 30, 1923, 1.

92. January 1924, 12.

93. November 19, 1923, 13.

94. Battling Siki (Louis M'barick Fall), "Résumé aux lecteurs de *L'Auto,*" *L'Auto,* September 29, 1922, 1.

95. Liebling, *Back Where I Came From,* 92.

96. *New York Evening Telegram,* November 20, 1923, 1; *New York World,* November 21, 1923, 7.

97. *New York Evening Post,* November 21, 1923, 11.

98. November 18, 1923, 61.

Chapter 4: "A First-Class Fighting Man"

1. *New York Evening Post,* November 21, 1923, 11.

2. *New York Evening Telegram,* November 21, 1923, 10.

3. *New York Tribune,* November 21, 1923, 19; *New York Evening Post,* November 21, 1923, 11.

4. Alan and Lois Gordon, *The Columbia Chronicles of American Life* (New York: Columbia University Press, 1995), 127.

5. *New York Evening Post,* November 20, 1923, 11.

6. *New York Evening Journal,* November 22, 1923, 20.

7. *New York Evening Journal,* November 22, 1923, 27; *New York Evening Telegram,* November 21, 1923, 10; *Boxing Blade,* December 8, 1923, 9.

8. *New York Evening Journal,* November 21, 1923, 10.

9. Scott Derks, *The Value of a Dollar: Prices and Incomes in the United States, 1860–1989* (Detroit: Gale Research, 1994), 175.

10. Gordon and Gordon, *The Columbia Chronicles of American Life,* 127.

11. Walker and Reichler, *Mickey Walker,* 139.

12. Goldstein and Graham, *Third Man in the Ring,* 165.

13. *The Black Lights: Inside the World of Professional Boxing* (New York: McGraw Hill, 1986), 119–20.

14. November 24, 1923, I, 9.

15. *New York Daily News,* November 21, 1923, 11; all my references to the *Daily News* account of the fight are from this source.

16. November 23, 1923, 24; all references to Newman's account of the fight are from this source.

17. *New York Evening Journal,* November 21, 1923, 1, 23; all references to the *Evening Journal* account of the fight are from this source.

18. *New York Evening Telegram,* November 21, 1923, 10; all references to the *Evening Telegram* account of the fight are from this source.

19. *New York Tribune,* November 21, 1923, 19; all references to Jack Lawrence's account of the fight are from this source.

20. *New York Evening Journal,* November 21, 1923, 23; all references to Mercer's account of the fight are from this source.

21. *New York Times,* November 22, 1923, 23.

22. Paul Meskil, "Seek Attacker of Costello in Midwest Cities," *New York World Telegram and Sun,* May 6, 1957, 1–2—clipping in Federal Bureau of Investigation Frank Costello file (Freedom of Information Act. Bu file no. 62–76543 Sub A); in 1936 Costello flew gangster Dandy Phil Kastel and Seymour Weiss, a close associate of Louisiana governor Huey Long, to New York for a Joe Louis title defense, putting them up at the New Yorker Hotel; in 1956 Costello would be charged, along with gangster Frankie Carbo, with rigging fights involving lightweight Art "Golden Boy" Aragon (clippings from the *New York Times,* October 16, 1957, 26C, and *Boston Globe,* March 22, 1956, 27, in Federal Bureau of Investigation Frank Costello file. Freedom of Information Act. Bu file no. 62–76543 Sub A).

23. Stuart, *Gangster #2,* 180.

24. Nown, *The English Godfather,* 35, 84–85.

25. Nat Fleischer, *How to Second and How to Manage a Boxer* (New York: Ring Publications, 1944), 45–46.

26. Pacheco, *Fight Doctor,* 37.

27. Fleischer, *How to Second and How to Manage a Boxer,* 44.

28. Pacheco, *Fight Doctor,* 36.

29. Fleischer, *How to Second and How to Manage a Boxer,* 45–47.

30. Fleischer, *Black Dynamite,* vol. 5, 189.

31. *New York Herald,* November 21, 1923, 24; all references to Wood's account of the fight are from this source.

32. Newman, *New York Daily News.*

33. *New York Evening Telegram,* November 21, 1923, 10; all references to Underwood's account of the fight are from this source.

34. Newman, *New York Daily News.*

35. Andre and Fleischer, *A Pictorial History of Boxing,* 116–17.

36. Fair, *Give Him to the Angels,* 46–47.

37. *New York Times,* November 21, 1923, 15.

38. *New York Times,* November 21, 1923, 15.

39. Jack Kearns and Oscar Fraley, *The Million-Dollar Gate* (New York: McMillan, 1966), 130.

40. Fleischer, *How to Second and How to Manage a Boxer,* 34.

41. Pacheo, *Fight Doctor,* 38.

42. Fleischer, *How to Second and How to Manage a Boxer,* 43–44.

43. Kearns and Fraley, *The Million-Dollar Gate,* 130.

44. A. J. Liebling, *A Neutral Corner* (New York: Farrar, Straus, and Giroux, 1990), 37.

45. *New York Times,* November 22, 1923, 23.

46. Newman, *New York Daily News.*

47. *New York Times,* November 21, 1923, 15.

48. *New York Tribune,* November 21, 1923, 19.

49. *New York Times,* November 21, 1923, 15.

50. Mercer, *New York Evening Journal.*

51. Newman, *New York Daily News.*

52. British Medical Association, *The Boxing Debate* (London: Chameleon Press, 1993), 14, 17.

53. British Medical Association, *The Boxing Debate,* 18–23.

54. Newman, *New York Daily News.*

55. *New York Times,* November 21, 1923, 15.

56. Newman, *New York Daily News.*

57. Mercer, *New York Evening Journal.*

58. Newman, *New York Daily News.*

59. British Medical Association, *The Boxing Debate,* 18.

60. Newman, *New York Daily News.*

61. *Boxing Blade,* December 8, 1923, 9.

62. Mercer, *New York Evening Journal.*

63. Newman, *New York Daily News.*

64. Newman, *New York Daily News.*

65. Mercer, *New York Evening Journal.*

66. *Cleveland Gazette,* November 24, 1923, 2.

67. Mercer, *New York Evening Journal.*

68. Newman, *New York Daily News.*

69. *New York Times,* November 21, 1923, 15.

70. *Chicago Defender,* November 24, 1923, 9.

71. Mercer, *New York Evening Journal.*

72. Underwood, *New York Evening Telegram,* November 21, 1923, 10.

73. Jack Lawrence, *New York Tribune,* November 21, 1923, 19.

74. *New York Evening Journal,* November 22, 1923, 27.

75. *New York Times,* November 22, 1923, 23.

76. *New York Daily News*, November 22, 1923, 23.

77. *New York Times,* November 22, 1923, 23.

78. *New York Herald,* November 22, 1923, 15.

79. *New York Evening Journal,* November 22, 1923, 27.

80. *New York Herald,* November 22, 1923, 15.

81. *New York Evening Journal,* November 21, 1923, 1.

82. *New York Evening Post,* November 21, 1923, 11.

83. *New York Herald,* November 22, 1923, 15.

84. *New York Evening Telegram,* November 21, 1923, 10.

85. *New York Evening Telegram,* November 23, 1923, 14.

86. November 21, 1923, 7.

87. *New York Evening Journal,* November 22, 1923, 27.

88. *New York Evening Telegram,* November 21, 1923, 10. Actually, Fall didn't win the latter honor.

89. See below, pages 165–66, 204–5.

Chapter 5: "Tough Luck!"

1. Shocket, "Battling Siki—the Man They Turned into a Joke," 58.

2. Dan Shocket most notable among them.

3. Niek Koppen, *Siki* (Documentary Video Production, Amsterdam, 1993).

4. As are Mouhamadou, Mamadou, and Mohammad. Malherbe and Sall, *Parlons Wolof,* 84.

5. Malherbe and Sall, *Parlons Wolof,* 84.

6. Koppen, *Siki.*

7. Fleischer, *Black Dynamite,* vol. 5, 73.

8. July 24, 1924, 30. *Le Matin* also gives "Baye Fall" as Siki's "*vrai nom*"(real name). September 25, 1922, 4.

9. Michael Crowder, *Senegal: A Study in French Assimilation Policy.* Rev. ed. (London: Methuen; New York: Praeger, 1967), 10, 14.

10. Nicolas Leca, *Les pêcheurs de Guet N'Dar,* vol. 17, no. 2 (April–June 1934): *Bulletin du comité d'études historiques et scientifiques de l'Afrique Occidentale Française,* 300–301.

11. Leca, *Les pêcheurs de Guet N'Dar,* 342–43.

12. Leca, *Les pêcheurs de Guet N'Dar,* 349–51.

13. Leca, *Les pêcheurs de Guet N'Dar,* 313–14.

14. Bénac, *Champions dans la coulisse,* 100; François Terbeen, with the collaboration of Claude Brezner, *Les géants de la boxe* (Paris: Editions Mondiales, 1962), 126, n.

15. Bénac, *Champions dans la coulisse;* Terbeen and Brezner, *Les Geants de la boxe;* George Peeters, *La boxe: 'noble art'* (Paris: Vigot Frères, 1944), 67.

16. Bénac, *Champions dans la coulisse;* Terbeen and Brezner, *Les Geants de la boxe,* 126; Green, *Shaw's Champions,* 122.

17. Fleischer, *Black Dynamite,* vol. 3, 74; Lardner, "The Battling Siki Murder," 54.

18. Ocania Chalk, *Pioneers of Black Sport: The Early Days of the Black Professional Athlete in Baseball, Basketball, Boxing, and Football* (New York: Dodd, Mead, n.d. [1975]), 164; *L'Auto* Special Edition, September 24, 1922; G. De Lafrete, *L'Echo de Paris,* September 25, 1922, 4.

19. Albert Stol, interviewed by Koppen, *Siki.*

20. Bénac, *Champions dans la coulisse;* Terbeen and Brezner, *Les Geants de la boxe,* 126.

21. *L'Auto,* December 17, 1925, 3.

22. Bénac, *Champions dans la coulisse,* 100.

23. Fleischer, *Black Dynamite,* vol. 3, 74; Collins, *Boxing Babylon,* 59.

24. John D. McCallum, *The Encyclopedia of World Boxing Champions* (Radnor, Pa.: Chilton Book Co., [1975]), 92; Lardner, "The Battling Siki Murder," 54; Chalk, *Pioneers of Black Sport,* 164.

25. Bénac, *Champions dans la coulisse*; Peeters, *La boxe*, 67; Collins, *Boxing Babylon*; Chalk, *Pioneers of Black Sport*; *L'Auto* Special Edition; De Lafrete, *L'Echo de Paris*, September 25, 1922, 4.

26. Green, *Shaw's Champions*, 122.

27. Bénac, *Champions dans la coulisse;* Fleischer, *Fifty Years at Ringside*, 91; De Lafrete, *L'Echo de Paris*, September 25, 1922, 4.

28. Bénac, *Champions dans la coulisse*; Terbeen and Brezner, *Les Geants de la boxe*; *L'Auto* Special Edition.

29. Bénac, *Champions dans la coulisse*.

30. Bénac, *Champions dans la coulisse*; *Le Petit Parisien*, September 22, 1922, 1.

31. Bénac, *Champions dans la coulisse*.

32. Lardner, "The Battling Siki Murder," 54; McCallum, *The Encyclopedia of World Boxing Champions*; Fleischer, *Black Dynamite*, vol. 3.

33. McCallum, *The Encyclopedia of World Boxing Champions*; Lardner, "The Battling Siki Murder," 54; Collins, *Boxing Babylon*; Fleischer, *Black Dynamite*, vol. 3; Fleischer, *Fifty Years at Ringside*.

34. Chalk, *Pioneers of Black Sport*.

35. Bénac, *Champions dans la coulisse*; Chalk, *Pioneers of Black Sport*; *L'Auto* Special Edition.

36. Fleischer, *Black Dynamite*, vol. 3.

37. Peeters, *La boxe*; *L'Auto* Special Edition.

38. Terbeen and Brezner, *Les géants de la boxe*; Bénac, *Champions dans la coulisse*; Fleischer, *Black Dynamite*, vol. 3; Chalk, *Pioneers of Black Sport*; *L'Auto* Special Pre-Fight Edition.

39. *Le Petit Parisien*, September 25, 1922, 1.

40. Bénac, *Champions dans la coulisse*; Allentown *Morning Call*, August 3, 1924, 1.

41. Peeters, *La boxe*; Collins, *Boxing Babylon*; *L'Auto* Special Edition; De Lafrete, *L'Echo de Paris*, September 25, 1922, 4.

42. Collins, *Boxing Babylon*; Bénac, *Champions dans la coulisse*; Chalk, *Pioneers of Black Sport*, etc.

43. Lardner, "The Battling Siki Murder," 54; see also Collins, *Boxing Babylon*, 59; Fleischer, *Black Dynamite*, vol. 3, 74.

44. McCallum, *The Encyclopedia of World Boxing Champions;* Lardner, "The Battling Siki Murder," 54.

45. Peeters, *La boxe*, 67.

46. De Lafrete, *L'Echo de Paris*, September 25, 1922, 4.

47. December 16, 1925, 1.

48. September 25, 1922, 1.

49. Peeters, *La boxe; L'Echo de Paris* and *L'Auto* Special Edition give the year as 1907, while other sources supply 1909.

50. Malherbe and Sall, *Parlons Wolof*, 90.

51. Bakary Diallo, *Force-bonté* (Paris: F. Riedier, 1926), 91.

52. Emil A. Magel, "Hare and Hyena: Symbols of honor and Shame in the Oral Narratives of the Wolof of the Senegambia"(Ph.D. diss., University of Wisconsin, 1978), 112–13.

53. Malherbe and Sall, *Parlons Wolof*, 99–101.

54. Oumy Ball, Personal interview, September 26, 2002.

55. Bénac, *Champions dans la coulisse,* 101.

56. Peeters, *La boxe,* 67; *L'Auto* Special Edition.

57. Bénac, *Champions dans la coulisse*; Terbeen and Brezner, *Les Geants de la boxe,* 125.

58. Bénac, *Champions dans la coulisse.*

59. *L'Auto* Special Edition—Bénac has him working with "Gontaud" before he went to Bordeaux.

60. *L'Auto* Special Edition; New York *Herald,* Paris ed., September 26, 1922, 6.

61. Robert July, *A History of the African People,* 4th ed. (Prospect Heights, Ill.: Waveland Press, 1992), 281, 352.

62. *L'Auto* Special Edition; Bénac, *Champions dans la coulisse.*

63. Tracy Callis ("Battling Siki (Louis Phal)." April 20, 1999. Cyber Boxing Zone. Internet. www:http://cyberboxingzone.com/boxing/Siki-b.htm) dates this fight earlier, prior to an October 13, 1912, loss to Louis Maria at Grasse, via technical knockout.

64. Peeters, *La boxe,* 67; *L'Auto* Special Edition.

65. Callis records fights in this period against Fernand Pratt (an eight-round draw, March 13, 1913), François Servat (an eight-round decision loss, March 27), and Frederick Henrys (a third-round loss on a foul, May 3).

66. *The Ring Record Book and Boxing Encyclopedia* (New York: Ring Book Shop, [Annual]) identifies the rival as Jules Perroud and has Siki winning both bouts by eighth-round knockout; Callis dates the bouts June 4 and 20, 1914, and has Siki winning one ten-round decision, losing another.

67. Bénac, *Champions dans la coulisse.*

68. Tracy Callis dates the fight January 9, 1914; both he and the *Ring Record Book* have Siki winning a ten-round decision. Callis says Siki lost on a foul in Narbone to Eugene Tajan on July 12, 1914, and won a ten-round decision over Roose July 27.

69. Callis makes Siki's record eight wins (four by technical knockout or knockout), two draws, and six losses (three by decision, two on fouls, one by technical knockout).

70. March 24, 1920, 2.

71. September 21, 1921, 1.

72. *L'Auto,* February 9, 1920, 2.

73. *New York Evening Telegram,* November 22, 1923, 10.

74. *New York Herald,* Paris, September 26, 1922, 6.

75. Sources for the description of this amphibious operation are: Marthe Du Bert, [Pseud. M. Dutrèb], *Nos Sénégalais pendant la grande guerre* (Metz: Maison d'Édition des "Voix Lorraines," 1922), 134–40; General A. Duboc, *Les Sénégalais au service de la France* (Paris: Editions Edgar Malfère, 1939), 103–6.

76. Sources for the description of this assault are: *Historique des troupes coloniales pendant la guerre, 1914–1918 (fronts extérieurs)* (Paris: Charles-Lavauzelle, 1931), 32–34; Eric Bush, *Gallipoli* (New York: St. Martin's Press, 1975), 162–63; Du Bert, *Nos Sénégalais pendant la Grande Guerre,* 140.

77. Diallo, *Force-bonté,* 83–84.

78. *Historique des troupes coloniales (fronts extérieurs),* 33.

79. Du Bert, *Nos sénégalais pendant la Grande Guerre,* 140–41.

80. Louis Guignard, "Les troupes noires pendant la guerre," *Revue des Deux Mondes* 51 (June 15, 1919): 864.

81. Lucie Cousturier, *Des inconnus chez moi* (Paris: Éditions de la Sirène, 1920), 57.

82. Du Bert, *Nos Sénégalais pendant la Grande Guerre,* 144.

83. Fleischer, *Black Dynamite,* vol. 3, 75.

84. *New York World,* December 16, 1925, 4.

85. *L'Auto* Special Edition.

86. Fleischer, *Black Dynamite,* vol. 3, 70.

87. Fleischer, *Fifty Years at Ringside,* 93.

88. Iba Der Thiam, *Le Sénégal dans la guerre 14–18, ou le prix du combat pour l'égalité* (Dakar: Nouvelles Editions Africaines du Sénégal, 1992), 23.

89. Shelby Cullom Davis, *Reservoirs of Men: A History of the Black Troops of French West Africa* (Geneva: Librairie Kundig, 1934), 144; Anthony Clayton, *France, Soldiers, and Africa* (London: Brassey's Defence Publishers, 1988).

90. See also Peeters, *La boxe,* 101.

91. September 25, 1922, 1.

92. *L'Auto* Special Editon; Peeters, *La boxe,* 67.

93. Charles Balesi, *From Adversaries to Comrades-in-Arms: West Africans and the French Military, 1885–1918* (Waltham, Mass.: Crossroads Press, 1979), 99.

94. Du Bert, *Nos Sénégalais pendant la Grande Guerre,* 140.

95. *Historique des troupes coloniales pendant la guerre, 1914–1918* (Paris: Charles-Lavauzelle, 1922), 83.

96. George Allen, *The Great War* (Philadelphia: George Barrie's Sons, 1919), vol. 4, 6.

97. Edmond Barthélemy Palat, *Les batailles d'Artois et de Champagne en 1915* (Paris and Brussels: G. Van Ouest, 1920), 142.

98. The description of this battle is drawn from Palat, *Les batailles d'Artois et de Champagne en 1915,* 142, 154–55; *Historique des troupes coloniales pendant la guerre, 1914–1918,* 82–83, 106–13.

99. *Storm of Steel,* trans. Basil Creighton (London: Chatto and Windus, 1929), 81.

100. The description of this battle is drawn from *Historique des troupes coloniales pendant la guerre, 1914–1918,* 114–15.

101. Eric J. Leed, *No Man's Land: Combat and Identity in World War I* (Cambridge: Cambridge University Press, 1979), 109, 112, 152, 156.

102. Fleischer, *Black Dynamite,* vol. 3, 75.

103. Georges Blond, *Verdun,* trans. Frances Frenaye (New York: Macmillan, 1964), 226.

104. Fleischer, *Black Dynamite,* vol. 3, 75–76.

105. Jünger, *Storm of Steel,* 99.

106. McCallum, *The Encyclopedia of World Boxing Champions;* see also Harry Mullan, *The Illustrated History of Boxing* (New York: Crescent Books, 1987), 167.

107. January 20, 1924, 10.

108. August 4, 1924.

109. August 2, 1924.

110. Peeters, *La boxe*, 51–52.

111. Victor Basquel and Alcide Delmont, *Le livre d'or de l'effort colonial français* (Paris: Presses Universitaires de France, 1923); *L'historique du 8ème régiment d'infanterie coloniale, 1914–1919* (Toulon: 1920).

112. Du Bert, *Nos Sénégalais pendant la Grande Guerre*, 100–102.

113. Henri Feuille, *Face aux Turcs: Gallipoli 1915* (Paris: Payot, 1934), 153–54.

114. Magel, "Hare and Hyena: Symbols of Shame in the Oral Narratives of the Wolof of Senegambia," 110–12.

115. Leed, *No Man's Land*, 105.

116. Henri Barbusse, *Le feu (Journal d'une escouade)* (Lausanne: Société Coopérative Editions Rencontre, 1917), 68.

117. François Ingold, *Les troupes noires au combat* (Paris: Editions Berger-Levrault, 1940), cited in Myron Echenberg, *Colonial Conscripts: The Tirailleurs Sénégalais in French West Africa, 1857–1960* (Portsmouth, N.H.: Heinemann; London: James Currey, 1991), 35.

118. In *"Caractères physiques et moraux du soldat nègre"* (Physical and moral characteristics of Negro soldiers), *Revue anthropologique* 10, 1–16.

119. Cited in Echenberg, *Colonial Conscripts*, 21; see also John Hoberman, *Darwin's Athletes: How Sport Has Damaged Black America and Preserved the Myth of Race* (Boston and New York: Houghton Mifflin, 1997), 189–90.

120. Du Bert, *Nos Sénégalais pendant la Grande Guerre*, 128–29.

121. Roger Cros, *La victoire des armées alliées en Orient 1918* (Montpellier: Causse, 1968), 90.

122. Rheinhold Eichacker, "The Blacks Attack!" *Current History* (April 1917): 110.

123. Eichacker, "The Blacks Attack!" 111.

124. Sources for the description of this assault are Balesi, *From Adversaries to Comrades-in-Arms*, 107–8; Holger H. Herwig, *The First World War: Germany and Austria Hungary, 1914–1918* (London: Arnold, 1997), 201; Palat, *La Grande Guerre sur le front occidental* (Paris: Librairie Chapelot, 1922), vol. 11, 32.

125. Allen, *The Great War*, 272.

126. Allen, *The Great War*, 200–201.

127. *Historique des troupes coloniales pendant la guerre, 1914–1918*, 146.

128. Palat, *La Grande Guerre sur le front occidental*, vol. 11, 32–33, 40.

129. Cousturier, *Des inconnus chez moi*, 73, 75.

130. Jünger, *Storm of Steel*, 83.

131. Albert J. Fyfe, *Understanding the First World War: Illusions and Realities* (Bern and New York: Peter Lang, 1988), 103; Tony Ashworth, *Trench Warfare, 1914–1918: The Live and Let Live System* (New York: Holmes and Meier, 1980), 211.

132. Vincent J. Esposito, *The West Point Atlas of American Wars, Vol II: 1900–1953.* (New York: Praeger, 1959), note to map 49.

133. Herwig, *The First World War*, 158.

134. Esposito, *The West Point Atlas of American Wars*, note to map 49; Fyfe, *Understanding the First World War*, 103–4.

135. *Historique des troupes coloniales pendant la guerre, 1914–1918 (fronts extérieurs)*, 99–100.

136. *Historique des troupes coloniales pendant la guerre, 1914–1918,*146.

137. Eric J. Leed, *No Man's Land: Combat and Identity in World War I* (Cambridge: Cambridge University Press, 1979), 114, 156.

138. Esposito, *The West Point Atlas of American Wars,* note to map 50.

139. *Historique des troupes coloniales pendant la guerre, 1914–1918 (fronts extérieurs),* 164–65.

Chapter 6: "A Hero, Perhaps . . ."

1. Roland Passevant, *Boxing business* (Paris: Éditeurs Français Réunis, 1973), 49–50.

2. (New York: Scribner's, 1926), 105–6.

3. Philippe Dewitte, *Les mouvements nègres en France: 1919–1939* (Paris: L'Harmattan, 1985), 27–29.

4. February 24, 1920, 1.

5. January 30, 1920, 2.

6. Bénac, *Champions dans la coulisse,* 101.

7. Passevant, *Boxing business,* 26, 178.

8. *La Dépêche,* June 8, 1914, 6.

9. December 28, 1919, 4.

10. March 21, 1920, 2.

11. February 3, 1920, 492.

12. *Le Sporting,* February 1, 1920.

13. Bénac, *Champions dans la coulisse,* 101.

14. April 2, 1920, 1.

15. *L'Auto,* March 24, 1920, 2, 3.

16. *La Boxe et les Boxeurs,* August 9, 1922, 9.

17. *L'Auto,* March 24, 1920, 2; March 26, 1920, 2; March 27, 1920, 2.

18. *L'Auto,* March 31, 1920, 2; April 2, 1920, 1.

19. *L'Auto,* April 3, 1920, 2; April 6, 1920, 2.

20. *L'Auto,* April 8, 1920, 2.

21. *L'Auto,* April 9, 1920.

22. *L'Auto,* April 10, 1920, 2.

23. *L'Auto,* April 28, 1920, 1.

24. *L'Auto,* April 29, 1920, 2.

25. Albert Stol, *Battling Siki: het levensverhaal van M'Barick Fall* (Amsterdam: In de Knipscheer, 1991), 71–72.

26. Walsh, *Men of Steel,* 54–55, 60–65.

27. May 13, 1920, 2.

28. As did Mbaye Gueye, the "tiger of Fass," and Tapha Gueye, the "new tiger of Fass," whom I saw in the arena of Dakar's Medina in 1992.

29. Gérard Salem, "La revanche des Fassois, la lutte sénégalaise," *Capitales de la couleur: Dakar, Abidjan, Douala, Kinshasa* (Paris: Editions Autrement, n.d. [1990]), 50.

30. Siki (Fall), "Résumé aux lecteurs de *L'Auto,*" *L'Auto,* September 29, 1922, 1.

31. Dewitte, *Les mouvements nègres en France,* 44, 45, 47.

32. *L'Auto,* May 29, 1920, 1; May 30, 1920, 2; June 10, 1920, 2.

33. *L'Auto,* June 3, 1920, 2.

34. Stol, *Battling Siki*, 64, 72.

35. Stol, *Battling Siki*, 72–73.

36. Stol, *Battling Siki*, 66–67.

37. Stol, *Battling Siki*, 67.

38. Stol, *Battling Siki*, 68.

39. Stol, *Battling Siki*, 63.

40. Stol, *Battling Siki*, 76.

41. Stol, *Battling Siki*, 77.

42. *L'Auto*, December 12, 1922, 1–2.

43. Orio Vergani, *Poor Nigger*, trans. W. W. Hobson (Indianapolis: Bobbs-Merrill, 1930), 7–8.

44. Stol, *Battling Siki*, 154.

45. Vergani, *Poor Nigger*, 155–56; a black heavyweight from Dallas, Texas, named Boykin really did campaign in American prize rings in the 1920s, but his first name was Joe, not George.

46. *Wretched of the Earth*, trans. Constance Farrington (New York: Grove Press, 1968), 39.

47. Frantz Fanon, *Black Skin, White Masks*, trans. Charles L. Markmann (New York: Grove Press, 1967), 72.

48. Fanon, *Black Skin, White Masks*, 70.

49. Germaine Guex, *La névrose d'abandon*, cited in Fanon, *Black Skin, White Masks*, 73–74.

50. Siki (Fall), "Résumé aux lecteurs de *L'Auto*," *L'Auto*, September 29, 1922, 1.

51. *Het Stadion*, July 24, 1920, 9.

52. *Het Stadion*, September 1, 1920, 52.

53. *Het Stadion*, October 27, 1920, 239.

54. *Het Stadion*, December 8, 1920, 375; in contrast, *L'Auto* said Siki, in top shape, waged "a vigorous combat" that he "almost constantly dominated." December 6, 1920, 2.

55. Dartnell, *Seconds Out*, 176–77.

56. *Le Sporting*, February 3, 1920, 492; he fought at Marseille, for instance, against Buisson. *Le Petit Provençal*, March 14, 1920, 3.

57. Stol, *Battling Siki*, 82.

58. *Het Stadion*, January 19, 1921, 547.

59. Stol, *Battling Siki*, 79–80.

60. Stanislas Jeannesson, *Poincaré, la France, et la Ruhr (1922–1924): Histoire d'une occupation* (Strassbourg: Presses Universitaire de Strassbourg, 1998), 169.

61. United States Department of State, *Colored Troops in the French Army* (Washington, D.C.: U.S. Government Printing Office, 1921), 12.

62. Echenberg, *Colonial Conscripts*, 35.

63. N.p. [3].

64. In the *Berliner Lokal-Anzeiger* and *Berliner Tageblatt*, for instance.

65. *Berliner Tageblatt*, January 13, 1921, n.p. [6]; *Berliner Lokal-Anzeiger* 25, January 16, 1921, n.p. [25].

66. January 16, 1921, n.p. [25].

67. *L'Auto*, January 17, 1921, 2.

68. January 17, 1921, 2.
69. *L'Auto,* January 17, 1921, 2.

Chapter 7: The Phantom Fighters at Salle Wagram

1. *Le Peuple,* July 4, 1921, 2.
2. Andre and Fleischer, *A Pictorial History of Boxing,* 101.
3. *Le Peuple,* July 2, 1921, 1.
4. The description in this paragraph is based on Manevy's column in *Le Peuple,* July 4, 1921, 2.
5. *Le Peuple,* July 4, 1921, 2.
6. July 6, 1921, 1.
7. *Le Peuple,* July 3, 1921, 1.
8. July 6, 1921, 1.
9. June 29, 1921, 2.
10. July 3, 1921, 3.
11. Stol, *Battling Siki,* 85.
12. Stol, *Battling Siki,* 83.
13. Stol, *Battling Siki,* 84–85.
14. *Het Stadion* hints Dutch boxers were loath to fight him, cowed by his speed. January 19, 1921, 547.
15. Even in Siki's era trainers had notions about how long a fighter needed to recuperate. Leo Bodner recalls declining a bout at Madison Square Garden with the avowal, "Sorry, none of my boys fight two weeks in a row." Alan Bodner, *When Boxing Was a Jewish Sport* (Westport, Conn.: Praeger, 1997), 108.
16. Stol, *Battling Siki,* 84.
17. January 19, 1921, 546–47.
18. M. J. Adriani Engels, *Honderd Jaar Sport* (Amsterdam: A. J. G. Strongholt, 1960), 116.
19. Stol, *Battling Siki.*
20. *Het Stadion,* January 19, 1921, 547.
21. *Berliner Tageblatt,* February 26, 1921, n.p. [7].
22. Mullan, *The Illustrated History of Boxing,* 168.
23. Douglas Gill and Gloden Dallas, *The Unknown Army* (London: Verso, 1985), 67, 152 n.
24. June 23, 1921, 2.
25. June 23, 1921, 2.
26. *L'Auto,* July 1, 1921, 2.
27. June 6, 1921, 2.
28. The *Ring Record Book* lists Siki as fighting both "Billy Balzac" and "Ercole Balzac" in 1921, but they were one and the same. In fact, Siki met Balzac just once, in September 1921.
29. August 30, 1921, 2.
30. September 21, 1921, 1.
31. *L'Auto,* September 3, 1921, 2.
32. *L'Auto,* September 15, 1921, 2.
33. September 22, 1921, 2.

34. *L'Auto,* September 23, 1921, 2.
35. *L'Auto,* September 26, 1921, 2; October 4, 1921, 3.
36. In 1919 he did knock out journeyman Dick Smith in Paris.
37. November 30, 1921, 21.
38. October 20, 1921, 3.
39. *New York Herald,* Paris, November 24, 1921, 6.
40. November 24, 1921, 2.
41. October 25, 1921, 4.
42. *L'Auto,* October 22, 1921, 2.
43. *L'Auto,* October 22, 1921, 2.
44. November 5, 1921, 4.
45. October 8, 1921, 2.
46. October 25, 1921, 4.
47. November 30, 1921, 2.
48. *L'Auto,* November 28, 1921, 1.
49. November 24, 1921, 2.
50. Including a four-rounder on the weekly boxing card for the Ardennes Boxing Club near his Charleville training camp. *La Boxe et les Boxeurs,* November 30, 1921, 8.
51. Fair, *Give Him to the Angels,* 38.
52. *La Boxe et les Boxeurs,* February 18, 1922, 24.
53. *La Boxe et les Boxeurs,* December 7, 1921, 7.
54. *New York Herald,* Paris, November 27, 1921, 6.
55. *L'Auto,* December 12, 1921, 3.
56. *L'Auto,* December 7, 1921, 6; December 4, 1921, 1.
57. *La Boxe et les Boxeurs,* December 7, 1921, 6.
58. December 4, 1921, 1.
59. *La Boxe et les Boxeurs,* December 7, 1921, 6.
60. December 4, 1921, 6.
61. *New York Herald,* Paris, December 4, 1921, 6; *L'Auto,* December 4, 1921, 1.
62. *Le Populaire de Paris,* January 12, 1922, 4.
63. The *New York Herald,* Paris, even repeated a rumor that he'd had a "nervous breakdown." November 29, 1921, 6.
64. Stol, *Battling Siki,* 91.
65. Dewitte, *Les mouvements nègres en France,* 27–28.
66. Malherbe and Sall, *Parlons Wolof,* 87–88.
67. Alassane Ndaw, *La Pensée africaine: recherches sur les fondements de la pensée négro-africaine* (Dakar: Nouvelles Editions Africaines, 1983), 238–40.
68. *La Boxe et les Boxeurs,* February 18, 1922, 24
69. Koppen, *Siki.*
70. *Le Populaire,* January 18, 1922, 4; January 19, 1922, 4.
71. *Le Populaire,* March 2, 1922, 4; March 21, 1922, 4.
72. *L'Auto,* January 18, 1922.
73. January 25, 1922, 5.
74. *La Boxe et les Boxeurs,* April 26, 1922, 7; *L'Echo des Sports,* April 17, 1922, 3.
75. *La Boxe et les Boxeurs,* May 10, 1922, 14.

76. *La Boxe et les Boxeurs*, May 10, 1922, 14.

77. *New York Herald*, Paris, September 7, 1922, 6.

78. May 1, 1922, 3.

79. Georges Carpentier, *Mon match avec la vie* (Paris: Flammarion, 1954), 135–36, 140–41.

80. Dempsey, Considine, and Slocum, *Dempsey*, 96, 98.

81. Carpenter, *Boxing: An Illustrated History*, 69–70.

82. It had appeared in *L'Express du Midi* in June 1919.

83. June 14, 1922, 19.

84. June 8, 1922, 11.

85. May 20, 1922, 3.

86. *L'Auto*, June 19, 1922, 2.

87. *La Boxe et les Boxeurs*, December 21, 1921, 3.

88. June 21, 1922, 2.

89. June 19, 1922, 2.

90. *L'Auto*, June 19, 1922, 2; June 21, 1922, 1; June 23, 1922, 1.

91. *L'Auto*, June 22, 1922, 1.

92. June 24, 1922, 2.

93. *New York Herald*, Paris, June 24, 1922, 2.

94. *La Boxe et les Boxeurs*, June 28, 1922, 5.

95. *L'Auto*, June 24, 1922, 2; *Mirroir des Sports*, June 29, 1922, 414.

96. *La Boxe et les Boxeurs*, June 28, 1922, 5.

97. *L'Auto*, June 24, 1922, 1; *La Boxe et les Boxeurs*, June 28, 1922, 5.

Chapter 8: "Yes, We Have No Bananas!"

1. Heller, *"In This Corner . . . ,"* 156.

2. Muhammad Ali and Richard Durham, *The Greatest: My Own Story* (New York: Random House, 1975), 215.

3. Peeters, *La boxe*, 70.

4. *New York Herald*, November 23, 1923, 14.

5. *New York Times*, November 22, 1923, 23.

6. Thomas Hauser, *The Black Lights: Inside the World of Professional Boxing* (New York: McGraw-Hill, 1986), 35.

7. *New York Evening Journal*, December 1, 1923, 17.

8. *New York Times*, December 16, 1923—I, 2, 3.

9. Walker and Reichler, *Mickey Walker*, 95–96; Fair, *Give Him to the Angels*, 53; Greb played Johnny Wilson the same trick to get a title match.

10. Fair, *Give Him to the Angels*, 38.

11. Koppen, *Siki*.

12. Fair, *Give Him to the Angels*, 89.

13. December 11, 1923, 24.

14. December 11, 1923, 26.

15. December 11, 1923, 10.

16. *New Orleans Times-Picayune*, January 20, 1924, 10.

17. *New York Times*, December 19, 1923, 17.

18. Derks, *The Value of a Dollar*, 178, 189.

19. *Le Peuple,* May 15, 1923, 3; Bénac, *Champions dans la coulisse,* 102.

20. Magel, *"Hare and Hyena,"* 117.

21. "The Battling Siki Murder," 60.

22. *New Orleans Times-Picayune,* January 20, 1924, 10.

23. *New York Times,* December 19, 1923, 17.

24. *A Neutral Corner* (New York: Farrar, Straus, and Giroux, 1990), 26–27.

25. Walker and Reichler, *Mickey Walker,* 237–38.

26. *New Orleans Times-Picayune,* January 21, 1924, 12.

27. Jack.Taylor, "From Jack Taylor, Coloured Ex-Light-Heavyweight Champion of the World," *Negro Anthology, 1931–1933,* ed. Nancy Cunard (London: Cunard and Wishart, 1934), 343.

28. *Chicago Defender,* December 29, 1923, 3.

29. *Philadelphia Inquirer,* December 26, 1923, 10.

30. *New York Times,* December 26, 1923, 3.

31. *New York Times,* December 30, 1923, 19.

32. *Cleveland Gazette,* January 12, 1924, 2; *New York Times,* January 3, 1924, 14.

33. *New York Times,* January 5, 1924, 17; January 3, 1924, 14.

34. *Buffalo Evening News,* January 7, 1924.

35. *New Orleans Times-Picayune,* January 21, 1924, 12.

36. January 8, 1924.

37. *Times-Picayune,* January 21, 1924, 12.

38. *Chicago Defender,* January 12, 1924, III, 2.

39. *Chicago Defender,* January 12, 1924, III, 2.

40. *Buffalo Evening News,* January 8, 1924.

41. *Buffalo Evening News,* January 8, 1924.

42. *Chicago Defender,* January 12, 1924, III, 2.

43. *New York Times,* January 28, 1924, 29.

44. *Buffalo Evening News,* January 8, 1924.

45. Cousturier, *Des inconnus chez moi,* 215.

46. Fleischer, *Fifty Years at Ringside,* 94.

47. Kearns, *The Million-Dollar Gate,* 51.

48. Jean Tourette, *Marseille ville de mon enfance* (Marseille: La Savoisienne, 1970), 143.

49. See *Chicago Defender,* February 23, 1924; Walsh, *Men of Steel,* 89.

50. Flesicher, *Black Dynamite,* vol. 3, 91.

51. *Memphis Commercial Appeal,* January 10, 1924, 13.

52. *Memphis Commercial Appeal,* January 13, 1924, I, 29.

53. January 10, 1924, 13.

54. January 6, 1924, 25.

55. January 13, I, 29.

56. January 14, 1924, 8.

57. January 16, 1924, 16.

58. *Chicago Defender,* January 19, 1924, I, 10.

59. *Memphis Commercial Appeal,* January 15, 1924, 15.

60. *Memphis Commercial Appeal,* January 16, 1924, 16.

61. *Memphis Commercial Appeal,* January 17, 1924, 16.

62. *Memphis Commercial Appeal,* January 10, 1924, 13.

63. *Memphis Commercial Appeal,* January 14, 1924, 12.

64. *Memphis Commercial Appeal,* January 15, 1924, 15.

65. *Memphis Commercial Appeal,* January 15, 1924, 15.

66. *Memphis Commercial Appeal,* January 17, 1924, 16; January 15, 1924, 16.

67. *Memphis Commercial Appeal,* January 16, 1924, 16.

68. *Memphis Commercial Appeal,* January 18, 1924, 17.

69. *Memphis Commercial Appeal,* January 13, 1924, I, 29.

70. *New Orleans Times-Picayune,* January 20, 1924, 10.

71. *New Orleans Times-Picayune,* January 22, 1924, 10.

72. Arche-Straw, *Negrophilia.*

73. *L'Auto,* September 29, 1922, 2.

74. Christopher L. Miller, *Blank Darkness: Africanist Discourse in French* (Chicago and London: University of Chicago Press, 1985), 17.

75. Hoberman, *Darwin's Athletes,* 102–3, 211–15.

76. *New Orleans Times-Picayune,* January 22, 1924, 10.

77. *New Orleans Times-Picayune,* January 22, 1924, 10.

78. Presaging Ali's famous "Ali shuffle."

79. Miller, *Blank Darkness,* 5.

80. January 19, 1924, II, 2.

81. April 1924, 12.

82. January 31, 1924, 18.

83. *Minneapolis Morning Tribune,* January 31, 1924, 18.

84. *Minneapolis Morning Tribune,* January 31, 1924, 18.

85. *Chicago Defender,* February 2, 1924, I, 10.

86. *Chicago Defender,* February 2, 1924, I, 10.

87. *Chicago Defender,* February 2, 1924, I, 10.

88. *Chicago Defender,* February 2, 1924, I, 10.

89. *Chicago Defender,* February 2, 1924, I, 11.

90. *St. Paul Pioneer Press,* February 1, 1924, 1; *Cleveland Gazette,* February 9, 1924, 2.

91. February 1, 1924, 14.

92. February 3, 1924, 16.

93. *St. Paul Pioneer Press,* February 1, 1924, 1.

94. *Minneapolis Tribune,* February 3, 1924, 16.

95. February 9, 1924, I, 11.

96. Now that Michigan had banned the Homer Smith bout, Canada looked like the next best bet—*Chicago Defender,* February 16, 1924, I, 11.

97. *Rochester Democrat and Chronicle,* February 8, 1924, 33.

98. The joke was that Hardin was black. Burns's loss of the heavyweight championship to Jack Johnson in 1908 had inspired a semi-ludicrous quest by a generation of novice white fighters, the so-called "white hopes," to "win the title back for the white race." See John Lardner, "The Jack Johnson Era of Boxing," *Negro Digest* 8, 1 (November 1949): 24–34, and *White Hopes and Other Tigers* (Philadelphia: Lippincott, 1951).

99. *Rochester Democrat and Chronicle,* February 7, 1924, 29.

100. *Rochester Democrat and Chronicle,* February 7, 1924, 29.

101. *Rochester Democrat and Chronicle,* February 9, 1924, 21.
102. *New York Times,* February 9, 1924, 9; *Rochester Democrat and Chronicle,* February 9, 1924, 21; *Chicago Defender,* February 16, 1924, I, 11.
103. February 16, 1924, 11.
104. *Columbus Dispatch,* February 14, 1924.
105. February 13, 1924.
106. February 15, 1924.
107. Dempsey, Considine, and Slocum, *Dempsey,* 87.

Chapter 9: "I No Fight"

1. February 19, 1924, 7.
2. Call to arms—the anniversary of the declaration of rebellion against Spain.
3. February 20, 1924, 10.
4. *La Discussion,* February 22, 1924, 6.
5. Lawrence's story is based on the report in the *New York Times,* February 22, 1924, 19.
6. *New York Times,* February 22, 1924, 19.
7. Dave Anderson, *In the Corner: Great Boxing Trainers Talk about Their Art* (New York: William Morrow, 1991), 149.
8. February 20, 1924, 8, 10.
9. *Havana Post,* February 22, 1924, 22.
10. *La Discussion,* February 23, 1924, 8; February 24, 1924, 4; *Havana Post,* February 24, 1924, 12.
11. February 27, 1924, 12.
12. *Passaic Daily Herald,* November 7, 1924, 14.
13. *Chicago Defender,* March 1, 1924, I, 11.
14. February 27, 1924, 9.
15. February 28, 1924, 8.
16. *Havana Post,* February 29, 1924, 1.
17. *New York Times,* March 15, 1924, 10.
18. *La Discussion,* March 9, 1924, 4.
19. *Havana Post,* March 2, 1924, 1.
20. *Havana Post,* April 27, 1924, 3.
21. *Havana Post,* April 7, 1924, 3; according to Anthony Summers and Robbyn Swan, mobster Frank Costello would later use Frank Sinatra and Jack Dempsey as couriers, sneaking millions of casino dollars into and out of Havana—"Sinatra, the Mob, and $3.5m," Timesonline, May 10, 2005 http://www.timesonline.co.uk/article/0,,923–1606133,00.html.
22. *La Discussion,* March 21, 1924, 8.
23. *La Disussion,* March 26, 1924, 18; *Havana Post,* April 7, 1924, 3.
24. *La Discussion,* March 26, 1924, 18.
25. *New York Times,* March 28, 1924, 11.
26. *Havana Post,* March 17, 1924, 1.
27. *Havana Post,* April 7, 1924, 3.
28. *Havana Post,* March 27, 1924, 3.
29. *Havana Post,* April 1, 1924, 3.

30. *Havana Post,* April 12, 1924, 3.
31. *New York Times,* April 8, 1924, 12.
32. *Havana Post,* April 20, 1924, 2.
33. *Havana Post,* April 27, 1924, 3.
34. *New York Times,* April 13, 1924, 1.
35. *New York Times,* May 1, 1924, 17.
36. *New York Times,* May 13, 1924, 16.
37. *Chicago Defender,* August 2, 1924, I, 10.
38. *Ring,* January 1925, 25.
39. *Wheeling Register,* July 11, 1924, 14; July 12, 1924, 14.
40. *Manchester Union Leader,* July 18, 1924, 10.
41. *Manchester Union Leader,* July 18, 1924, 10.
42. July 24, 1924, 3.
43. Readers who doubt such quips made the rounds are referred to McCallum, *The Encyclopedia of World Boxing Champions,* 92; Mullan, *The Illustrated History of Boxing,* 168; and Lardner, "The Battling Siki Murder," 54.
44. *New York Sun,* July 23, 1924, 1; *New York World,* July 24, 1924, 1; the description of the wedding is based on these two reports.
45. *New York Sun,* July 23, 1924, 1.
46. *New York Mirror,* July 23, 1924, 3.
47. *New York American,* July 25, 1924, 6; *New York Daily News,* July 25, 1924, 5.
48. *New York American,* July 24, 1924, 3.
49. *New York Times,* July 24, 1924, 30; *New York American,* July 24, 1924, 3.
50. July 24, 1924, 39.
51. July 24, 1924, 27.
52. July 24, 1924, 16.
53. *New York Sun,* July 24, 1924, 1.
54. *Chicago Defender,* July 26, 1924, I, 10.
55. *New York Herald Tribune,* July 25, 1924, 6; *New York Evening Post,* July 25, 1924, 12; *New York World,* July 25, 1924.
56. *L'Auto,* December 12, 1922, 1—actually, since Wolof doesn't have an exact equivalent for "brother" they could have been cousins, half-brothers, brothers, or other male relatives.
57. *L'Auto,* December 12, 1922, 1–2.
58. Siki (Fall), "Résumé aux lecteurs de *L'Auto,*" *L'Auto,* September 29, 1922, 1.
59. July 5, 1922, 18.
60. *New York Daily News,* July 26, 1924, 3; *Chicago Defender,* August 2, 1924, 1.
61. *New York Herald Tribune,* July 25, 1924, 6; see also *New York Times,* July 25, 1924, 4; *New York Evening Post,* July 25, 1924, 12; *New York Daily News,* July 25, 1924, 3.
62. July 25, 1924, 2.
63. *Providence Journal,* August 2, 1924.
64. *New York American,* July 24, 1924, 3.
65. *New York Times,* August 2, 1924, 10.
66. *New York Times,* August 2, 1924, 10.
67. *Providence Journal,* August 2, 1924.

68. *New York Herald,* Paris, September 27, 1922, 12.
69. *New York Times,* August 2, 1924, 10.
70. *Providence Journal,* August 3, 1924.
71. *Allentown Morning Call,* August 4, 1924.
72. *Allentown Morning Call,* August 3, 1924, II, 1.
73. *Buffalo Evening News,* August 12, 1924, 18, 22.
74. The description in this and the following paragraphs is based on a report in the *Lorain Times-Herald,* August 21, 1924.
75. "Looking like nothing so much as an angry ape," sneers the *Lorain Times-Herald,* August 21, 1924.
76. *New York Times,* June 30, 1924, 9.
77. The *Cleveland Gazette* made it $800—August 30, 1924, 2.
78. *Cleveland Plain-Dealer,* August 21, 1924.
79. *New York Times,* August 18, 1924, 23.
80. *Chicago Defender,* August 23, 1924, I, 11.
81. *New York Times,* September 12, 1924, 18.

Chapter 10: Apes and Peacocks

1. The dialogue here has been recast from indirect to direct quotation; but it is based closely on the report in *Passaic Daily Herald,* November 7, 1924, 14.
2. *Passaic Daily News,* November 6, 1924, 10; *Passaic Daily Herald,* November 7, 1924, 14.
3. *Passaic Daily News,* November 6, 1924, 10
4. *Passaic Daily Herald,* November 7, 1924, 14.
5. *Passaic Daily Herald,* November 7, 1924, 14.
6. *Passaic Daily Herald,* November 7, 1924, 14.
7. *Passaic Daily Herald,* November 7, 1924, 14.
8. Heller, *"In This Corner . . . ,"* 154–55.
9. Walker and Reichler, *Mickey Walker,* 99–100.
10. Early, *The Culture of Bruising,* 81–82.
11. *Ring,* May 1924, 38.
12. Andre and Fleischer, *A Pictorial History of Boxing,* 188–89.
13. *Passaic Herald,* November 8, 1924, 6.
14. *Passaic Daily News,* November 8, 1924, 8.
15. *Passaic Daily News,* November 8, 1924, 8.
16. Nine—Greb, Tunney, Walker, Loughran, Delaney, Berlenbach, Carpentier, Gibbons, and Stribling—are enshrined in the International Boxing Hall of Fame in Canastota, New York.
17. *New York Age,* November 22, 1924, 6.
18. A national amateur champion, he went to the 1920 Antwerp games as a representative of the New York Athletic Club, though an injury prevented him from competing—Pete Ehrmann, "Setting the Record Straight on Paul Berlenbach," *Ring Magazine,* February 2005, 69–70.
19. Vernon Pizer, *Glorious Triumphs: Athletes Who Conquered Adversity* (New York: Dodd, Mead, 1966), 114–24.

20. Hickey had turned Berlenbach, a natural left-hander, around to fight out of a right-handed stance.

21. *Ring,* September 1924, 41.

22. *New York Times,* November 14, 1924, 22.

23. *New York Evening Journal,* November 14, 1924, 41.

24. *New York Herald Tribune,* November 13, 1924, 18; *New York Daily News,* November 14, 1924, 35.

25. *New York Evening Journal,* November 14, 1924, 41; November 15, 1924, Sports Section, 1.

26. *New York Herald Tribune,* November 15, 1924, 15.

27. *New York Daily News,* November 15, 1924, 23.

28. *New York Herald Tribune,* November 15, 1924, 15.

29. *New York Age,* November 22, 1924, 6.

30. *New York Evening Journal,* November 14, 1924, 41.

31. Harry Newman, *New York Daily News,* November 15, 1924, 23.

32. Sid Mercer, *New York Evening Journal,* November 14, 1924, 41.

33. *New York Evening Journal,* November 14, 1924, 41.

34. *Syracuse Post-Standard,* November 26, 1924, 15.

35. *Syracuse Herald Journal,* November 26, 1924.

36. November 28, 1924.

37. *Syracuse Herald Journal,* November 28, 1924.

38. *Syracuse Post-Standard,* November 28, 1924; *Syracuse Herald Journal,* November 28, 1924.

39. *Syracuse Post-Standard,* November 28, 1924.

40. Randy Roberts, *Papa Jack: Jack Johnson and the Era of White Hopes* (New York: Free Press, 1983), 26.

41. *Everlast Boxing Record* (New York: Everlast Sport Publishing, 1924).

42. Michael DeLisa, ed. "Theodore 'Tiger' Flowers (the 'Georgia Deacon')," Cyber Boxing Zone (April 14, 2000), www.cyberboxingzone.com/boxing/flowers.htm.

43. December 4, 1924, 45.

44. December 4, 1924, 14.

45. *Brooklyn Daily Times,* December 5, 1924, 17.

46. *Brooklyn Standard Union,* December 5, 1924, 18.

47. *Brooklyn Standard Union,* December 5, 1924, 18.

48. *Brooklyn Daily Eagle,* December 5, 1924, 24.

49. Bénac insists he overheard Levy refer to such deals. Bénac, *Champions dans la coulisse,* 117.

50. *Chicago Defender,* December 20, 1924, 2, 9.

51. Sources for the description of this incident are: *New York Times,* December 22, 1924, 3; *Memphis Commercial Appeal,* December 22, 1924, 14; *Memphis Commerical Appeal,* December 23, 1924, 15; *National Police Gazette,* January 17, 1925, 11.

52. Ali and Durham, *The Greatest,* 65.

53. *Memphis Commercial Appeal,* December 19, 1924, 24.

54. December 23, 1924, 15.

55. Siki's ploy may have been disloyal but was probably legal. Levy's contract

was valid for New York State. Doc Kearns, Dempsey's manager, avoided a rival claimant to his services, John "the Barber" Reisler, who held a valid New York contract, by the simple expedient of signing Dempsey for a fight on the Weehawken, New Jersey, ferry, just outside New York waters. Kahn, *A Flame of Pure Fire,* 46.

56. *Atlanta Constitution,* January 18, 1925, 1C.

57. *Atlanta Constitution,* January 18, 1925, 1C.

58. *Atlanta Constitution,* January 21, 1925, 11.

59. *Atlanta Constitution,* January 23, 1925, 7.

60. He would one day, in fact, face Max Schmeling for the heavyweight title.

61. *New York Times,* January 8, 1925, 30.

62. Walker and Reichler, *Mickey Walker,* 81–82.

63. Fleischer, *Black Dynamite,* vol. 3, 89–90.

64. Fleischer, *Black Dynamite,* vol. 3, 88.

65. Fleischer, *Fifty Years at Ringside,* 92.

66. Fleischer, *Black Dynamite,* vol. 3, 90.

67. Fleischer, *Fifty Years at Ringside,* 92–93.

68. June 10, 1925, 18.

69. Fleischer, *Fifty Years at Ringside,* 93.

70. Fleischer, *Fifty Years at Ringside,* 92.

71. Fleischer, *Black Dynamite,* vol. 3, 88.

72. As Early points out, *The Culture of Bruising,* 81–82.

73. Fleischer, *Black Dynamite,* vol. 3, 71–72.

74. Fleischer, *Fifty Years at Ringside,* 93.

75. March 14, 1925, 14.

76. The photos are in the *New York Journal,* March 14, 1925, 1, and *New York American,* March 14, 1925, S1.

77. March 14, 1925, 1.

78. March 14, 1925, 15.

79. *New York American,* March 14, 1925, S1.

80. March 14, 1925, 15.

81. *New York Times,* March 13, 1925, 17.

82. *New York Evening Journal,* March 13, 1925, 10.

83. March 13, 1925, 15.

84. March 14, 1925, 1.

85. March 14, 1925, 14.

86. March 14, 1925, S-1.

87. Sources for the description of the fight are: *New York Journal,* March 14, 1925, 1; *New York Telegram,* March 14, 1925,15; *New York American,* March 14, 1925, S1; *New York Times,* March 14, 1925, 9; *New York World,* March 14, 1925, 7.

88. March 14, 1925, 7.

89. Mercer, *New York Journal,* March 14, 1925, 1.

90. *New York Telegram,* March 14, 1925, 15.

91. *New York World,* March 13, 1925, 17.

92. Underwood, *New York Telegram,* March 14, 1925, 15; *New York Times,* March 14, 1925, 9.

93. Farnsworth, *New York American,* March 14, 1925, S-1.

94. Jack Kofoed, *New York Evening Post,* March 14, 1925, 15.

95. *New York Telegram,* March 14, 1925, 15.

96. *New York American,* March 14, 1925, S-1.

97. *New York Journal,* March 14, 1925, 1; *New York American,* March 14, 1925, S-1.

98. *New York American,* March 14, 1925, S-1.

99. *New York Journal,* March 14, 1925, 1.

100. *New York Journal,* March 14, 1925, 1.

101. *New York World,* March 13, 1925, 17; *New York Journal,* March 14, 1925, 1; *New York Telegram,* March 14, 1925, 15.

102. *New York American,* March 14, 1925, S-1.

103. Andre and Fleischer, *A Pictorial History of Boxing,* 189.

104. *New York World,* December 16, 1925, 4.

105. Paul Sann, "Kill the Dutchman! The Story of Dutch Schultz," www.paulsann.org/killthedutchman/chapter X.htm (accessed April 25, 2003).

106. Allan May, "Waxey Gordon's Half Century of Crime," Crime Magazine: An Encyclopedia of Crime, http://crimemagazine.com/waxey.htm (accessed January 15, 2005).

107. Memo to J. Edgar Hoover from SAC, New York, December 20, 1957. Federal Bureau of Investigation. Frank Costello file. Freedom of Information Act. Bu file no. 92–2869 Section 1.

108. June 30, 1925.

109. *Brooklyn Citizen,* July 10, 1925, 8; *Brooklyn Standard Union,* July 11, 1925, 8.

110. *Jersey Journal,* July 23, 1925, 12.

111. Joe Gould didn't chauffeur West Side mob boss Owney Madden home from prison out of mere friendship. Years later, in 1937, Gould would only give Joe Louis a title shot against Braddock in return for ten percent of future heavyweight title promotions at the Garden—over the next ten *years!* He would divide the money, of course, with Madden and his mob cronies. When Gould worked on the waterfront during World War II, he got caught taking part in a million-dollar scam diverting contracts for life rafts and life jackets intended for the military. He was sentenced to three years in prison. Braddock, who spent the war years "assisting in moving material through the Port of New York," was called to testify at Gould's trial. A few years earlier a political candidate had charged Braddock with using political connections in Hudson County to get illegitimate welfare relief for his children. When Braddock made his famous comeback in 1935, he and Gould headed off criticism for this lapse by rushing with suspicious alacrity to the Union City and Hudson County relief offices to pay back the money he'd taken on the dole. In 1938 Madden's mob crony Bill Duffy would brazenly list himself as the copyright holder to the film of the Braddock / Tommy Farr fight. The unscrupulous Gould liked to brag of once sneaking boxer Jack Herman out of the hospital, where he was being treated for appendicitis, handing him a sack of ice to hold against his side to dull the pain, and putting him on a train for Florida so he could fight Luis Angel Firpo for $5,000. Michael C. DeLisa, *Cinderella Man: The James J. Braddock Story* (Wrea Green, UK: Milo Books, 2005), 50, 52, 171–72, 187–88, 205, 236, 244. Stern, *Bill Stern's Favorite Boxing Stories,* 59.

112. Kahn, *A Flame of Pure Fire,* 413–15.

113. Helene Stapinski, *Five-Finger Discount: A Crooked Family History* (New York: Random House, 2001), 63, 69.

114. Dayton David McKean, *The Boss: The Hague Machine in Action* (New York: Russell and Russell, 1967), 217.

115. *New York Times,* August 25, 1925, 21.

116. Michael Immerso, *Newark's Little Italy: The Vanished First Ward* (New Brunswick and Newark: Rutgers University Press and Newark Public Library, 1997), 111; Mark. A. Stuart, *Gangster # 2: Longy Zwillman, the Man Who Invented Organized Crime* (Secaucus, N.J.: Lyle Stuart, 1985), 48; Thomas L. Jones, "A Single Strand of Hair," *The Crime Library.* http://www.crimelibrary.com/gangsters/genovese/index.htm (accessed January 9, 2003).

117. Phil Berger, *Blood Season: Tyson and the World of Boxing* (New York: William Morrow, 1988), 220.

118. *Hudson Dispatch,* July 23, 1925, 17; July 24, 1925, 12.

119. *Jersey Journal,* July 23, 1925, 12; *Hudson Dispatch,* July 23, 1925, 17.

120. *Jersey Journal,* July 24, 1925, 17, 19.

121. *Hudson Dispatch,* July 24, 1925, 12.

122. Details in this and the succeeding paragraph are drawn from the *New York Evening Journal,* July 27, 1925,18.

123. *New York Times,* July 27, 1925, 15.

124. *New York Evening Journal,* July 27, 1925, 18.

125. *New York Times,* July 28, 1925, 23.

126. *New York Times,* July 27, 1925, 15

127. *New York Times,* July 28, 1925, 23.

128. Richard O'Connor, *Hell's Kitchen: The Roaring Days of New York's Wild West Side* (New York: Old Town Books, 1958), 214, 217.

129. *National Police Gazette,* July 1924, 10.

130. *New York Age,* August 15, 1925, 6; my description of the fight is from this source.

131. Ronald K. Fried, *Corner Men: Great Boxing Trainers* (New York: Four Walls Eight Windows, 1991), 293.

132. *New York Times,* August 13, 1925, 17.

133. *New York Times,* August 13, 1925, 17.

134. *Hudson Dispatch,* August 14, 1925, 16; the entire conversation and description here closely follow this source.

135. *Hudson Dispatch,* August 14, 1925, 16.

136. August 19, 1925, 16.

137. *New York Times,* August 19, 1925, 15.

138. August 19, 1925, 20.

139. *Jersey Journal,* August 19, 1925, 8.

140. *New York Times,* August 13, 1925, 17; August 28, 1925, 29.

141. *New York Times,* November 6, 1925, 27.

142. Several sources, including the *Ring Record Book* and Tracy Callis, list Siki as facing two further opponents in New Jersey in late August and early September, George LaRocco (or Rocco) and Harold Mays. But these bouts were contested not by the Battling Siki whose real name was Louis M'barick

Fall but by another boxer borrowing his ring name. The *Newark Evening News* refers to the boxer in question as "*Young* Siki" and identifies him as "the Newark boy" and "the Newark negro heavyweight"—September 9, 1925, 16. The *Newark Star-Eagle* refers to Young Siki as "the latest colored sensation in the local circle" and a "huge colored fighter" whose victory over Rocco was a "big surprise." It also makes references to this fighter's record that do not jive with the record of the real Battling Siki—September 9, 1925, 20.

Chapter 11: "Trop de Cinéma"

1. *New York Evening Sun,* December 16, 1925, 1; I've changed their indirect representation of the conversation here to direct quotation.

2. The *New York Herald Tribune,* December 16, 1925, and *New York Times,* December 16, 1925, 3, are among various sources quoting Siki's words directly, with small variations in the wording.

3. *Baltimore Sun,* November 14, 1925, 13; *Baltimore Afro-American,* November 21, 1925, 8.

4. November 14, 1925, 7.

5. *Baltimore Afro-American,* November 21, 1925, 8.

6. *New York Telegram, Evening Sun,* December 15, 1925, 1.

7. *New York Amsterdam News,* September 9, 1925, 4.

8. *New York Evening Sun,* December 16, 1925, 1.

9. *New York Times,* December 17, 1925, 27.

10. *New York World,* December 16, 1925, 1.

11. *New York World,* December 16, 1925, 1; other sources for the description of Lillian's evening are: *New York Evening Sun,* December 16, 1925, 1: *New York Post,* December 15, 1925, 1; *New York Daily News,* December 16, 1925, 3; *New York Times,* December 16, 1925, 3; *New York Telegram,* December 16, 1925, 1.

12. *New York Daily News,* December 16, 1925, 3.

13. Eduardo Arroyo, *Panama Al Brown* (Paris: Bernard Grasset, 1998), 37.

14. Sources for this description are: *L'Echo de Paris,* December 6, 1922, 1; *Boxing Blade,* December 16, 1922, 12; *New York Evening Journal,* December 6, 1922, 1.

15. *L'Humanité,* September 25, 1922, 2.

16. *L'Auto,* September 22, 1922, 1; *L'Echo de Paris,* September 25, 1922, 1.

17. *New York Herald,* Paris, September 26, 1922, 6.

18. *New York Times,* December 5, 1922, 23.

19. Carpentier, *Mon match avec la vie,* 233–34.

20. *Le Petit Parisien,* September 25, 1922, 1; *New York Herald,* Paris, September 25, 1922, 1

21. Bob Scanlon, "The Record of a Negro Boxer," *Negro Anthology, 1931–1933,* ed. Nancy Cunard (London: Cunard and Wishart, 1934), 339–40.

22. Scanlon, "The Record of a Negro Boxer," 341.

23. Gordon and Gordon, *The Columbia Chronicles of American Life,* 127.

24. Olivier Merlin, *Georges Carpentier, gentleman du ring* (Paris: Hatier, 1975), 85.

25. *New York Herald,* Paris, September 26, 1922, 6.

26. *L'Echo des Sports,* September 25, 1922, 2; *Petit Parisien,* September 25, 1922, 1; *L'Echo de Paris,* September 25, 1922, 1.

27. September 30, 1922, 1.

28. September 25, 1922, 1.

29. *L'Echo des Sports,* September 26, 1922, 1.

30. *New York Times,* December 5, 1922, 23; *Boxing Blade,* December 16, 1922, 12.

31. Koppen, *Siki.*

32. *L'Echo de Paris,* September 25, 1922, 1; *Le Populaire,* September 25, 1922, 1.

33. *Le Matin,* September 25, 1922, 1; *L'Echo de Paris,* September 25, 1922, 1.

34. *Boxing Blade,* December 16, 1922, 12.

35. *L'Eclair,* December 5, 1922, 1; *L'Auto,* December 5, 1922, 1.

36. Scanlon, "The Record of a Negro Boxer," 341.

37. Passevant, *Boxing business,* 145.

38. December 6, 1922, 1.

39. *L'Auto,* December 5, 1922, 1.

40. *L'Auto,* December 5, 1922, 1; December 6, 1922, 1.

41. *Boxing Blade,* December 16, 1922.

42. September 30, 1922, 493.

43. *Boxing Blade,* December 16, 1922.

44. *Le Populaire,* September 25, 1922, 1.

45. *New York Herald,* Paris, September 25, 1922, 1.

46. *L'Echo des Sports,* September 25, 1922, 2; *Le Matin,* September 25, 1922, 4.

47. Carpentier, *Mon match avec la vie,* 230.

48. *La Boxe et les Boxeurs,* November 8, 1922, 14.

49. *La Boxe et les Boxeurs,* November 8, 1922, 14.

50. *Le Miroir des Sports,* November 30, 1922, 351.

51. *Le Populaire,* September 26, 1922, 4.

52. *Chicago Defender,* October 7, 1922, 1; *Newark Evening News,* September 27, 1922, 18.

53. November 16, 1922, 306.

54. September 25, 1922, 2.

55. Carpentier, *Mon match avec la vie,* 227.

56. September 25, 1922, 1.

57. *L'Echo des Sports,* September 26, 1922, 1.

58. *New York Times,* September 26, 1922.

59. *Le Petit Parisien,* September 26, 1922, 1.

60. *L'Echo des Sports,* September 28, 1922, 1.

61. *Chicago Defender,* September 30, 1922, 1.

62. *Chicago Defender,* September 30, 1922, 1.

63. September 27, 1922, 1, 2.

64. *New York Times,* November 13, 1922, 17.

65. *New York Herald,* Paris, September 28, 1922, 6.

66. Green, *Shaw's Champions,* 128.

67. *New York Herald,* Paris, September 25, 1922, 1.

68. September 25, 1922, sec. 1, 12.

69. Rpt. in *Illustrated London News,* September 30, 1922, 490–91.

70. Green, *Shaw's Champions,* 127.

71. Green, *Shaw's Champions,* 128–29.

72. *New York Times,* September 25, 1922, 1.

73. Scanlon, "The Record of a Negro Boxer," 342.

74. October 7, 1922, 2.

75. *L'Echo des Sports,* September 2, 1922, 3.

76. *Le Populaire,* September 30, 1922, 2.

77. *New York Times,* November 10, 1922, 21; *L'Echo des Sports,* November 10, 1922, 1; *Le Populaire,* November 10, 1922, 3.

78. *L'Auto,* December 19, 1922, 3.

79. *L'Auto,* October 4, 1922, 3.

80. *L'Auto,* October 7, 1922, 3.

81. *L'Auto,* October 7, 1922, 3; *New York Times,* October 4, 1922, 20; *Chicago Defender,* October 7, 1922, 1.

82. October 14, 1922, 4.

83. James J. Martine, "Hemingway's 'Fifty Grand': The Other Fight(s)," *Journal of Modern Literature* 2 (September 1971): 125.

84. Ernest Hemingway, *The Sun Also Rises* (New York: Scribner's, 1954), 71.

85. Hemingway, *The Sun Also Rises,* 72.

86. *The Short Stories of Ernest Hemingway* (New York: Scribner's, 1953), 325.

87. *The Short Stories of Ernest Hemingway,* 321.

88. *New York Herald,* September 27, 1922, 12; *New York Times,* September 26, 1922, 23.

89. October 17, 1922, 1.

90. *L'Echo des Sports,* October 18, 1922, 1.

91. *L'Auto,* October 18, 1922, 1.

92. November 9, 1922, 3.

93. *L'Echo des Sports,* November 10, 1922, 1; November 11, 1922, 1.

94. Including *La Boxe et les Boxeurs, Le Populaire,* and *Le Gaulois.*

95. November 10, 1922, 3.

96. *Le Gaulois,* November 10, 1922, 3.

97. November 11, 1922, 1.

98. *Le Miroir des Sports,* November 30, 1922, 351.

99. *L'Echo des Sports,* November 11, 1922, 1.

100. *New York Times,* November 12, 1922, 3.

101. *Le Peuple,* December 1, 1922, 3.

102. *Le Populaire,* November 11, 1922, 1; January 5, 1923, 2; *L'Humanité,* January 5, 1923, 2.

Chapter 12: Tagged

1. *New York Times,* December 16, 1925, 3; *New York Daily News,* December 16, 1925, 44.

2. *L'Echo de Paris*, December 1, 1922, 2.

3. Robert July, *The Origins of Modern African Thought* (London: Faber and Faber, 1968; New York: Praeger, 1967), 366.

4. *Le Peuple,* November 30, 1922, 1.

5. *Le Petit Parisien,* December 1, 1922, 1.

6. *Le Populaire,* December 1, 1922, 1.

7. *Le Petit Parisien,* December 1, 1922, 1–2; *Le Populaire,* December 1, 1922, 1; *L'Humanité,* December 1, 1922, 2.

8. *Le Populaire,* December 1, 1922, 1.

9. *Le Peuple,* December 1, 1922, 3.

10. *Le Petit Parisien,* December 1, 1922, 1–2.

11. *Le Peuple,* December 1, 1922, 3.

12. *Le Petit Parisien,* December 1, 1922, 1–2.

13. *L'Echo de Paris,* December 1, 1922, 2.

14. *Le Petit Parisien,* December 1, 1922, 1–2.

15. *Le Petit Parisien,* December 2, 1922, 4.

16. *L'Auto,* December 5, 1922, 1.

17. *L'Eclair,* December 5, 1922, 1.

18. *New York World,* December 16, 1925, 4.

19. *L'Eclair,* December 5, 1922, 1.

20. December 6, 1922, 1–2.

21. *New York Times,* December 5, 1922, 23.

22. *L'Auto,* December 6, 1922, 1.

23. *L'Auto,* December 6, 1922, 1.

24. *Le Miroir des Sports,* October 12, 1922, 226.

25. *L'Echo des Sports,* October 1, 1922, 2.

26. *New York Times,* December 4, 1922, 22.

27. *New York Amsterdam News,* December 6, 1922, 1.

28. *L'Auto,* December 6, 1922, 2.

29. December 12, 1922, 4.

30. December 16, 1922, 3.

31. *Le Temps,* January 17, 1923, 4; *New York Herald,* Paris, January 16, 1923, 8.

32. December 12, 1922, 2.

33. *L'Auto,* December 13, 1922, 1.

34. *L'Auto,* December 13, 1922, 1.

35. *Le Canard Enchaîné,* December 13, 1922, 4.

36. *L'Auto,* December 16, 1922, 2.

37. *L'Auto,* December 20, 1922, 3, 4.

38. *New York Post,* December 16, 1925, 1; *New York Times,* December 16, 1925, 3; *New York Evening Sun,* December 16, 1925, 1.

39. *New York Amsterdam News,* December 9, 1925, 6.

40. *New York Amsterdam News,* December 9, 1925, 6.

41. This description is drawn from various sources, most notably: *New York World,* December 16, 1925, 1; *New York Evening Sun,* December 16, 1925, 1; *New York Telegram,* December 16, 1925, 1; *New York Post,* December 16, 1925, 1; *New York Daily News,* December 16, 1925, 3; *New York Times,* December 16, 1925, 3; *New York Herald Tribune,* December 16, 1925, 1.

42. *New York World,* December 16, 1925, 1; *New York Evening Sun,* December 16, 1925, 1.

43. *New York Daily Mirror,* December 16, 1925, 4; *New York American,* December 16, 1925, 1; *New York Daily News,* December 16, 1925, 3; *New York Age,* December 19, 1925, 1.

44. *New York Post,* December 16, 1925, 1.

45. *New York Evening Sun,* December 16, 1925, 1.

46. *New York Telegram,* December 16, 1925, 1.

47. *New York Daily News,* December 16, 1925, 4.

48. *New York Evening Sun,* December 16, 1925, 1.

49. Sources for this paragraph are: *New York Post,* December 16, 1925, 1; *New York Evening Sun,* December 16, 1925, 1; *New York Times,* December 16, 1925, 1; *New York Herald Tribune,* December 16, 1925, 1.

50. *New York Times,* December 16, 1925, 1.

51. December 17, 1925, 4.

52. *New York American,* December 16, 1925, 1.

53. December 16, 1925, 1.

54. François Terbeen and Claude Brezner, *Les géants de la boxe* (Paris: Editions Mondiales, 1962), 126; Bénac, *Champions dans la coulisse,* 118.

55. December 16, 1925, 1.

56. December 19, 1925, 1.

57. *New York Evening Sun,* December 16, 1925, 1; *New York Times,* December 16, 1925, 1.

58. December 17, 1925, 2.

59. December 20, 1925.

60. Bénac, *Champions dans la coulisse,* 117.

61. Bénac, *Champions dans la coulisse,* 117.

62. Bénac, *Champions dans la coulisse,* 117.

63. A confidential memorandum by a *New York Post* reporter to the FBI, dated October 23, 1935, would report that Luciano's bodyguard had confided, "Luciano has made a treaty with the Longies [Zwillman's gang] which permits the latter to operate in Manhattan." Federal Bureau of Investigation Frank Costello file. Bu file no. 87–30 Section 5.

64. Walsh, *Men of Steel,* 82–83; Andrew M. Kaye, *The Pussycat of Prizefighting: Tiger Flowers and the Politics of Black Celebrity* (Athens: University of Georgia Press, 2004), 149.

65. Craig Thompson and Allen Raymond, *Gang Rule in New York* (New York: Dial Press, 1940), 45.

66. Nown, *The English Godfather,* 43, 47.

67. Bénac, *Champions dans la coulisse,* 117.

68. *New York World,* December 16, 1925, 4.

69. *Witness to a Century: Encounters with the Noted, the Notorious, and the Three S.O.B.s.* (New York: Random House, 1987) 367; Nown, *The English Godfather,* 181.

70. Rpt. Ward Greene, ed., *Star Reporters and Thirty-four of Their Stories* (New York: Random House, 1948), 300–301.

71. Early, *The Culture of Bruising,* 82.

72. Early, *The Culture of Bruising,* 68–69.

73. Early, *The Culture of Bruising,* 79.

74. *New York Amsterdam News,* December 23, 1925, 6.

75. *New York World,* December 16, 1925, 4; other sources for this description include: *New York Daily Mirror,* December 17, 1925, 10; *New York Evening Journal,* December 17, 1925, 1; *New York Times,* December 19, 1925, 9.

76. *New York World,* December 16, 1925, 4.

77. *Salah: the Muslim Prayer* (Elmhurst, New York: Islamic Books and Tapes, n.d. [1998?]).

78. *New York Times,* March 9, 1926, 8; the description of Maroney's capture closely follows this source.

79. *New York Times,* March 9, 1926, 8.

80. John Lardner, "This Was Pugilism: Battling Siki," *New Yorker,* November 19, 1949, 108.

81. Charles Van Devander, "How Costello Made Kennedy Boss of the Hall" (clipping in Federal Bureau of Investigation Frank Costello file. Bu file no. 62–76543 SUB A); undated FBI memorandum, ca. 1953, summarizing Costello's activities (Federal Bureau of Investigation Frank Costello file. Bu file no. 62–76541 Section 1); memo to J. Edgar Hoover, from New York SAC, December 20, 1957 (Federal Bureau of Investigation Frank Costello file. Bu file no. 92–2869 Section 1); Robert H. Prall, "Costello Got Rich on Rum," *New York World Telegram and Sun,* May 11, 1957 (clipping in Federal Bureau of Investigation Frank Costello file. Bu file no. 62–76543 SUB A).

82. Andrew Sinclair, *Era of Excess: A Social History of the Prohibition Movement* (New York: Harper and Row, 1962), 228, 230.

83. *New York Times,* October 5, 1926, 8.

84. Greene, *Star Reporters,* 298.

85. Early, *The Culture of Bruising,* 82.

Afterword

1. Jill Stone, *Times Square: A Pictorial History* (New York: Macmillan, 1982), 33–34, 37–38.

2. Abner "Longy" Zwillman interviewed by Special Agent in Charge A. P. Kitchin, Newark, N.J., November 9–10, 1938 (Federal Bureau of Investigation, Abner Zwillman file, Part 2, Bu file nos. 92–3105, 62–36085, 58–4441).

3. Memorandum from special agent in charge ("RHP"), Newark Office, FBI, to J. Edgar Hoover, June 7, 1950 (Federal Bureau of Investigation, Abner Zwillman file, Part 2, Bu file nos. 92–3105, 62–36085, 58–4441).

4. *New York Leader,* October 12, 1923, 7.

5. Clipping dated June 1, 1935, in Federal Bureau of Investigation, Frank Costello File no. 87–30 SUB A .

6. Summary Report, December 27, 1957, Federal Bureau of Investigation, Abner Zwillman file, Part 2, Bu file nos. 92–3105, 62–36085, 58–4441.

7. General Investigative Intelligence file, April 17, 1954, Federal Bureau of Investigation, Abner Zwillman file, Part 2, Bu file nos. 92–3105, 62–36085, 58–4441.

8. Federal Bureau of Investigation, Abner Zwillman file, Part 2, Bu file nos. 92–3105, 62–36085, 58–4441.

9. *Washington Times-Herald,* March 8, 1944, 5; Robert H. Prall, "Costello Pals Go to Doom," *New York World Telegram and Sun,* May 15, 1957, 1, 18 (clippings in Federal Bureau of Investigation, Frank Costello File 62–76543 SUB A).

10. Memorandum from special agent in charge ("RHP"), Newark Office, FBI, to J. Edgar Hoover, June 7, 1950 (Federal Bureau of Investigation, Abner Zwillman file, Part 2, Bu file nos. 92–3105, 62–36085, 58–4441). Robert Lacey, *Little Man: Meyer Lansky and the Gangster Life* (Boston: Little, Brown, 1991), 45.

11. Summary Report, December 27, 1957 (Federal Bureau of Investigation, Abner Zwillman file, Part 2, Bu file nos. 92–3105, 62–36085, 58–4441).

12. Summary Report, December 27, 1957, Federal Bureau of Investigation, Abner Zwillman file, Part 2, Bu file nos. 92–3105, 62–36085, 58–4441; Summary Report, June 18, 1958, Federal Bureau of Investigation, Abner Zwillman file, Bu file no. 58-4441.

13. Stuart, *Gangster #2,* 159.

14. Walker and Reichler, *Mickey Walker,* 190–93.

15. *New York Call,* September 1, 1923, 2.

16. Ali and Durham, *The Greatest,* 324.

17. Shocket, "Battling Siki—the Man they Turned into a Joke," 59.

18. Shocket, "Battling Siki—the Man they Turned into a Joke," 58.

19. See Dave Anderson, "Battling Siki Finally Finds His Way Back Home," *New York Times,* March 28, 1993, 5.

20. Nick Tosches, *The Devil and Sonny Liston* (Boston: Little, Brown, 2000), 38–48, 177–78, 193–94, 197.

21. Peter Heller, *Bad Intentions: The Mike Tyson Story* (New York: Da Capo Press, 1995), 111–12, 292–93, 297.

22. *New York American,* December 16, 1925, 1.

23. Richard Hoffer, *A Savage Business: The Comeback and Comedown of Mike Tyson* (New York: Simon and Schuster, 1998), 45, 66.

24. Heller, *Bad Intentions,* 341.

25. Heller, *Bad Intentions,* 352–53.

26. Ashe, *A Hard Road to Glory,* 32.

27. Hoffer, *A Savage Business,* 264.

28. Hauser, *Muhammad Ali: His Life and Times* (New York: Simon and Schuster, 1991), 39.

29. Hauser, *Muhammad Ali,* 328.

30. Hauser, *Muhammad Ali,* 41.

31. Hauser, *Muhammad Ali,* 85, 264.

32. Jack Newfield, *Only in America: The Life and Crimes of Don King* (New York: William Morrow, 1995), 232.

33. Phil Berger, *Blood Season: Tyson and the World of Boxing* (New York: William Morrow, 1988), 20–21.

34. Hoffer, *A Savage Business,* 188–89.

35. Gilmore, *Bad Nigger,* 134–35; Kahn, *A Flame of Pure Fire,* 422.

36. Roberts, *Papa Jack,* 225.

37. Newfield, *Only in America,* 104–5, 147.

38. Newfield, *Only in America,* 54, 224, 333; Kahn, *A Flame of Pure Fire,* 46.

39. Newfield, *Only in America,* 39.

40. Newfield, *Only in America,* 228; Heller, *Bad Intentions,* 147.

41. Newfield, *Only in America,* 88.

42. Kahn, *A Flame of Pure Fire,* 37; Heller, *Bad Intentions,* 38; Newfield, *Only in America,* 113.

43. Hauser, *Muhammad Ali,* 405.

Works Cited

Ali, Muhammad, and Richard Durham. *The Greatest: My Own Story.* New York: Random House, 1975.

Allen, George H. *The Great War.* 4 vols. Philadelphia: George Barrie's Sons, 1919.

Anderson, Dave. *In the Corner: Great Boxing Trainers Talk about Their Art.* New York: William Morrow, 1991.

Andre, Sam, and Nat Fleischer. *A Pictorial History of Boxing.* Rev. ed. Secaucus, N.J.: Citadel, 1959.

Anglade, Jean. *La vie quotidienne des immigrés en France de 1919 à nos jours.* Paris: Hachette, 1976.

Arche-Straw, Petrine. *Negrophilia: Avant-Garde Paris and Black Culture in the 1920s.* London: Thames and Hudson, 2000.

Arroyo, Eduardo. *Panama Al Brown.* Paris: Bernard Grasset, 1998.

Asbury, Herbert. *The Gangs of New York: An Informal History of the Underworld.* New York: Alfred A. Knopf, 1927.

Ashe, Arthur R. *A Hard Road to Glory: Boxing.* New York: Amistad, 1988.

Ashworth, Tony. *Trench Warfare, 1914–1918: The Live and Let Live System.* New York: Holmes and Meier, 1980.

Auger, Jean. *La boxe anglaise.* Paris: Librairie Garnier Frères, 1923.

Balesi, Charles. *From Adversaries to Comrades-in-Arms: West Africans and the French Military, 1885–1918.* Waltham, Mass.: Crossroads Press, 1979.

Ball, Oumy. Personal interview. September 26, 2002.

Barbusse, Henri. *Le feu (Journal d'une escouade).* Lausanne: Société Coopérative Editions Rencontre, 1917.

Barrow, Joe Louis, Jr., and Barbara Munder. *Joe Louis: Fifty Years an American Hero.* New York: McGraw Hill, 1988.

Barthes, Roland. "Le monde où l'on catche." *Mythologies,* 13–24. Paris: Editions du Seuil, 1957. 13–24.

Basquel, Victor, and Alcide Delmont. *Le livre d'or de l'effort colonial français.* Paris: Presses Universitaires de France, 1923.

Batchelor, Denzil. *British Boxing.* London: Collins, n.d. [1948].

"Battling Siki as a Dark Cloud on the Horizon." *Literary Digest,* October 14,1922. 61–65.

Bénac, Gaston. *Champions dans la coulisse.* Toulouse: L'Actualité Sportive, 1944.

Benot, Yves. *Les députés africaine au Palais Bourbon de 1914 à 1958.* Paris: Editions Chaka, 1989.

Benson, Peter E., C.W.O., U.S.M.C., ret. Personal interview. Manchester, Conn., July 24, 1997.

Berger, Phil. *Blood Season: Tyson and the World of Boxing.* New York: William Morrow, 1988.

Big Fights: Siki vs. Carpentier, September 24, 1922. Video recording, created from 16 mm film. Big Fights, Inc., New York.

Big Fights: Siki vs. McTigue, March 17, 1923. Video recording, created from 16 mm film. Big Fights, Inc., New York.

Big Fights: Siki vs. Nilles, July 8, 1923. Video recording, created from 16 mm film. Big Fights, Inc., New York.

Blond, Georges. *Verdun.* Trans. Frances Frenaye. New York: Macmillan, 1964.

Boahen, A. A., ed. *Africa under Colonial Domination.* Vol. 7 of *UNESCO General History of Africa.* London: Heinemann; Berkeley and Los Angeles: University of California Press, 1981.

Bodner, Alan. *When Boxing Was a Jewish Sport.* Westport, Conn.: Praeger, 1997.

Brailsford, Dennis. *Bareknuckles: A Social History of Prizefighting.* Cambridge: Lutterworth, 1988.

Breslin, Jimmy. *Damon Runyon: A Life.* New York: Ticknor and Fields, 1991.

Bretonnel, Fred, and A. Dethès. *La boxe.* Paris: S. Bornemann, n.d. [1928].

British Medical Association. *The Boxing Debate.* London: Chameleon Press, 1993.

Bush, Eric. *Gallipoli.* New York: St. Martin's Press, 1975.

Callis, Tracy. "Battling Siki (Louis Phal)." April 20, 1999. Cynber Boxing Zone. Internet. www:http://cyberboxingzone.com/boxing/Siki-b.htm.

Cangioni, Pierre. *La fabuleuse histoire de la boxe.* Paris: Nathan, 1990.

Carpenter, Harry. *Boxing: An Illustrated History.* New York: Crescent Books, 1982.

Carpentier, Georges. *Carpentier by Himself.* Trans. Edward Fitzgerald. London: Hutchinson, 1955.

———. *Ma vie de boxeur.* Amiens: R. L. Eveillard, 1921.

———. *Mes 80 rounds.* With the collaboration of Jacques Marchand. Paris: Oliver Orban, 1976.

———. *Mon match avec la vie.* Paris: Flammarion, 1954.

Chalk, Ocania. *Pioneers of Black Sport: The Early Days of the Black Professional Athlete in Baseball, Basketball, Boxing, and Football.* New York: Dodd, Mead, n.d. [1975].

Chemin, Michel, and Gilles Lanier. *La boxe dans son siècle.* Paris: La Sirène, 1991.

Chevalier, Louis. *Montmartre du plaisir et du crime.* Paris: Editions Robert Laffont, 1980.

Clark, Peter B. *West Africans at War, 1914–1918, 1939–1945: Colonial Propaganda and Its Cultural Aftermath.* London: Ethnographia, 1986.

Clayton, Anthony. *France, Soldiers, and Africa.* London: Brassey's Defence Publishers, 1988.

Cohen, William B. *The French Encounter with Africans: White Response to Blacks, 1530–1880.* Bloomington: Indiana University Press, 1980.

Collins, Nigel. *Boxing Babylon.* New York: Citadel Press, 1990.

Cousturier, Lucie. *Des inconnus chez moi.* Paris: Editions de la Sirène, 1920.

Cros, Charles. *La parole est à M. Blaise Diagne, premier homme d'état africain.* Paris: Editions Chaka, n.d. [1990].

Cros, Roger. *La victoire des armées alliées en Orient 1918.* Montpellier: Causse, 1968.

Crowder, Michael. *Senegal: A Study in French Assimilation Policy.* Rev. ed. London: Methuen; New York: Praeger, 1967.

Dartnell, Fred (Lord Medford). *Seconds Out!* London: T. Werner Laurie, n.d. [1924].

Davis, Shelby Cullom. *Reservoirs of Men: A History of the Black Troops of French West Africa.* Geneva: Librairie Kundig, 1934.

DeLisa, Michael C. *Cinderella Man: The James J. Braddock Story.* Wrea Green, UK: Milo Books, 2005.

————, ed. "Theodore 'Tiger' Flowers (the 'Georgia Deacon')." Cyber Boxing Zone. April 14, 2000. www.cyberboxingzone.com/boxing/flowers.htm.

Dempsey, Jack, Bob Considine, and Bill Slocum. *Dempsey: By the Man Himself.* New York: Simon and Schuster, 1960.

Derks, Scott. *The Value of a Dollar: Prices and Incomes in the United States, 1860–1989.* Detroit: Gale Research, 1994.

Dewitte, Philippe. *Les mouvements nègres en France: 1919–1939.* Paris: L'Harmattan, 1985.

Diagne, Blaise. *Blaise Diagne: sa vie, son oeuvre.* Dakar: Nouvelles Editions africaines: Sonapress: Editions des Trois Fleuves, n.d. [1974].

Diallo, Bakary. *Force-bonté.* Paris: F. Rieder et Cie, 1926.

Dieng, Amady Aly. *Blaise Diagne, Deputé noir de l'Afrique.* Paris: Editions Chaka, 1990.

Douglas, Ann. *Terrible Honesty: Mongrel Manhattan in the 1920s.* New York: Farrar, Strauss, and Giroux, 1995.

Droussent, Claude. *L'Encyclopédie de la boxe.* Paris: Famsay, 1990.

D'Souza, Dinesh. *The End of Racism: Principles for a Multi-Racial Society.* New York: Free Press, 1995.

Du Bert, Marthe [Pseud. M. Dutrèb]. *Nos Sénégalais pendant la Grande Guerre.* Metz: Maison d'Edition des "Voix Lorraines," 1922.

Duboc, General A. *Les Sénégalais au service de la France.* Paris: Editions Edgar Malfère, 1939.

Early, Gerald. *The Culture of Bruising: Essays on Prize-fighting, Literature, and Modern American Culture.* Hopewell, N.J.: Ecco Press, 1994.

Echenberg, Myron. *Colonial Conscripts: The Tirailleurs Sénégalais in French West Africa, 1857–1960.* Portsmouth, N.H.: Heinemann; London: James Currey, 1991.

Eco, Umberto. *Semiotics and the Philosophy of Language.* Bloomington: Indiana University Press, 1986.

Ehrmann, Pete. "Setting the Record Straight on Paul Berlenbach." *Ring,* February 2005, 66–73.

Eichacker, Rheinhold. "The Blacks Attack!" *Current History,* April 1917: 1101–2.

Encinosa, Enrique G., and Hank Kaplan. *Boxing—This Is It!* Palm Springs, Calif.: ETCV Publications, 1985.

Engels, M. J. Adriani. *Honderd Jaar Sport.* Amsterdam: A. J. G. Strongholt, 1960.

Erenberg, Lewis A. *Steppin' Out: New York City's Restaurants and Cabarets and the Decline of Victorianism, 1890–1925.* Chicago: University of Chicago Press, 1984.

Esposito, Vincent J. *The West Point Atlas of American Wars, Vol II: 1900–1953.* New York: Praeger, 1959

Everlast Boxing Record (Annual). New York: Everlast Sport Publishing.

Fair, James R. *Give Him to the Angels: The Story of Harry Greb.* New York: Smith and Durrell, 1946.

Fall, Mar. *Le Bordeaux des africaines.* Talence, France: Maison des Sciences de L'Homme d'Aquitaine, 1989.

Fanon, Frantz. *Black Skin, White Masks.* Trans. Charles Lam Markmann. New York: Grove Press, 1967.

———. *Les damnés de la terre.* Paris: François Maspero, 1968.

———. *Peau noire, masques blancs.* Paris: Editions du Seuil, 1952.

———. *The Wretched of the Earth.* Trans. Constance Farrington. New York: Grove Press, 1968.

Faragher, John Mack, Mari Jo Buhle, Daniel Czitrom, and Susan H. Armitage. *Out of Many: A History of the American People.* Vol. 2. Englewood Cliffs, N.J.: Prentice Hall, 1994.

Farwell, Byron. *The Great War in Africa: 1914–1918.* New York: Norton, 1986.

Federal Writers Program: Negroes of New York. Schomburg Center typescript. New York, 1939. N. pag.

Feuille, Henri *(Capitaine). Face aux Turcs: Gallipoli 1915.* Paris: Payot, 1934.

Fleischer, Nat. *Black Dynamite: The Story of the Negro in the Prize Ring from 1782 to 1938.* 5 vols. New York: Ring Athletic Library, n.d. [1938–1947].

———. *Fifty Years at Ringside.* New York: Fleet Publishing, 1958.

———. *How to Box.* New York: Ring Athletic Library, n.d. [1929–1932].

———. *How to Judge and How to Referee a Fight.* New York: Ring Athletic Library, 1933.

———. *How to Second and How to Manage a Boxer.* New York: Ring Publications, 1944.

———. *Leonard the Magnificent: Life Story of the Man Who Made Himself King of the Lightweights.* Norwalk, Conn.: O'Brien Suburban Press, 1947.

———. *Jack Dempsey, the Idol of Fistiana: An Intimate Narrative.* New York: Ring Athletic Library, 1929.

Freire, Paolo. *Pedagogy of the Oppressed.* Trans. Myra Bergman Ramos. New York: Continuum, 1995

Fried, Ronald K. *Corner Men: Great Boxing Trainers.* New York: Four Walls Eight Windows, 1991.

Fyfe, Albert J. *Understanding the First World War: Illusions and Realities.* Bern, N.Y.: Peter Lang, 1988.

Gajdusek, Robert E. *Hemingway's Paris.* New York: Charles Scribner, 1988.

Gill, Douglas, and Gloden Dallas. *The Unknown Army.* London: Verso, 1985.

Gilmore, Al-Tony. *Bad Nigger! The National Impact of Jack Johnson.* Port Washington, N.Y.: Kennikat Press, 1975.

Golding, Louis. *The Bare-Knuckle Breed.* New York: A. S. Barnes, 1954.

Goldstein, Ruby, and Frank Graham. *Third Man in the Ring.* Westport, Conn.: Greenwood Press, 1972.

Golsworthy, Maurice. *Encyclopedia of Boxing.* 8th ed. London: Robert Hale, 1988.

Gordon, Alan, and Lois Gordon. *The Columbia Chronicles of American Life.* New York: Columbia University Press, 1995.

Gorn, Elliott J. *The Manly Art: Bare-Knuckle Prize Fighting in America.* Ithaca, N.Y.: Cornell University Press, 1986.

Gouin, Gustave. *L'armée d'Orient des Dardanelles au Danube. La victoire d'Orient.* Marseille: F. Detaille, 1931.

Green, Benny. *Shaw's Champions: George Bernard Shaw and Prizefighting, from Cashel Byron to Gene Tunney.* London: Elm Tree Books, 1978.

Greene, Ward, ed. *Star Reporters and Thirty-four of Their Stories.* New York: Random House, 1948.

Grombach, John V. *The Saga of Sock: A Complete Story of Boxing.* New York: Barnes, 1949.

Guignard, Louis. "Les troupes noires pendant la guerre." *Revue des Deux Mondes* 51 (June 15, 1919): 849–79.

Haldane, R. A. *Champions and Challengers: One Hundred Years of Queensberry Boxing.* London: Stanley Paul, 1967.

Hauser, Thomas. *The Black Lights: Inside the World of Professional Boxing.* New York: McGraw Hill, 1986.

———. *Muhammad Ali: His Life and Times.* New York: Simon and Schuster, 1991.

Hay, Ginette. *Georges Carpentier.* Arras: Les Dossiers de Guaheria 4, 1993.

Heller, Peter. *"In This Corner . . . !": Forty-two World Champions Tell Their Stories.* New York: Da Capo Press, 1994.

———. *Bad Intentions: The Mike Tyson Story.* New York: Da Capo Press, 1995.

Hemingway, Ernest. *Selected Letters.* Ed. Carlos Baker. New York: Scribner's, 1981.

———. *The Short Stories of Ernest Hemingway.* New York: Scribner's, 1953.

———. *The Sun Also Rises.* New York: Scribner's, 1954.

Herries, Bill. *The Old Westside Hell's Kitchen.* N.p., n.d. [New York, 1954].

Herwig, Holger H. *The First World War: Germany and Austria Hungary, 1914–1918.* London: Arnold, 1997.

L'Historique du 8éme régiment d'infanterie coloniale, 1914–1919. Toulon: 1920.

Historique des troupes coloniales pendant la guerre, 1914–1918. Paris: Charles-Lavauzelle, 1922.

Historique des troupes coloniales pendant la guerre, 1914–1918 (fronts extérieurs). Paris: Charles-Lavauzelle, 1931.

Hoberman, John. *Darwin's Athletes: How Sport Has Damaged Black America and Preserved the Myth of Race.* Boston and New York: Houghton Mifflin, 1997.

Hoffer, Richard. *A Savage Business: The Comeback and Comedown of Mike Tyson.* New York: Simon and Schuster, 1998.

Hurdman-Lucas, F. *From Pit Boy to Champion Boxer: The Romance of Georges Carpentier.* London: Ewart, Seymour, n.d.

Immerso, Michael. *Newark's Little Italy: The Vanished First Ward.* New Brunswick and Newark, N.J.: Rutgers University Press and Newark Public Library, 1997.

Ingold, François. *Les Troupes noires au combat.* Paris: Editions Berger-Levrault, 1940.

Isenberg, Michael T. *John L. Sullivan and His America.* Urbana and Chicago: University of Illinois Press, 1988.

Jackson, Kenneth T. *The Ku Klux Klan in the City.* Oxford: Oxford University Press, 1967.

Jeannesson, Stanislas. *Poincaré, la France, et la Ruhr (1922–1924): Histoire d'une occupation.* Strasbourg: Presses Universitaire de Strassbourg, 1998.

Johnson, G. W. *The Emergence of Black Politics in Senegal.* Stanford: Stanford University Press, 1971.

Johnson, Jack. *Jack Johnson—In the Ring—and Out.* Chicago: National Sports Publ., 1927.

Jones, Thomas L. "A Single Strand of Hair." *The Crime Library.* http://www.crimelibrary.com/gangsters/genovese/index.htm (accessed January 9, 2003).

Journal of African History. Special issue on Africa in World War I, 19. 1 (1978).

July, Robert W. *A History of the African People,* 4th ed. Prospect Heights, Ill.: Waveland Press, 1992.

———. *The Origins of Modern African Thought.* London: Faber and Faber, 1968; New York: Praeger, 1967.

Jünger, Ernst. *Storm of Steel.* Trans. Basil Creighton. London: Chatto and Windus, 1929.

Kahn, Roger. *A Flame of Pure Fire: Jack Dempsey and the Roaring Twenties.* New York: Harcourt, 1999.

Kann, Réginald. "Les troupes indigènes en France." *Le Temps,* April 26, 1923, 3.

Kaye, Andrew M. *The Pussycat of Prizefighting: Tiger Flowers and the Politics of Black Celebrity.* Athens: University of Georgia Press, 2004.

Kearns, Jack, and Oscar Fraley. *The Million-Dollar Gate.* New York: McMillan, 1966.

Kenny, Harold J. *The Boxing Manual.* Philadelphia: Fred Herbstrith, 1945.

Kisselhoff, Jeff. *You Must Remember This: An Oral History of Manhattan from the 1890s to World War II.* San Diego, New York, and London: Harcourt, Brace, Jovanovich, 1989.

Koppen, Niek. *Siki.* Documentary Video Production, Amsterdam, 1993.

Lacey, Robert. *Little Man: Meyer Lansky and the Gangster Life.* Boston: Little, Brown, 1991.

Lardner, John. "This Was Pugilism: Battling Siki." *New Yorker,* November 19, 1949, 97–108.

———. "The Battling Siki Murder," *New Yorker,* November 19, 1949. Rpt. *Negro Digest* 8, 6 (April 1950): 52–63.

———. "The Jack Johnson Era of Boxing," *Negro Digest* 8, 1 (November 1949): 24–34.

———. *White Hopes and Other Tigers.* Philadelphia: Lippincott, 1951.

Leca, Nicolas. *Les pêcheurs de Guet N'Dar.* Vol. 17, no. 2 (April–June 1934) of *Bulletin du comité d'études historiques et scientifiques de l'Afrique Occidentale Française.*

Leed, Eric J. *No Man's Land: Combat and Identity in World War I.* Cambridge: Cambridge University Press, 1979.

Leibling, A. J. *Back Where I Came From.* San Francisco: North Point Press, 1990.

————. *A Neutral Corner.* New York: Farrar, Straus, and Giroux, 1990.

————. *The Sweet Science.* Westport, Conn.: Greenwood, 1956.

Lunn, Joe Harris. "Kande Kamara Speaks: An Oral History of the West African Experience in France, 1914–1918." In *Africa and the First World War.* Ed. Melvin E. Page. Houndmills, Basingstoke, Hampshire: Macmillan Press, 1987, 28–53.

McCallum, John D. *The Encyclopedia of World Boxing Champions.* Radnor, Pa.: Chilton Book Co., [1975].

McKean, Dayton David. *The Boss: The Hague Machine in Action.* New York: Russell and Russell, 1967.

Magel, Emil A. "Hare and Hyena: Symbols of honor and Shame in the Oral Narratives of the Wolof of the Senegambia." Ph.D. diss., University of Wisconsin, 1978.

Malherbe, Michel, and Cheikh Sall. *Parlons Wolof: langue et culture.* Paris: Editions L'Harmattan, 1989.

Martine, James J. "Hemingway's 'Fifty Grand': The Other Fight(s)." *Journal of Modern Literature* 2 (September 1971): 123–27.

Masson, Paul. *Marseille pendant la guerre.* Paris: Presse Universitaire de France; New Haven, Conn.: Yale University Press, 1926.

Maurel, Jean François. *Blaise Diagne et son temps.* Catalogue from the Senegalese National Archives Exhibition. Dakar, 1972.

May, Allan. "Waxey Gordon's Half Century of Crime." *Crime Magazine: An Encyclopedia of Crime.* Http://crimemagazine.com/waxey.htm (accessed January 15, 2005).

Merlin, Olivier. *Georges Carpentier, gentleman du ring.* Paris: Hatier, 1975.

Michel, Marc. *L'appel à l'Afrique: contributions et réactions à l'effort de guerre en A.O.F. (1914–1919).* Paris: Publ. de la Sorbonne, 1982.

Miller, Christopher L. *Blank Darkness: Africanist Discourse in French.* Chicago and London: University of Chicago Press, 1985.

Moorehead, Alan. *Gallipoli.* New York: Harper and Brothers, 1956.

Mullan, Harry. *The Illustrated History of Boxing.* New York: Crescent Books, 1987.

Ndaw, Alassane. *La pensée africaine: recherches sur les fondements de la pensée négro-africaine.* Dakar: Nouvelles Editions Africaines, 1983.

Newfield, Jack. *Only in America: The Life and Crimes of Don King.* New York: William Morrow, 1995.

Nown, Graham. *The English Godfather.* London: Ward Lock, 1987.

Oates, Joyce Carol. *On Boxing.* Hopewell, N.J.: Ecco Press, 1994.

————, and Daniel Halperin, eds. *Reading the Fights.* New York: Prentice Hall, 1990.

O'Connor, Richard. *Hell's Kitchen: The Roaring Days of New York's Wild West Side.* New York: Old Town Books, 1958.

Pacheco, Ferdie. *Fight Doctor.* New York: Simon and Schuster, 1976.

Page, Melvin E., ed. *Africa and the First World War.* Houndmills, Basingstoke, Hampshire: Macmillan Press, 1987.

Pálat, Edmond Barthélemy. *Les batailles d'Artois et de Champagne en 1915.* Paris and Brussels: G. Van Ouest, 1920.

————. *La Grande Guerre sur le front occidental.* Paris: Librairie Chapelot, 1922.

Palmer, Joe. *Recollections of a Boxing Referee.* London: John Lane—The Bodley Head, 1927.

Passevant, Roland. *Boxing business.* Paris: Editeurs Français Réunis, 1973.

Peary, Gerald. "Missing Links: The Jungle Origins of King Kong," www.geraldpeary.com /essays/jkl/kingkong-1.html (accessed March 7, 2003).

Peeters, Georges. *La boxe: 'noble art.'* Paris: Vigot Frères, 1944.

———. *Pleins feux sur les rings.* Paris: La Table Ronde, 1970.

Pegler, Westbrook. "Pegler among the Platonians," *Star Reporters and Thirty-four of Their Stories.* Ed. Ward Greene, 298–301. New York: Random House, 1948.

Petit, Marcel. *Boxe: Technique—Entrainement.* Paris: Editions Amphora, 1972.

Philonenko, Alexis. *Histoire de la boxe.* Paris: Critereon, 1991.

Pizer, Vernon. *Glorious Triumphs: Athletes Who Conquered Adversity.* New York: Dodd, Mead, 1966.

Quiminal, Catherine. *Gens d'ici, gens d'ailleurs.* Paris: C. Bourgois, 1991.

Reiss, Stephen A. "In the Ring and Out: Professional Boxing in New York, 1896–1920." *Sport in America: New Historical Perspectives.* Ed. Donald Spivey, 95–128. Westport, Conn.: Greenwood, 1985.

Reynaud-Lacroze, Eugene. *Méharistes au combat.* Paris: France-Empire, 1983.

Reynolds, Francis J., Allen L. Churchill, and Francis Trevelyan Miller. *The Story of the Great War.* 6 vols. NewYork: P. F. Collier and Son, 1916.

The Ring Record Book and Boxing Encyclopedia. New York: Ring Book Shop, [Annual].

Roberts, Randy. *Papa Jack: Jack Johnson and the Era of White Hopes.* New York: Free Press, 1983.

Robinson, Sugar Ray, and Dave Anderson. *The Sugar Ray Robinson Story.* New York: Viking, 1970; rpt. New York: Da Capo, 1994.

Rose, C. *Boxing Taught through the Slow-Motion Film.* London: Athletic Publications, n.d. [1924].

Salah: the Muslim Prayer. Elmhurst, New York: Islamic Books and Tapes, n.d. [1998?].

Salem, Gérard. "La revanche des Fassois, la lutte Sénégalaise." *Capitales de la couleur: Dakar, Abidjan, Douala, Kinshasa,* 48–50. Paris: Editions Autrement, n.d. [1990].

Sammons, Jeffrey T. *Beyond the Ring: The Role of Boxing in American Society.* Urbana and Chicago: University of Illinois Press, 1988.

Sann, Paul. "Kill the Dutchman! The Story of Dutch Schultz," www.paulsann.org/killthedutchman/chapter X.htm (accessed April 25, 2003).

Sante, Luc. *Low Life.* New York: Random House, 1992.

Sawyer, Tom. *Noble Art: An Artistic and Literary Celebration of the Old English Prize Ring.* London: Unwin Hyman, 1989.

Scanlon, Bob. "The Record of a Negro Boxer." *Negro Anthology, 1931–1933.* Ed. Nancy Cunard, 339–42. London: Cunard and Wishart, 1934.

Seldes, Gilbert. *Witness to a Century: Encounters with the Noted, the Notorious, and the Three S.O.B.s.* New York: Random House, 1987.

Senghor, Leopold Sédar. *Poèmes.* Paris: Editions du Seuil, 1964.

Shocket, Dan. "Battling Siki—the Man They Turned into a Joke," *World Boxing* September 1974, 32–33, 58–60.

Smith, Kevin. "The Black Thunderbolt—Kid Norfolk." *Cyber Boxing Zone.* Internet; www:http://cyberboxingzone.com/boxing/norfolk.htm (April 20, 1999).

Stapinski, Helene. *Five-Finger Discount: A Crooked Family History.* New York: Random House, 2001.

Stern, Bill. *Bill Stern's Favorite Boxing Stories.* New York: Pocket Books, 1948.

Stol, Albert. *Battling Siki: het levensverhaal van M'Barick Fall.* Amsterdam: In de Knipscheer, 1991.

Stone, Jill. *Times Square: A Pictorial History.* New York: Macmillan, 1982.

Stovall, Tyler. *Paris Noir: African Americans in the City of Light.* Boston and New York: Houghton Mifflin, 1996.

Stuart, Mark A. *Gangster #2: Longy Zwillman, the Man Who Invented Organized Crime.* Secaucus, N.J.: Lyle Stuart, 1985.

Taylor, Jack. "From Jack Taylor, Coloured Ex-Light-Heavyweight Champion of the World." *Negro Anthology, 1931–1933.* Ed. Nancy Cunard, 342–43. London: Cunard and Wishart, 1934.

Terbeen, François, and Claude Brezner. *Les géants de la boxe.* Paris: Editions Mondiale, 1962.

Thiam, Iba Der. *Le Sénégal dans la guerre 14–18, ou le prix du combat pour l'égalité.* Dakar: Nouvelles Editions Africaines du Sénégal, 1992.

Thomas, Louis. *L'Armée de la guerre.* Paris: Librairie Payot, 1916.

Thomason, John W. *Fix Bayonets.* New York: Scribner's, 1926.

Thompson, Craig, and Allen Raymond. *Gang Rule in New York.* New York: Dial Press, 1940.

Tosches, Nick. *The Devil and Sonny Liston.* Boston: Little, Brown, 2000.

Tourette, Jean. *Marseille, ville de mon enfance.* Marseille: La Savoisienne, 1970.

U.S. Department of State. *Colored Troops in the French Army.* Washington: U.S. Government Printing Office, 1921.

"*L'Utilisation des troupes noires.*" *Revue de Paris,* December 15, 1917, 872–94.

Vergani, Orio. *Io, povero negro.* Milan: Fratelli Treves, 1929.

———. *Poor Nigger.* Trans. W. W. Hobson. Indianapolis: Bobbs-Merrill, 1930.

Walker, Mickey, and Joe Reichler. *Mickey Walker: The Toy Bulldog and His Times.* New York: Random House, 1961.

Wallace, Irving. *The Fabulous Showman: The Life and Times of P. T. Barnum.* New York: Alfred A. Knopf, 1959.

Walsh, Peter. *Men of Steel: The Lives and Times of Boxing's Middleweight Champions.* London: Robson Books, 1993.

Watkins, Mel. *On the Real Side: A History of African American Comedy.* Chicago: Lawrence Hill, 1999.

Wynter, Leon E. *American Skin: Pop Culture, Big Business, and the End of White America.* New York: Random House, 2002.

Archival Sources

Federal Bureau of Investigation. Frank Costello file. Freedom of Information Act.

Federal Bureau of Investigation. Abner Zwillman file. Freedom of Information Act.

Periodicals

Les Annales (Paris)
Atlanta Constitution
L'Auto (Paris)
Baltlimore Afro-American
Baltlimore American
Baltlimore Post
Berliner Lokal-Anzeiger (Berlin)
Berliner Tageblatt (Berlin)
La Boxe et les Boxeurs. (Paris)
The Boxing Blade (St. Paul)
Brooklyn Citizen
Brooklyn Daily Eagle
Brooklyn Standard-Union
Buffalo Evening News
Le Canard Enchaîné (Paris)
Chicago (Ill.) *Broad Ax*
Chicago (Ill.) *Defender*
Cleveland (Ohio) *Gazette*
Cleveland (Ohio) *Plain Dealer*
Columbus (Ohio) *Dispatch*
La Dépêche du Midi (Toulouse)
La Discussion (Havana, Cuba)
L'Echo de Paris
L'Echo des Sports (Paris)
L'Eclair (Paris)
L'Express du Midi (Toulouse)
Le Gaulois (Paris)
Havana (Cuba) *Morning Post*
Hudson Dispatch (Jersey City, N.J.)
L'Humanité (Paris)
Illustrated London News
L'Illustration (Paris)
Irish Times (Dublin)
Jersey Journal (Jersey City, N.J.)
Key West (Fla.) *Citizen*
London Times
Lorain (Ohio) *Times-Herald*
Manchester (N.H.) *Union Leader*
Le Matin (Paris)
Memphis (Tenn.) *Commercial Appeal*
Minneapolis Tribune

Le Miroir des Sports (Paris)
Montreal (Canada) *Gazette*
Montreal (Canada) *Herald*
National Police Gazette (New York)
Newark (N.J.) *Evening News*
Newark (N.J.) *Star-Eagle*
New Orleans Times-Picayune
New York Age
New York American
New York Amsterdam News
New York Call
New York Daily News
New York Evening Journal
New York Evening Post
New York Herald
New York Herald (Paris ed.)
New York Leader
New York Telegram and Evening Mail
New York Times
New York Tribune
New York World
Passaic (N.J.) *Daily News*
Passaic (N.J.) *Daily Herald*
Le Petit Journal (Paris)
Le Petit Parisien (Paris)
Le Petit Provençal (Marseille)
Le Peuple (Paris)
Philadelphia Inquirer
Pittsburgh Courier
Le Populaire (Paris)
The Ring (New York)
St. Paul (Minn.) *Pioneer Press*
Le Soir (Paris)
Le Sportif (Paris)
Le Sporting (Paris)
Het Stadion (Amsterdam)
Summit Herald and Summit Record (N.J.)
Syracuse (New York) *Post-Standard*
Le Temps (Paris)
Wheeling (W.V.) *Register*

Index